Liberalism
in the
Bedroom

Christine Hunefeldt

Liberalism in the Bedroom

Quarreling Spouses in Nineteenth-Century Lima

The Pennsylvania State University Press
University Park, Pennsylvania

Library of Congress Cataloging-in-Publication Data

Hünefeldt, Christine
 Liberalism in the bedroom : quarreling spouses in nineteenth-century Lima / Christine Hunefeldt.
    p.   cm.
 Includes bibliographical references and index.
 ISBN 0-271-01935-2 (cloth : alk. paper)
 ISBN 0-271-01936-0 (pbk. : alk. paper)
  1. Marital conflict—Peru—Lima—History—19th century. 2. Marriage—Peru—Lima—History—19th century. 3. Women—Peru—Lima—Social conditions—19th century. I. Title.
 HQ606.15.L5H86 2000
 306.872'0985'2509034—dc21   98-55336
                                                                    CIP

Copyright © 2000 The Pennsylvania State University
All rights reserved
Printed in the United States of America
Published by The Pennsylvania State University Press,
University Park, PA 16802-1003

It is the policy of The Pennsylvania State University Press to use acid-free paper for the first printing of all clothbound books. Publications on uncoated stock satisfy the minimum requirements of American National Standard for Information Sciences—Permanence of Paper for Printed Library Materials, ANSI Z39.48–1992.

For my parents,
Helga and Joachim

Contents

List of Tables	ix
Acknowledgments	xi
List of Abbreviations	xv
Glossary	xvii
Introduction	1
1. Lima in the Nineteenth Century	17

Part I: Couples, Barrios, and the Church

2. At Home and in the Streets	61
3. The People and the Church	79
4. The Canonic Interstices: Dissent, Consent, Incompatibility	109
5. Guarding Marriage from Conflicts: Couples and Beaterios	147

Part II: Couples and Everyday Life

6. Women and the Dangers of Premarital Sex	179
7. Dowries and Marriage in Civil Court	223
8. Strategies for Survival: Struggles over Assets and Earnings	273
9. Redefining Female Domains	315
10. The End of the Century and Backward	347
Bibliography	369
Index	385

List of Tables

1.1.	Population growth and ethnicity in Lima, 1792–1920	19
1.2.	Children and fertility in Lima, 1810–1900	23
1.3.	Natality/mortality in municipal records, 1826–1924	24
1.4.	Legitimacy/illegitimacy in Lima's matrimonial licenses, 1800–1900	25
1.5.	Natural children declared in Lima's wills, 1810–1900	26
1.6.	Wills registering legitimacy/illegitimacy, 1810–1900	26
1.7.	Number of children alive when parents wrote their wills, 1810–1900	27
1.8.	Place of birth of men married in Lima, 1800–1890	28
1.9.	Place of birth of women married in Lima, 1800–1890	28
1.10.	Prisoners in the Lima penitentiary, crimes, 1862–1876	38
1.11.	Race and criminality, 1890s	40
5.1.	Family intervention in matrimonial conflicts, 1800–1910	150
5.2.	Women's location when filing a divorce and who opened the files, 1800–1910	151
5.3.	Male ethnicity among quarreling couples, three periods, 1800–1910	156
5.4.	Male occupations among quarreling couples, three periods, 1800–1910	157
7.1.	Dowries mentioned in wills, 1810–1900	233
7.2.	Average dowry, 1810–1900	233
7.3.	Dowries, acquest, and will executors, Lima, 1810–1900	237
7.4.	Contributions to marriage by sex, 1810 and 1900	252
8.1.	Marriage and remarriage, men, 1800–1910	278
8.2.	Marriage and remarriage, women, 1800–1910	280

8.3.	Demand reason and who presents the demand, 1800–1820	288
8.4.	Demand reason and who presents the demand, 1840–1860	288
8.5.	Demand reason and who presents the demand, 1890–1910	289
9.1.	Working women and race, 1908	345

Acknowledgments

I began work in Lima's archives for this book in 1983 with a generous grant from the Deutsche Forschungsgemeinschaft (DFG). By stretching resources, I was able to work in Lima's archives almost daily for three years and was even able to pay for at least one and occasionally three research assistants to help me gathering materials from Lima's very rich repositories. Most notably, Marcela Calisto—currently a professor at Ohio State University— was always near at hand, and her help and thoughts are part of the book. She is almost as guilty as I am both for the flaws and for the insights that this book contains. An initial side result from this research—a book on slavery, family, and abolition in Lima in the first half of the nineteenth century—was published by the University of California Press four years ago. Over the past several years I have presented portions of the book in conferences, and some ideas have been published in Spanish elsewhere. Conferences and papers gave me much feedback from colleagues, who helped to shape the present manuscript. Steve Stern's extensive comments on the dowries chapter (Chapter 7) at a conference in Mexico City (1996) have greatly helped to broaden its scope and content. At an earlier stage (1994) my colleague Michael Monteon read the whole manuscript and provided detailed comments on each page, including not only help with editing, but also pinning down for me in his own very special direct way the essential messages of the manuscript. His comments allowed for a rethinking of the overall organization of the manuscript. At one point (1996), I received additional sharp criticisms from an anonymous reader, which helped me push the arguments still further and to rewrite portions of the manuscript. The whole statistical package would not have seen daylight without the decided support from my husband, Nelson Altamirano. To all these kindred, colleagues, and friends, I am very thankful.

A thorough polishing hand came with the copyediting process I decided to engage in even before submitting the manuscript to Penn State Press. Throughout a whole year Patricia Rosas helped me "translate" English into English and to find the middle ground between my own Spanish-influenced metaphoric presentations of the argument and the desired directness and systematicness for North American eyes. A final polishing came with the press's copyeditor, Elizabeth Yoder. All along it has been a route of cultural discoveries mediated by the uses of language. Finally, some interesting comments reached me through Sanford Thatcher, Penn State University Press's efficient and charming general editor. The anonymous comments he gathered for me have helped to sharpen the liberalism side of the argument.

When I began this research, there were not many people in Lima engaged in similar projects. It was rather a solitary endeavor, and it was not always easy to convince friends and colleagues about the rewards of a gender and family perspective in historical research. Strolling along in Mexico City's streets, Ruggiero Romano—well known for his interest and continued support of Peruvian historians—actually scolded me, in his very accentuated Italian style, for not doing the "real thing"—economic history. Matters have changed a little since 1983, and despite Ruggiero's scolding, I still think it was the right thing and the right time to engage in this research. In contrast to Mexican historiography, for example, Peru (and the Andean region more generally) is still a "neglected" place in terms of family history, herstory, and social history.

The key repositories for this research were the Archbishopric Archive and the National Archive in Lima. The old priest in charge of the Archbishopric Archive had mixed feelings about a *gringa* wearing pants looking through the ecclesiastical secrets and treasures and would use his power (he held the keys to the door) to let me know. I understood. There was not much I could do about my green eyes, but I could certainly comply with a dress. Quite in contrast to the old priest, the personnel in the archive, who knew exactly what I was looking for, helped me uncover the marvels of the archive. We engaged in much talk and exchange of ideas. In those days there were not many researchers in this archive. Besides the genealogists hired to trace the elites' family trees and an occasional researcher from the United States (I still remember Sabina McCormack's sniffing nose during those cold winter days), there was a great deal of silence. Matters were different in the National Archive, where a lively crowd of students gathered to find materials for theses and papers, and national and foreign historians always found time to go across the street, have a coffee, and chat about their most recent findings. These outings were invaluable because they gave an outlet to immediate enthusiasm (often also deception) and allowed for a very fresh and continued exchange of ideas. Talking to Alberto Flores Galindo, Memma Mannarelli, Margarita Suarez, Nils Jacobsen, Paul Gootenberg, and Mario Cardenas in this setting has always been an enlivening experience.

I still admire the patience of the personnel in the archive. The civil and criminal court cases *(expedientes)* for the nineteenth century are bundles of chronologically organized papers. Package after package had to be carried upstairs from the basement to the reading room. Having me look through these bundles month after month meant a major physical burden for the archivists.

Last but not least, this book is dedicated to my parents, the living denial of the key argument of the book. After fifty years of marriage, for them marriage is still happiness, not conflict.

After so much help from so many different people, I am willing to let go, conscious that some flaws remain and still doubting whether the *beaterios,* the dowries, and the dispensations sections should be here or there. Such doubts, however, only show that life is just that . . . intertwined.

Abbreviations

AA	Archivo Arzobispal
ACR	Actas de la Sesiones de la Comisión Reformadora del Código Civil Peruano
AGN	Archivo General de la Nación
AML	Archivo Municipal Lima
APPu	Archivo de la Prefectura de Puno
BN	Biblioteca Nacional
C	Cuaderno
CCI	Causas Civiles
CCR	Causas Criminales
CD	Causas de Divorcio
CDIP	Colección Documental de la Independencia del Perú
CS	Corte Superior
L	Legajo
LicM	Licencias Matrimoniales
LM	Litigio Matrimonial
NM	Expedientes de Nulidad de Matrimonio
PR	Protocolo
RA	Real Audiencia

Glossary

Aguador	Water carrier
Alcalde	Mayor
Alcalde de barrio	Neighborhood mayor
Almidonería	Store in which clothes are starched
Aniversario	Payments to the church based on landed property (in this context)
Arancel	Fixed payments to the church for services, also custom duty
Balneario	Residential unit, neighborhood usually located outside city limits, suburb
Beaterio	Monastery-like institution for divorcing women
Cacique	Ethnic lord
Cajón	Store usually located at the central plaza of a city
Callejón	Residential alley
Capellanía	Money the church received to carry out masses on behalf of landowners
Casa mantequería	Lard producing workshop
Casa solar	House on the outskirts of the city
Casa tambo	*Tambo* with an attached house
Casita	Small house
Casta	Mixed-blood person with black ancestors
Caudillo	Political/military leader
Celador	Jail warden
Chacra	Small plot of land, vegetable garden
Chicha	Low alcohol beverage made of corn
Chichería	Store or pub in which chicha is expended
Chingana	Popular word for *pulpería*
Chisme	Gossip

Chocolatería	Small store in which hot chocolate and pastries are sold
Comadre	Godmother
Comisario (de cuartel)	Police officer (in charge of a cuartel), district police commissioner
Compadrazgo	Ritual kinship tie through baptism, first communion, or marriage
Compadre/Comadre	Persons linked by *compadrazgo* ties
Corregidor	State appointed administrator in charge of a *corregimiento*
Corregimiento	Real estate with a significant assignment of Indian laborers controlled by a *corregidor*
Costumbrista	Literature genre depicting local traditions and customs
Cuadra	House block
Cuarta marital	The one-fourth of a spouse's wealth accumulated throughout marriage
Cuarta conyugal	The one-fourth of a spouse's wealth before marriage
Cuartel	Administrative compound in the city encompassing several *barrios*
Cupo	Imposed monetary payment
Defensor de matrimonios	Marriage defense attorney
Diputado	Deputy
Encomendero	Colonial bureaucrat, wholesale supplier
Esponsales	*Sponsalia*
Finca	Small landed property
Fiscal	Prosecutor
Gananciales	Half of the accumulated wealth throughout marriage
Gente decente	"Decent," well-off people
Guano	Bird droppings
Hacienda	Small to medium-sized landholding
Hijuelas	Inventory of heirloom
Huerta	Garden plot, vegetable garden
Instrumento dotal	Notarially recorded dowry acknowledgment
Limeña, Limeño	Man or woman from Lima
Litis Expensas	Costs of a trial
Maricón	Homosexual
Mayordomo	Supervisor in a *hacienda;* also, person in charge of organizing patron-saint festivities
Obraje	Textile workshop
Parroquia	Parish
Partido	Administrative unit, province

Patente	Taxes imposed on street vendors and cottage industries
Peso	Spanish currency
Plata labrada	Silverware
Procurador protector fiscal	State-assigned lawyer for Indians
Protector de Naturales	Colonial bureaucrat, Protector of Indians
Provisor	Church bureaucrat in charge of handling marital conflicts
Pulpería	Small store in which often alcohol is expended
Real	Spanish currency, one peso usually equals eight reales
Regidor	Municipal bureaucrat
Ronda	Citizen patrol
Saya y manto	Typical *limeña* dress during the colonial period and the nineteenth century
Sereno	Night watchman in a neighborhood
Servicios menores	People working as domestics
Sol	Peruvian currency since 1872
Solar	Urban lot
Sponsalia	Premarital notarized marriage agreement
Tambo	Small store in rural settings
Teniente de cura	Local priest assistant
Tienda	Store
Tinterillo	Lawyers without a professional degree, legal trafficker
Visitador general	State-appointed inspector

Introduction

This is the story of women and men in nineteenth-century Lima, about how they lived in urban neighborhoods and rural hinterlands, and how they dealt with the problems of daily life. Above all, it is an account of how women became "sly creatures" in the eyes of men, and men became "irresponsible fathers" in the eyes of women.

In nineteenth-century ecclesiastical and civil court cases, Peruvian men and women described their daily encounters, used existing laws to argue their cases, and constantly interpreted and reinterpreted legal and social rules.[1]

I reviewed 1,070 conjugal suits in Lima's archbishopric. In some cases, wills in notarial records could be evaluated in order to ascertain what had happened to quarreling couples at the end of their lives. In exceptional cases, a couple began a suit at the ecclesiastical court, then started one in civil or criminal court, and many years later wrote a will. Such cases allow for a reading of several decades of conjugal strife.[2]

These court cases reveal a dialogue about couples' relationships, attitudes, and perceptions of gender, life cycle, race, and class; about changing

---

1. As will become evident in the following chapters, such interpretations were often more radical and straightforward than the more cautious "feminist" arguments brought forward by women writers in nineteenth-century Lima. Peruvian women writers, especially Juana Manuela Gorritti (born 1818) and Clorinda Matto de Turner (born 1854), are portrayed by Denegri (1996).

2. In Lima many women went to court. I hesitate to agree with Silvia Arrom's assertion that women "never enjoyed [their right to protection] because they failed to go to court to enforce it" (1985b, 81). This discrepancy may have to do with differences between Mexico City and Lima. However, I suspect it has more to do with the availability of sources. Arrom's study is based on 81 ecclesiastical court cases (1985b, 207 and 279, appendix III).

moral expectations; and about the varying paces of social change. They illustrate three levels of social life: the concrete details of couples' daily lives; the discourses that evolved in day-to-day situations to challenge prevailing expectations and existing laws; and how these discourses, emerging out of personal experiences, social expectations, and legal devices, synthesized economic, social, political, and moral power struggles in society at large.

The examination of these court records expands our picture of women historically. This study of the interactions of couples and their families, neighbors, judges, and parish priests also sheds new light on Peruvian nineteenth-century history and, more generally, on the worldwide surge of liberalism, as we can observe its effects on interpersonal and gender relationships. The ecclesiastical and civil cases illuminate the contours of nineteenth-century liberal ideas in the domestic realm and in intimate relationships. From the perspective of present-day liberalism, it is interesting to consider the possible long-term repercussions of liberalism on gender and family relations—a topic usually pushed aside by the more obvious economic and political troubles attached to liberal policies.

This is an urban study as it reveals gender and family relations within the city of Lima; however, it is also based on documentation beyond the city walls.[3] Records from the Peruvian viceroyalty, and, starting in 1825, from the newly founded Republic of Peru, were archived in Lima, the ecclesiastical and civil headquarters of a vast territory, including many rural provinces.[4] Although provincial judges and courtrooms existed, most lawsuits were resolved in the city of Lima, especially when the matter at stake required the intervention of a next higher judicial or ecclesiastical authority. Claimants came to Lima from remote provinces in order to pursue legal matters, in part because provincial politics and provincial elite networks among provincial notables were often so entrenched that "justice" for those excluded from such networks had to be sought elsewhere. Administrative reforms throughout the 1850s, 1860s, and beyond continued to create new archbishoprics, thus reducing the number of people who would resort to Lima's ecclesiastical court. Both the changing administrative boundaries

---

3. Remains of Lima's colonial wall are still visible today, although the city has expanded far beyond it.
4. While in 1850 Lima's archbishopric had the highest number of inhabitants per parish and included the departments of Lima, Callao, Ancash, and Junín, totaling 590,776 residents, by 1865 this vast geographical area had been greatly reduced and included only the department of Lima and the littoral provinces of Callao and Ica, totaling 205,000 residents (García Jordán, n.d.).

and mobility resulting from the pursuit of legal matters explain why this book reflects many cases from remote coastal and highland provinces as well as the more common urban lawsuits.[5]

Questions and Perspectives

Research on family, gender relations, and social change finds its theoretical underpinnings in a wide range of recent historiographical discussions: family history, feminism—and within these realms, power relations and resistance, and the redefinition of public and private spaces. Different opinions in each set of discussions are increasingly intertwined, and there is a continued search for a "middle ground" geared toward a better understanding of the workings of power relations in society. Feminists' understanding of gendered power stands in stark contrast to postmodern ungendered technology of power. One approach—that of feminists—leads to an understanding of the systematic oppression of women by men, an understanding of the workings of patriarchal domination, and, consequently, to a political agenda of women's historical vindication. The other approach—postmodernism—denies the overall existence of cleavages (including gender divisions), locates expressions and discourses of power at all levels of social interaction, and, consequently, enhances our understanding of an individual's exposure to power but does little to explain the systematic and long-term inequalities between social groups (including men and women).

Maureen Mahoney and Barbara Yngvesson, who take a stand with Michel Foucault, Pierre Bourdieu, and Michel de Certeau, put it succinctly: "That subordinates have resisted relations of domination is clear. Explanations of such resistance are unsatisfying, however, because they [the authors mentioned] emphasize the force of political economy and dominant cultural discourses and shy away from theorizing about the way relationships of power (whether based on class, gender or legal entitlement) are constructed psychologically and reproduced through everyday practice. Without an account of how subjects experience these relationships of power, we cannot

---

5. The spatial contraction of the archbishopric helps to explain why so many of my "rural cases" refer to the first half of the nineteenth century, whereas they tend to diminish in the second half of the century. I have decided to incorporate them, nevertheless, because so many migrants from Lima's rural provinces lived in Lima throughout the nineteenth century (Tables 1.8 and 1.9).

explain what impels them to resist domination and to make change" (1992, 44–45). And they conclude: "An explanation of resistance requires a theory of the subject as not being simply produced in relations of power but as making meanings in her relationships with others" (70).

Thus desire, knowledge, and agency need to be connected if we want to explain power and—more specifically—gender relations. Agency implies the construction of strategies based on individual knowledge and longings. Individuals are constantly trying to deal with their own worlds by interacting with others; they are, in Mahoney's and Yngvesson's wording, "active meaning-makers." Consequently, it is not the case that institutions undermine the family by interfering with intimate morality; rather, it is the opposite: the worst kind of tyranny is the intimate kind, and no real family life is possible where it rules. And this is no less true of secular than of religious society. Thus, individually constructed psychological meanings need to be evaluated to detect their systematicness. Translating this definition of historically constructed power relations back into Lima's marital conflict cases means that only if we can observe men and women using changing arguments to illustrate their cases, may a shift of power relations be detected. Moreover, in contrast to postmodernism, and in spite of class and ethnic cleavages, in nineteenth-century Lima gender *was* an argumentative divide.

Historiography in Europe and the United States that recognizes the close links between family history and broader contemporary issues, such as women's liberation and proletarian consciousness, has impelled family history to add new dimensions to already developed historical subjects. But not all scholarly approaches agree that the family, and with it the history of gender relations, is the crucial unit of analysis for understanding society's larger social structures and changes. Marxism considers the family as a dependent variable—that is, dependent on the overall socioeconomic transformations in society. A different view on the family informs us that the family is only intelligible in and by itself; its functions, roles, and internal dynamics have a different logic than that of the overarching society: "The family is different from the economy not simply in the functions it performs for the society but in the quality of the relations it contains. For this reason, the theory of the family cannot be functionalist. . . . The family is the social space where generations confront each other directly and where the two sexes define their differences and power relations" (Poster 1978, 143). Thus, both Marxist and family-centered perspectives question the validity of using family history as a basis for understanding society. In the first perspective, the family is defined by overarching socioeconomic processes; in the second, the family exists beyond society's reach.

Work on the family and women has shown that both approaches need to be reconciled if our goal is to understand society. Human beings are created by various sets of social relations, including families; and "the 'economy' can only be understood within the context of a society textured in these kinds of ways [inheritance practices, dowry, developmental cycle]; the 'public' life arises out of the dense determinations of the 'domestic' life" (Thompson 1978, 7). In this synthesizing view, class actions are seen as embedded in a political development and in daily (family) life conditions. At different times and places, families fulfill different roles. The family and its members should not be disconnected from society. Doing so leads to the emergence of false theorems, such as claiming that the family has suffered from a decrease of its social functions or that women have been passive victims of patriarchy, of their husbands' or their children's domination.[6] Following Thompson's synthesizing approach, the accent of our questions has shifted toward an understanding of the binding links between society, the family, and its individual members.[7]

A relatively new dimension in the trend of recognizing the dialectical relationship between family and wider social processes is the inclusion of the psychosocial aspects of domestic life across classes and cultures (Medick and Sabean 1982, 91–100). Conjugal property, for example, cannot be defined solely as the expression of individual material interests, because it is also a social communication that expresses the distribution of wealth within society and power relations within the family. Women challenging existing laws about who should administer conjugal goods are redefining socially and culturally constructed power relations, gender roles, and the institution of marriage. Thus, when women in Lima and elsewhere fight to rescue their conjugal assets from their husbands' squandering, they are not only trying to ensure their own and their children's survival, but by acting on their interests, they help define wider social processes. The gender-specific

---

6. Rosenbaum (1980 [1978], 19–20) and Mitterauer and Sieder (1980 [1977], 110) warn about the consequences of "disconnecting" family and socioeconomic development.

7. This tendency has been acknowledged across disciplines as we have witnessed a shift from women to gender issues, a wider assessment of the links between gender, class, and race, and new ways of representing women's voices (Acosta-Belén 1994, 12). Not surprisingly, given the complexity of race, class, and gender relations, a relatively high percentage of the works in this new direction in Latin America are twentieth-century-Peru-based. See especially Bourque and Warren (1981), Bunster and Charney (1989), Deere and León de Leal (1982), Babb (1989).

discourses built up in Lima's courtrooms—as we will see—reflect systematic connections between women's allegations in court, changing perceptions on women and the family, and changes in society.

Beyond general questions provided by trends in feminist/postmodernism debates and family historiography, more specific questions have arisen out of a growing literature on Latin American family history. In Latin America, historians and social scientists of gender and family issues have long viewed families as a part of encompassing social changes; that is, the family has been connected to overarching social processes.[8] By the 1970s scholars had recognized the peculiar political, social, and economic functions of extended family networks among the upper classes in Latin America (Cancian, Goodman, and Smith 1978, 337–60). Latin America's notable families deserved special attention because family networks among elites fill gaps left by the state.[9] Elites have often acted as corporate groups—reproduced by "family" mechanisms including the manipulation of marriage alliances—to maintain their economic and social power. In the lower echelons of society, the extended family (including ritual kin) replaces a deficient social security system and has helped to resolve political, economic, and emotional uncertainties (Golte and Adams 1987). Dependent economies and weak political structures appear to call for supplemental levels of support to make societies work. At the same time, the need for family-based support bestowed specific rules on families and, within them, on women.

Families exerted economic and moral control on society at large, and family-based notions of morality and order became the ideological pillars of the Latin American republics evolving from political instability. Elite families, especially, imposed sets of values on society at large that were codified in terms of honor, morality, and virtue. The regulation of gift exchange among family members, the organization of ceremonies and parties for rites of passage, the preservation of their daughters' virginity, and the strict control on with whom one was seen—all were part of the duties of wives within the scheme of a family-based social organization that helped integrate extended families and society.

8. For recent assessments in this direction, see Blom (1991), Stoner (1989, 101–34), Arrom (1991, 389–99, especially 396–99).

9. For research on Peru, see Bourricaud (1972) and Gilbert (1982). For other Latin American countries, especially Mexico, see Saragoza (1990), Lizaur and Lomnitz (1987), Kicza (1985), and Ladd (1976). On Argentina, see Socolow (1978), and for a comparative approach on three countries, see Balmori, Voss, and Wortman (1984).

Although the workings of elite family structure are well documented, overall we know much less about middle- and lower-class families, or families from specific ethnic and racial groups. Even less well documented is the interaction among upper, middle, and lower classes during their daily routines and the outcome of this interaction. Did lower-class families and women imitate the honor and virtue codes common among elites? Did upper-class women engage in lawsuits similar to the ones pursued by their lower-class sisters? There is still little evidence about how women from all classes and racial groups lived, with or without husbands or families. Without pretending to answer to all of these questions, this book will trace the interaction between classes and ethnic groups and will illustrate commonalties and divergences among them.

Following the trends of Latin American historiography of the 1970s, Latin Americanists in the 1980s perceived patriarchal structures and honor codes as being embedded in wider economic and social systems. However, a more nuanced interpretation was added. Historians publishing research on Latin America, especially social historians, favored the analysis of society's honor codes in regard to sustaining family life and subjugating women (Seed 1988; Gutiérrez 1985, 1991; Arrom 1985b; Szuchman 1988; Lavrin 1989). How and when did parents agree to marriages? How and when did children protest or act against parental will? How did different social groups comply with behavioral expectations? The answers to these questions provide a means of understanding how society framed attitudes and actions, and how, within these codes, lives were constrained or enhanced through the trials of free will. Such questions will also be addressed for Lima in the nineteenth century.

Recent studies show a strong tendency to envisage women's history as part of the general evolution of society and to accentuate women's participation in society, especially in regard to their participation in the labor market and to how they have undermined or complied with patriarchal rules. Nevertheless, we know little about women's pleas and about how to interpret them in the light of deeply entrenched race and class violence. Contrary to a widespread generalization that women were among the last groups to develop a social consciousness, they had—as I will argue in Chapters 5, 6, 7, and 8—such a consciousness as early as slaves and Indians (male and female) did. Lower-class women tied their work to their sense of rights even before the law granted such a connection; and more often than not, race and class arguments were implicit, if not explicit, in their allegations.

I have chosen to illustrate the subtle workings of a highly stratified society through the lens of gender relations. This decision is premised by the closeness between society and family in Latin America and by my perception that many different kinds of gender relations and discourses were created, not only in the course of time, but also according to who was using what kind of arguments and in which context. This decision, in turn, implies a reassessment of one of the most insistent arguments brought forward over the past two decades by Latin American feminists and feminists researching Latin America: that because developing countries exemplify oppression and exploitation at their worst, the feminist agenda is inevitably embedded in this general oppression (Acosta-Belén 1994, 5). However, eighteenth- and perhaps nineteenth-century Latin American economies approximated those of Europe and the United States. Given the similar economic performance, feminists' concerns in earlier times may have been similar to the ones promoted in Europe or the United States. From an eighteenth- or nineteenth-century perspective, the more obvious question is why the expressions of feminine (if not feminist) vindication sound so different from vindications put forward in Europe and in the United States.

Part of the problem is, I think, that feminists and social historians have looked in the wrong direction by trying to find European or North American feminist expressions in Latin America. Although there are similarities, especially in Latin American countries with large percentages of European immigrants (above all Argentina) later in the nineteenth century, this is not the case for areas such as Peru, where European migration was slight and where strong indigenous, African, Chinese, and mestizo populations prevailed. My sense is that the political activism that characterized the initial stages of feminist involvement in Europe and the United States only explains a part of the story. We need to look into the less obvious manifestations of feminine reasoning—for instance, into the "hidden transcript" behind many court cases; that is, the systematic changes in which complaints in court were forwarded by men and women of different walks of life. In 1994 Acosta-Belén wrote: "The contemporary stage, commonly referred to as the 'second wave' of the Latin American and Caribbean women's movement, is still challenging the patriarchal order of things and advocating increased rights, but searching more deeply than ever before into the historical roots of women's oppression and the social constructions of gender, segregated sex roles and double standards of sexuality, and denouncing the many forms of violence that women confront daily in both the domestic and public spheres" (10).

Denunciation and historical understanding of oppression are one side of the coin; the other calls for understanding women's reactions through an interpretation of the meaning of these reactions from a historical and statistical point of view.[10] Published work in the 1990s shows a clear tendency to examine how "domestic" issues were brought to the public arena. This has blurred the more traditional analytical separation between the private and the public spheres, and the transformation of "domestic" issues into political arguments (see especially Stoner 1991 and Lauderdale-Graham 1988). Thus, a redefinition of private and public spaces leads to a broader understanding of domestic work, and production and reproduction are seen as two sides of the same coin. In redefining the private and public spaces, more traditional views of the domestic division of labor are challenged, and a new approach to women's and the family's historical role is called for.

A parallel notion is that the comparatively high percentage of women heads of households working in the formal economy has much to do with how marriage was perceived (many women had been abandoned by their lovers or husbands) and with how lower-class women were catalogued in the honor/virtue pyramid (many women were expected to work or to be sexually compliant because they were black or Indian).[11] It was, above all, women from the lower classes who had to push "domestic" issues into the public domain. They were the ones who were sexually assaulted and put to work (Chapters 6, 7, and 8). These ongoing debates enlarge our understanding of present and past social processes by incorporating increasingly complex layers, new questions, and new sources with which to answer them.

Overall, this book is not a study of the "modernization" of the family in the usual sense (from patriarchy to individualism and the nuclear family) or a lament of the gendered restrictions imposed on women by patriarchs. Rather, it reveals the construction of a new terminology, and especially nineteenth-century liberal ideas imported from England and France, and how this terminology found its way into domestic life—with all

---

10. As far as possible and plausible, conflict cases have been represented both by illustrating individual life stories and by a summarized statistical form to account for more general tendencies. It is one way to meaningfully summarize the enormous amount of available court cases.

11. Very much in line with this interpretation, in presenting the articles by Potthast-Jutkeit, Salinas Mesa, Kuznesof, Ramos, Metcalf, Diaz, and Stewart in the 1991 no. 3 edition of the *Journal of Family History*, McCaa (1991, 215) writes: "Although it has been argued that these pathologies [i.e., women as householders and its consequences] were the first products of protoindustrialization in Latin America, they seem more likely the maturing of Iberian colonialism in multi-racial societies."

the contradictions and problems this implied—and how women conquered ever-new spaces and languages to counter and adapt to such changes.[12]

The core of this book is about women within families in trouble; and this vantage point, seeing women argue their rights and humanity in court, provides a new window from which to observe nineteenth-century Peruvian liberalism. Such an analysis requires an abundance of case studies because many different voices must be heard within a wide chronological framework. Changes in social perceptions, morality, and mentality are less obvious and harder to delineate than changes in balance of payments or trends in literary production. In the wake of reassessing liberalism from a reading of changing male/female relationships, much needs to be said about the objectives and mechanisms women used to make life livable well before womanhood was "discovered" by feminists. Women's history, based on women's real and imagined history, reveals popular-based feminine reasoning. In this sense, the portrayal of male/female relationships is an attempt to identify the subtle workings of female vindications, especially among women of the popular classes. At the same time, these gender-based struggles in the courtroom influenced historical outcomes in a multiethnic society.

Peru in the Nineteenth Century

Over the last decade the historiographical debate in and on Peru has focused on the content and significance of nineteenth-century economic and political liberalism. Between 1780 and 1910 (the "long nineteenth century"), Peru witnessed profound changes. This period saw border and civil wars, urban growth, and a new insertion into international markets. Nation building was a convoluted endeavor permeated with upheavals by Indian peasants, rural workers, and artisans.

Throughout the colonial period Lima had been one of the centers of the Spanish empire, but by the end of the nineteenth century it had lost much of its former preeminence, especially when compared to the burgeoning ports and cities on the Atlantic coast. Beginning with the Bourbon Reforms aimed at tightening Spain's control over its colonies, Lima's importance decreased.

---

12. An especially clear example of liberal contradictions and women's reactions to them is the transformation of the dowry system discussed in Chapter 7.

The establishment of new viceroyalties increased taxes on intracolonial trade, and the displacement of Creole bureaucrats from decision-making positions in the colonial state not only shifted the geographical locus of political power but also unleashed the struggles for independence. The wars of independence (1820–25) were fought in the name of liberal political ideas. However, political unrest and economic uncertainty caused a retreat from such ideas, which accounts for the perpetuation of colonial devices to extract surplus labor from Indian peasants and black slaves that lasted at least until midcentury, and for the disastrous financial situation of the Peruvian state and its urban and rural municipalities. Economic and political changes were slow and went hand in hand with the blocking of class, ethnic, and—as will be shown—gender claims. Women were victims—and occasionally heroes—of the wars of independence; however, they were not seen as part of the "imagined community" of the new nation-state (Pratt 1990, 51).

In the first decades after independence, Lima's population decreased—in contrast to what happened in other Latin American cities.[13] Numerous *caudillos* disputed political power, and presidencies were short-lived. After two decades of civil strife, some stability returned in the 1840s when Peru's *guano* deposits became valued in European markets. Mid-nineteenth century was a period of dramatic economic growth. The revenues obtained from *guano* exports provided the republican state with the income to lower import duties, build railroads and jails, improve the infrastructure of cities, abolish slavery and Indian tribute, and import laborers from China to work on coastal sugar plantations, construct the railroads, and dig on the guano islands. New migration policies appeared, fiscal revenues gave credence to liberal innovation, and political stability allowed the government to envisage social reform and even to promote education and sponsor writers.

---

13. For an assessment of Lima's population censuses in the nineteenth century, see R. Miller (1988) and Gootenberg (1990). In the available bibliography, authors agree that in comparison with other Latin American cities, Lima's demographic evolution was slow and that major demographic growth did not occur until the second half of the nineteenth century. The prime censuses for the nineteenth century are those of 1792 and 1876. The next major census was not carried out until 1940. Population figures from interim periods should be considered with skepticism because they were based on partial registers in some parishes or entirely on calculations. In spite of the censuses' flaws, it is probably true that Lima's population more than doubled between the end of the eighteenth century and the beginning of the twentieth century. See also Haitin (1983, 199). Available statistics on population between 1792 and 1940 are summarized in Table 1.1.

Many European businesses participated in the booming export economy by engaging in commerce and financial treaties with the Peruvian state. Peru's external debt soared until the 1873 financial crisis undermined the optimistic outlook of earlier decades. European merchants, some of whom were consular representatives, lived in Lima, interacting with each other and with Peru's political authorities and elites. Through them, news and ideas found their way to Peru's elites.[14] Henry Meiggs, the American engineer who built Peru's railroads, became the sponsor of intellectual organizations; President Manuel Pardo, their supporter. The writings of European liberal thinkers were translated into Spanish and became a part of Peru's political and economic philosophy. As they shaped Peru's liberal philosophy, these ideas were often transmuted, adapted, and sometimes rejected.[15] With living standards rising between 1845 and 1870, Lima's elites engaged in a modernization project, developed new tastes, and pursued European fashions. Although they increased their demands for social order, they did not open up political participation to the popular classes or acknowledge women's role in society. To the contrary, as will be discussed, the control on women was severed in the wake of the midcentury economic growth to make them fit the ideal of the domestic angel. Consuming British tea instead of "old-fashioned" chocolate was easier than producing new citizens.

The 1873 financial crisis and the War of the Pacific (1879–84) brought new economic hardships for the country. Between 1890 and 1910 the country underwent a slow export diversification, a more inward-looking economic development, and the political consolidation of the coastal export-oriented landed elite.

14. Heinrich Witt (1992), a Danish consul-merchant who lived in Lima for over thirty years after independence, describes such daily encounters in his diary in great detail.

15. For a thorough analysis of how liberal economic ideas became introduced and adapted to Peru during the nineteenth century, see Gootenberg (1994). My sense is that in a much more radical denial of liberal ideas, the enlightened *modernistas* of the eighteenth century had rejected and/or selectively and conveniently absorbed liberal ideas of their age. A reading of Lima's newspapers in the years preceding the wars of independence, as proposed by Macera (1977, 2:325–42), clearly sustains this interpretation: "La confusión y hasta la hibridez de estas posiciones son extensivos a la totalidad de las posiciones ideológicas del periodismo revolucionario. No podían vencer al pesimismo de su inducido complejo de inferioridad frente a los europeos. La construcción de una sociedad nueva no les parecía empresa difícil sino imposible, 'colocados como estamos, decía uno de ellos, en climas de perezosa influencia.' Pero al mismo tiempo creían en una ley de progreso continuo e indefinido, como lo dijo El Tribuno en su artículo sobre la Aptitud civil de la República Peruana *(sic)*. 'Oh generaciones futuras, rezaba el clérigo Larriva, la actual os envidia' " (Macera 1977, 2:340).

It was only toward the end of the nineteenth century that new avenues to express women's plight and women's thoughts were slowly opened up. The turn of the century saw the emergence of the first unions and feminist organizations.

The Messages

My archival research concentrates on these three crucial moments in Peruvian history: 1800–20, the end of the colonial period; 1840–60, the age of guano; and 1890–1910, the period of reconstruction after the War of the Pacific. My reading of gender relations thus relates the bedroom to the cycles of the political economy. Dramatic changes occurred in the arguments used by divorcing spouses toward the middle of the century, but less change occurred after that. Between 1890 and 1910 the arguments remained the same, the voices became louder, and many couples relinquished church and state intervention and control, attempting instead to resolve conflicts on their own.

In the broader historical picture, the changes in institutional settings throughout the nineteenth century involved the decline of the church as an arena of conflict and arbiter of marital strife and its replacement by the more secular state (Chapters 2, 3, and 4). Changes in social attitudes were reflected by the transformation of traditional instruments for protecting women and the family, such as dowries and inheritance practices (Chapters 5, 6, and 7). The character of litigation that took place over such issues as divorce,[16]

---

[16]. Throughout the nineteenth century, divorce in Peru meant a temporal separation of the spouses with ecclesiastical court approval and not the dissolution of marriage. For a very detailed discussion on divorce in Hispanic America and Mexico up to the mid-nineteenth century, see Arrom (1985, 206–58). Goody (1983, 41) offers a brief synthesis of divorce law in different cultures and time periods: "But Christianity decreed otherwise [in contrast to Roman, Greek and Hebrew law], and in this case the change goes back to the words of Christ himself (Mathew 19:3–9): 'What therefore God has joined together let no man put asunder.' Divorce became virtually impossible in Europe until Luther declared marriage a 'worldly thing' and allowed dissolution at least for adultery. The Church of England, on the other hand, inherited Roman canon law unchanged in this respect. While marriage was no longer a sacrament, it was still Holy Matrimony, and hence indissoluble—except for a brief period of fifty years after the Reformation and then again after 1857 when jurisdiction over matrimonial causes was taken away from the ecclesiastical courts. During the intervening period divorce was hard and remarriage impossible, creating the problem not so much of setting aside a spouse, since this

demand for compensation for sexual wrongs and abandoned marriage proposals (Chapter 5), property settlements, and alimony (Chapters 8, 9) mirror these changes.

Following the legal-cultural approach of the book, I draw some conclusions on how and why Lima's society moved from a religious-legal code, with its fusion of the moral and the material and its treatment of women as moral and intellectual inferiors, to the conflicts characteristic of breaking down the religious code and replacing it with a secular and liberal code, triumphant but embodying the patriarchal and religious assumptions that continued to subordinate women.

In sum, this study shows how nineteenth-century men and women continually redefined their roles in society, in the family, and in marriage through mediation by families and neighbors, and in civil and ecclesiastical court proceedings, where they expounded their views on society's often contradictory values and attitudes. These defining arguments appear in many lawsuits involving marital behavior and domestic assets. Women from different walks of life exposed their anger, suffering, impotence—and sometimes their victories—in court. Conjugal conflicts and outcomes are the lens illuminating women's participation in reformulating society's moral and economic schemes, and with them the boundaries of domesticity. Courtroom conflicts reveal the growing questioning of male predominance and show the limits of affection and bargaining between couples to resolve such conflicts. The cases not only plot how the rhetoric changed but also how urban life, popular ideology, and intimate possibilities evolved. The result was not "modern" in any evolutionary-sociological sense. Instead, layer after layer of expectations, arguments, and finally laws gradually laid new grounds on which women could contest their rights as human beings and, eventually, as citizens.

Modernity had little to do with women's consciousness. With uneven intensity and success, women criticized and changed racial perceptions and undermined social hierarchies through their allegations in court. Women, stigmatized by their sex and their race, have voices in the twentieth century,[17]

---

could be done informally, but dissolving the marriage legally and then being in a position to remarry." For an extraordinarily detailed and sophisticated account of divorce in Europe and the United States, see Phillips (1988).

17. For recent publications that underline the varying degrees of women's political involvement according to race and class background, see Jacquette (1989), de Oliveira (1989), Fisher (1993), Jelin (1990), F. Miller (1991), Escobar and Alvarez (1992), and Marks (1993).

but it must be recognized that women in the nineteenth century and earlier also had many voices.

Liberalism, far from opening doors for women, shifted the ground on which women waged battles for survival—while maintaining women's inferior legal status. By the end of the nineteenth century and the beginning of the twentieth century, many women had concluded that basic patriarchal and Christian arrangements were a fraud and that they had to think seriously about survival within this hypocrisy.

In the following chapters we will find many women and children made destitute by intimate tyranny as well as many who challenged this tyranny by constructing new avenues of defense and new social support systems.

1

Lima in the Nineteenth Century

Dramatic economic changes often produce an opening of the political realm in which more encompassing populist discourses challenge political exclusion.[1] In Lima economic changes came more slowly than in places like Mexico City, Buenos Aires, or Santiago. Lima's population only doubled during the nineteenth century, and even then its occupational structure scarcely altered. Still, the many social groups living in the city exerted pressures and expressed their willingness to be included in political life. The underclass, the many different racial groups, and women found new ways to challenge established customs, rules, and perceptions. In response, those groups that upheld the status quo forcefully propagandized racial and gender stereotypes and translated those perceptions into judicial rulings that excluded large segments of the population from the benefits of a full-fledged citizenship.

Economic and Demographic Changes

At the end of the colonial period—and in spite of the implementation of the Bourbon reforms—Lima's economy was stagnant: "For all practical

---

1. This argument is also forwarded by Lavrin (1995) to explain the development of feminism and social change in Argentina, Chile, and Uruguay between 1890 and 1940.

purposes industry was nonexistent in late eighteenth-century Lima. There were a number of water-powered flour mills, some looms for production of passementerie, a little soap manufacturing, a few mills for grinding cacao beans into chocolate, and a rather active earthenware works. These economic activities were more in the nature of a cottage industry than a full-fledged business enterprise. The city boasted only one factory—producing gunpowder—worthy of that name" (Haitin 1983, 117). Lima's physical structure reflected its decline. An earthquake in 1746 had destroyed about 90 percent of Lima's buildings. Reconstruction had been slow and costly, and the ruins were still visible at the beginning of the nineteenth century.[2]

In 1790, 52,627 people resided in Lima: 32.7 percent were white; 6.1 percent, Indian; 17.0 percent, black; and 44.1 percent, mestizo (Bromley and Barbagelata 1945, 76ff; see Table 1.1). Of those, 1,027 were artisans organized in guilds, although many more artisans labored independently.[3] Slaves made up 26 percent of the population. These groups earned their livelihood largely in the "mechanical arts," that is, within the service and manufacturing sectors. Most urban poor worked as servants,[4] day laborers, or peddlers for subsistence-level wages. Around 1800 most of the population experienced a decline in their standard of living (Haitin 1983, 117ff). Attempts to improve social well-being, forwarded by enlightened thinkers such as Ladrón de Guevara and Lequanda, were blocked by rigid social structures (Macera 1977, 3:186). Women were especially hard hit.

Lima's monasteries spent over 16,000 pesos per year to feed the city's poor. When the new archbishop took office in 1806, he followed a longstanding tradition by inviting poor and sick Spanish women in Lima to petition for monthly allowances.[5] About 4 percent of Lima's female population at the time—some 910 women—sent letters asking for financial aid. Many were widows, single, and/or sick; they had children and parents to care for, and because of their status, they could practice only needlework to earn money.[6] The lack of options was a part of the rigid traditional structures in

---

2. See, for instance, Domingo Angulo, Jorge Guillermo Leguía, Pablo Patrón, José de la Riva Agüero, and Horacio H. Urteaga, *Monografías históricas sobre la Ciudad de Lima, tomo II* (Lima: Librería e Imprenta Gil S.A.), 1935.

3. According to Macera (1977, 2:187) there were 1,155 artisans, day laborers, and "others."

4. Among servants, the 1790 census counted 2,903 "castas" (not including slaves) and 474 whites (Macera 1977, 2:186).

5. Macera (1977, 2:183–85, n. 59) mentions a similar document containing twenty-two petitions filed in Huamanga in 1792.

6. AA, Pobres, Siglos 18 y 19.

Table 1.1 Population growth and ethnicity in Lima, 1792–1920

Year	Total	White	Indian	Black	Casta	Mestizo	Slave	Asian
1792[a]	61,605	19,986	4,332	8,960	10,023	4,807	13,497	—
1812[d]	64,900	18,210	10,643	—	13,287	4,879	17,881	—
1841[b]	54,802	19,593	5,292	—	24,126	—	5,791	—
1857[ae]	94,195	38,394	32,083	10,683	—	13,035	—	—
1862[e]	89,434							
1876[a]	100,156	42,694	19,630	9,088	—	23,120	—	5,624
1876[e]	101,488							
1884[b]	101,488	10,506 (+56,628 creoles)	13,832	18,320	—	—	—	2,202
1891[ae]	103,956	47,645	18,660	7,494	—	25,481	—	4,676
1893[e]	107,114							
1896[e]	100,194							
1903[a]	130,202	55,918	19,878	7,275	—	43,559	—	3,572
1903[e]	130,829							
1908[ae]	140,539	58,683	21,473	6,763	—	48,133	—	5,487
1920[a]	172,567	70,350	18,248	6,608	—	71,688	—	5,673

Percentage Change in Racial Group Composition in Lima:				
White	Indian	Black/Casta/Slave	Mestizo	Asian
32%–41%	7%–11%	53%–4%	8%–42%	0%–3%

SOURCES:
[a] Bromley/Barbagelata (1945, 76ff.).
[b] *Informe Demográfico* (1972).
[c] Estadística: Municipalidad de Lima (n.d.).
[d] Moreno Cebrián (1977, 723).
[e] Miller (1988, 2).

urban society. As Hipólito Unánue, a progressive thinker of the early 1800s, noted, many Creole women were unwilling to be obstetricians because they considered it an "oficio vil" (dirty work).[7]

The wars of independence further worsened living conditions. Between 1821 and 1825 the armies of the contending political parties occupied Lima several times, and many people fled or died. Demographic recovery took at least until midcentury, the period of booming guano exports. The 1876 census counted 46,582 persons earning a living from agriculture, representing 45.2 percent of the city's population and 7.4 percent of the nation's economically active population (EAP). Independent professions, domestic

---

7. Unánue (1805), quoted in Macera (1977, 2:182).

servants, and others in the service sector accounted for 16.5 percent of the city's population (16,958 people) and 20.4 percent of national EAP.[8]

For Lima's white and mestiza women, however, not much had changed since the beginning of the century. Around 1895, Capelo (Morse and Capelo 1973, 69) calculated that Lima's 6,000 seamstresses (about 10 percent of the female population) earned, when they were lucky to find some work, a monthly income of only 13 soles, barely enough to buy meager amounts of food and pay for cheap lodgings. He commented: "Lima's seamstress is the being most worthy of protection that there can be." These women included wives, mothers, and daughters of impoverished or deceased white men. The real or alleged status of white and mestiza women limited their job opportunities. In the meantime, their darker-skinned sisters were earning higher incomes by working in factories (around 1,000 women), cooking (around 3,000), and as laundresses (around 1,000) (Morse and Capelo 1973, 22–23).

By 1900 about 30 percent of Lima's population was employed in *servicios menores* (men and women working as domestics).[9] Of these 30,000 people, 11,000 were men, and 19,000 were women, which included the 3,000 cooks and the 1,000 laundresses. At the turn of the twentieth century, approximately 70 percent of the female population in Lima worked in low-paying, typically female jobs, while natural population growth and migrant labor were partially absorbed into preexisting occupations.

Throughout the century the ideal of progress was interwoven with demographic issues. For contemporaries, economic stagnation resulted from labor shortages (more so on rural estates than in the city) and Peru's "inadequate" racial composition. Legal measures and civil codes reveal a concern about Lima's demographic development. In the 1830s Manuel Vidaurre, a judge in the Supreme Court, proposed that people still single at age thirty-five should be considered legal offenders and be sentenced to pay maintenance for three children in an orphanage. He also suggested that people advocating chastity or encouraging women to join convents should be punished by withholding their citizenship for ten years. Homosexuality he considered high treason against the country, and having sexual intercourse with old women he interpreted as a waste of semen

---

8. Pinto and Goicochea (1977, 19).

9. Capelo (Morse and Capelo 1973, 99) divided Peru's labor force into those participating in "producción primaria," and "producción derivada." The first group includes: *agricultores, industrias domésticas, oficios, empresas industriales, artistas, transportadores, comerciantes, transeúntes.* The second group includes: *servicios menores, profesiones especiales, oficinistas, funcionarios, militares, contratistas, rematistas, rentistas,* and *parásitos.*

(Trazegnies 1980, 154–55). Such extreme "liberal" approaches found little audience.

However, Vidaurre's concern over fertility levels was somewhat justified. In the first half of the nineteenth century, life expectancy at birth was about thirty years (Haitin 1983, 245). By 1859 it still averaged only thirty to thirty-two for men and thirty-two to thirty-four for women.[10] Death was particularly common among newborns and remained at approximately 23 percent well into the twentieth century. As Rory Miller put it: "The contemporary concern with disease and death was not misplaced. Lima, in short, was an extremely unhealthy place in which to live, with high infant mortality and a wide range of endemic and epidemic disease" (1988, 12).[11]

In spite of an increasing respect for hygiene and slow infrastructural expansion, the municipal government was concerned about Lima's population. In 1884 officials made a head count at the five main gates to the in-wall city. On average, 2,295 people entered Lima each month, whereas 2,815 left, a monthly loss of 520 inhabitants (6,240 residents each year, an equivalent of 6.1 percent of the city's 1884 population). A continuous flow of immigrants from Peru's rural provinces and from abroad did not stop pessimistic observers from using these statistics and birth and death rates to calculate that Lima would disappear on the fifth of July at midnight in the year 2074 (Clavero 1885, 37). This negative assessment proved inaccurate: Lima boasted 130,289 people by 1903 and—well beyond the former city walls—8 million people in 1990.

Although Lima was not densely populated overall, the poorest neighborhoods—such as Barrios Altos[12]—were overcrowded. Migrants from other regions in the country crammed into less expensive interior city areas, and migrants increasingly settled *outside* the city walls, in the *balnearios*. Until the end of the nineteenth century, Lima's physical expansion happened mainly in the suburbs. Between 1848 and 1876 growth in Lima's suburbs was much higher than in the city itself.[13] On average, the suburbs witnessed a 7.3

---

10. Informe Demográfico (1972, 108). See also Haitin (1983, 245), who states that infant mortality in Lima must have exceeded 200 per 1,000 births.
11. Haitin also notes that the faults in the registration system make it impossible to give exact figures on infant mortality. "The estimates made in the first decade of the [twentieth] century, however, concur in suggesting that the infant mortality figures for Lima were among the highest in the world." For example, in 1903 there were 276 deaths in the first year of life per 1,000 births; in 1908, 319 deaths in the first year per 1,000 births, plus an additional 125 deaths before the children reached two years of age.
12. Eyzaguirre, cited in R. Miller (1988, 12).
13. Data presented in Informe Demográfico (1972, 87–88).

percent population increase between 1848 and 1876, whereas Lima's population grew only by 0.8 percent between 1841/1856[14] and 1876. The populations of Ate, Magdalena, and Carabayllo increased 12.5 percent; Chorrillos, Surco, Miraflores, and Ancón, 6 percent; and Lurin and Pachacamac, 2.5 percent. Lima eventually absorbed these outlying areas. Toward midcentury, Peru's booming export economy attracted more migrants, which accounts for the more rapid population growth in the latter part of the century in addition to slight increases in rates of reproduction in spite of the still-high infant mortality rates and low fertility and life expectancy.

Between 1810 and 1900, 73 percent of all testators in Lima[15] declared that they were either married or widowed, and of these 33 percent had no children (see Table 1.2). In other words, one third of Lima's wives never bore children. Fertility was extremely low, lower than in other cities in Latin America and the rest of the Western world in this period.[16] For those testators with children (the remaining 67 percent), on average only 1.7 children were living at the time of the making of the will. Thus, during the 1800s too few children survived to replace the parents' generation. Lima reached a replacement rate (2.0 children per married or widowed testator) only in 1870 with a slight increase (2.1 children) by 1880. Dramatic drops in childbirth rates are visible first in 1830 (probably signaling the consequences of the wars of independence) and again in 1890 (as a result of the War of the Pacific) (see Table 1.2). Moreover, there are no clearly discernible surges in fertility, which indicates that natural growth had little to do with the doubling of Lima's population toward 1900. Meager municipal records for the nineteenth century show that birth/death ratios were negative except in 1826, the period between 1887 and 1894, and after 1917 (Table 1.3).[17]

Indicators derived from a reading of wills and municipal records may underrepresent natural growth in two ways: parents with children were not

14. To bring Lima's average growth near to the 1848 calculations provided in the Informe Demográfico, an average has been taken of the population figures given for Lima in the 1841 and 1856 censuses (see Table 1.1).

15. This data is based on a recording of 1,394 wills from all available notarial records existing in the AGN for every ten years between 1810 and 1900.

16. For a discussion of fertility, conception, and birth in the Western world, see Gottlieb (1993, 113–31). Haitin (1983, 222) has calculated a fertility rate of 6.2 children per legal marriage in Lima and concludes that the city (as well as León in Mexico, Buenos Aires in Argentina, and Santiago in Chile) had high fertility rates. My own findings—based on a reading of wills—sharply contradict his conclusions on fertility for Lima.

17. R. Miller (1988, chart between pp. 5 and 6) shows strong fluctuations until 1881 and stabilizing trends beginning at the end of the War of the Pacific and in 1918, and records the difficulties in establishing accurate figures.

Table 1.2 Children and fertility in Lima, 1810–1900 (percentage)

	No Children	Fertility/Mortality	Natural Children
1810	36.3	1.5	15.8
1820	35.8	1.6	19.7
1830	31.2	1.3	14.6
1840	35.7	1.8	15.5
1850	23.8	1.7	16.5
1860	33.8	1.9	21.3
1870	33.0	2.0	20.8
1880	32.7	2.1	17.2
1890	22.5	1.7	18.9
1900	47.9	1.6	21.7

SOURCE: AGN, Notarial Records, Wills.

compelled to write a will because the law dictated how an estate was to be divided among surviving children; and, perhaps more significantly, many children were born out of wedlock. Soaring percentages of illegitimacy throughout the 1800s not only reveal frequent premarital or extramarital sexual relationships but also indicate the presence and problem of natural children.

Wills and matrimonial licenses reflect illegitimacy rates.[18] In matrimonial licenses the registered illegitimacy rate is 19.1 percent for men and 24.1 for women (Table 1.4). Between 1800 and 1820 the percentage for men and women was 22.3; from 1840 to 1860 it rose slightly to 22.9 percent; and at the end of the century—1880 and 1890—it fell to 16.7 percent. The drop of the illegitimacy percentage in this last period seems to reflect an increased wariness to record illegitimacy rather than a drop of illegitimate births. These figures confirm the broad tendencies registered in wills, but overall the percentages reflected in marriage licenses are higher.

---

18. Given the uncertain and dubious nature of available population censuses, wills and matrimonial licenses prove to be more trustworthy sources. However, we need to remember that not all of Lima's inhabitants knew about the existence of notaries or went to one to sign their wills. A high percentage of *limeños* never opened a matrimonial license file—an obligatory procedure defined in canon law—to petition the church for approval for their impending marriage. Many couples did not marry at all, and many did so only after the birth of one or more children. Nevertheless, wills and matrimonial licenses have definite advantages. In the case of wills, individuals—approaching the Final Judgment—were morally compelled to admit to illegitimate and natural offspring. In the case of matrimonial licenses, data is confirmed by witnesses' declarations.

Table 1.3 Natality/mortality in municipal records, 1826–1924

Year	Annual Natality	Annual Mortality	Natality/Mortality Ratio
1826[a]	2.940	2.668	1.1019
1827	2.940	3.171	0.9271
1838–47[b]		3.044	
1848–57		3.981	
1864[c]	4.180	4.625	0.9037
1867	3.186	3.797	0.8390
1870	4.380	4.715	0.9289
1874	3.896	4.091	0.9523
1877	4.767	4.854	0.9820
1880	3.450	6.291	0.5484[d]
1884	3.528	4.214	0.8372
1887	4.268	3.659	1.1664
1890	4.137	3.924	1.0542
1894	3.964	3.756	1.0553
1897	3.728	4.171	0.8937
1900	3.845	4.473	0.8596
1904	3.762	4.088	0.9202
1907	4.604	4.758	0.9676
1910	4.111	4.899	0.8391
1914	4.169	4.618	0.9027
1917	5.665	4.948	1.1449
1920	7.028	5.908	1.1895
1924	7.337	5.250	1.3975

SOURCES: Several scattered papers in AML, paquete 65.
[a] In 1820, 3.930 people died; in 1821, 4.505; in 1822, 5.568; in 1826 (which after the wars of independence was the first "normal" year), 2.668; in 1827, 3.171. In these two last years it has been calculated that 2.940 children were born (natality/mortality ratio ranging between 1.1019 and 0.9271) (BN, *La Prensa Peruana*, 12 August 1828 [kindly provided by Paul Gootenberg].)
[b] *Informe Demográfico* (1972, 116).
[c] Indicators between 1864 and 1884 were published by Clavero (1884, 65).
[d] This sharp drop was a consequence of the battles against Chilean occupation and reached its peak in 1881, when the birth/death ratio was 0.3779.

Matrimonial licenses also indicate differences between men and women in regard to illegitimacy rates. Long-term trends apply to both, but overall, marrying women had substantially higher illegitimacy rates. At the beginning of the century, 20.1 percent of the men were illegitimate in contrast to 24.6 percent of the women. Thirty years later the figures were 19.4 and 26.3 percent respectively, and toward the end of the 1800s the gap widened still further: 13.2 percent of marrying men declared themselves to be illegitimate compared to 20.5 percent for the women. Within the overall trend toward

Table 1.4 Legitimacy/illegitimacy in Lima's matrimonial licenses, 1800–1900

Year	% Men	Total Marriages	Cases with Data	% Women	Total Marriages	Cases with Data
1800	17.6	889	783	20.6	889	767
1810	19.8	445	258	24.2	445	260
1820	22.8	222	114	28.9	222	114
1830	20.7	326	222	20.1	325	234
1840	16.0	167	156	26.1	167	157
1850	17.8	206	197	24.9	206	189
1860	24.5	384	330	28.0	384	339
1870	22.4	509	407	27.2	509	426
1876[a]						
1880	15.3	333	300	24.6	333	321
1890	11.1	352	332	16.5	352	345

SOURCE: AA, Licencias Matrimoniales, parroquias: Santa Ana, San Sebastián, San Lázaro, Huérfanos, San Marcelo, Sagrario.
[a] 1,185 of 2,196 men and 1,046 of 2,083 women; based on the 1876 census for the parishes of Santa Ana, Sagrario, San Lázaro, Cercado, San Sebastián, and San Marcelo.

high illegitimacy rates around 1850, followed by a slow decline toward the end of the century, women's illegitimacy rates at the end of the century had barely dropped to the level of percentages registered by men in the early 1800s. In the tightening moral climate of the nineteenth century, illegitimacy was (still) considered a social stain that went hand in hand with low birth, and the higher percentage of illegitimate women in matrimonial records may indicate that more illegitimate women married legitimately born men. This may be statistical evidence of a subtle, morally defined female hypergamy and an expression of women's desire to cleanse their offspring from this social stigma.

Wills corroborate these trends. Almost one fifth (18.2 percent) of Lima's children were born out of wedlock between 1810 and 1900, ranging from 17.8 percent between 1810 and 1820 and between 1840 and 1860, and rising to 19.3 toward the end of the century (from Tables 1.5 and 1.6). A comparison of the marriages/illegitimacy ratios shows that natural parents had as many natural children as married parents had legitimate children (Tables 1.5 and 1.7). In other words, fertility was low throughout, but population growth calculations must take into account both legitimate and illegitimate/natural children.

Migration also explains population growth. A look at migration patterns throughout the period shows that a coincidence of slightly higher fertility

Table 1.5 Natural children declared in Lima's wills, 1810–1900

Year	Married	Abandoned	Divorced	Widowed	Single	Total	%a
1810	7	0	2	4	26	39	15.8
1820	22	0	1	11	20	54	19.7
1830	8	0	0	0	16	24	14.6
1840	8	0	1	4	17	30	15.5
1850	12	0	0	4	12	28	16.5
1860	9	1	0	13	13	36	21.3
1870	8	5	11	8	26	58	20.8
1880	16	0	5	4	25	50	17.2
1890	6	3	0	9	17	35	18.9
1900	7	0	1	11	24	43	21.7
Total	103	9	21	68	196	397	
Percentage	25.9	2.3	5.3	17.1	49.4	100.0	18.2

SOURCE: AGN, Notarial Records, Wills.
a Of all children (legitimate and natural) declared in wills.

Table 1.6 Wills registering legitimacy/illegitimacy, 1810–1900

Year	Illegitimate	Legitimate	N/A	Total
1810	22	154	16	192
1820	18	148	8	174
1830	15	136	3	154
1840	16	98	8	122
1850	13	107	5	125
1860	14	71	6	91
1870	18	100	33	151
1880	18	113	28	159
1890	7	77	18	102
1900	11	73	40	124
Total	152	1,077	165	1,394
Average %	10.9	77.3	11.8	100.0

SOURCE: AGN, Notarial Records, Wills.

rates and rural-urban and international migration account for the slow increase of Lima's population around 1870.

The Peruvian state answered its demographic challenge by encouraging immigration. It brought laborers from China to solve the rural shortage of labor (especially after the abolition of slavery and Indian tribute during the mid-1850s) and from Europe to "improve" the racial mix and bolster

Table 1.7 Number of children alive when parents wrote their wills, 1810–1900

Year	No. of Couples with					6 or More Children	Total Children per/Year	Annual Average
	1	2	3	4	5			
1810	21	23	16	6	4	8	207[a]	2.6
1820	23	23	20	6	5	7	220	2.6
1830	16	10	12	9	4	2	140	3.3
1840	14	13	7	11	2	8	163	3.0
1850	17	8	12	4	3	7	142	2.8
1860	11	9	1	6	7	7	133	3.2
1870	15	13	11	7	7	14	221	3.3
1880	15	17	13	13	7	11	241	3.2
1890	13	9	8	4	5	9	150	3.1
1900	8	8	9	7	2	11	155	3.4
Total	153	133	109	73	46	84	598	3.1
Average %	25.6	22.2	18.2	12.2	7.7	14.0	100.0	

SOURCE: AGN, Notarial Records, Wills.
NOTE: Here I am only considering those spouses that declared themselves married or widowed when they wrote their will.
[a] Total amount of children involved, divided by the number of will declarations.

the labor pool. The steady growth of the white population, particularly after 1850, suggests that demographic changes resulted from European immigration and perhaps from higher fertility and lower mortality rates in this group. However, it may also reflect "cultural whitening."

Beginning in the 1850s, immigrants from all over the world transformed Lima into a more cosmopolitan city. Immigrants from neighboring countries (those classified as South Americans), Chinese, and Europeans joined the existing black, white, and Indian populations. Among Europeans, Italians were the single largest group (Worral 1973). Irish and Spaniards also arrived, along with Germans, who colonized small areas in the Amazon basin and worked in mines and haciendas. Some groups, such as the Polynesians, suffered complete disaster, and those lucky enough to survive very quickly returned home (Sacchetti 1904).

Although African slaves substantially increased Lima's population between 1792 and 1812, Africans had "disappeared" by midcentury. The slave trade was abolished in 1808, and slavery itself in 1854. The first Chinese immigrants disembarked in Callao in 1849, but the "coolie" trade was suppressed shortly afterward and reestablished only in 1863. Peruvian census takers counted the Chinese (called "Asians") only after 1876. Chinese immigrants had to redeem their labor contracts before being free to choose a new living site (Rodriguez 1989), which may account for the lag between their first arrival and their appearance in Lima's censuses (Table 1.1).

I have extrapolated migration indicators from matrimonial licenses for each decade from 1800 to 1890 (Tables 1.8 and 1.9). Wills—in contrast to matrimonial licenses—tend to minimize migration indicators because they were usually recorded in the place of birth of the testator. Similarly, it may be assumed that couples marrying in Lima intended to remain there. This assumption is further reinforced throughout the nineteenth century by the

Table 1.8 Place of birth of men married in Lima, 1800–1890 (percentage)

Origin	1800	1810	1820	1830	1840	1850	1860	1870	1880	1890
Peru	82.1	71.4	76.5	75.3	81.3	76.0	81.7	82.3	64.5	75.4
Rural	41.2	33.1	34.9	29.4	23.8	35.8	40.2	50.6	27.4	38.7
Lima	40.9	38.3	41.6	45.9	57.5	40.2	41.5	31.7	37.1	36.7
Foreign	17.9	28.6	23.5	24.7	18.8	24.0	18.3	17.7	35.5	24.6
Europe	65.2	48.5	43.6	37.0	40.0	57.1	60.3	43.2	69.3	58.8
South Am.	23.2	22.3	48.7	42.5	36.7	36.7	30.9	39.8	13.2	24.7
North Am.	1.9	1.0	0.0	2.7	3.3	0.0	2.9	4.5	1.8	2.4
Asia							5.9	11.4	11.4	12.9
Others	9.7	28.2+	7.7	17.8+	20.0	6.2	0.0	1.1	4.3	1.2
Total	889	445	222	325	167	206	384	509	333	352

SOURCE: AA, Licencias Matrimoniales.

Table 1.9 Place of birth of women married in Lima, 1800–1890 (percentage)

Origin	1800	1810	1820	1830	1840	1850	1860	1870	1880	1890
Peru	95.3	87.1	92.9	93.9	96.3	95.1	93.2	95.5	85.9	93.1
Rural	36.9	26.6	25.4	26.3	22.6	27.5	37.0	55.3	31.5	39.6
Lima	58.5	60.5	67.5	67.6	73.8	67.6	56.2	40.2	54.4	53.5
Foreign	4.7	12.9	7.1	6.1	3.7	4.9	6.8	4.5	14.1	6.9
Europe	51.3	4.4	25.0	15.8	33.3	30.0	40.0	31.8	58.7	66.7
South Am.	28.2	22.2	75.0	57.9	66.7	70.0	56.0	54.7	26.1	29.2
North Am.	2.6	0.0	0.0	0.0	0.0	0.0	4.0	4.5	2.2	0.0
Asia								4.5	4.3	0.0
Others	17.9	73.4	0.0	26.3	0.0	0.0	0.0	4.5	8.7	4.1
Total	889	445	222	325	167	206	384	509	333	352

SOURCE: AA, Licencias Matrimoniales.

existence of ecclesiastical regulations that required that a woman marry in her parish of birth (Valverde 1942, 215).

Taking an annual average for 1800 to 1890, 41.1 percent of the men and 60 percent of the women registered in the matrimonial licenses were born in Lima. Averaged together, only about 50 percent of the people marrying in Lima were born there. Men migrating from elsewhere in Peru represented 35.5 percent of the total, and women, 32.8 percent. The narrow gap between these percentages confirms that migrants tended to marry each other. Moreover, these couples usually came from the same region or even the same town. Thus, about one third of all marriages in Lima took place between individuals who had been born in other regions of Peru. Immigration from rural provinces surged around 1800 and again in 1870 for both sexes. These surges broadly coincide with the slightly rising fertility rates, especially around 1870.

Throughout the nineteenth century about 15 percent of all marriages in Lima involved foreigners, but there were differences between men and women. More foreign men (23.4 percent of all marriages) than women (7.2 percent) married in Lima.[19] Among foreign men, Europeans were the most numerous (52.3 percent), followed by men from other South American countries (31.9 percent). For women the reverse was true: South American women (barring temporal fluctuations) represented the largest group (48.6 percent), followed by European women (35.7 percent). Military or political unrest was linked to marriage with foreigners. In 1810 and 1830, marriage to Africans predominated; in 1820, during the wars of independence, and again in 1880, during the War of the Pacific, marriage with migrants from the interior was common. Overall, in the 1870s the coincidence of more stable immigration patterns with slightly increasing fertility rates may account for Lima's population growth in the last third of the century. As the century progressed, conjugal conflict cases—as will become obvious in the following chapters—not surprisingly involved an increase of men and women of European origin and a steady presence of couples born in other regions of the country in spite of the reduction in size of Lima's archbishopric.

Faced with an increasingly heterogeneous population, census takers found it more and more difficult to categorize the many racial types resulting

---

19. According to the 1876 census (cited in Pinto and Goicochea 1977, 9), the foreign population in Lima was 35,518. Of these 27,188 were employed men, 5,034 were unemployed men. From a total of 3,296 foreign women, only 600 were employed.

from miscegenation. Thus, information regarding race is deficient in Lima's censuses.[20] Nevertheless, the censuses between 1792 and 1920 (see Table 1.1) reveal general tendencies in Lima's demography: a steady increase in whites, a highly fluctuating Indian presence that reflected migration patterns from rural provinces, a decrease in the number of blacks as part of the quickening manumission process, and a steady growth of the mestizo population. In 1812 whites and mestizos accounted for 44.1 percent of Lima's total population; by 1920 they represented 82.1 percent. This dramatic increase in the mestizo population reflects not only miscegenation but also the perceptions of the census takers and the desire on the part of those being counted to belong to a whiter social group ("cultural whitening").

In spite of Lima's relatively slow demographic growth, ethnic diversity multiplied rapidly, and racially defined boundaries became more blurred. In spite of the spreading belief that "order and progress" went together, municipal authorities, the police, and even priests often found it difficult to fulfill this mandate.

Policing the City

The municipality attempted to remake life in the city as part of its effort to organize state power, spur economic growth, and gain control over the expanding population. The many different initiatives, few of which were successful, show how difficult it was to establish social, political, and budgetary control.[21] For most of the nineteenth century, the state was far removed from people's more private interests. As a consequence, people enjoyed some leeway in organizing their lives but also suffered from the consequences of "social disorder."

According to the 1792 census, the province[22] of Lima had 16 districts, 3 villages, 9 towns, 18 hamlets, and 169 haciendas. Around that time Lima

---

20. Criteria used to classify people racially were not applied consistently from census to census or even within one single census. Racial, cultural, and economic criteria overlapped; thus, census information on race should be considered with care.

21. Lima was no exception. Similar attempts have been made in other cities in Latin America. For Argentina, see L. C. Johnson (1990) and Szuchman (1988); for Brazil, see Holloway (1993).

22. Each department had several provinces. Provinces, in turn, were divided into districts, villages, towns, hamlets, and haciendas.

proper counted 3,641 houses on 355 streets. Although the city was divided into four *cuarteles*, and those *cuarteles* into 35 *barrios* (Haenke 1808, 55–68), people identified themselves first as belonging to a *barrio* or to one of Lima's six parishes,[23] a demonstration of the importance of the neighborhood and the church in people's minds, of their unwillingness to accept administrative changes, and of how slowly encompassing administrative changes reached people's awareness.

Throughout the nineteenth century the province of Lima retained much of its rural character. The number of haciendas in Lima's outskirts actually increased; the 1876 census registered 247 haciendas.[24] As noted earlier, almost half of Lima's population earned a livelihood from agriculture. People who worked and lived on haciendas traveled to Lima to sell their produce in the markets, make purchases, promenade, see relatives, or visit one of the city's many *pulperías* (liquor stores).

Toward midcentury economic growth and state consolidation allowed government officials to pursue administrative changes. In 1861 districts were reduced to ten. The number of doors in the city had grown to 14,000, but the number of streets had diminished to 346. One more *cuartel* existed, and the number of *barrios* had increased by eleven (Haenke 1808, 55–68). Still, by 1861 the city within walls was no larger than 5.7 square kilometers, although this figure almost doubles to 9.4 square kilometers if the parish of San Lázaro, one of Lima's most densely populated parishes beyond the walls, is included. About half of the city space was either owned by the church, was under municipal control, or was part of the rural landscape.[25] Despite the many administrative changes, city authorities had a difficult time in implementing what they called "social order."

In 1785 the *visitador general* and superintendent, Jorge Escobedo, deemed Lima a social disaster and declared he would take action. On April 17 he ordered the city's subdivision into *cuarteles* and *barrios*. Shortly afterward he appointed *alcaldes de barrio* (*barrio* mayors), who were each in charge of a

23. These were Santa Ana, San Marcelo, San Sebastián, Huérfanos, Sagrario, and the Cercado. A seventh parish, San Lázaro, was located outside the city walls.

24. Toward the beginning of the twentieth century, when international sugar prices dropped dramatically, Italian immigrants were able to buy almost all of Lima's outlying haciendas (Trazegnies 1980, 69).

25. Within the city's walls, churches and convents occupied 8.3 percent of the land, and plazas and squares another 1.6 percent. If the walled city and the parish of San Lázaro are considered together, about 36.3 percent of the total 9.4 square kilometers consisted of orchards, vegetable gardens, and garbage dumps. None of this space was actually available for habitation, which means that only about 53.8 percent of the city's total area was inhabitable.

small police force. Such measures were meant to safeguard tranquility and order in the city. The *alcaldes de barrio* were chosen from among "persons of distinction," and subordinate to them were *serenos* or watchmen, who actually patrolled the streets. The *serenos* became a part of daily life in the city as they walked through each *barrio* and shouted out the time on the hour. They also witnessed matrimonial disputes, rescued desperate wives from beatings by drunken husbands, and espied all kinds of adulterous behavior. By 1806 the *serenos* were allowed to use firearms, but only after 10:00 P.M.[26] Supposedly the citizens in the *barrios* paid the salaries of the *serenos*, but there were no means to enforce this. Consequently, neither the *alcaldes de barrio* nor the *serenos* had the necessary financial support to enforce municipal regulations.

Although social disorder was already a central concern to Peru's viceroy and Lima's elites at the end of the eighteenth century, the wars of independence brought even more disorder. The wars displaced many people, either because of the military draft or because of hunger. At their conclusion, weapons and ammunition fell into the hands of robbers, often former soldiers; and organized bands attacked people and property, even in the cities.[27]

During the wars married men could not be drafted, so the law was changed to prohibit marriage. Concubinage increased dramatically and threatened troop morality.[28] The number of marriages declined around 1820 (see Tables 1.8 and 1.9) in response to the new law, and in spite of the ruling against drafting married men, many husbands were forced to leave their wives and families behind. Some established new families elsewhere and never returned. In 1845 one abandoned wife remembered: "The separation caused by the wars bent my husband's feelings. In his heart he harbored many different passions and instead of finding out where I was in order to fulfill his marital obligations, he engaged in a dubious relationship in Huancayo [central highland city], where he has been living over the past twenty-one years, scandalizing the whole neighborhood."[29]

The ordeals of another woman, Bernardina Chaves, reveal the uncertainties brought about by the war. She was the daughter of a priest in one of

26. AGN, RA, CCR, L 108, C 1301, 1806.
27. Organized bands and robbers were already widespread prior to the wars of independence, but gained momentum during and after the war. See Walker and Aguirre (1990), especially the chapter by Flores Galindo.
28. CDIP, 5:462–63, Comunicación del Doctor José M. del Piélago al Comandante Paula Otero, Cerro de Yauricocha, 19 November 1821.
29. AA, LM, L 9 (1820–49), 1845, Lagardía vs. Collazos.

Lima's rural provinces. During the war her father found her in bed with her lover, Sebastián Villar, and insisted that they marry. Witnesses were brought in, and Bernardina and Sebastián agreed to marry. The day after the marriage, Sebastián was drafted into the army. Bernardina's father forced the witnesses not to tell anyone about the marriage, so that nobody would know that it ever took place. After seven years Bernardina and her father assumed Sebastián was dead, and Bernardina remarried. Bernardina had several children in her new union, but four years after the second marriage, Sebastián appeared. Everyone involved agreed that nothing could be done; Sebastián was willing to let Bernardina go and to marry another woman. Soon afterward, Bernardina's second husband died. After four years of widowhood, she began a new relationship. But her father—knowing that her first husband was alive—did not agree to a third marriage. Bernardina and her new lover married in a different parish to escape her father's control. One year after the third marriage, Bernardina's father received a letter from Sebastián inquiring about his wife. For more than eight years, Bernardina hid the knowledge of Sebastián from her third husband by moving from town to town. Around 1852, Bernardina fell ill. Believing she would die, she confessed the whole story to her husband. Bernardina survived, and she and her third husband sought advice from a priest. This local priest absolved them of their sins, but only a few months later, Lima's archbishop declared the union between Sebastián and Bernardina valid and ordered Bernardina to separate from her third husband.[30] We do not know if Bernardina followed the archbishop's directive or the whereabouts of Sebastián after 1850. Nevertheless, Bernardina's story epitomizes the uncertainties arising from years of war.

Banditry, illegitimacy, and irregular marital status were all signs of turbulent political times and, as perceived by liberals and conservatives alike, of social and moral decay. Efforts to deal with this disorder were unsuccessful. By 1827 police inspectors asked the municipality to enlarge their power and to provide them with more and better equipment to deal with the city's turmoil.[31] *Serenos* were allowed to carry firearms at all hours but still lacked the authority to incarcerate public offenders. That same year, the inspector general of *Cuartel II* answered questions raised by the office of Lima's prefect (the city's highest police authority) in response to complaints

---

30. AA, Comunicaciones Oficiales de Curas, L 6 (1848–53), 1850, Comunicación de Juan Bautista Gusmán, Parroquia de Hatun Yauyos, January 23, 1850.
31. AGN, PJ, Prefectura, L 117, 1827.

concerning the inefficiency of *serenos* and police inspectors. The inspector general defended his subordinates and claimed that "the deplorable state of the capital" resulted not from the *serenos'* inefficiency, but because even "the most abject underclass [*plebe*][32] knew that *serenos* and inspectors had no real power" and that "they were but insignificant agents, because they could not incarcerate delinquents even if they were caught red-handed, because there were no safe places in which to confine them." It followed—the inspector argued—"people felt free to commit all sorts of crimes . . . [and] the general public knows that there is no authority and no police to call upon in case of an insult and at nights there are only few *serenos* in the streets."[33] Rich people confronted what in their eyes was a chaotic situation, but few were willing to pay money to a state that was not able to guarantee their personal safety or the safety of their property. Until the 1840s the Peruvian state even lacked the resources to pay salaries to its employees.[34]

Contemporaries complained that other attempts at imposing order did not work any better than the *sereno* system. Lima's citizens organized *rondas* (citizens' patrols), but many hesitated to join them because they feared losing their lives. According to the inspector general, the *barrios* under his command contained three kinds of people, none of them qualified to participate in the *rondas*: "Some are *mosos* [*sic*, young men], and they are either part of the urban militias or employees in the state's offices, and the rest are either old and thus excluded from this service by the law, or the handicapped who, by reason of health, are not able to stay up all night." This left only slaves and the *plebe*. For obvious reasons, slave owners would not run the risk of arming their slaves; and the *plebe* could not be trusted as guardians of moral and social order because they were the ones who had to be restrained. Understandably, *rondas* were never implemented.

In 1835 a Lima newspaper published an editorial that again revealed police negligence and severely criticized the lack of order in the city.[35] This editorial was inspired by the daily assaults on private property perpetrated by

---

32. According to Flores Galindo's (1984) definition: "[la plebe] carece de lazos con las asociaciones corporativas y se resiste a reproducir la célula familiar." More than a resistance to constitute families, I would argue for the impossibility of doing so following bourgeois standards.

33. AGN, PJ, Prefectura, L 117, 1827.

34. AGN, Corte Suprema de Justicia (1842–55) PJ 80, Visita realizada por José Marurí de la Cuba a la Corte Superior de Justicia y de los Jusgados de Alzadas tanto del Tribunal del Consulado como del de Minería. Lima, 24/12/1846.

35. Decreto emitido por el coronel de los Ejércitos Nacionales, Miguel Angel Bujanda, *Gaceta del Gobierno*, no. 17, del 22/4/1835.

bandit gangs. In responding to these accusations, the municipality decreed that district governors, police inspectors, prison guardians, and *serenos* were to be placed under the command of the Tribunal de la Acordada. This court would deploy a constabulary squadron, distributed along the city's streets according to "the conveniences of public security." Patrolling became more centralized and bureaucratized, but Lima's inhabitants were not necessarily better protected. José Gálvez (1931:n.i.) portrays Lima around 1840 thus: "Socially Lima was still a colonial city. But in order to be fair, it is necessary to recognize that there was more disorder than in colonial times. Liberty was a mask for licentious behavior, full of abuses and a lack of authority. With a badly equipped and undersized police force, assaults at night were frequent in the houses of the rich and on the trails to the *haciendas*. Even bandits imposed their ways and their sinister grip." Gálvez's comments connect "liberty" and "licentious behavior." In the following decades, this perception would be extended to show how the urban underclass misinterpreted the new age of liberalism.

Police forces were reorganized again in 1854.[36] Officials considered organizing a *serenos*' battalion, independent of the police force and with its own officials and chiefs in command. The new battalion was to be composed of five companies, one for each of the five *cuarteles*, under the command of *cuartel* inspectors and Lima's highest police authority, the prefect. The *celadores* (wardens) were in charge of carrying out the inspectors' mandates. A new position, the *comisario de cuartel* (district police commissioner), would be aided by inspectors. *Serenos* would now be in charge of the city's tidiness.[37]

During General Ramón Castilla's presidential administration at midcentury, complaints about robberies and assaults in the city diminished considerably. Either the city's police department was at last able to impose some order and prevent gang activities, or perhaps improved economic conditions had led to a decline in the crime rate. Although Lima was safer, incursions by bands from the surrounding rural areas continued.

During Castilla's second presidency in the 1860s, the government dedicated itself to improving jails.[38] Prisoners were counted, their felonies

---

36. BN, D 2218, 1854.
37. Later, those in charge of city sanitation were called *baja policia*, meaning, literally, the lower echelons of the police force.
38. These attempts were preceded by an 1853 report on the U.S. penitentiary system written by Mariano Felipe Paz Soldán, a Peruvian reformist, at the request of President Rufino Echerique (Aguirre 1991, 12ff).

evaluated, and new prisons planned and built. Lima inaugurated its first penitentiary on July 23, 1862,[39] and it quickly became the city's most important corrective facility. However, the penitentiary soon came under attack. The arguments brought forward reveal interesting facets of the Peruvian state's notion of social and moral control and also disclose changing economic conditions and shifting interpretations of criminality.

Reports on the devastating conditions in Lima's jails around 1878 reveal disastrous mismanagement and living conditions at least as terrible as those described in less liberal times (Flores Galindo 1984, 162–63). Gratings, pipes, and even walls were falling apart, which "in great measure compromised the prisoners' security."[40] Everything—including the director's and the matron's offices—was filthy.[41] Only one matron, acting as director, warden, and instructor, supervised all women prisoners. Her main task was to prevent male prisoners from coming in contact with her wards. In spite of all precautions, several women became pregnant while in jail.[42]

The 25 centavo daily per capita subsistence allowance paid by the Treasury in 1871 was far less than necessary. Prices of two basic food staples—meat and rice—had increased by about 60 percent since the 1860s.[43] In 1863, annual expenses of the penitentiary were calculated at more than 40,000 pesos;[44] in 1868, the budget had increased to 91,978 pesos (now called "libras peruanas"),[45] and still expenses by far exceeded available funding.

---

39. "Lima had three main places serving as prisons or transitory sites of confinement. They were the Presidio de Casas-Mata, the jail called Carceletas located in the old building of the Inquisition, and the Cárcel de Policía or Depósito de Guadalupe, built in 1822 inside the Intendancy building. Eventually, military or police headquarters—Santa Catalina, Dragones de Policía, and others—were used as transitory jails. There was also a jail in the San Lorenzo island where criminals—especially black slaves—were sent out to cut stones" (Aguirre 1991, 8–9).

40. AGN, PJ, Penitenciería Lima, L 246 (1877–78).

41. AGN, PJ, Penitenciería Lima, L 246 (1877–78), Memorandum from the Director of the Penitentiary to the Director of Justice, Lima, 5 June 1878.

42. AGN, PJ, Penitenciería, L 242 (1863–68), Pedido de la Matrona de la Penitenciería Dolores Seguín de Henriquez por aumento de haber. Lima, 19 June 1866. See also AGN, PJ, Penitenciería de Lima, L 242 (1863–68), Letter from the Director of the jail to the Minister of Justice. Lima, 27 August 1867; and AGN, PJ, Penitenciería de Lima, L 246 (1877–78), Letter signed by Francisco de Bustamente. Lima, 12 April 1878.

43. AGN, PJ, Penitenciería de Lima, L 243 (1869–72).

44. AGN, PJ, Penitenciería, L 242 (1863–68), Budget signed by Ramón de Figuerola.

45. AGN, PJ, Penitenciería, L 242 (1863–68), Budgets for October, November, and December 1868, presented by Pedro B. Alarco. One Peruvian pound was almost equivalent to the late colonial peso. Both had a one to one exchange rate to the British pound.

Some contemporaries strongly advocated the replacement of brutal punishment (such as cold showers, meager rations, and isolation) with reform-oriented measures (such as the creation of artisan workshops).[46] Partly because tools could be turned into weapons, the reforms were not generally implemented.[47] Some directors tried to justify the reinstatement of corporal punishment, which had been abolished by General San Martín in 1821. The penitentiary director stated in 1867 that "flagellation could be imposed on serfs and the rabble and was tolerated in the family and in the schools." Claims for harsher punishments, in turn, were born out of a growing anxiety and impotence in the face of social and moral disorder.[48]

In 1864 the penitentiary had 215 prisoners (188 men, 27 women).[49] Between 1862 and 1876, 740 individuals (677 men, 63 women) had been sentenced and transferred to the penitentiary, out of which 245 had served their sentence, 104 had died (two-thirds because of tuberculosis), and some had escaped or had been sent to other institutions. In 1876, 277 people were being held in the penitentiary, and 170 in other corrective institutions (Casa Matas and the Cárcel). Thus, a total of 447 sentenced offenders were in jail in 1876, or approximately 1 percent of Lima's adult population.

The distribution by nationality of offenders reflects immigration patterns, but the percentages for each group do not correlate proportionally to the size of ethnic groups living in Lima. Those incarcerated were predominantly "Peruvians" (81.2 percent). Foreigners (18.8 percent) had recourse to their consulates or could be extradited rather than imprisoned, and Europeans and North Americans in particular were firmly inserted into Lima's eco-

---

46. AGN, PJ, Penitenciería Lima, L 244 (1872–74), Informe sobre la Penitenciería que presenta al Supremo Gobierno la Comisión nombrada por decreto del 29 de agosto de 1872. In this report, the commission asked for greater surveillance and expressed concerns about the fact that work (which was perceived to be the only way to redeem these "bad elements") was not considered to be an obligation. In a similar vein, the commission mentioned that the salaries paid were not even enough to pay for the prisoners' food and that both prisoners and their families had complained about this situation.

47. AGN, Letter from Francisco Valdizán to the Coronel Director, Lima, 9 September 1866.

48. In 1827 Congress approved flagellation for disobedience in the marine corps. Quote from AGN, PJ, Penitenciería Lima, L 242 (1863–68), Memoria de la Penitenciería al Sr. Ministro de Estado en el Despacho de Justicia, 7 March 1867.

49. AGN, PJ, Penitenciería Lima, L 242 (1863–68), Estado general de los presos existentes en esta prisión, 1864. Among men, 40.9 percent were incorporated into the shoemaker workshop and 15.9 percent (the second largest group) in the carpenter workshop. All women were either washing, ironing, or cooking.

nomic life, which diminished the attractiveness of criminal activity. It is not surprising, for example, to find Europeans (5.1 percent of all inmates in the penitentiary in 1876) and North Americans (0.7 percent) often accused of money forgery.[50] Money forgery represented 2.0 percent of all recorded crimes in 1876 (Table 1.10), and although severely punished, was technologically a more sophisticated crime.

Homicide accounted for 65 percent of all convictions, followed by robbery and assault (21.3 percent) and rebellion (4.5 percent). Crimes involving family members (patricide, infanticide, and fratricide) and rape accounted for 3.6 percent of all convictions (Table 1.10). In other words, Lima was a society in which "rebellion"—the expression of political discontent and social injustice—accounted for almost as many cases as those involving gender and family issues. Other "family issues," such as vaguely defined "physical abuse" against a spouse or marital abandonment, were left to the ecclesiastical court. These acts were not considered a crime unless a spouse was killed; only then would the perpetrator be accused in criminal court.

Misdemeanors such as vagrancy, molestation, or defamation were common and did not usually involve imprisonment. Since the early years of

Table 1.10 Prisoners in the Lima penitentiary, crimes, 1862–1876

Crime	Women	Men	Total	%
Homicide	47	434	481	65.0
Robbery/assault	4	154	158	21.3
Rebellion	0	33	33	4.5
Injuries	4	14	18	2.4
Forgery	1	14	15	2.0
Rape	0	13	13	1.8
Patricide	3			
Infanticide	4	3		
Fratricide	2	0		
Filicide	1	0	13	1.8
Rustling	0	6	6	0.8
Others	0	3	3	0.4
Total	63	677	740	100.0

SOURCE: AGN, PJ, Penitenciería Lima, L 245 (1875–76), Memoria de la Penitenciería de Lima, 1876.

---

50. AGN, PJ, Penitenciaría Lima, L 245 (1875–76), Memoria de la Penitenciería de Lima.

the new Republic, Lima's political authorities had expressed annoyance with high vagrancy rates. Decrees on September 16, 1829, and July 3, 1849, stipulated that vagrants should be sent to either the army or the marine corps. To some observers this would tarnish the prestige of these military forces without achieving any positive results.[51] By the end of the War of the Pacific in 1884, Lima's police department employed 1,415 people (Clavero 1885, 30). But in the 1890s young men identified as vagabonds still endangered Lima's tranquility. Thus, bad municipal organization and increasing numbers of migrants to the city led to a renewal of "disorder" in the city.[52]

Parallel to a doubling of homicides between 1892 and 1893, 474 people were imprisoned for vagrancy in 1892; and by 1893, 663 vagrants had been convicted. People arrested for drunkenness increased from 1,828 in 1892 to 5,031 in 1893. Given the large numbers involved (about 14.1 percent of Lima's total population in 1891,[53] of which 16.9 percent were women and 83.1 percent men), it seems that the prison-shortage problem had been solved. In some cases, criminals were forced into labor assignments. It is probably no coincidence that out of the 14,678 people arrested in 1893, 56.7 percent were classified as artisans and day-laborers, whereas only 6.2 percent had no occupation. Similarly, 62.6 percent of the total were literate (38.7 percent among women and 67.5 percent among men). This indicates that people may have been taken into custody, not because they had committed an offense, but because "vagrants" were a cheap labor source, and police and municipal guardians, performing their duties in a heightened moral climate, judged "disorder" on a broader scale.

51. AGN, H6–0873, Memoria de la Subprefectura e Intendencia de Policía de Lima, 1897, Anexo 27, p. 128. See also AGN, PJ, Penitenciería Lima, L 245 (1875–76), Razón de los presos existentes en el Establecimiento, con espresión del oficio á que actualmente se dedican. Among the male prisoners, 35.6 percent were in the shoemaker workshop and 15.8 percent in the tailoring workshop. The other prisoners (59) were either in special isolation or sick when the count was carried out. AGN, Penitenciería Lima, L 246 (1877–78). The largest group was the shoemakers (31.7 percent), and, what is more surprising, there were more skilled laborers than apprentices (55.2 percent to 22.0 percent). A complaint filed at that time by one of the convicts, Benito Rodríguez, who worked in the shoemaker shop, showed how little these workers could accumulate; he had earned only 20.40 soles in ten months. Such minimal earnings could scarcely improve living conditions for an average of 250 inmates.

52. AGN, Memoria del Prefecto de Lima, Coronel Pedro E. Muñiz (Lima: Imprenta del Universo), 1893. Also see AGN, H6–0873, Memoria de la Subprefectura e Intendencia de Policía de Lima, 1897, Anexo 27, p. 129.

53. In the periods 1896–97 and 1897–98, 12,821 and 15,174 people were involved respectively (representing 12.3 percent and 14.6 percent of the total population in 1891; and 9.8 percent and 11.6 percent of the 1903 census). See Table 1.1.

The ruling class and the church firmly associated crime, including moral trespasses, with the lower class and with vagrancy. These notions had been building up throughout the century and gave credence to racist attitudes. In a city with few job opportunities, lower class people were accused of *falta de amor al trabajo* (lacking love for labor). How race related to crime at the end of the century is noteworthy (Table 1.11). Taken together, whites and mestizos accounted for 42.3 percent of the 14,678 people accused of a felony. Indians, blacks, and Asians (the lower classes) together accounted for 56.7 percent. Because of their retail activities in the city, it may be more appropriate to include Asians with the economically better-off racial groups (mestizos and whites). This gives an almost perfect equilibrium between both groups. However we group them, populations accused of a crime show a descending incidence among Indians, blacks, mestizos, Asians, and whites. More than one-third of the Indian population living or working in Lima in 1892 in some way or another had trouble with the police. Because they continuously entered and left the city to sell agrarian produce, it is understandable that they fell prey to vagrancy accusations. A similar explanation also holds true for accusations against blacks who labored on their own plots or as workers in nearby *haciendas*.

A majority of those arrested were taken into custody during weekdays at daytime (55.0 percent), while drunk (53.0 percent), walking down the street (78.7 percent) or in rented houses and rooms (11.3 percent). The single most common felony was public drunkenness (34.3 percent of all registered cases), followed by noisy quarreling (9.9 percent), homicide (9.8 percent), thievery (9.4 percent), and scandalous behavior (8.1 percent). Following a long-standing nineteenth-century "tradition," 663 (4.5 percent) cases refer

Table 1.11 Race and criminality, 1890s

		White	Indian	Black	Mestizo	Asian
Total population: 1891[a]	103,956	47,645	18,660	7,494	25,481	4,676
People arrested: 1892–93[b]	14,678	2,006	6,625	1,345	4,192	349
		13.7%	45.2%	9.2%	28.6%	2.4%
% pop. arrested	14.1%	4.2%	35.6%	17.9%	16.5%	7.5%

SOURCE: Muñiz, 1893. This report covers from July 1, 1892 to June 30, 1893.
[a] From Bromley/Barbagelata (1945, 76ff.). Also in Miller (1988, 2).
[b] From Muñiz (1893).

to disrespect toward policemen. No matter how real or faked the accusations, Lima was a highly quarrelsome society in which policing was difficult.

Overall, it seems that by the end of the century some degree of social control had been successfully implemented, in part because more people were behind bars. On the other hand, registered rates of "deviation" also were alarming. It may not be a mere coincidence that increased export activity between 1890 and 1905 came at the same time as increasing "criminality." In the wake of export-led growth, social control was tightened and some groups were marginalized. With the strengthening of economic liberalism, value systems, and economic interests clashed,[54] and some individuals landed in jail, while others benefited from the increasingly uneven distribution of wealth. Criminality was being redefined to justify police and judicial intervention. Holloway (1993, 1) noted that in Brazil the "historical development of the police . . . through a dialectic of repression and resistance, was part of a more general transition from the traditional application of control through private hierarchies to the modern exercise of power through public institutions." The same was true for Lima. This transition is illustrated in a varied set of arguments in encounters with the police, in the circumvention of municipal decrees, in the emphasis on spatial segregation between different social groups, in overt racism, and last but not least, in marital strife.

Municipal Decrees

As shown by problems of policing and prison management, municipalities suffered the trials of liberalism. Municipal officials to some degree regulated street vendors and cottage industries by making them pay taxes (*patentes*). Yet, lack of revenue was a persistent feature of city budgets even during the guano boom. Institutional inertia and unwillingness often lay at the heart of fiscal gaps. The search for remedies to financial distress eventually led to the betrayal of the liberal ideals that were the legacy of the struggle for political independence from Spain. Indian tributes, perceived as a denigrating colonial practice, were not abolished until 1854, because together with import duties, they still were the main source of revenue to the state and city councils since 1821.

---

54. Long ago, Rodman proposed this idea (1969, 673–83) when evaluating the meaning of illegitimacy in the Caribbean social structure.

One amusing vignette provides a sense of the subtle changes and continuities following the wars of independence. Since colonial times, profits from the Plaza de Acho (Lima's magnificent bullfight arena) had been part of viceregal rents, which the viceroy distributed to the poorhouse (Hospicio de Pobres).[55] In 1810 eight bullfights at Acho brought in 42,686 pesos and 3½ reales, not counting earnings from the sale of bull meat.[56] Then, as an expression of anti-Spanish sentiment, Acho was shut down shortly after the declaration of independence in 1821. Bullfights had become "irreconcilable with the present era imbued by the achievements of culture and civilization."[57] General Simón Bolívar, the Libertador, nevertheless cherished bullfights. When he arrived in Lima, the local notables arranged a series of splendid festivities to express the people's gratitude. Of course, these festivities included the lifting of the bullfight ban. Consequently, "beyond the advantage of satisfying Bolivar's wishes, the government found—with no doubt—a viable way to collect funds."[58]

Bullfight revenues had always benefited the poorest segments of urban society, and after independence these funds covered part of the municipal deficit. Bullfights, believed to be barbaric, and a colonial leftover, continued because Lima's municipality depended on their rent. Budgetary necessity was complemented by the popularity of the bullfights, a beloved diversion—no matter how barbaric—shared by all of Lima's inhabitants.

Following the wars of independence, the new republican state emerged from political and military turmoil with a weak bureaucratic infrastructure and little money to try to put one in place. Urban development was hampered by the general lack of investment funds, both public and private. Lima's inhabitants were reluctant to pay for progress and renewal when the municipality invited them to share the costs of building needed public lighting and sewage systems. In the 1820s there was no public lighting system.[59] Every house was required to keep a light at the front door because darkness was an invitation to robberies and assaults. However, many

55. "Todas las rentas efectivas del hospicio de Pobres se reducen á 2.602 pesos, en esta forma, 1.372 que da el asentista de la plaza de Toros" (Fuentes 1861, 3:176, n. 1).
56. BN, D 8862, 1810. At that time, this amount could buy at least a big hacienda or one hundred slaves.
57. Similar decrees were issued under the same reasoning in other Latin American cities (see Collier 1967, 225–36).
58. CDIP, t. XXVII, 2:266–67.
59. Public lighting was scarce and consisted of oil lamps; there were eight street lamps for each block (*cuadra*). This changed during the guano boom. In 1851 a contract was signed with Don Luis Melchor Charon y Cia., and in 1855 Lima's first gas lamp was ignited.

complaints were filed against neighbors who did not comply. In January 1847 Dr. Don Juan Mariano Cosío, a member of the Supreme Court, was accused of violently resisting to pay his share for the construction of the Otero aqueduct. When asked for his contribution, Don Mariano attacked the neighborhood guard who was in charge of collecting the money. In the ensuing public scandal, Don Mariano tried to protect his position by alleging that the guard had been drunk and had attacked him.[60] Lima's citizens had little respect for municipal regulations; the longing for progress very literally ended at one's porch.

Limeños also knew that *chicherías* and *pulperías* sold alcohol and allowed prohibited games. These "noisy and violent" places flourished in spite of continued attempts to curtail them. In 1815 one of Lima's notables, Don Marcos Tagle, complained to the Real Audiencia, asking that the *alcalde* from the Barrio de Espíritu Santo close down a *chichería* on Chillón street owned by Josefa Bazán. According to Don Marcos, this *chichería* had terrible effects on his servants: "My dependents abandon their duties, lose respect for my house, and thus harm my interests. We are continuously exposed to insults, like the one my wife had to go through last Thursday when I went to look for the Indian owner of the *chichería,* who was laboring on his plot. I needed to find him in order to bring home three of my servants who were sitting in the *chichería* drinking and playing cards. All this leads to licentiousness and other disorders."[61]

It was widely assumed that alcohol consumption led to increased violence, above all among the lower classes. Responding in 1816 to yet another complaint from citizens and to an initiative undertaken by the *pulperos'* guild, the municipality decreed the "extinction of *chinganas* [another word for *chicherías* and *pulperías*] which had no official license from the Cabildo [the city's council]." The city actually made an attempt to enforce this decree, but people found ways and means to escape official threats. They pretended to sell other products or simply shut off the main entrance and continued to distribute liquor and amusement through the rear door.[62] Oftentimes people requesting help from policemen were told to avoid "frequent fights and complaints." Eventually a high-level police officer might threaten to

---

60. AGN, Prefectura Lima, L 121, Comunicación del Coronel Intendente de Policía al Ministro de estado en el despacho de Justicia, Lima, 13/2/1847. In fact, it took many more years before this vital aqueduct was completed.
61. AGN, RA, CCI, L 128, C 1308, 1815, 14f.
62. AGN, RA, CCI, L 128, C 1308, 1815; AGN, Cabildo, CCI, L 33, C 555, 1816.

impose a fee if the person continued to complain.[63] As late as 1898, *chicherías* were an important source of municipal revenues (if detected by government officials) and were an integral part of social life. In the different *barrios* complaints were raised over and over again, a sign of the municipality's impotence in controlling "immorality and fighting" in these popular places. Blacks and Indians, including many women, owned most *chicherías* and *pulperías*, and this emphasized the connection between social disorder and the lower classes.

The incapacity of the municipality (and of the state itself) to create order and bureaucratic organization must be placed in a context of empty coffers and unwillingness of individual citizens, rich and poor, to make an effort to improve the general condition of *all* citizens. It was difficult to organize a police force; and even when such a force was in place, it had a difficult time implementing municipal decrees, preventing assaults, or controlling "scandalous behavior." Ideals of progress were translated into concrete actions only with difficulty.

Social Interaction and Spatial Segregation

People from many different social and cultural backgrounds interacted on a daily basis in homes, on streets, in open-air marketplaces, and in Lima's many churches. Compared to other nineteenth-century cities, Lima was small, and contacts and interaction among different racial groups were unavoidable. Nevertheless, there was definite physical segregation, which hardened as migrants from other Peruvian regions settled in Lima's outskirts and European immigrants reinforced the white population in the heart of the city. On one hand, there were integrating impulses, as people intermarried and interacted economically. On the other hand, certain spaces in the city and its outskirts were settled by specific racial groups, and economic differentiation among them widened social gaps.

Lima's elite used their coaches, and the number of mules hauling them, to display their status. Much-watched Sunday promenades, involving as many as three hundred coaches, provided an opportunity to exhibit wealth and power. By focusing on the number of mules, the British traveler William B. Stevenson recognized that social hierarchies manifested themselves in social

63. AGN, Corte Superior de Justicia, CCI, L 757, 1860. No title.

activities, and that both the state and the church participated in this hierarchical display: "The rich merchant would show up in his coach with one mule; nobility would be hauled by two; those featuring a Castile entitlement would occupy coaches with four mules, and the viceroy and the archbishop would be seated in one steered by six."[64] A matching number of mules placed the church and the viceroy in the top level of the hierarchy, followed by the nobility and Lima's big merchants.

Promenades and encounters in public spaces had become common toward the end of the eighteenth century. The cockfight ring opened in 1762. One of Lima's boulevards, the Vieja Alameda, inaugurated in 1611, was supplemented by the Alameda de Acho in 1773 and the Alameda de Callao a few years later. The Acho bullfight arena was built in 1768. Lima's first cafe opened its doors in 1771 in the Calle Santo Domingo[65] and was quickly joined by many others. The parade grounds of Paseo de Aguas (inaugurated in 1772) and the Paseo Militar (1773) provided *limeños* a place to interact, look for a spouse, and fight to redeem their honor (Córdova y Urrutia 1839, 31–32). Poor and rich could gather in these places to observe each other. Nevertheless, each group also had its own pastimes and recreations. Often migrants hailing from one place lived together on one block or street.[66] The elite found entertainment and took vacations in the suburbs of Chorrillos, Miraflores, and Lurín. The underclass, on the other hand, met at the city's *pulperías* or gathered on sidewalks. Few had time and money to vacation, although if they did, it meant that they were eager to be seen and talked about, and eventually to interact with the well-off.

Even in segregated areas, however, interaction was unavoidable. Chorrillos and Lurin, for example, were old Indian towns. The upper class vacationing there coexisted with Indians earning their living through fishing and agriculture. Another traveler, Gabriel Lafond (1840, 131), described this scene:

64. Stevenson (1829); CDIP, t. XXVII, 3:164.
65. For locations in Lima, see map, pp. 46–47.
66. This is still a widespread residence pattern. For a documented case in 1857, see AA, CD, L 93 (1857–59), Melchor vs. Abalos, in which all witnesses called in by Manuela Melchor had been neighbors in Lima and in Pachacamac, the town were she had been born. In other cases, spouses referred to their witnesses as *paisanos*, presumably meaning—as it does today—that they had been born in the same rural province or town. See Case 846, AGN, CS, CCR, L 113, 1851, Arias vs. Herrera; and for a case involving Chinese *paisanos*, see Case 851, AGN, CCR, s.n. (39ff), 1854, Expediente seguido contra José Cardosa, 19 años, por homicidio perpetrado en la persona del chino Antonio.

I-V. Cuarteles
1. archbishopric
2. municipality
3. Plaza de Independencia (Plaza de Armas)
4. Tribunal del Consulado
5. Santo Domingo
6. Desamparados
7. San Francisco
8. Plaza Bolívar
9. La Caridad
10. congress
11. jail
12. Central Market
13. Santa Rosa
14. San Andres Hospital
15. Santa Ana Hospital
16. Refuge for the Incurable
17. Puerta de Maravillas
18. Copacabana
19. Concepción
20. San Pedro
21. Huérfanos
22. penitentiary
23. Puerta de Guadalupe
24. Puerta de Juan Simón
25. Encarnación
26. Railroad (Lima-Callao)
27. La Merced
28. San Agustín
29. San Marcelo
30. Mercenarias
31. Cocharcas
32. Puerta de Cocharcas
33. Barbones
34. Puerta de Monserrate
35. Puerta del Camal
36. Puerta del Callao
37. Beaterio del Patrocinio
38. Descalzos
39. Pedregal
40. Quinta de Presas
41. Puerta de Guía
42. San Lázaro
43. Paseo de Aguas
44. Plaza de Acho
45. San Sebastián
46. Nazarenas
47. theater
48. railroad (Lima-Chorrillos)
49. military headquarters
50. military hospital
51. Buena Muerte
52. River Rimac
53. government/tribunals
54. cemetery
55. gunpowder mill
56. Puerta Santa Catalina
57. asylum for orphans
58. Beaterio de Copacabana
59. Beaterio de Amparadas
60. Baños de Piedra Lisa y Tivoli

Lima, Peru's capital city, adapted from the map by the state engineer and architect Antonio Maria Dupard, 1859 (Facsimile: Lima, INDUSTRIALgráfica S.A.)

Indians have had the good idea of robbing these rutinary citizens [as he referred to Chorrillos vacationers]. They sell them fish they angle right there and in their very noses at a much higher price than in Lima's market places. Indian women wait for the summer season to begin to have their children baptized, awaiting to make the rich Europeans their godparents. Europeans in turn—half out of benevolence and half out of self-interest—are willing to accept this deal and comply with Indians' wishes. The priests' revenues in this parish are also highly lucrative. Indian women judge their fellow citizens well and their opinions are fully justified, where a Peruvian becomes entangled with them; they spend prodigiously for fear of being thought cheap. They will then throw coins to the children to hear them scream: Long live the generous godfather! But yet honor is not satisfied. When the generous godfather returns to Lima, it will not take long before the new *comadre* knocks at his door to remind him of his duties toward the godchild. She will bring along a fish which scarcely costs between eight and ten reales and, in return, she will obtain a thousand times that even and manifold favors from her investment from the godfather. This first visit will soon be followed by a second one, in which the *comadre* will lament her mistakes and bad luck: either she has lost her fishing utensils, or a child died, for which she will ask the godfather to lend her 25 to 30 *piastras* [pesos] even if only for a short time.[67]

Compadrazgo was a widespread mechanism that obligated disparate economic and racial groups to each other, albeit with different goals.[68] The rich used these alliances to build a network of dependents and gain access to cheap labor and goods. By allowing them to help their Indian or mestizo *compadres*, whom they considered inferior, *compadrazgo* made the elite feel morally superior. For the poor, *compadrazgo* was a way to gain marginal access to power. Indian migrants' experiences were not always as one-sided as those portrayed by Lafond, however. More often than not, daily life for them was charged with racism and exploitation based on their inability to deal with city life.

67. The original version of this travelogue is in Italian. This passage was translated from the Spanish version in the CDIP.
68. For a more detailed assessment of Indian-Spaniard *compadrazgo*, see Charney (1991, 295–314).

Indians from nearby provinces arrived at the city's gates with their fish or agrarian produce; some also brought an unresolved judicial case or complaint in the hope of obtaining justice. Unfortunately, their efforts were usually far less successful than those of their cousins in Chorrillos and Lurín who carried fish to Lima's well-fed vacationers. As seen earlier, some ended up behind bars under vagrancy charges. Inevitably these migrants had to suffer the extortion of unprofessional legal traffickers (*tinterillos*), usually mestizos with some knowledge of legal procedures. These legal efforts invariably meant a loss of time and money, and more often than not a lost case as well. A contemporary observer stated that *tinterillos* abounded "as if there were not enough 'paper makers' out there, who stand at the city's gates to seduce Indians, to betray them as soon as they arrive. Furthermore, Indians would have fewer distractions without them and they would better live from what they earn with their honest work. I feel worried watching them return to their villages without the money they obtained from selling their products."[69]

Indians were geographically the least stable social group.[70] Many maintained their rural links, and their migration between the city and their homes partly explains why travelers perceived Lima's population, and within it the Indian population, as highly unstable. Indians looking for employment in the city were underpaid. Because blacks were artisans—an effect of the hiring-out system involving slaves—Indians did not have many employment options. They preferred to live and work in the Cercado parish and the suburb of Chorrillos. Other alternatives open to Indians were odd jobs (particularly in the services), day labor, or small retail ventures. A common employment was working for small merchants to distribute goods to Indian customers in the city and in the outlying areas, the *chacras* and *haciendas*. Because they rarely had enough starting capital to engage in independent mercantile activity, Indians depended on a patron—a merchant—and a steady supply of consumers to develop distributorships. Although some Indians participated in the urban trade in the markets or sold small amounts of manufactured goods or agrarian produce house to house, their commercial

69. AGN, RA, CCR, L 123, C 1506.

70. At times, Indians made up more than 30 percent of Lima's population (as in 1857), but at the end of the eighteenth century and the beginning of the twentieth century, they accounted for only about 9 percent (Table 1.1). Although these differences may be explained in part by the subjectiveness of the census takers, they also seem to indicate a strong propensity for migration. As shown in Tables 1.8 and 1.9, percentages of both male and female spouses from other Peruvian provinces marrying in Lima is high.

activities occurred on the fringes of urban life, on the streets and in Lima's suburbs.

Tambos, small grocery stores, existed both in Surco and Chorrillos and were located on the travelers' routes into the city. These were places where people from the suburbs could buy basic household goods. Transactions in the *tambos* involved minimal amounts of money, which explains why wealthier merchants (mestizos and whites) did not invest in them, leaving this enterprise open to Indians. The municipality leased the *tambos* to the highest bidders for a stated period of time in exchange for a monthly payment.

In 1827 Francisco Ruiz made the best offer on one of the many *tambos* in Lima's outskirts. At that time monthly rent was 40 pesos. When Ruiz took over, he asked for a rent reduction to 30 pesos. His reasoning gives us some insight into the limits of Lima's mercantile activity—one of the few occupations open to Indians, mestizos, and the descendants of the black population. First, Ruiz explained, there were maintenance costs that included money paid to the rural police in charge of protecting against frequent assaults by highwaymen. Next, the products sold in the *tambos* were largely the same as those produced domestically. Because domestic production had low maintenance costs, it was cheaper to produce goods at home than to buy them in *tambos*. Furthermopre, urban salaries were insufficient to sustain the Indian labor force, let alone supply it with disposable income, so production of many necessary items had to be transferred to the domestic sphere, with many Indian women working in productive tasks. Even if they had wished to shop at the *tambo*, Indian women had no option but to produce the needed goods themselves. Thus, Ruiz wrote, "the *tambo* can not sell products as cheaply, because buying them costs more money." In sum, tambo rental was subject to serious domestic competition, did not necessarily provide an income, and was often a money-losing proposition. Domestic production was still an important component of urban life, undercutting profits from retail commerce. It also meant that municipal revenues derived from the control of these activities were low.[71]

The gradual decay of slavery in the course of the first half of the nineteenth century increased competition in the labor market. Former slaves migrated to the city—mainly to the San Lázaro parish. In the city they competed with European immigrants for artisan or service-sector jobs. A "typical" black occupation was the *aguador* (water carrier). Lima had clay

71. AGN, PJ, Prefecturas, L 175, 1828.

water pipes in only a few neighborhoods. *Aguadores*, mostly *casta* or black men, used mules to bring water in barrels and jugs from public fountains to each house. Each trip cost one real. There was a guild that registered *aguadores* by parish, and water carriers were not allowed to sell water beyond their parish boundary. *Aguadores* began to disappear around the middle of the century when the administration of President Castilla built iron pipes. Still today, however, one can observe water carriers in Lima's *barriadas* (shanty towns), although some water carriers nowadays drive trucks.

Plantation and hacienda owners, in turn, sought alternative sources of cheap labor and finally succeeded in bringing Chinese laborers to Peru. By the 1870s the Chinese were a small minority in Lima, and they established small stores all over the city, frequently displacing Indians and mestizos. Shopkeeping created the deeply entrenched cultural image of the *chino de la esquina* (Chinese on the corner). In fact, the word *chino* became synonymous with a small store. Accumulated anger against the *chino* owners led to looting by Indians, blacks, and *mestizos* during the War of the Pacific (Arona 1891; Bonilla 1982).

Status, color, and occupation went together in nineteenth-century Lima. People could be robbed of their earnings because the color of their skin rendered them second-class citizens or noncitizens. Difficult living conditions in the city and racial difference allowed for numerous forms of coercion and conflict, further reinforcing racism. A racially segmented occupational structure limited people's job opportunities, and job exclusion coupled with the lack of jobs reinforced that segregation. As prices for consumer goods increased in the course of the nineteenth century,[72] many individuals—including women—worked several jobs simultaneously, and at times they had to adopt, with uneven success, several racial identities to circumvent racial constraints.

Juan Azabache, an Indian who called himself a "Don" and had an African last name, associated himself with a merchant to distribute goods. His relations with the merchant soured, and eventually the merchant accused Juan of owing a debt of 100 pesos, which Juan claimed was arbitrary and untrue. When the Indian-black "Don" refused to repay these alleged debts, the merchant locked Juan up in his house and, after flagrantly insulting him, threatened to turn him in as a thief. In his declaration, Juan assures us that his only crimes were not knowing anyone in the city who could help

---

72. According to our information on food for prisoners in Lima's penitentiary, rice and meat prices doubled between 1850 and 1870.

him and not having the resources to defend himself against his employer's accusations. According to his initial contract, Juan was to receive a monthly salary of 17 pesos for distributing merchandise, but Juan claimed that the merchant had never paid him. Having hired Juan to sell merchandise, the merchant had also used him as a rural laborer in his garden plot (*huerta*), work for which Juan should have earned 6 reales a day. The merchant was not able to prove that he had paid Juan; and Juan, for his part, could prove that he actually had carried out both tasks. Thus, the amount the merchant said Juan owed him was less than what the merchant owed Juan. Denying all evidence to the contrary, the merchant simply stated that Juan's debt—or as he put it, his theft—amounted to not one hundred, but two hundred pesos.[73]

We do not know if the merchant's twisted logic convinced the judge, but this case reveals the exposure of Indians (supposing Juan really was one) to extortion. Because Juan worked simultaneously distributing goods and as a rural laborer, it is also clear that Indians had to pursue multiple occupations in order to survive—often because employers arbitrarily requested them to carry out any job at hand.

Nearly a century after Stevenson observed the display of power in the mule-team promenades of merchants, nobility, the archbishop, and the viceroy—if we continue to use mules as a measurement of the pace of change—we see that around 1884 almost half of Lima's mules were used for public or commercial activities. The government, the military, hotels and restaurants, railroads and tramways, and even some European artisans all owned mule teams.[74] The ownership of mules now incorporated public and private services, and some people sitting in the coaches had "changed" color.

Parallel to such visible economic and social changes, elites constructed a racial and moral ideology meant to accentuate differences that—economically—were becoming increasingly blurred. "The greater the wealth and more even the distribution in a given society," Stone (1965, 61) wrote, "the emptier become titles of personal distinction, but the more they multiply and are striven for." Accentuating ethical demands and racist stereotypes was the typical political answer to counterbalance state inefficiency and to prevent urban turmoil by controlling the demands of different social groups. Consequently, it became commonplace to attach moral taint to certain racial traits. Although racial stereotypes had existed all along, in

73. AGN, CCI, L 10, 1854.
74. Clavero (1885, 56) registers a total of 1,619 horses, 2,008 mules and 460 donkeys.

the nineteenth century they dramatically gained leverage and in some way were "internationalized" when used to explain economic backwardness.

Moral Taint and Racial Traits

An array of stereotypes concerning women and races signaled real, perceived, and constructed social hierarchies. European consuls, merchants, and travelers shared with Lima's elite their apprehensions about urban and rural popular classes. According to them, fomenting European immigration and improving moral attitudes and working habits among the popular classes would put Peru on the path to modernity and progress. Miguel de Eyzaguirre, the *Protector de Naturales* (Indian Protector) provided a noteworthy exception to this line of thought. In the early 1800s, he favored Indian education and criticized the abusive behavior of local authorities and other social groups toward the Indian population. However, even Eyzaguirre proposed to alleviate the Indians' terrible lot by distributing adequate portions of land to them—but only if they married someone white (Macera 1977, 2:224–25).

Most Europeans praised Peru for its vast natural resources and potential, but when comparing Peru to their own countries, they found much to criticize. They explained the gap in the level of "modernization" in terms of race and culture. Travelogues and consular reports reflecting this thinking were widely read and thus helped to spread ideas about the link between race and modernization. In contrast to massive European immigration to Chile, Argentina, and Brazil beginning in the 1850s, European migration to Peru was always slight. In spite of their relatively small numbers (Tables 1.8 and 1.9), European influence was critical. Their ideas blended views on progress and modernity; moreover, in marrying elite Peruvian women, they hardened the already existing link between whiteness and power. Beyond some folkloric glimpses, the writings of European travelers and businessmen do not give details about the popular classes or about their living conditions, expectations, needs, and political outlooks.[75]

When European travelers mentioned Peruvian elite women, they praised them for their greater intelligence when compared to elite men. At the

---

75. It is only in recent years that historians working on Peru have started to address these issues. See Mallon (1995); Gootenberg (1990); Méndez (1987); Giesecke (1978); Manrique (1987); and Oliart (1994).

same time, they condemned lower-class women for their inclination toward prostitution (among black and *casta* women) and dreadful child-rearing practices (among Indian women). Such stereotypes found their way into novels and newspapers (Oliart 1994, 73–85). Much of what was defined as "popular" was, in fact, expressed in racial terms.

In a widely disseminated nineteenth-century literature, Indian and black men were portrayed as inadequate partners, even for women from their own race. These accounts denied Indians their masculinity and represented them as sinister, dirty, and cowardly semihumans, who loved their cows more than their wives. Ongoing peasant upheavals in the highlands and some violent outbursts during the War of the Pacific (1879–84) confirmed Indian grossness. Indians were considered unredeemable; the only solution was extinction or racial mixing. Such well-entrenched perceptions, in turn, deepened the gap between Indian peasants and white elites.

Indian women were portrayed as somewhat better. As mates of soldiers (*rabonas*) in the armies, their courage was exalted. Indian women were sturdy, hard workers who returned to work immediately after giving birth. Black women were represented as loving, sensual, and noisy creatures. They prepared delicious repasts in Lima's streets and marketplaces; they were house servants and wetnurses to white children; and they were the desired sexual partners of white men. Moreover, nannies' horror-filled bedtime stories and silly nicknaming—according to this way of thinking—accounted for the frailty of white males. In contrast, black men, feared when free, were only good as slaves and as conveyors of colonial traditions. Artisans and highwaymen were by definition black.

These well-known stereotypes had historical roots. Long before independence, miscegenation had blurred social boundaries and weakened status attributes defined by race and class. To counter increasingly blurred racial and economic boundaries, elites reinforced segregation by adding rules of honor and morality to the requirements for status. Tautologically, subordinate social groups were defined as being unable to understand the benefits of status requirements (descent, ethnicity, religion, profession, property) because they were subordinate. By this token, they were excluded (or excused) from elites' honor codes, while at the same time, such God-given requirements justified exploitation and enslavement (Gutiérrez 1985, 82). Throughout the nineteenth century, written records compared blacks, Indians, and Chinese in regard to their capacity to work and their moral and social traits. Ultimately, such comparisons judged all these groups to be undeserving and thus helped to maintain and deepen social distances.

However, racial stereotyping was not only an "elite issue." Episodes in Lima's streets and bedrooms[76] reveal the downward prolongation of entrenched racial stereotypes. Most defamation suits in the nineteenth century involved people from the lower and middle classes and were related to racial insults. Even insults between spouses often reflected racial stereotypes and were intended to denigrate the "opponent" (Lavalle 1986, 31).

In a telling episode in 1816, Manuela Solís and Manuel Sancho Dávila, both *castas*, were strolling along Malambo street when they decided to buy a piece of cake in a chocolate store (*chocolatería*). Lacking an underground sewage system and paved streets, *barrios* were continuously flooded. Because the street was full of water, Manuel and Manuela could not reach the store, so they asked the owner to throw them the cake wrapped in a napkin with a stone in it. The couple and the owner were loudly joking about the situation, and just as the baker threw the cake, a *sereno* walked by. The napkin with the cake and the stone in it hit his head. Furious, he turned immediately to Manuela; he was convinced she had purposely thrown the stone at him. Manuel defended his wife but was dragged to jail by the *alcalde de barrio*. Witnesses attested to what had happened, Manuel was set free, and the mayor and the *sereno* were told to be more thoughtful about their actions.[77] Public quarrels, which were common, often had a strong racial ingredient: the *sereno* blamed the woman because she was dark-skinned and thus, he assumed, inclined to be boisterous and rude.

Some forty years later, in 1855, when a poor tailor witnessed his eighteen-month-old son killed by a passing mule-cart, he blamed the owner of the cart for hiring black—and thus inexperienced and careless—drivers just to save a few pesos.[78] The driver was sentenced to two months in jail, and the owner of the cart paid 50 pesos to help toward the funeral costs.

Racial anxieties were also present in the bedroom. María del Rosario Pino, the *casta* wife of *mestizo* Victor Espín, was convinced that her husband brutally mistreated her because of her race. "The inequality of our color has caused my husband to hate me, his faithful wife."[79] Not even children

---

76. In Lima's AGN there are many lawsuits for defamation (*juicios de difamación*), and most of them were opened by people defending themselves from what they thought were racial insults.

77. AGN, RA, CCR, 1816. For another episode some years later, see also AGN, CS, CCR, 1855, Don Gerónimo Abísqueta contra Doña María de Morales por injurias graves y conato de homicidio.

78. AGN, CS, CCR, 1855, Querella criminal de Don Juan Mariano Cuerbo contra Don José Valencia por haber pisado y matado con su carreta a su hijo de 18 meses en la puerta de su casa.

79. AA, CD, L 93 (1857–59), 1858, Pino vs. Espín.

escaped the racial grip. Describing an episode in Cusco at the beginning of the twentieth century, a traveler, Edward A. Ross (1915, 170–71), wrote: "Not merit but caste determines social consideration. When an American organized a football team among lads, he found that the son of the blacksmith [was] liable to be roundly scolded for tackling hard the son of a gentleman: 'How dare you knock over your patron!' the other boys would exclaim."

Racial ingredients appear in all situations. Arguments used publicly and in the bedroom often included race as a way to denigrate an opponent or even—as in María del Rosario's case—as a way of self-denigration: her racial inferiority explained her husband's brutality. Stereotyping implied connecting racial features to a certain kind of behavior, a behavior that could be anticipated by judging one's skin color. The reverse was also true: if people behaved in a certain way, the reasoning went, they must belong to a given racial group. The underlying racism was not only a strategy used by elites to substantiate social distances; but the connection between behavior and race also became interiorized by the targets of the segregation and appeared in bedroom conversations. These stereotypes prevented couples and classes from recognizing common battlegrounds. First and foremost, behavior was explained by resorting to skin color, rather than as the result of street flooding, tense neighborhood relations, a distortion of gender relations, the inherent roughness of a boys' football game, or an accident that might happen to anyone. Such subtle implicit racism found its way into court cases and even influenced sentences passed by judges. Often the law was bent to convey social messages to litigants. Justice had and has a color; only the language has changed. The colonial *gente indecente* became the early republican *plebe*, and the *plebe* became the twentieth-century *chusma*, *populacho*, and *cholada*.

Women in general, and wives in particular, were another group that was thoroughly stereotyped. Although gendered racism existed—as seen above—images and perceptions of women as wives cut across class and race lines.

Changes and Continuities

The nineteenth century saw gradual development toward a more "modern" Peruvian economy. But development meant more than just economic and demographic growth. For Peruvian elites, nation-building and progress were the outcome of an export-led economy that increased economic differentiation and created a racially more complex population. Economic growth and industrial development was ideologically embedded in the accentuation of racial and gender stereotypes. This was especially true in the cities, where the races coexisted. Racism and conjugal conflict resolution became ideological weapons to deal with blurred racial boundaries and women's growing participation in the urban economy. Decency and correct moral behavior became mechanisms to separate women from men and women from each other to maintain class boundaries and political exclusion.

Such long-term tendencies appear in the way people in the city interacted socially and spatially. They are also reflected in how certain jobs came to be available only to a specific race or gender. Each group had "preferred" occupations, or—perhaps more accurately—were systematically excluded from certain occupations. Competition in the labor market increased with Lima's demographic expansion, and—as will be documented in the following chapters—moral pressures on women from all walks of life increased. Women, in turn, reacted by challenging their husbands' moral superiority. Wives pointed to the contradictions between the moral expectations they were subjected to and their husbands' transgressions of the same moral expectations. Men viewed women as "sly creatures"; women viewed men as hypocrites. Both views became mutually reinforcing. Abandoned, divorced, or poor women found it hard to live up to ideal womanhood, and they had to be "sly" to survive. Some married women had to resort to a "shadow economy," or "penny capitalism,"[80] not only to avoid starving but also to keep up a socially constructed image of the good wife.

Many worries about moral and social disorder at the beginning of the nineteenth century prevailed and even increased later in the century. What changed was the tune that went with the music: more jails were built; the police force was expanded; the discourse about the "good citizen" became louder. However, many of these changing mechanisms for creating "social order" were geared toward reasserting social control rather than solving social inequality or expanding political participation. People's reactions to increased economic and moral pressures also changed; and in the wake of

---

80. A detailed description of both concepts is given in Roberts (1986, 223–48) as one of the many strategies European women found to compensate for their husbands' low wages. More often than not, the shadow economy involved wives' income or savings hidden from their husbands. The still-current use of the expression "*schwarze Kasse*" (black coffer) in Germany contains the same idea.

such changes, women's voices denouncing the male double standard also became louder, especially among women from Lima's popular classes. If all this was part of a "liberal project" in nineteenth-century Peru, we will find that liberalism was challenged not only by artisans demanding protective tariffs but also by women questioning their husbands' prerogatives. Many such challenges were phrased in racial and gender terms; often they were inseparable.

PART I

Couples, Barrios, and the Church

2

At Home and in the Streets

Although women were idealized as virgins and mothers, wives were creatures who had their own ways. For many husbands, wives were sly creatures. Male discourse on wives expressed a shared understanding and established an alliance in daily life and in the courtroom. Men, although separated by socioeconomic differences, shared their perceptions of wives. Wives were evaluated through the lens of ideal womanhood but were also seen as a threat to male prerogatives. Thus, wives stood at the crossroads of female attributes and male fears.

"I Am Always The One Who Gives In" is the title of a short story written by Manuel A. Segura, one of Peru's most widely read *costumbrista* writers of the 1860s. What the author describes is a common domestic conversation among spouses (in this case a conversation between the author and his wife). In the absence of diaries, literary accounts are useful because, as Segura intended, this personal story unveils common perceptions of female traits, albeit with exaggerations for the purpose of moral reform.

Segura and his wife belonged to Lima's middle class. He was a professional writer; she was—according to Segura—a spoiled housewife, not particularly pretty, but with bewitching, dark black eyes, small adorable feet, and a pace that made everyone turn their heads.[1] Segura praises his wife's moral virtues with an irony clearly addressing common male fears: "She has never betrayed me, at least I have never come to know about it."[2] Physical beauty and moral virtue were, in fact, the ascribed qualities of womanhood throughout the nineteenth century. However, husbands could never be sure about their wives' virtue.

Segura convinces his readers that no matter how hard he tried to persuade his wife to spend less—to stop buying clothes and perfumes, and to refrain from summer vacations in Chorrillos[3]—she ignored him. If he argued with her, she accused him of not loving or caring about her. She even claimed that he didn't provide for her material comfort. No matter whether he was happy or sad, in her eyes his every mood was wrong. If he was happy, she would say he was a fool and was having affairs; if he was sad, she would accuse him of skipping domestic duties and of bringing home his anger. According to Segura, not even the guano islands[4] in their entirety would have sufficed to soothe her claims.

In describing facets of his conjugal life, Segura emphasized society's perception of wives. He defined four typical female domains: women's power in the home based on sexual bargaining, women's frivolous material longings, women's secret weapons to convince men, and women's basically unstable, emotional opinions. To these traits one may add women's deep religiosity.[5] Segura's story was addressed to female readers. In his introductory paragraph, he cautions, "My said wife had a bad temper, as do many who will pretend they do not understand what I mean." They—Lima's wives—would recognize such domains and so, of course, would men.

My own findings show that Segura's assumptions found their way into the complaints presented by men and women in court—or vice versa, that his assumptions blended perceptions one could hear in the streets, the bedroom, and the courtroom.

---

1. The description of Segura's wife is taken from another short story "Me voy al Callao" (Segura 1968, 17–22).

2. The Spanish version reads: "no me ha sido infiel nunca, o al menos no he tenido noticia de que lo haya sido" (ibid., 23).

3. Chorrillos was the vacation site for Lima's elites. One could own or rent a house, and people spent their time visiting each other. Going or not going to Chorrillos was a sign of upward or downward social mobility. Many travelers, among them Witt (1992), describe social life—especially among women—in Chorrillos.

4. Bird droppings from the guano islands were exported between 1845 and 1870, and this income represented Peru's primary revenue.

5. They were described as participating in every procession and attending mass regularly. See, for example, Witt (1992, 63, 190, 207, 378).

In *beaterios* (places of refuge for divorcing women),[6] ecclesiastical court, and even in the streets of Lima, "right" and "wrong" were daily defined, challenged, and at times redefined.

Living Together in the *Barrio*

The nineteenth-century Peruvian "sea of disorder"—of which conjugal quarrels in homes and streets were an important part—was calmed to some degree by what people did in their neighborhoods, the *barrios*. An inefficient police force and an insufficient municipal budget gave people leeway to do things *their* way, even when that meant disregarding municipal decrees or the dictates of brotherly and conjugal love, as exhorted by parish priests and neighbors.

The degree of diversity in households reveals the social composition of a *barrio*. The 1831 census carried out by Lima's municipal government and fragments of a household census carried out in the parish of Santa Ana in 1808 counted many small shops (*tiendas*), which were also family residences; houses; small houses (*casitas*); several *callejones*, in which many families lived one next to another in small rooms; and resort-style houses, called *casas solares*.[7] Of the shops, which accounted for 49 percent of all residential units, *pulperías* or *chinganas* and artisan workshops were the most numerous.

A "house" was not always a one-family residential unit. Slaves, skilled workers, and apprentices lived in these stores and artisan workshops in addition to the nuclear family, and they were often witness to conjugal conflicts. Widows and widowers, as well as single men and women, rented rooms in family homes.[8]

---

6. Toward the mid-nineteenth century, Fuentes (1861, 3:122) succinctly described *beaterios* as the only places in the city in which "innocence could be preserved, weakness compensated, dishonor remedied and crimes punished." In Lima, "casa de recogimiento" and *beaterios* were synonymous and interchangeable during the colonial period (see Van Deusen 1987, 7) and later on.

7. The Santa Ana census of 1808 registered 74 *casitas*, 171 *casas*, 271 *tiendas*, 16 *callejones*, 2 *cocheras*, 14 *casas solares*, and 4 *esquinas*, a total of 552 residential units. AA, Padrón Residencial de Santa Ana, 1808.

8. Some descriptions show the extreme fragmentation of living space. See, for example, AGN, RA, CCI, L 102, C 1079, f. 28: "Esta finca se halla construída y compuesta á la moda, con su patio, sala, quadra, quarto de dormir, y su cosina con un techo ó campo que, suficientemente le sirve de traspatio y corral, ademas de la oficina mantequería que e labrado nuevamente con bastante desaogo para la matansa de las cabesas y composición de manteca, ademas de dos

64   Liberalism in the Bedroom

In crowded living conditions, the feeding of dependents strained the household budget and added to the tensions between a husband and wife. In a complaint about mistreatment and adultery filed in Lima's ecclesiastical court in 1815, Eulalia Martínez, the wife of Francisco Chungcipoma, a gunsmith, described her life in his gunsmith shop:

> In spite of the money he earns as a gunsmith, a trade he knows very well, and in spite of the fact that I have an annual income of one hundred and forty-two pesos from the rent of an *esquina-pulpería* I own, my underwear is of the most miserable kind, worse than a beggar's. With only twelve reales, I am supposed to pay for all daily household expenses, including feeding and clothing a daughter and a servant, and feeding five apprentices. It never is enough. I have to perform miracles by multiplying bread and fish like our adorable Jesus in the desert. Meals lead to continuous arguments and fights, since there is never enough money left to buy food, whereas he [my husband] has enough money to spend on prostitutes.[9]

Houses (*casas*), which accounted for 30.9 percent of all residential units in the 1808 census, could be subdivided into different living spaces: the first or second floor could be rented to another family, as could individual rooms facing on one of the patios; a porch could be turned into a shop. The decision to rent a small room or apartment inside a bigger house was a way of minimizing subsistence costs, but it also enhanced social interaction, thus gaining some protection for wives and children subject to abuse. Many civil court cases over unpaid rents reveal that the pattern of subleasing was widespread and that many people in Lima earned a living from renting out portions of their homes.

Physical closeness in a house or a *callejón* made neighbors witness to conjugal quarrels, beatings, and adulterous behavior. In court, a witness would describe how close he or she lived to a quarreling couple to explain (or

---

piezas utiles que tiene en el patio, otro en la Sala, y su respectivo Callejón." This fragmentation was also seen in the houses belonging to Lima's upper class. See, for example, AGN, RA, CCI, L 23, C 242, f. 28: "[. . .] los Altos de una casa, cituada en la Calle de Concha, en cuio arrendamiento se incluye toda la vivienda Alta, la cochera, que está a la mano Izquierda de su frente, el quarto que le es contiguo y está en el segundo Arco, la parte del patio que necesita para poner una Calesa, y la Pazadera que está al pie de la escalera." This mixture of rooms and garage brought in 500 pesos annually. See also, AGN, RA, CCI, L 17, C 174, f. 15.

9. Case 335, AA, CD, L 87 (1815–20), Martínez vs. Chungcipoma.

excuse) their familiarity with a neighbor's private life. Next-door neighbors could not only tell that a couple was quarreling, but they could also repeat what had been said and how long the quarrel had lasted.[10] At times these neighbors were called upon to restrain a violent husband. As one woman put it, her neighbors "were the protecting angels worried about my safety."[11]

After a big party one night, Eulalia Martínez, the gunsmith's wife, could not find her husband. She had suspected that he was having an affair with a single woman, María Corpancho, who rented one of the workshop's patio rooms. Eulalia immediately knew that something odd was happening. She went to the room and found her husband in bed with María. "Leaving them in this situation, I went back to my room full of contempt and despair," she said. "When he later came home, he felt guilty. He was caught *in flagranti*, and his guilt was obvious from the marks of sexual intercourse he had on his underwear, and I told him so."

Enraged, he beat her. In court, Eulalia declared that he would have killed her had her little daughter not begged him on her knees to stop and a female slave and a sturdy apprentice from the workshop not physically intervened on her behalf.

People lived closely together, and neighbors' brawls were on everyone's tongue. Brisk city gossip could involve a jealous wife and her husband's lover living next door to each other,[12] but also sets of families quarreling with each other. One Sunday night in 1891, a woman called her neighbor a "*cholo sinverguenza*" (a brazen half-breed) and accused his wife and daughter of immoral behavior. Insults against a family's honor were followed by a bedpan flying through the air. Although Doña Trinidad Pareja later claimed that the bedpan contained flower water, not urine, the judge was unconvinced.[13] Possibly worse were accusations touching on the moral behavior and the racial qualifications of the individuals. Doña Petronila Beserra was accused of calling her neighbor "a prostitute and saying that she made love to a black man while her husband was asleep." One witness, a Chilean woman

---

10. Case 976, CD, L 91 (1848–53), 1853, Rodríguez vs. Flor. More recent interviews with working-class women published by Laura Miller (Miller et al. 1987, 15–152) show a very similar pattern.
11. Case 437, AA, CD, L 83 (1802–4), 1804.
12. AGN, CS, CCR, L 62, 1840, Evangelista vs. Mendoza. The wife and the husband's lover both worked in a butcher's booth at the local market.
13. Case 0101, AGN, Expedientes Judiciales, CCR, L s.n., 1891, Juicio por querrella y contraquerella seguidos entre Don Manuel Alejos y su esposa Doña Dominga Aguirre de Alejos con Doña Trinidad Pareja por injurias.

Fig. 1. Plaza Mayor, Lima, in the 1850s.

Fig. 2. Around the Plaza Mayor were (and partially are) the cathedral, the municipality, the seat of government, many "cajones," and elite residences. It was the place to be seen, to observe, to pray, and to purchase, the place where men and women publicly interacted.

living on the same street, testified that Doña Petronila called her neighbor a "*choclito verde y bieja bruja y puta*" (an overripe wench and a witch). Another witness, a baker, claimed that Petronila had been drunk while making these accusations. The judge sentenced her to jail for four days.[14]

Among the upper classes, neighbors in the *barrio* and slaves living in the household were more important than tenants, both as witnesses and as sources of conflict. In 1811 Doña Antonia Guisado and her husband, Don Julián García Gonzáles, both Spaniards, had a terrible fight in their bedroom. Together they owned a big store in the Calle de Mercaderes, right on Lima's central plaza. After brutally beating her, "he grasped a knife to stab her. But Andrea [a servant] wrenched the knife away from him. Andrea knew that this would not be enough to calm him down, and to avoid further tragedy, she ran down to the patio and shouted for help. Neighbors immediately came to the rescue."[15] Close living quarters also provided protection for servants who lived in big households. Masters and homeowners would intercede when a servant couple had come to blows. When a Chilean-born shoemaker was trying to kill his wife, a domestic worker in an elite household, her master accused the shoemaker of attempted homicide. The shoemaker was sent to prison and later extradited for four years, in spite of his lawyer's allegations that he had been drunk, implying that he was unaccountable.[16] Living under the cover of a master and houseowner provided protection against unruly husbands.

Neighbors sometimes arrived unbidden if the quarreling was so loud that it could not be overlooked. Such spontaneous involvement reveals the existence of a reliable social support network centered in the *barrio*. María Dolores Barrera sued her husband in 1809 out of fear that his continued beatings would end her life. Her neighbor, Gaspar Ganderillas, had rescued her many times, and in court he described the latest scene he had witnessed: "I have lived in the same house with the said Juan Guzmán and his wife. One morning I heard screams and beating. I ran over. The couples' children opened the door of the room. I entered to find María Dolores on the floor in her underwear. The said Juan Guzmán, also in underwear, was holding a brick in his hand ready to throw it at his wife."[17]

---

14. Case 0118, AGN, Expedientes Judiciales, CCR, L s.n., 1890, Juicio criminal seguido por Don Eduardo Ríos y su Esposa contra Doña Petronila Beserra por injurias.
15. Case 245, AA, CD,L 86 (1810–14), 1811, Guisado vs. Gonzáles.
16. Case 844, AGN, CS, CCR, L 108, 1850, Guzman vs. N.
17. Case 69, AA, CD, L 85 (1808–9), 1809, Barrera vs. Guzmán.

Children were an essential link among neighbors because they interacted with each other even more than adults did. While playing together in the streets and patios, they could share experiences and anxieties. When their parents fought, children sought help from the parents of their playmates.

Neighbors would even break down doors to help a desperate wife.[18] One night when Casimira Vega was beaten by her husband, Ambrosio Redeo, an Indian woman and her husband went to her aid. As in other cases, this was not the first time they had interceded. In the witness stand, the Indian woman declared that "on another occasion, he did the same at midnight when all in the neighborhood were asleep. When we heard the screams, my husband and I got up to help her. We broke the door, entered the room, and separated them."[19] Clearly, husbands, despite their many male prerogatives, did not have unlimited freedom to beat or cheat on their wives. No matter how many locks a man put on the door to his home, neighbors would step in.[20] When screams were heard, neighbors would come closer, listen, and take sides.[21] Domestic violence was hard to hide from the public eye.

Even when the quarreling couple was living in an "illicit relationship," as the law called it, neighbors were willing to get involved. Pedro Sánchez, a thirty-six-year-old widower, had been dismissed by his concubine, Josefina Barzo, a twenty-six-year-old seamstress. One day he came back to the Calle Malambo to recover his mattress..and when Josefina barred his entrance, he forced his way in, and infuriated by her resistance, set fire to the room. Neighbors had been watching and rushed to help Josefina extinguish the blaze. Pedro was sent to jail for six months.[22] Neighbors also helped Andrés Oliva's concubine. In spite of the fact that they had called in the police,

---

18. See also case 14, AA, CD, L 87 (1815–20).

19. Case 624, AA, CD, L 83 (1802–4). See also case 834, AA, CD, L 93 (1857–59), 1857, Gonzales vs. Tejada.

20. Josefa Fuentes accused her husband of purposefully closing the door so that nobody could hear her scream while he tried to kill her. Her neighbors managed to break in only with great difficulty. AA, LM, L 10 (1850–69), 1853, Fuentes vs. Risco.

21. Case 606, AA, LM, L 7 (1800–1809). In this case, we have the declarations of a husband who accuses his wife of quarreling with him all the time: "en la noche de ese propio dia, provocandome a una riña, no solo con las mas vulnerantes expresiones, sino aun llegando a levantarme airadamente las manos que me fue inevitable procurar repelerlas, y al alborozo del Barrio que se agolpó a nuestra habitación que habia cerrado para ocultar del modo posible su escándalo."

22. Case 0241, AGN, Expedientes Judiciales, CCR, L s.n., 1890, De oficio contra Pedro Sánchez Porras por Incendio, 1890.

Andrés hurt her so badly that she had to be brought to the Santa Ana hospital.[23]

In especially violent struggles, neighbors too used violent means to put a husband in his place. In 1809, when Juana Murga resorted to the ecclesiastical court to obtain a divorce on the grounds of mistreatment and adultery by her husband, Antonio Sarmiento, she had already suffered many years of brutal beatings. They lived in a room in a *callejón*, with many neighbors living close by. Those neighbors had observed the precautions she took to visit her parents against her husband's wishes. One day, when Juana's parents had sent a caleche to pick her up and had even asked her friend Melchora Sotomayor to accompany her, Antonio appeared just as they were leaving. Then, according to witnesses, he uttered words they dared not repeat for the court record. He tried to drag his wife inside the house, all the while shouting that he meant to kill her. The neighbors stepped in. Antonio kicked and knocked everyone around, the neighbors fought back, but in the end Antonio jumped on his wife and beat her until she fainted.[24] The witnesses were scandalized by this heinous behavior.

Serenos and mayors were called in when quarrels outgrew the neighbors' capacity to handle them and when neighbors felt that some official intervention was necessary to mitigate violence and restore peace in the neighborhood.[25] Around 1806, Paula Calderón and her husband, Santiago Castro, lived in a shoemaker *tienda-habitación* in the Barrio de la Quadra Peña Dorada, near the Encarnación monastery. Their neighbors, and even the *barrio* mayor, had witnessed how, in one of fight, Santiago had not only threatened his wife with a knife but had actually torn out one of her braids.

23. Case 0237, AGN, Expedientes Judiciales, CCR, L s.n., 1891, De oficio contra Andrés Oliva por lesiones. In another case, neighbors in a *callejón* intervened to save Jesús Solis from an acutely alcoholic husband, Pedro Lecas, a thirty-two-year-old mestizo barber. Previously neighbors had seen him running naked through the streets. AGN, Expedientes Judiciales, CCR, L s.n., 1891, De oficio contra Pedro Lecas por lesiones.

24. Case 394, AA, CD, L 85 (1808–9), 1809, Murga vs. Sarmiento.

25. A similar case occurred in 1853 in a *casa-chingana* owned by an Indian couple. Tomasa Valdez accused her husband of "beating, pulling out her hair, and piercing her body by blows and bites." One night she climbed up on the roof, and an Indian neighbor provided her with a ladder to get down and hide from her husband while he called in the *sereno*. Case 052, AA, CD, L 91 (1848–53), 1853, Valdes vs. Dias. A free *moreno*, a witness in the Almonaci vs. Samudio case, remembered that Cosme Samudio beat his wife so badly that the *sereno* could not pull them apart and had to call in the *alcalde*. It seems, though, that not all *serenos* complied with this rule. In 1806 José Uceda, a resident in the *barrio* of Malambo, filed a complaint against the *barrio sereno* in the Real Audiencia. José alleged that his face had been severely cut by the sword of the *sereno*, and even worse that it happened before 10:00 P.M. AGN, RA, CCR, L 108, C 130, 1806.

When the other neighbors heard what had happened, they arrived on the scene and snatched the braid out of Antonio's hands. In the fracas, one neighbor was seriously injured. In their declarations, witnesses emphasized that the husband had gone beyond the pale, and they fully sided with Paula in her suit for a divorce. Santiago's behavior, the mayor declared, threatened public tranquility, and worse yet, had made the apprentices working with them lose all respect for them too. Because Paula and Antonio continuously quarreled, the apprentices could and would not see them as models of proper behavior. Thus, the mayor reasoned, this behavior undermined proper hierarchy.[26]

Conflicts like these were beyond acceptable limits because of their brutality and because they upset people's lives. Living in close proximity to neighbors provided women with a reasonable degree of protection against violent husbands or lovers. There were limits to what *barrio* residents and authorities were willing to accept for the sake of a man's domestic prerogatives. Neighbors had a sense of what constituted excessive physical abuse, and they would not tolerate it. The limit was defined by the degree of violence: husbands should be more sensitive, wives should not be treated like slaves; moreover, pregnant women should not be beaten at all.[27] In this way, neighbors not only helped desperate wives, but they also compelled moral discipline in a wider sense.

Restricted Privacy: The Force of Gossip

Despite Lima's sweltering climate, doors and windows had to be shut to insulate the bedroom from the eyes and ears of *barrio* residents. Husbands and wives worried about what the neighbors thought, because their ostracism could turn a husband, a wife, or the entire family into outcasts. Neighborhoods could, indeed, become oppressive and morally demanding. In 1857, as an example, a lawyer was so ashamed that he left town when his sexual problems with his wife had made him the neighborhood laughing stock.[28] In 1808 María Josefa de Lara sued her husband, Martín Mendieta, a drunk who frequently beat her. In her complaint, she declared that her

---

26. Case 112, AA, CD, L 84 (1805–7), 1806, Calderón vs. Castro.
27. Case 136, AA, LM, L 7 (1800–1809), 1808, Collazos vs. Portilla.
28. Case 868, AA, NM, L 65 (1857–59), 1857, Loyola vs. Valdez.

husband had raped one of their daughters, and it "is common knowledge. As a result I am considered a scandal in my own neighborhood."[29] In public opinion, María Josefa was deemed as guilty as her husband—how *could* she have allowed it to happen? Blame and disgrace fell on the entire family.

Gossip destroyed more than one marriage. Don José Mercedes Contreras found out through neighborhood gossip that his wife was behaving "improperly." She had been walking at night on the streets in Callao, Peru's main port city. The "hearsay in Callao is that my wife is wandering about at six o'clock in the morning, and this is terribly sad for a husband who duly fulfills his marital duties," he said. Neighbors even knew that his mother-in-law was the one who came to pick her up,[30] thus marking him as a man who had no control over what was happening in his own household.

A wife might come to accept her husbands' adultery, but she would not tolerate being the object of street gossip in her own *barrio*. *Barrios* were very tightly knit, and peoples' lives depended on being accepted by their neighbors. Francisca Inostrosa knew that her husband was betraying her. He and his concubine had been seen together in *caleches,* the bullfight arena, and *pulperías*. But the last straw came when the husband rented a room for his lover in the *barrio* where he lived with Francisca. As far as Francisca was concerned, the *barrio*—as she wrote to the judge—was just too small for the both of them.[31] About forty years later, in 1848, Camila Sotomayor's trials were even worse. Her husband brought his concubines not only into the *barrio* but into the matrimonial bed. On several occasions when he went to bed with one of his many lovers, Camila found herself locked out all night, sitting at the entrance waiting for morning when he would let her in. Neighbors observed the different women entering and leaving the house and would also see Camila "humbly returning to hide [her] shame and disgrace."[32]

Husbands, of course, were opposed to meddling that interfered with what they considered to be their marital prerogatives. Some men even ventured to accuse the priest of trespassing conjugal rights. But even such private conversations were overheard. In the Calle del Baratillo, the neighbors of Doña Manuela Vargas and Don Francisco Bernardo Sánchez de la Concha had interceded in quarrels on several occasions. Finally, Doña Manuela filed

29. Case 286, AA, CD, L 85 (1808–9), 1808, Lara vs. Mendieta.
30. Case 896, AA, LM, L 10 (1850–69), 1852, Meri vs. Contreras.
31. Case 272, AA, CD, L 86 (1802–4), Inostroza vs. N.
32. Case 011, AA, CD, L 91 (1848–53), 1848, Sotomayor vs. Saldarriaga.

a complaint against her husband in the ecclesiastical court and asked the priest to come to their home to talk to her husband. Don Antonio Neda, one of the neighbors, testified that as he was walking down the street near the couples' house, he overheard "shrill screams and horrible words. [Don Francisco] was yelling at his wife telling her she was a whore and a wretched something or other and that she would no longer be allowed to go to church. 'I—[Don Francisco said]—don't give a damn about the priest. Maybe he has something to say in his church, but I have the say in my house.' Out of curiosity I asked the neighbors what was going on, and they said that her husband was shouting at her because she had gone to the priest of the parish of San Lázaro."[33] Another witness, a *mestiza* who lived in the same *callejón*, mentioned that the couples' continuous fighting disturbed everyone in the *barrio*.

When husbands thought they could get away with it, or when their anger outweighed their moral scruples, many did not hesitate to question the rights of the church to intervene in marital conflict. In extreme cases of anger, some men even claimed they had an alliance with the devil. The church's exhortations on spousal love could be shredded by a husband's whip. For many husbands, violence was a conscious assertion of their male prerogatives. Antonio Farfan was a hatmaker, and Faustina Soto sold food. When she was five month pregnant with their third child, her husband had thrown a heap of logs at one of their children, and had she not blocked this onslaught with her own body, the child would have been killed. After the incident, Faustina ran away in disguise, but Antonio chased her through Lima's streets. When she finally hid in a lawyer's house, Antonio stood at the door, screaming that "he did not obey Jesus Christ, that he only had one soul and this he had sold to the devil."[34]

When husbands were prosecuted, they frequently reacted to the social control by accusing neighbors, *serenos*, *alcaldes* and even priests of being sexually interested in their wives. After all, they were men too. An arbitrator who rescued a wife too often could end up accused of trying to seduce her. However imaginary, husbands used these moral accusations to constrain intervention and assert their domain.[35] Sometimes, as we will see, their suspicions proved right.

33. Case 616, AA, CD, L 86 (1810–14), 1810, Vargas vs. Sánchez.
34. Case 586, AA, CD, L 83 (1802–4), 1803, Soto vs. Farfan.
35. Case 322, AA, CD, L 84 (1805–7), Maldonado vs. Jordan.

Couples even fought in Lima's streets,[36] screaming, biting, whipping, and insulting each other. In these fights, wives were dubbed "prostitutes" and *putas de sambos y negros* (whores for *sambos* and blacks), and in turn they called their husbands "dark-skinned bastards."[37] *Serenos*, passersby, and neighbors intervened to stop a battering, whether the aggressor was the husband or, as in some cases, a jealous wife. Women also fought each other in public, and passersby would restrain one from biting off the other's finger or pulling out her hair. Sometimes onlookers went as far as forcing an adulterous wife to return to her husband.[38] At other times they might get involved in order to stop an angry husband from dragging his wife back home.[39] *Serenos* declared in court that some couples, carried away by the quarrel, even fought in the streets in underwear.[40] Without a doubt, the line was blurred between private and public expressions of anger and the resolution of conflict.

As newcomers to Lima, migrants found in the neighborhood a social environment that helped them replace lost support networks. Oftentimes neighbors' assistance went beyond stopping physical violence. Husbands were prone to vanish, sometimes leaving on long business trips to rural provinces or abandoning the home altogether to live with a new lover. A wife in this predicament turned to her neighbors for sustenance and compassion. Especially when a woman was sick and could not take care of herself, or when her survival was threatened, individuals did not hesitate to step in.[41] In the absence of state-sponsored institutions to deal with such cases, neighbors and the extended family might be a woman's only recourse.

The *chisme* (gossip) over initially isolated neighborhood events could spread throughout the *barrio* or even across the city, as more and more people sided with one or the other of the spouses. Interpretations of right and wrong constantly evolved from the discussion, intermediation, and resolution of these events. In 1849 Doña Margarita La Torre de Belaúnde

---

36. Case 57, AA, LM, L 7 (1800–1809), 1804, Balverde vs. Barbosa. She was a free *samba* laundress married to a free *moreno*. Witness to this fight was Ramón Arias, a free mulatto living next to the couple on the Calle de Ormeño.

37. See, for example, case 51, AA, CD, L 87 (1815–20), 1817, Baca vs. Rios; and case 738, AGN, Corte Superior, CCI, 1854, Causa seguida por Doña Martina Benegas contra Don Agustín Repeto por difamación.

38. Case 806, AGN, CS, CCR, L 121, 1852, Don José Burgos, zapatero, 40 años, contra Don Pedro Benavides, comerciante, 38 años, por seducción de su esposa y robo de valores.

39. Case 373, AA, LM, L 8 (1810–15).

40. Case 14, AA, CD, L 87 (1815–20), Almonaci vs. Samudio.

41. Case 394, AA, CD, L 85 (1808–9), Murga vs. Balcasar.

of Arequipa wrote a letter to her uncle, Javier Luna Pizarro, archbishop of Lima, on behalf of Doña Martina Mendoza. In her letter, she pleaded that her uncle ratify Doña Martina's divorce. The core of her argument was that everyone in Arequipa and Moquegua (two cities in southern Peru) knew how much Doña Martina had suffered in her marriage. The husband beat and mistreated her and had even attempted to muddy her honor in the local newspapers. This woman—Doña Margarita concluded—deserved to escape her husband's repellent cruelty and the gossip, which by then involved the newspapers in two major cities. A mounting social pressure and, certainly, the timely letter from the niece to her powerful uncle alerting the archbishop to the "bad example" set by the Arequipa elite couple, led to a quick divorce to avoid further commotion. Lima's archbishop complied with his niece's and the people's wishes.

Collective action borne out of a neighborhood event also had more subtle expressions. Especially dramatic events were kept alive in people's memories over long periods of time. One means of recollection arose by naming a street or a corner in the city after what had happened there. Often, a name perpetuated itself in the collective memory to the point that it became the official street or place name. For example, the "Calle del Suspiro" (the Street of the Sigh) was remembered as the street in which a woman had stabbed her lover when he told her he would marry someone else (A. Gálvez 1905, 81). Later, a man stabbed to death under similar circumstances would be dubbed "the man of the sighing street." Such socially constructed images and stories were rooted in real life, but through reiterated collective memory, they became warning posts to demarcate neighborhood ethics.

The plebeian public sphere (*plebejische Offentlichkeit*) was at work in nineteenth-century Lima.[42] Before conflicts reached the courtroom, much had already transpired in the *barrios* (in all likelihood, more conflicts were dealt with through alert *barrio* mediators than in formal courtrooms). People resisted filing suits because they knew that in court—even more so than in the neighborhood—their problems would become a part of common gossip and of official, usually harsh, reprimands. Such fears were common among men and women, and quite a few couples abandoned their divorce suits because they feared social scandal: "Our trivial discord is now behind us, and it no longer merits the court's attention, always a scandalous event,

---

42. See Medick (1983). His use of this concept neatly fits my description of meddling neighbors.

which is so detrimental for the children and always gives rise to unfavorable comments."[43] As we will see, the dropping of court actions became more frequent as the century progressed, whereas the neighbors' intervention did not subside.[44]

People from the *barrio* helped to solve conflicts and in doing so constructed a *barrio* ethic about expected marital and—more generally—social behavior. In homes and in the streets, neighbors, friends, and relatives set limits to male abuse and to the rovings of adulterous women. This ranged from using force to providing needed food and money. While not necessarily following liberal principles of individual freedom, affective individualism, or citizen rights, these *barrio* interactions created an evolving ethic of social duty. Although neighbors were gossips who could make or break an individual's reputation, *barrio* intervention was overwhelmingly helpful, especially for women in despair. Couples listened to what neighbors had to say.

Despite its constricting aspects, for many women the *barrio* played the role of the "good angel." *Barrio* expectations, as expressed through daily interactions among neighbors, carried greater weight than the ideal, moralistic recommendations of canon law, the church and priests, or state policies and civil law. The testimony of neighbors was extremely important to the outcome of a lawsuit. Only when witnesses corroborated a wife's accusations of abuse would a judge take the suit seriously. A single occurrence usually got the husband only a lecture on better behavior, but certainly no decree of divorce followed. Witnesses helped judges to understand the dimensions of the conflict by reconstructing past conflict scenes and by providing their opinions on such scenes. In a sense, then, *barrio* ethics (customs) guided the outcome of a suit (the practice of law); and customs, in turn, were informed by assumptions and understandings on the role of men and women as described by Segura.

In the absence of efficient mechanisms of social control, morality was *the* weapon to maintain order. This control was acted out in the realms of family and marriage but, as illegitimacy rates show, with uneven success. In a similar vein, *barrio* morality was continuously reinterpreted as people judged

---

43. Case 038, AA, CD, L 93 (1857–59), 1859, Ureta vs. Geraldino.
44. The intervention of neighbors in Lima stands in stark contrast to what happened in Europe during the same time period. Europe saw "the rise of affective individualism" and a decline in the influence of extended kin, friends, and community (Hareven 1973). When looking at conflict resolution in Lima, we see that neighbors mediated, and that there was little "bonding" to resolve marital conflict.

"what was going on next door." For the church, marriage was a sacrament and a bond based on love; for the *barrio*, it was a sacrament that entailed conflict and could leave women, in particular, at risk. Neighbors—following their own interpretation of right and wrong—translated the church's holistic moral recommendations to fit the particular needs of couples.

3

The People and the Church

Changing socioeconomic and demographic patterns made even the most impassioned liberals recognize the church's role in preserving order in Peru. Liberals, conscious of their social distance from the popular classes, recognized that the church was the only national entity with access to all social groups (Klaiber 1992, 61). Church and state had different means of establishing control, but on both sides there was a clear sense of interdependency based on the necessity to sustain public order and morality. Beyond this ideological convergence, the state depended on the church for information collected during confessionals (which would reveal the plots for revolts) and census taking in the parishes. Church and state were mutually supportive, particularly when it came to the control of subordinate social groups. Harmony between these institutions was not always complete, however. At the heart of their conflicts lay a struggle over power and concrete material interests. Power parity—as ideally expressed by the number of mules pulling the coaches of the archbishop and the viceroy—was not easy to achieve in the daily bargaining over control of peoples' lives.[1]

Secularization occurred very slowly during the nineteenth century. The Peruvian church retained most of its economic and political prerogatives

---

1. For an analysis of church-class relations at the end of the eighteenth century based on a reading of the *modernistas*, see Macera (1977, 3:9–78).

and never lost control over the most intimate spheres of individual and family life. The church defined religious behavior, but it also had a say in how work, economic behavior, and social hierarchies should be understood. Throughout the nineteenth century, the church attempted to reconcile its condemnation of excessive earnings (*lucro*) with the prevalent patterns of social mobility by interweaving its universalistic principles about brotherhood and humanity with its sense of God-given social hierarchy. This meant an unresolved conflict between two ideals, the ancient Christian asceticism and the more recent aristocratic paternalism (Macera 1977, 3:158ff).

Religious authority pervaded Lima. The church either owned or administered many of the city's buildings.[2] Church holdings represented 8.3 percent of Lima's total area. In 1791, out of a total of 3,941 buildings, 1,135 (28.8 percent) in some way or another belonged to the church (Bromley and Barbagelata 1945, 76).[3] Clergymen and nuns lived in the city's cathedral, six parish churches, eleven hospitals, fifteen nunneries, nineteen monasteries, and several retreat houses (among them the *beaterios*), as well as an oratory, various novitiates, and colleges (Ganster 1990 [1986], 138–40). From these buildings they professed and passed condemnation on Lima's inhabitants. Manuel A. Fuentes (1861, 3:147–50), based on earlier findings by Murillo and Calancha, claimed that "in the whole world there was no other city in which charity and the distribution of alms was as widespread as in Lima."[4] By 1839, 9,549 masses were held in twenty-eight religious institutions during the year's eighty-nine holidays (Córdova y Urrutia 1839, 61–62). According to Flora Tristán (1986 [1838], 277), a well-known anticlericalist, around that time people went to mass two to three times a day and participated in at least two processions every week. However, in spite of the church's very firm grip on people's lives, the nineteenth century witnessed what Macera (1977, 3:205) called the "dissolution of Christian asceticism."

The church was not a monolithic entity. Different opinions and tendencies coexisted within it. Beyond the well-known rivalries between regular

---

2. Macera's claim about how little we know about the church's wealth still holds true (1977, 2:195).

3. In Mexico City this percentage was even higher. "The Church as a whole owned 47.08 percent of all urban property, and within the church no other institution controlled as much of this property as did the nunneries" (Lavrin 1989, 182).

4. Fuentes' count of religious institutions is even higher than the ones given by Ganster. According to Fuentes, there were 56 churches, 26 public chapels, 19 schools (12 of which were for girls), 14 monasteries for nuns, 5 *beaterios*, 4 poor houses, and one house for abandoned children (1861, 3:147–50).

orders and secular clergy, or (particularly before and during the wars of independence) between Spaniards and Creoles, even written ecclesiastical law was subject to many interpretations when it came to resolving individual cases and situations. Moreover, although the church preached unity and meant to include everyone, it reflected divisions of Peruvian society at large. "The highest posts were reserved for the *peninsulares* (Spanish) and for trusted Creoles. Very rarely was an Indian ordained to the priesthood, and the *mestizos* could ascend the ecclesiastical ladder only with difficulty" (Klaiber 1992, 14).

Priests and lay brothers alike were very involved in the city's economic life. They lent money at interest, were slumlords, invested in artisan workshops, and were often called in to substitute for lawyers or university faculty. As in Mexico City, home ownership and rental agreements with individuals and families put the church and the convents in contact with a spectrum of urban society and made ecclesiastics a prominent part of the city's social fabric (Lavrin 1986). After independence, "the Church survived, its mission defended if inert, its assets real if diminished, its offices intact if often unfilled. This was not a Church in decline, and, if it was temporarily weak, the state was weaker. . . . In the aftermath of independence the Church was more stable, more popular and apparently more wealthy than the state" (Lynch 1989, 303).

Between 1850 and 1875 the physical and economic dominance of the church diminished.[5] As a reaction to the 1855–56 liberal convention, however, a more militant church was born (Klaiber 1992, 62–63). Tithes were reduced during the wars of independence and abolished in 1859, the *leyes de ex-vinculación* cancelled interest on loans made by the church, and much of the church's property was transferred into private hands. Nevertheless, by 1878 the church controlled fifteen monasteries (there were thirteen in 1847 and in 1853) and three *beaterios* (in contrast to five in 1847 and seven in 1853).[6] The number of nuns, *donadas*, *beatas*, and lay women living in these

---

5. In 1790, after the implementation of decrees aimed at reducing the church's presence in Peruvian society, there remained in Lima 565 monks and nuns, lay brothers, and choristers. In the jurisdiction of Lima's archbishopric, there were 11 more convents, with a total of 103 monks and nuns (AA, Estadística, L 2, 1790). According to an ecclesiastical census in 1841, in Lima's five parishes there were 101 members of the secular clergy, while in the provinces of the archbishopric there were 233 (AA, Estadística, L 8, 1841). Some rough estimates of the number of clergymen show that at the end of the colonial period in several cities throughout Latin America (including those in Mexico and Peru), approximately one in every eleven white men were clerics (Ganster 1990 [1986], 138).

6. In all periods, though, only three *beaterios* were used by divorcing women.

places had increased from 580 in 1853 to 1,033 in 1878 (García Jordán n.d., 77).

During this gradual secularization, church and state continuously clashed on issues the church considered its prerogatives—from the sacramental character of matrimony to the timing of municipal burial registration and the appointment of priests. "Cemeteries were laicized in 1869, civil marriage for non-Catholics was recognized in 1897, freedom of worship for all confessions was established in 1915, and obligatory civil marriage for all and the right to divorce were upheld in 1910" (Klaiber 1992, 20).

In 1888 the church founded the Unión para Mujeres (Union for Women), which, under the guidance of Bishop Francisco de Sales Soto, built schools, helped the poor, and engaged in missionary activities. With the advance of liberalism, the church grew more conservative. It also increasingly became associated with "feminine qualities": love for tradition, sentimentalism, and passive subordination to authority. By contrast, the political program of liberalism acquired *machista* nuances (Klaiber 1992, 75–79). As I will show, Klaiber's assessment that "perhaps what some freethinkers termed 'ignorance' or 'submission' in judging Catholic [and] women's behavior was in reality a display of feminine independence against *their* [husbands'] authority," can be corroborated through a reading of ecclesiastical and civil court cases.

In spite of the protest of liberal voices, Peruvians in general defended the church's economic and moral prerogatives. Everything that, or anyone who, challenged such prerogatives—including Protestants—were satanized. Even at the Higher Court (*Corte Superior*) in 1826, fifteen out of seventy-six lawyers were ecclesiastics.[7] At the end of the nineteenth century, criminal lawsuits, condemnation, and persecution were still carried out against people who tried to assume functions traditionally controlled by the Catholic Church.[8] Immigration from Europe—an utmost priority for the state to promote growth and development—was delayed because the church and the liberal forces in society wished to suppress other religions and different social and political ideas (García Jordán 1987). Peru was (and is) a Catholic country

---

7. AGN, CSJ, L 45 (1825–28). Peru's judicial system included the "Jueces no letrados," "Jueces de Primera Instancia," "Corte Superior," and "Corte Suprema." One Corte Superior existed in each of the twenty-three departmental capitals, but there was only one Corte Surprema, in Lima.

8. See AA, Notas del Supremo Gobierno, L 16, 1890–1898, Escrito del Ministerio de Justicia, Culto e Instrucción, a case initiated because an evangelist appeared in Callao in 1896. For a discussion on the liberty of cults and immigration policy, see García Jordán (1987, 37–61).

with a constitutional recognition of its religion, and one of the world's most long-standing and ardent defenders of the holiness of matrimony.

In Lima's bustling city life, parish priests and the church guided the lives of Lima's inhabitants, especially when it came to family life and conjugal relations. The church tried to maintain its control over the life led in Lima's homes, women's essential realm. The church regulated family life and gender relations; granted dispensations and absolution for transgressions; administered counseling in the confessional regarding punishment of children, wife beating, and sexual sins; and controlled the granting of divorce or annulment (Lowry 1988, 21).[9] Parishes were divided into sections, each under the supervision of an ecclesiastical official. Every priest carried in his pocket a checklist with the name of each parishioner—man, woman, and child—on which he recorded their behavior and the fulfillment (or not) of their Christian duties. Tibesar (1970, 359) notes that the *padrones*—as these check lists were called—show that "the vast majority of the people not only attended mass on the required days but also received the sacraments of confession and communion out of obligation and even frequently out of devotion."

However, church control over men and women was far from complete. People frequently did not comply with church standards of neighborly, familial, and conjugal love. On the contrary, social life was sometimes marred by desperate or willful rejection of rules that were incompatible with the possibilities and restrictions of real life. These deviations resulted in a multifaceted array of situations and conflicts. This was true for interpersonal relations, especially in the domestic sphere, where one would expect that the church's ideals of respect, love, devotion, understanding, and forgiveness had their strongest foothold. In Lima, as elsewhere, the family was not always a haven of freedom and comfort.

Marriage, Ecclesiastical Fees, and Secularization

Matrimony was a major issue that heated the debate between state and church.[10] Although there was an ongoing fight over the sacramental versus

---

9. These issues will be discussed in detail in the following chapters.
10. The following discussion is based on ACR. On civil marriage, see especially pp. 64–70; for a discussion on which people resorted in which ways to civil marriage, see pp. 99–110; and on obligatory marriage, see p. 168.

civil character of marriage, Peru was one of the last countries in the world to accept civil marriage. For a long time the church managed to keep the upper hand on matrimonial issues. In the 1852 Civil Code, matrimony as a religious sacrament was placed above the idea of matrimony as a civil contract.[11] As a sacrament, matrimony was indissoluble. Thus, the state willingly "sacrificed its sovereignty and the liberty of conscience to a positive religion."[12] In forwarding this opinion, the 1852 Civil Code lagged behind some earlier and more liberal proposals published by Manuel Lorenzo Vidaurre, president of the Supreme Court of Justice in 1834. In his project, Vidaurre had defined matrimony as a legal and natural contract.[13] The 1923 report of the Comisión Reformadora (ACR), the body responsible for reforming the civil code, explained why, after one hundred years, Vidaurre's proposals still had not resulted in radical change: "A violent change from one system to another that was radically different—from an exclusively canonic matrimony, which had prevailed uninterruptedly for four centuries, to a civil obligatory matrimony, still little practiced in Europe and little known in American positive law—created, as one would expect, the complete triumph of conservative reaction. In the parliamentary commission, inaugurated by a decree dated June 7, 1851, the canonists' thesis defended by Manuel López Lissón and Manuel Pérez de Tudela was accepted with no debate whatsoever."[14] Through most of the nineteenth century, the church monopolized jurisdiction over marriage, quite in contrast to England, for example, where several different jurisdictions—sometimes following contradictory laws—coexisted to solve conjugal disputes (Stone 1990, 26).

In Peru marriage was celebrated according to ceremonies prescribed by the church. It was indissoluble, and divorce (until 1930, only a temporary separation of the spouses) and annulment had to be approved by the church. The secularization of marriage was not approved until 1918. Until then, only some legal aspects of marriage were dealt with in civil court. *Sponsalia* (a notarized record of promise of future marriage), alimony, dowry, and inheritance issues resulting from marriage and divorce were handled by secular judges (Valverde 1942, 41). Only in extreme cases of physical violence were the criminal courts called into action. According to legal analyst Emilio F. Valverde, the "sacramentalist doctrine" of canonists

11. For a reading of family law in Peru, see Emilio F. Valverde (1942, vol. 1)
12. ACR, 2d fasc., 99.
13. ACR, 2d fasc., 8, 14, 17, 18, 36.
14. ACR, 2d fasc., 106.

dominated all "legal precepts." This meant that in Lima the prevailing laws regarding marriage were those issued by the Council of Trent almost four hundred years earlier, by which "matrimony was considered not only as a relationship among spouses and their children, but also with society and God" (Valverde 1942, 35–36). A note in the 1923 reformist discussions attempting to justify this interpretation stated that "the real enemies of the good doctrines always had been those who had pushed too hard to implement them, that is, before society was prepared to receive them.... In the middle of the nineteenth century, the secularization of matrimony was an action ahead of time. But some changes were necessary, because simply adjusting to outlived molds would be living behind the times."[15]

In this abstract and vague assertion lies a message: although there were few alternatives, toward the end of the century the more enlightened thinkers were not willing to submit to a canonic victory. To do so would have meant to ignore "a renovating ferment: the liberty of conscience." Nevertheless, decisions continued to come from Rome. In 1864 Pius IX published the encyclical *Quanta Cura* with an appendix, the *Syllabus on Errors*, in which liberalism, secularism, freedom of thought, and tolerance were condemned. Shortly afterward a Peruvian liberal priest, Gonzáles Vigil, was excommunicated because he advocated for a more national and liberal church, believed in religious tolerance, had denied that the Roman Catholic faith was the only true belief, and preferred clerical marriage to celibacy (Lynch 1989, 315–16).[16]

Between 1871 and 1890, civil matrimony spread throughout the world unhampered. "With the speed of an ink spot on a blotter," Switzerland and Prussia (1874), Germany (1876), Mexico (1859?), Chile (1884), Uruguay (1885), and Argentina (1889, 1890) decreed the validity of civil matrimony.[17] In spite of these precedents, Lima's commissioners in charge of reviewing the civil code decided to cling to traditional rules. Civil matrimony was partially introduced in Peruvian legislation when the 1852 Civil Code incorporated an article permitting non-Catholics to resort to civil matrimony.

15. Ibid., 106–7.
16. Gonzáles Vigil was probably the last priest in the nineteenth century to dare challenge Rome's power. The colonial preeminence of Madrid over Rome (Véliz 1980, 216) was replaced by the preeminence of Rome over Lima.
17. Lavrin (1995) shows how in Argentina, Chile, and Uruguay the recognition of civil marriage and the possibility of divorce were matters of continuous bargaining between different political factions between 1880 and 1930. Liberal bills were often proposed in congress, but they were then put aside when opposed by the church.

By 1897 the only liberal sign was the formal recognition of the two forms of matrimony: the one based on canon law for those who were part of the recognized Catholic community, and the other based on civil law for those who were foreigners and non-Catholics.[18] Until 1897 foreigners could not have a church wedding unless they converted to Catholicism.[19] Even as late as 1928, Peruvian citizens were subject to exclusively ecclesiastical jurisdiction over matrimony. Any dissension was denounced as impious by the clerical opposition. Reformers timidly began to claim that civil marriage was a "solution stemming from scientific knowledge," and it could no longer be considered a by-product of liberal euphoria (as it had been in the middle of the nineteenth century). Civil marriage had become an idea that had matured and was now ingrained in "human legal conscience."[20]

Thus civil marriage was technically possible, but the state's lukewarm backing explains why it was rarely used. Between 1897 and 1922 only 35 (of 112) provinces performed civil marriages, and foreigners accounted for almost 50 percent of these civil ceremonies.[21] The state's submissiveness to the church (quite in contrast to the perceived "feminization" of the church) and longstanding traditions left it uninterested in promoting civil marriage registrations. Such an incapability or unwillingness left a gap in the bureaucratic infrastructure. The uncertainties and oscillating decisions of state building made open confrontation with the church impractical and fiscally dangerous.

Several attempts to implement reforms failed. The 1852 Civil Code ordered the establishment of civil registers (including marriage registers) under the control of the district governors, but when municipalities were created in 1856, the registration process was turned over to them. A law dated April 9, 1873, which created local administration councils (*concejos de administración local*), further indicated how urgent it was to establish registration agencies, not only in Lima, but also in more remote rural provinces. However, it was necessary in 1892, and even in 1928, to ratify and reiterate the 1856 propositions because earlier decrees were never

18. ACR, 2d fasc., 108–9.
19. Valverde (1942, 46) interprets this as follows: "Se solucionó de ese modo el delicado problema social que creaba para la población extranjera, de distintos cultos cada día más numerosa, la imposibilidad de contraer matrimonio, por ser tan sólo válido el católico."
20. ACR 2d fasc., 119 and 115.
21. In Lima there were no civil marriages, whereas in Callao (Lima's port, with a high percentage of European immigrants) there were 775 registered (approximately 40 percent); in Chiclayo, 77; Bajo Amazonas, 95; Moquegua, 48; Pasco, 47. These were all areas in which economic growth was linked to exports and European immigration.

implemented. Shifting jurisdictions and the absence of clear ideas about how to finance reforms meant that most decrees rolled right into the trash baskets. Contemporaries knew that in many districts the prescribed registers were never opened, and in others organization was so deficient that there was no provision to pay civil servants to carry out the job.[22]

The inadequacies in the registration system were impossible to ignore by the beginning of the twentieth century, when Lima and other departmental capitals confronted an increasing population: "The population growth in our main cities, that is, the departmental capitals, . . . overburdens our civil register offices, and it cannot be properly dealt with by the municipal officials; this in turn causes tremendous shortcomings and irregularities in the service and with great harm to individuals, whose family rights often remain legally unproven."[23]

Thus, in the course of time, more and more people were affected by the lack of civil registers. Official inertia was rampant. The church had been in charge of these matters for a long time, and it would require a lot more pressure from state institutions before attitudes changed and higher levels of efficiency emerged.

Registration and matrimony were not the only causes of disputes between church and state. Education, for example, was almost entirely under the aegis of the church. Although some private schools existed, school curricula stressed courses on morality and religion, and no school text could be used without the approval of the archbishop.[24]

Since colonial times, the church had charged a fixed amount of money (*aranceles*) for baptisms, marriages, and burials. Although *aranceles* were accepted, parishioners complained about the extra money, goods, and free services that priests required from the community. In spite of protests from all over the country, there was little that provincial and departmental political authorities (or for that matter the state itself) could do to control or prevent abusive activity. Although petitions to lower payments were forwarded to Lima's archbishop toward the end of the 1860s,[25] it was only around 1890 that the state dared to propose that the church lower its burial fees. Eloquently,

22. ACR, 2d fasc., 64–65.
23. ACR, 2d fasc., 66.
24. AA, Notas del Supremo Gobierno, L 16, Ministerio de Justicia, Culto e Instrucción al Arzobispado. Lima, 15 January 1890.
25. BN, Juan Ambrosio Huerta, "Informes que el Illmo. S.D.D. Juan de la Huerta Obispo de Puno dirije al Illmo. S.D.D. José Sebastián de Goyeneche Dignísimo Arzobispo de Lima sobre los Proyectos de Ley de Reducción de los derechos de Matrimonios . . . (entre otros)," 1869. Huerta's comments were inspired by his belief that lowering fees for marriage would help to

state officials argued that such a consideration would only be fair, given the church's commitment to social deeds. The government was not concerned about the payments for baptisms and marriages because they were "family events" that people could celebrate when and where they wanted. But burials were something different. Death occurred after families had already spent considerable sums of money to care for the dying person.[26] The state made it clear to church officials that a subtle blackmail was involved. Burials could not be postponed. One year after this petition, surprisingly, the state was in charge of fixing *aranceles,* and the provincial and departmental political authorities were authorized to control their observance.[27]

Secularization thus was not a "big" issue; it was anticlerical rather than antireligious. It was never openly endorsed or part of an explicit political agenda. But gradually the church's influence over the shape of the state declined.[28] Piece by piece, in Lima as elsewhere in Latin America, the "state assumed control of the educational system, lay cemeteries were established everywhere; fees were abolished for religious ceremonies, and civil marriage was universally instituted" (Véliz 1980, 193).

Despite the smooth transition to a more secular society, many people, especially women, felt the changes. The specific cases that follow show some of the less obvious disputes between the church and the state and reflect ways in which seemingly general disputes had concrete effects on people's lives.

---

moralize people, especially artisans and Indians, who could not pay the high costs and were thus doomed to live in concubinage, and that it would thus speed population growth.

26. It was stated thus: "No preocupan al Gobierno los derechos actuales para el bautismo y el matrimonio, tanto porque el arancel es en esta parte equitativo, cuanto porque ambos sacramentos esencialmente religiosos dependen en cuanto á su fecha, de la voluntad de los interesados que los celebran como fiesta de familia. Pero los derechos de entierro, hoy que no existe funeral de cuerpo presente, se han convertido en equitativa concesión á favor de los párrocos. . . . La muerte sobreviene generalmente despues de extraordinarios desembolsos. . . . Ya que la autoridad civil no expide papeletas de entierro para los cementerios católicos que ella sostiene, sin la prévia constancia del pago de derechos parroquiales, y haciendo asi eficaz la recaudación que sin tal apoyo sería casi nula, no puede menos de insistir en la justiciera rebaja que concibe la modesta congrua sacerdotal con los derechos y necesidades de nuestra sociedad" (AA, Notas del Supremo Gobierno, Ministerio de Justicia, Culto, Instrucción y Beneficencia al Arzobispado, Lima, 18 January 1890). According to normal procedures, local civil authorities issued permits to bury the dead after ecclesiastical fees had been paid. In other words, if the church was asking for too much money to bury the deceased, such a permit could not be obtained and corpses were doomed to remain in the streets and houses.

27. AA, ibid., Lima, 2 February 1894.

28. According to Véliz (1980, 193), anticlerical activities lasted for over a century and reinforced control by the central state.

Public Morality: Prostitution and Homosexuality

Although Lima's inhabitants and institutions were reluctant to talk about prostitution and homosexuality, isolated comments reflect the way in which the people, the church, and the state envisaged these "social diseases," as they called them.[29] As with other "city matters," it seems that the worries over the number of prostitutes and homosexuals in Lima did not subside in the course of the nineteenth century.

Prostitutes, by definition, were women; homosexuals, by definition, were men. Not all men condemned prostitution, and in order not to contravene social expectations and contradict moral discourse, prostitution itself was redefined to justify a double standard.

In 1815 Don Manuel Cañedo, a fifty-five-year-old guard, was married to Doña Juana Masa, a seamstress, and they lived Bajo el Puente. Accused by his wife of visiting prostitutes, Don Manuel was forced to justify his actions. He argued:

> If a relationship with a prostitute was a crime, every man, no matter how respectable his social standing or character, would be a lawbreaker simply because he visits one of those women. This would hamper social relations, and many churchmen and honest people would be considered criminals. I ask myself: Is it because of her occupation a prostitute carries a leper-like stigma on her shoulders that pollutes others who greet her or visit her? This cannot be, because we see these women engaging in business, appearing in the church and in court.... Neither the priests who make them listen to mass, nor the merchants who sell them their goods, nor their friends and family members can be accused of any crime. Therefore, the issue is not whether one deals with prostitutes, but rather the means by which one deals with them.[30]

Doña Juana, presenting her accusation in the ecclesiastical court, was supported by twenty-four witnesses, all neighbors, who testified that Don

---

29. Macera (1977, 3:297–98) argues that at the end of the eighteenth century and the beginning of the nineteenth, there was a scientific interest in sexual life and ample public debate on issues related to sexuality. However, in the same article he agrees that "el silencio parece ser la regla tácita acordada respecto de esos temas vedados" (340).

30. Case 345, AA, CD, L 87 (1815–20), 1815, Masa vs. Cañedo.

Manuel had beaten his pregnant wife and visited prostitutes. Don Manuel circumvented his wife's accusations by asserting that many other "respectable" men could be blamed for the same offense, if visiting a prostitute was an offense at all. By "de-sexualizing" prostitution (in his wording buying sex was the same as attending mass or purchasing goods), Don Manuel made it a normal social act. Although Don Manuel requested that the court send his wife to a *beaterio*, she was allowed to stay with her parents. One year afterward, in 1816, the court found that there was not enough proof to order a divorce. In 1817 Doña Juana reopened the case, arguing that she had wanted to appeal the court decision earlier, but had had no money to do so. No final sentence was passed. However, it is striking that the accounts of the many witnesses who supported Doña Juana's assertions were not enough to decree a divorce; adultery involving a prostitute was less of a crime than "public adultery." Moreover, by emptying prostitution of its moral dimension, it became a worldly issue in the realm of men. Thus, it could not be subjected to moral criticism and, consequently, did not merit attention in an ecclesiastical court. Such social-gender logic ran against the usual moral outrage against prostitution, *amancebamiento* (living together without being married), homosexuality, the spread of syphilis, abortion, child abandonment, or other acts considered to be "pathological phenomena" (Macera 1977, 3:187).[31]

In only one case in the ecclesiastical and civil suits did a woman accuse her husband of "adultery" with another man. In contrast to the judges' leniency when husbands resorted to prostitutes, in this case the wife obtained a quick divorce. In 1846 Josefa Murillo and Juan Calderón had been married for twenty-six years and had had several children. Juan mistreated her and had never provided for the family; even her smaller children worked for their daily food. Josefa's arguments reveal a whole set of ideas concerning homosexuality; she termed it "her husband's preference for sodomitic sexual relationships":

> Perhaps my husband's excesses could be concealed if they happened with a person of the proper sex. Men's natural propensity toward women, the stimuli of nature, and the attraction beauty exerts on

---

31. An interesting comment on this issue is provided by Guy (1990, 89–115) for Buenos Aires between 1875 and 1937, where such "social diseases" were interpreted as part of a "hereditary inferiority" and thus as an inescapable moral taint attached to the lower classes. In contrast, in Lima these manifestations of "social disease" were subject to reform.

men can upset the brain of the most commensurate man and launch him to actions that, although criminal in the eyes of the law, can be understood. But when dealing with a crime like the one committed by Calderón, what can be said to explain it? Absolutely nothing. His depravity is against nature itself, the result of corruption, and a proof of the perversity of his soul.[32]

Wives could understand adultery or prostitution, but not a husband's sodomy. Men were weak because by nature they had a strong and irresistible drive to which they succumbed. The only natural outlet for this drive was intercourse with a woman. Extramarital sexual relations with the opposite sex were the result of male anatomical weakness; sexual relations with the same sex, however, were the result of a "perverse soul," and thus merited condemnation by the church. In Josefa's case, one of her witnesses declared that her husband slept in one bed with his lover, while Josefa and her children slept in another. Moreover, one night Juan and his lover Martín had a fight. Martín left the house, and Juan called the *serenos* to force him to come back. The mayor, the *serenos*, and the neighbors knew what was happening. This "public knowledge" probably explains why Josefa and her witnesses were willing to accuse her husband of sexual transgressions.

Homosexuality was dealt with in civil court. However, the arguments brought forward by wives, neighbors, and *barrio* guards were of a moral kind: women could not be expected to continue living with husbands who showed strange sexual inclinations, and public order was endangered when men behaved and dressed like women. Clearly, there was a strong overlap between church and civil court jurisdiction on the issue of homosexuality. Men's "perverse" actions threatened public morale and thus required police intervention. Women's responses to male perversity challenged the continuity of marriage and thus required the priest's intervention.

In 1803 the soldiers of the *Comisión de Capa* saw Francisco Pro walking on Lima's streets wearing *saya* and *manto*.[33] When they realized that he was a man, they jailed him. Francisco explained that he was out for some fun in Lima's Alameda, but he had no cape and hat at hand, so he used those of his sister, María. Walking on the Alameda, he encountered her and showed her his disguise. María got angry and hit him. It was then that soldiers walking

32. Case 912, AA, CD, L 90 (1843–47), 1846, Murillo vs. Calderón.
33. This was the typical, very provocative dress used by women throughout the colonial period and until around 1850.

by recognized what was happening. Asked by the judge why he was known as a *maricón*, Francisco answered that people had nicknamed him this for his pale complexion and delicate facial features. Furthermore, he was well known as a good cook and could sew and do the laundry. However, he insisted, "this does not mean that I behave like a *maricón*. I do not move like one of those real *maricones* with their feminine gestures. I have never tried to be different from what nature made me." As a final argument, Francisco mentioned that using a disguise was not a crime. "During the day and at night in *caleches* and in public places women from all walks of life disguise themselves as men. Nobody thinks that this is a crime, so—I thought—why should it be a crime if I do the same?" But Francisco was wrong; it was not the same. He was identified by the soldiers as one of the many *maricones* who were on Lima's streets, and the proof was that he—contrary to his own assertions—had feminine gestures and used "women's words." Francisco was condemned to public exposure in the clothes he had been found in, and to have his hair cut. Later on he was sentenced to two years of public works.[34] Although Francisco tried to argue on similar lines as Don Manuel Canedo had (everyone used disguises, everyone resorted to prostitutes), Francisco was punished, whereas Don Manuel left the courtroom with a smile on his face.

Seemingly, homosexuals were a part of the city's daily life, to a point where they organized their own parades. On August 14, 1827, the newspaper *El Telégrafo* published a special edition containing a letter to Lima's prefect that accused *maricones* of parading in Amancaes. Homosexuality was defined as a "corruption that is the worst enemy of the human species." The anonymous writer threatened that he would not stop his campaign until these "degraded and perverse beings" had shackles on their feet and shovels in their hands. Furthermore, he encouraged Lima's prefect to engage in broader cleansing actions[35] to protect Lima's youth and children from "such dreadful

34. Case 481, AGN, RA, CCR, L 98, C 1191, 1803, Causa seguida contra Francisco Pro por habérsele encontrado vestido de mujer, 21 ff. For a case involving two mulatto slaves who engaged in a publicly sodomitic relationship, see AGN, RA, CCR, L 90, C 1107, 1800, Escrito de Manuel Rubio, Teniente Coronel de Dragones. Punishments seem to have become harsher as the century progressed. In 1890 two men initially accused of robbery were sentenced to four years of jail, not because of the robbery but because the medical record showed that they were "passive" homosexuals. AGN, Expedientes Judiciales, CCR, 1890, Autos seguidos de oficio contra Manuel Rivas (natural del Callao, 21 años, soltero, cargador) y Belisario Enciso (natural de Lima, 24 años, soltero, jornalero) por lesiones inferidas a Santos Tapia (natural de Chota, 26 años, soltero, jornalero) y Manuel Gonzales (natural de Chile, 20 años, soltero), 38 ff.

35. *El Telégrafo*, no. 109 (Lima: Imprenta de la Instrucción Primaria), 1827.

examples."³⁶ Still, at the end of the 1860s, Fuentes (1866, 59ff) claimed that games, drunkenness, homosexuality, and syphilis were part of a sad social panorama in Lima.

Even if there were attempts to curtail transgressions against "public morality," much escaped the attention of city authorities, and probably much more than anyone was willing to admit occurred in more than one bedroom. The public display of sexual options, such as the *maricón* parade or the husband who sought the *serenos'* help to bring back his male lover, indicates that people were not entirely constrained by traditional morality. Despite campaigns against deviation, the moral realms of life were hard to control. Moreover, court decisions made it increasingly clear that adultery with a woman was "preferred" to adultery with a man, that engaging with prostitutes was acceptable for men, but that "adultery"—committed by women for sheer survival when husbands refused to provide for them—was a sin. Thus, attempts to impose moral control were followed by the emergence of a moral double standard.

Marital consent, parental dissent, or dispensations involving one of the impediments stipulated by the Council of Trent became the arena in which state and church ideals, wishes, and interests clashed. More than a vague notion of "public morality"—as in the case of prostitution and homosexuality—the debate over dispensations reveals the church's involvement in the life of couples and families. Moreover, this debate unravels "aristocratic-paternalist" traits or, stated differently, how dispensations (and, as will be seen in the following chapter, dissent and consent) were handled according to who was involved. Race, class, and gender did matter.

Impediments and Dispensations in Lima and Its Rural Parishes

The church itself perceived that in the course of the nineteenth century priests were losing control over their parishioners as a result of increased immigration and a rise in the number of people each priest had to serve. Still, it was the parish priest who was relied on to identify and check out

---

36. It is noteworthy that in only one civil court case have I found an accusation of pederasty (AGN, Expedientes Judiciales, CCR, 1891, Juicio seguido a Leopoldo Valiente por delito de pederastía).

individuals petitioning to marry by opening a matrimonial license file. The presence of an increasing number of strangers in the city (Tables 1.8 and 1.9) made it more difficult for priests to recognize bigamists and others involved in deceit. But some supervision could be imposed: priests talked to people and listened to their confessions.

Everyone wishing to marry in church had to fulfill rituals designed to control marriage and the conditions of marriage. There was nothing easy about getting married. According to canon law, marriages had to be announced and publicized. Banns (public announcement of the proposed marriage) had to be published in widely read newspapers, read aloud in one of Lima's main squares, or posted on the church's doors. People were expected to step forward if they knew of any impediment to the marriage.

An important impediment was kinship. Kin to the fourth degree, both in the ascending and in the descending line; collateral kin (that is, one's future spouse's relatives); and even those people who had ritual kinship as godparents in baptism and marriage were off-limits in regard to sexual intercourse and marriage. If the bride or groom had had sexual intercourse within this kinship network prior to marriage, they needed a written dispensation to excuse the sin,[37] and this document was included in the matrimonial license file after penitence had been decreed upon the transgressors. The closer the kinship, the stricter the church's imposed sanctions and penitence.

Religious vows, a promise to serve God as a priest or a nun, were another impediment. Holy promises could not be easily retracted and called for thorough soul-searching for all involved before a dispensation could be granted. Another impediment was physical and mental illness, which included sexual impotence and diseases; various forms of heresy, such as witchcraft, atheism, and professing non-Catholic beliefs; and, more generally, madness. If deviations or sicknesses could be proven, the couple could not obtain a dispensation to marry. These impediments, particularly sexual impotence, were used to annul marriages as well (presumably there was no way of being aware of this impediment before marriage).

Catholic premarital rituals also required consent declarations from both fathers for those who married before reaching twenty-five years of age (after 1830, age twenty-one). If the father had died, the mother stepped in or, in her absence, the closest paternal male relative. When parents did not agree to the impending marriage, they expressed their dissent in writing. Church authorities carefully scrutinized the objections. The church was aware that

---

37. Peru's 1852 civil code explicitly stated that granting dispensations was the exclusive domain of the church. See art. 143.

women were sometimes forced into marriage by their parents, so a written consent signed by the bride was also required.[38]

Couples also presented to their priest birth certificates stating their parishes of birth. If born in different parishes, they had to marry in the woman's parish. At least two witnesses per person had to be present at the ceremony. Moreover, witnesses declared in writing how and for what length of time they had known each of the partners or both. Church officials processed matrimonial files with great care, not only because they gave the church moral leverage and control over people's lives, but also because once the marriage had taken place, the presence of unexcused impediments could be used by a spouse to petition for an annulment. Because marriage was a sacrament, the church was interested in avoiding allegations in hindsight.

Transgressions against these carefully elaborated rules are a measure of the degree to which people complied with ecclesiastical dictates. Records of transgression reflect the evolution of these rules. How people used dispensations, consent, and dissent helps explain resistance to church rules and reveals the intricacies of a highly fragmented society and the manifold interstices of canon law.

Dispensations Among Elites

A fundamental conflict existed between the church's impediment to marry kin and economic interests. Especially for the upper classes, spouses were often chosen from among second-degree relatives (cousins, nieces, and nephews). The closer that family kinship networks were knit, the greater the likelihood that the family would be able to concentrate, accumulate, and retain property and wealth (Kuznesof and Oppenheimer, 1985, 219). Exclusion of outsiders through strategic marriage alliances turned "family business" into a class strategy, and throughout the nineteenth century created the foundations of a state structure based on networks of families (Balmori, Voss, and Wortman 1984, 10). This assertion holds for most (if not all) Catholic Latin American countries.

Obviously, the kinship impediment contradicted class interests, and thus the church had great power in determining the patterns of wealth accumulation.[39] By granting dispensations, the church was aiding the concentration

---

38. For a detailed description of marriage procedures and transgressions, see Lavrin (1986, 47–85) and Rípodas Ardanaz (1977).

39. Until the beginning of the European Middle Ages, the church had forbidden marriage up to the fourteenth degree of kinship without its approval (Goody 1983). The practical

of wealth. For secular interest groups, the only way to rid themselves of ecclesiastical control over family organization and reproduction was by promoting secularization. By granting paid exceptions, the church revealed its need and willingness to compromise with the state and the elite groups that partly controlled it.[40] Although over time the church showed itself more lenient in administering marriage regulations and in lowering the degree of relationship allowed for marriage, dispensations still played a crucial role in the maintenance of class-based power structures, which included the church itself.

The importance of dispensations went beyond relieving spouses from kinship impediments. Dispensations were also handed out to allow people to skip the banns and to marry in a different parish from the one in which they had been born (both requirements of the Council of Trent). In a way, dispensations made certain transgressions possible, particularly for those willing and able to pay for these special certificates. Dispensations could be issued before or after marriage. In the latter case, they could reaffirm an existing marriage. By dispensing with the very guilt its rules created, the church asserted its authority over marriages even if people did not comply with its all-embracing regulations. Beyond the exercise of moral control, the granting of dispensations also allowed the church to earn cash.

The use of dispensations tells us much about the church's involvement in people's lives, and it also gives us an idea of people's behavior. In Lima few dispensations were denied, signaling that the church basically followed people's wishes. More complex is the question about people's behavior. The number and nature of the dispensations reveal how certain social groups closed ranks. Many dispensations issued because of existing affinity (one's spouse's family) and consanguinity (one's own family) means that marital choices were highly restricted; few dispensations may mean either

---

consequence was that very complex genealogies had to be provided, an endeavor that now allows for a fascinating reconstruction of past social groups and classes. Such close control hampered social reproduction, particularly in small towns in which everyone became blood-related. People had to marry outside their own group, and in many cases this meant the dispersal through inheritance of wealth (especially land) as well as a weakening of communities' social control. If no outside marriage partner was available, people remained single, and in the absence of heirs, property was bequeathed to the church, thus augmenting the church's wealth (Goody 1983). After the Middle Ages, when emigration and general mobility became more common, people found it easier to find marriage partners outside their own kin group.

40. There seems to be a general agreement on this assertion. See Balmori (1985); Balmori and Oppenheimer (1979, 231–61); Blank (1974); Kuznesof (1980, 571–92). It is also true that bishops and archbishops more often than not were sons of the elite.

a compliance with existing church regulations or a basically free choice of marriage partners.

Two crucial questions arise in regard to Lima's inhabitants. Did the church handle impediments and dispensations differently according to race and/or class? To what degree did people comply with church regulations, and to what degree did they perceive compliance as a moral issue?

Information concerning dispensations in Lima is fragmentary. There are only two sources. The first is a book that records all dispensations for the Lima archbishopric between 1807 and 1809.[41] The second book records so-called secret marriages for the last decades of the nineteenth century. The latter source shows couples attempting to avoid the reading of banns out of fear of negative public opinion and possible reprisal. These are very different sources, and they are not comparable. Significant, however, is the fact that they were different. While at the beginning of the century there was a systematic recording of dispensations, by the end, any impediment was registered as "secret." Moral concerns were replaced by social concerns.

In 1807, 121 dispensation requests were filed; in 1808, 115; and in 1809, 112. Of these, only 59.4 percent involved residents of Lima; the rest came from the archbishopric inland provinces, reflecting the migratory patterns discussed earlier (see Tables 1.8 and 1.9). Using matrimonial licenses, we find that approximately 12 percent of all marriages[42] required some type of dispensation. Of this 12 percent, 26.8 percent mentioned consanguinity to the fourth degree as an impediment; 66.2 percent, affinity to the fourth degree; and only 7.0 percent referred to other impediments set by the Council of Trent, such as vows of chastity and spiritual kinship (0.9 percent) or crime, adultery, or promise of marriage to another person (6.1 percent). Indians and Spaniards, in contrast to mestizos and blacks, resorted more frequently to dispensations, albeit—as we will see—for quite different reasons and under different circumstances.[43]

Between 1868 and 1910, 307 secret marriages were recorded. Of these,

---

41. Ideally, I would have wanted to find similar information for the end of the nineteenth century, but the archives where my research was carried out yielded nothing comparable.

42. The total number of marriages (889 and 445, respectively) is taken from Tables 1.8 and 1.9. The dispensations granted between 1807 and 1809 averaged 116 annually.

43. Although in about 18 percent of the cases race is indicated, there is no convincing way of relating race (and/or class) to the types of dispensations issued. In those few cases in which race is identified, most refer to Spaniards and Indians. Only five cases involving mestizos are recorded, and only three involving blacks. For this reason, I had to rely more on qualitative than on quantitative evidence on the racial issue.

76 (24.8 percent) had no impediment recorded. Another 132 declared that impediments had been discussed verbally with the priest, but no written record was considered necessary. This leaves only 99 marriages (32.2 percent) for which some kind of impediment was identified. This may indicate that the church handled impediments with greater leniency at the end of the century. The impediments mentioned include consanguinity (13 cases, or 13.1 percent), affinity (3 or 3.0 percent), or social considerations (47, or 47.5 percent), which ranged from displeasing the family because one of the spouses was Protestant, to the fact that the couple had been living together, had had children, and were generally believed to be already married. In quite a few cases (24, or 24.2 percent), the lack of time excused the reading of banns. For whatever reason, none of these couples or their relatives wanted banns to be published.

In the course of time, it seems that more dispensations were sought in order to safeguard and validate a marriage rather than to compensate for problems of consanguinity or affinity.[44] This may reflect the changed administrative boundaries of the archbishopric and the altered demographic composition of Lima, which resulted from higher immigration rates from Europe and the United States and from Peru's rural provinces. Given the paucity of cases, we cannot draw a statistical model of class-related behavior, and we cannot determine the degree to which the elite intermarried in the nineteenth century. The reasons for many secret marriages *remained* secret, making it difficult to know why and how people shielded themselves from social view. Secrets were revealed only occasionally because of changed social circumstances. Thus, there are some specific cases in which the silence behind the secret is recognizable. Selected petitions for dispensations uncover some of the trends.

Doña Jacoba del Real had been married for over seventeen years when, in 1840, she finally disclosed the circumstances that had led to her marriage to her uncle, Don José Manuel Salas. A dispensation for consanguinity had been negotiated by those interested in bringing about this marriage. She had neither participated in these negotiations nor was she asked if she was willing to marry her uncle. In fact, she had resisted the marriage because she

---

44. A similar argument is made for medieval England. Here, the great majority of matrimonial cases presented at court were geared toward validating a marriage rather than seeking divorce. When the marriage proceedings were more carefully defined around the fifteenth century, the number of matrimonial cases diminished considerably (Helmholz 1978, 27, 30, 72, 167).

thought that her kinship tie to Don José was an insurmountable hurdle.[45] In his dispensation request, Don José had alleged "severe causes," without specifying them. Probably he whispered them into a priest's ear. Following the granting of the dispensation, he had to confess twice, take communion, fast, and provide alms on six Fridays.

Doña Jacoba claimed that the dispensation injured her reputation, especially because no marriage banns had been published. In contrast to the seventeenth-century perception that reading of the banns indicated questionable honor (Rípodas Ardanaz 1977, 80), around 1840 Doña Jacoba used the absence of banns to prove that her honor had been damaged. She explained that her lips had been sealed because of a premarital pregnancy. Doña Jacoba did not wish to ruin the life of her daughter. The penalties imposed on Don José before the dispensation was granted were quite harsh by prevailing standards, and show that in addition to the consanguinity impediment, he had had sexual intercourse with his niece before marriage. Now, however, their daughter had died, so after seventeen years, Doña Jacoba went to court. She expressed general criticism of the dispensation system when she found that hers was not a unique case, but that "many times ecclesiastical prelates have resorted to dispensations simply considering the difficulties some women face finding a spouse of their same class and circumstances, and this probably was the reason put forward [in this case] to exempt the impediment of kinship."

Critics of the system blamed the church for causing unhappiness and for allowing socioeconomic considerations to influence its decisions regarding a dispensation, sometimes even to the point of circumventing the formal requirement of consent. In the long run, dispensations (or the lack of them) could be used to annul a marriage even if (as in Doña Jacoba's case) improper moral behavior had to be disclosed. A dispensation could be obtained, and, if nothing dramatic happened, a family (particularly an elite family) could marry off its children, preserve its good social image, reproduce itself, and count on the church's alliance. But there were no guarantees that social circumstances would remain the same, and when

45. She wrote: "En febrero del año pasado de 1823, contraje matrimonio con el Sr. D. José Manuel Salas mi tio carnal, de mérito de la dispensa del impedimento legal, obtenida en esta curia eclesiástica por las personas interesadas en que se verificase dicho enlase. En la consecusión de esta dispensa no tuve yo la menor parte; por que nunca presté mi consentimiento para que se efectuase este matrimonio al que siempre me opuse con la más firme resistencia. Los estrechos vínculos de parentesco que me unen al Sr. Salas fueron en mi concepto un obstáculo insuperable."

they changed, the church could side with an unhappy wife and thus limit patriarchal control.[46] The rules that enabled certain people to manipulate marriages to their own ends could, under the right circumstance, also be used to benefit unhappy spouses. Such decisions were an open door to reconsider the once-and-forever character of marriage. Dispensations cemented the church's stronghold over people's marriage choices, but often they also provided reasons for an annulment.

Dispensations in Lima's Provinces and Among Popular Classes

In spite of high immigration rates, couples tended to follow patterns of racial and even geographical endogamy. Men and women from Lima's rural provinces, other South American countries, and Europe married spouses from their same town of origin or were already married by the time they settled in Lima. Thus, physical immobility was not a reason for the existing marriage endogamy among white elites and among other social groups. Other taboos existed. Peru's multiethnic society with its strong racial prejudices created its own endogamous boundaries. Peoples' perceptions of differences set intrinsic limits to marriage choices.[47]

From early in the colonial period, marriages across race were discouraged. To a great degree, *mestizaje* resulted from extramarital relationships. And when people tend to choose spouses from within their own ethnic group, the number of potentially available partners diminishes. For racial, class, and psychological reasons, the number of men and women is not equivalent to the number of available spouses. For smaller racial groups— such as whites in the provincial towns and Indians in Lima—marriage choice was thus much more restricted than for other ethnic groups, and this helps explain the higher incidence of dispensations for white and Indian populations.

In the dispensation records mentioned above, we saw that 59.4 percent of the petitions between 1807 and 1809 came from people living in Lima.

---

46. A similar thought on racial intermarriage is provided by Kuznesof (1991, 378–79): "El derecho canónico estaba marcadamente en favor de la libertad de matrimonio entre fieles, y no establecía nada en contra de las uniones interraciales. Sin embargo, la política real hacia el matrimonio interracial fue un tanto ambigua." See also Seed (1988) for an assessment of this issue for colonial Mexico.

47. Similar racial endogamy in Mexico has been documented: "Aunque muchos estudiosos han informado de descubrimientos similares, varios de ellos subrayan la constante importancia del matrimonio dentro del propio grupo racial. A finales del siglo 18, pese a los niveles de miscegenación y a unas pautas residenciales sumamente variadas, es poderoso el testimonio de que la *calidad* seguía siendo una gran fuerza en la sociedad mexicana" (Kuznesof 1991, 387).

By midcentury some priests and members of provincial elites noted that dispensation petitions came primarily from the interior, the smaller provincial capitals in Lima's archbishopric. It seems that the percentage coming from the interior grew for the reason already mentioned, namely, the restrictions on marriage choice resulting from class and race considerations.

In 1851 Hipólito Soto, a merchant from Nazca who wished to marry his second-degree cousin, commented in a letter to the *provisor*: "If one sits back and thinks, one cannot but see that in the towns of the interior of Peru, such as Nazca, the wealthy people are commonly kin-related, and one has to admit that in this case dispensations have to be more frequent and necessary. This is so in contrast to the big cities, like Lima, in which many *gente decente* [people of high social standing and good reputation] make dispensations less necessary, given that consanguinity and affinity have a wider range, and fewer people are blood-related."[48]

Lima was clearly perceived as a place where the *gente decente* had a better chance to marry without needing a dispensation, whereas in a provincial setting it was difficult to find socially adequate spouses outside one's own close kinship group. More restricted marriage choices were especially important in the provinces to maintain political and economic control based on family networks. For the white population in Lima, and in spite of ethnic endogamy and class boundaries, the possibilities of finding spouses outside one's extended family were relatively higher. Still, kinship dispensations were necessary. The availability of dispensations for a price made it easy for elites in both Lima and the provinces to consolidate their interests through intermarriage.

Although most dispensations had to be purchased, many were simply handed out, allowing the church to confirm the moral principle lying behind the request. Among the poorer segments of society, particularly Indians, dispensations represented yet another means to spread Catholicism. Thus for some people (above all whites), dispensations were social-survival and accumulation strategies, while for others (those defined as "legal minors" and culturally different), they indicated a complicated relationship to the church itself.

Canon law transferred responsibility for dispensations to the local priests and did not prescribe consultations with the bishops or archbishops. Because parish priests knew the local circumstances best, they were to decide.[49]

---

48. BN, D 10326.
49. According to García Calderón Sr. (1879, 775) this happened even earlier: "Por la bula de San Pio V, expedida en 4 de Agosto de 1571 se concede á todos los prelados diocesanos de

Nevertheless, priests could seek advice from high ecclesiastical authorities when they had doubts about granting a dispensation. High ecclesiastical authorities feared revelation of the leniency with which they themselves handled dispensations. In almost every response to a consultation coming from towns and villages, these authorities added a paragraph asking the local priest to be cautious and silent about the approval of his request. The church was willing to dispense, but it was also committed to preserving discipline and preventing moral decay. When a priest wrote a letter to his superiors, he did not even mention the names of the individuals involved (they were often referred to as "Ns," meaning "anybody and nobody"). This gave the ecclesiastical authorities the sense that deliberations were of an abstract theological nature, with no relation to real people. However, local knowledge of the transgression affected the final judgment of the case. If the public was unaware of an impediment, things were easy because discussion of the transgression was limited to those involved and the priest. On the other hand, if the impediment was public knowledge, and especially if it had provoked social criticism, the church's options were much more limited.

Some examples may help to illustrate the manifold implications at stake. Writing from a village of Yauricocha to Lima, one priest commented: "I feel urged to resort to your Highness' pastoral zeal to dispense benignly the impediment of first-degree affinity contracted through illicit copulation in the direct line, so that it will become possible to marry N. with whom N. lives in concubinage and whom he now wants for a spouse, after having copulated carnally with the mother. The said impediment is not of public knowledge. Since he met the daughter he has not again dishonestly treated her mother, and although the mother is still alive, they do not live together. The communication with the daughter, who knows nothing about the impediment, has been of public knowledge."[50]

Lima's ecclesiastical authorities granted the dispensation, because doing otherwise would have brought about "grave and scandalous inconveniences" and "harm to third parties." The final paragraph of this letter added "we discharge our conscience in yours," thus endorsing the moral responsibility

---

Indias la facultad de dispensar, no solo para las órdenes, sino tambien para obtener beneficios eclesiásticos, en casi todas las especies de irregularidad. Los Ordinarios, en uso de estas facultades y de las sólitas, deben conceder las dispensas en los casos que ocurran. Solo se puede dar pase á las dispensas que se eleven á Roma, cuando conste que se han interpuesto ante el respectivo Ordinario y que éste se ha negado á concederla por algun motivo."

50. AA, Comunicaciones Oficiales de Curas, L 1 (1765–1818), Consultation from the priest of Yauricocha to Lima's Archbishop, 24 March 1807.

of the decision to the priest. Nevertheless, canon law had been transgressed, and some kind of punishment had to be handed out: "Although we grant the dispensation, the person who created the impediment will confess and take communion this year three times on days of his devotion, and he will also fast on three days that are convenient to him [!]."[51]

For Indians, recommendations were especially lenient. Pope Gregory XIII had long before suggested that Indians be defined as legal minors deserving protection. In the nineteenth century, the church was still trying to impose its dispensation rules on the Indian population. "An Indian"— wrote the priest from Iguasi—"wants to marry an Indian. Both belong to my parish. Having read the banns, it was revealed that they have an impediment in the second-degree for illicit intercourse. She has had sexual relations with a first-degree cousin of the man she now intends to marry. No children were born. As you know, Pope Gregory XIII gave the Bishops in the Indies the ability to issue dispensations for Indians no matter their kinship relationship, if and when the divine law is not offended."[52] And the priest added: "For me it is very difficult to halt their promiscuous ways; it is also not easy to tell them to leave town."[53]

Despite four hundred years of indoctrination, differences in kinship terminologies made it difficult for priests and Indians to establish impediment and dispensation regulations. The Indians' communal solidarity also worked against priests' efforts to separate those who lived "in the offense of God." Traditional land-inheritance patterns even prescribed "endogamy," and the whole Indian community would have protested if a priest separated a couple that according to him was living in sin. From the priests' point of view, poverty and ignorance were the core explanation of this behavior; their parishioners were simply "poor Indians who lived with each other in dishonesty."[54]

Priests were prominent figures in Indian parishes. In some cases, watchfulness was especially "paternal," as when they themselves helped to reproduce the *mestizo* population. In the eyes of Indians, such behavior led to mistrust and the perception of moral contradictions in the declared Catholic rules.

Dispensation consultations sent to Lima took a long time, and until a decision was forthcoming, priests tried to ensure that no more offenses

---

51. AA, Comunicaciones Oficiales de Curas, L 1 (1765–1818).
52. AA, Comunicaciones Oficiales de Curas, Inquiry from the priest of the Iguasi parish to Manuel Arias, secretary in Lima's Archbishophric, 12 August 1809.
53. AA, Comunicaciones Oficiales de Curas, L 1 (1765–1818).
54. AA, Comunicaciones Oficiales de Curas, L 1 (1765–1818). Lima, 30 April 1816.

occurred by at least temporarily impeding contact between the prospective spouses. Consequences of a priest's meticulous inquiries could be unexpected. In 1812 Nazca's priest separated an already married couple because he found out that they had had a double impediment when they married—one of affinity for illegal sexual intercourse in the third degree and the other of consanguinity in the fourth degree—and no dispensation had been granted. After several months of separation, the couple agreed that they would rather remain separated than return to marital life. But to their great distress, the marriage was validated through the corresponding postnuptial dispensations.[55] In the eyes of the church, marriages had to be rescued by any means; and dispensations were one way of doing so, even when, as in this case, couples preferred an annulment. Marriage was more important than individual happiness.

In Lima, couples who recognized an impediment, including blacks and Indians, actively sought a dispensation. In the provinces, such requests were mediated by the local priest, who scrutinized people before marrying them. It is highly probable that the further removed from a priest's surveillance an area was, the fewer the dispensations issued for peasants and Indians, many of whom were unaware of the impediment rules. Thus, in the provinces, among the lower classes, dispensations were much more an issue of social and religious control. In Lima and among provincial elites, impediments had been interiorized and were part of a whole structure of morality refereed by the church and social conveniences. Thus, dispensations had quite distinct implications for each class and were shaped by where people lived.

Morality and Dispensations in People's Life

Melodramatic instances reveal that dispensations were necessary, useful, and part of people's lives. In 1857 Don Manuel Corballido, a repentant soul and a member of the elite in the provincial town of Casma, wrote to the dean and head vicar of the archdiocese to justify his desire to marry his first cousin and thus save her honor. Although it was the kinship relationship that had to receive dispensation, the core arguments of Don Manuel's allegations focused on premarital sex and pregnancy:

55. AA, Comunicaciones Oficiales de Curas, L 1 (1765–1818). Lima, 3 August 1812.

By one of those accidents of the human species, I am today in the imperative situation of having to repair the honor of Señorita Doña Magdalena Corballido, my first degree cousin who is pregnant and whose child deserves to see the light of day under happier auspices than those that preceded its conception. Señorita Corballido belongs to a distinguished family in Huaraz and deserves for her education and good habits a place in society she would be deprived of, if church and religion do not take her under their protection, thus putting a veil on her disgrace which should only be known in the domestic sphere and in her conscience. It is on behalf of the honor of this family, my own, and the interests of the ill-fated creature . . . this woman carries in her womb, that my marriage should proceed immediately, unless a young lady's moral and honor be harmed instead of being protected by the church.[56]

Don Manuel ardently beseeched the church to help him save the family's honor as well as that of his cousin and the child she carried. By allowing him to marry her, the church would restore their honor and social standing. It was in the interest of both church and family to solve such situations in the most expedient and silent way. Making this issue one of social salvation reinforced the need for a quick resolution because the church recognized that a bad example to lower classes had to be wiped out. Moral control depended on the church's willingness and expediency. Social considerations are at the forefront of Don Manuel's petition, whereas the moral issue is presented in terms of an obvious and thus understandable human weakness.

In those cases in which "social disaster" could be prevented, the church was quick to give dispensations; but where moral transgressions had persisted over long periods of time and were publicly known, the church was much more reluctant, even in cases where a refusal would subject those involved to severe social discrimination. In 1871 José de la Rosa Cueto was denied a dispensation to marry a second-degree niece of his dead wife. José was fifty years old and his wife's niece was thirty. Since his wife had died, José and the niece had had three children together. Eight children survived from his first marriage. José now wanted to legitimize his relationship, in order "not to be a bad example for my large family without abandoning a woman whom nobody will pick up."[57] By not allowing this marriage, the

---

56. Case 764, AA, Particulares, L 2 (1840–1922).
57. AA, Particulares, L 2 (1840–1922), 13 February 1871.

church condemned three children to illegitimacy and made it difficult for the couple to become accepted socially. At the same time, the eight children from the first marriage were left with the stigma of having bastard brothers and sisters and a father whose moral conduct was blameworthy (and this is without mentioning that the children found themselves without a mother's care). From the point of view of everyone—except the church—this was a cruel decision. It is understandable only when we recall that the couple had been living together for many years and that everybody knew they were not lawfully married. Three children were more than enough proof of their willful flouting of church doctrine. From the church's perspective, granting a dispensation—even to the humblest people—would be an endorsement of concubinage. Concubinage or "sinful" extramarital sexual relationships, and their resulting illegitimacy rates, had changed little in the course of the nineteenth century. To the contrary, they were very widespread and on the rise until at least the 1860s, despite the fight against them mounted by the church (Table 1.5).

In spite of the vibrant moral rhetoric that accompanied dispensation petitions, many people found it possible to live "in sin" for long periods of time. From early in the colonial period, *barraganía* was an accepted form of marriage with the advantage or disadvantage (depending on who was asked) of avoiding the once-and-forever clause in Catholic vows. *Barraganía* was acknowledged in the Siete Partidas, where it was even stipulated that a man could not have two *barraganas* simultaneously, thus complying with the rule of monogamy. According to Ripodas Ardanaz (1977, 12–13), the recognition of *barraganía* was an admission of the existence of "irregular" domestic situations that needed to be regulated. If, in spite of such well-entrenched forms of behavior, people resorted to dispensations, it was usually to satisfy a specific social need or alleviate unbearable personal remorse. Many people could do without legal or ecclesiastical recognition of their living arrangements.

As mentioned earlier, the *castas* and Indians of Lima were imbued with Catholic moral ideals. The church stringently imposed its doctrine on them and on the elite but was more lenient with people living in Lima's rural provinces. Living in the city brought individuals from different ethnic backgrounds nearer to the priests' observant eyes. However, even within the city, Indians and *castas* were socially less visible, so unlike the elite, they were less likely to seek official sanction for their unions.

Only when Agustín Rivilla, a free mulatto and skilled potter, wanted to get married in 1803 did he admit to having had sexual relations with Hipólita Peres, a *quarterona*. They had been living together for two years, and when

Hipólita insisted on getting married, Agustín was forced to search secretly for a dispensation: "In all this time I would have fulfilled my promise to marry her were it not that, as a result of my frailty and because I often went to her house, I had acquired the impediment of affinity with her mother. The shame to declare my crime and my ignorance have made me delay this petition until today, when I feel persecuted by the afflictions of my conscience." In this case the church granted the dispensation, while imposing prayers, confessions, and penitence.[58]

In a similar case in 1854, Maria Bruque found out, after fifteen years of marriage, that her husband had had sexual relations with her mother and that this was known to everyone but herself. The marriage was annulled because no dispensation had been requested at the time of the wedding and because the couple had married in a different parish from that in which María had been born. All three—the daughter, the mother, and the son-in-law—claimed ignorance due to their low social status.[59] María's and the potter's arguments sound quite different from the ones recorded by the elite classes. It is noteworthy that Agustín is aware of a "crime," but at the same time claimed ignorance. Lower-class people knew that white elites perceived them to be ignorant. In Agustín's case, the recognition of some sort of crime coupled with his claim of ignorance led to a positive response.

There were universal rules for dispensations, but the arguments brought forth in hopes of obtaining them reveal manifold social circumstances. The church was willing to bend its rules accordingly and to adapt them to the requirements of geography, race, ethnicity, and the socioeconomic status of its petitioners. Flexibility was made possible by assessments of individual cases, thus creating "permanent exceptions" to the rules. The church's solutions of individual cases varied according to who the petitioner was, quite frequently following generally held prejudices. Indians, by definition uncivilized, had their own customs and behaved like children, and thus their misdemeanors enjoyed a general pardon from the outset. By the same logic, Indians had to be closely watched. Priests knew that many couples among *castas,* lower-class mestizos, and even whites had "marital arrangements" that did not match the church's ideal of matrimony. *Castas,* in particular, were considered ignorant (just as were the Indians), and that perception became a device in its own right when they wanted to obtain a dispensation. In other words, the church had different images of the classes of people living in the archbishopric, but people who knew how they were perceived by the

58. AA, Esponsales, 1803.
59. Case 744, AA, LM, L 10 (1850–69), 1854, Bruque vs. Salazar.

church and society at large used these images to obtain what they wanted. The lower classes played the game. While they occasionally complied with the rules, they also claimed exceptional status following their own logic and requirements, even when their behavior was viewed negatively by the church and some segments of urban society. There were class-imposed limitations to the church's efforts to morally control intimate life. Guilt and moral standards had differentiated effects on people's lives.

Dispensations and the moral concerns behind them represented one of the many fields of negotiation with the church. In this sense, the church validated social status by certifying "correct" moral behavior. Moral issues—as enacted through dispensations—were the church's area of strength, perhaps more than the futile attempts to combat prostitution and homosexuality; but it seems that in the course of the nineteenth century the importance of moral considerations decreased, and the focus shifted toward social considerations. Dispensation arguments based on problems of individual conscience evolved into those made for the sake of social cleansing. The church played a crucial, albeit inadvertent, role in the shift. In spite of the church's fear of divulging the leniency with which it handled dispensations, people from all social strata knew of it. The general moral relaxation that the church feared materialized; and this may help explain why, in addition to the contraction of the archbishopric's boundaries, the number of dispensations decreased, while illegitimacy rates increased.

If people wanted the church's approval of their relationships, they had to be increasingly watchful, leave fewer traces behind, and retreat into the secrecy of their own four walls. Anything could happen, but nobody should know. Thus, morality became more a social convention, rather than a reflection of the improvement (according to ecclesiastical standards) of Lima's morality. In the course of the century, morality bore less resemblance to social reality than it had earlier in the century. Proper moral behavior became a prerogative for those who could afford privacy. Those who could not were caught and criticized, thus helping to perpetuate race and class prejudice. For some, a dispensation meant pardon for human weakness; for others it meant an imposition of the will of others and a slick means of segregation. Thus, in a much more sophisticated way than physical separation (which was visible in the distribution of race and wealth in Lima's *cuarteles* and *barrios*), upholding "right" morality—expressed in how and when different kinds of people petitioned dispensations—was a way of accentuating and reproducing social boundaries.

4

The Canonic Interstices

Dissent, Consent, and Incompatibility

In regard to marriage, two kinds of consent existed legally. The first, given by the male head of household (or if deceased, by the female head of household), allowed underage children to marry.[1] Parents opposed to the marriage could actively withhold their consent or go as far as to write a claim of dissent, justifying their opposition. Although a child could contravene parental wishes, he or she ran the risk of losing an inheritance.[2] A second kind of consent was given by the future spouses, especially brides, when opening a matrimonial file (*pliego matrimonial*). Aware of the many

---

1. According to the Pragmática de Matrimonios of 1776, men under 25 and women under 23 years of age could not marry without their father's consent. If the father was dead, the mother had to give her consent, and a mother's consent was required for men under 24 and women under 22 years of age. If both parents were dead, men under 23 and women under 21 needed their maternal and paternal grandparents consent. If no tutors or grandparents were available, the local judge (*juez de domicilio*) had to grant consent for men under 22 and women under 20 (BN, D 10901, 1803, 2 ff., Testimonio de una circular referente a matrimonio de menores de edad. Aranjues, 10 April 1803). According to Arrom (1985b, 148), "In the late colonial period the Crown increasingly restricted the freedom of marriage sanctioned by the Catholic Church. Members of the militia, nobility and government bureaucracy needed official permission to marry after 1728; minors needed parental consent after 1776; those wishing to contract interracial marriage needed a dispensation from civic authorities after 1805."

2. Laws referring to dissent and consent issues are in Civil Code 1852, art. 146–55, and are defined as *impedimentos impedientes* (García Calderón 1879, 1096).

impositions on women, the church required that within each matrimonial file the bride certify that she had not been forced or coerced. This requirement was strictly kept. Although some women were still forced into marriages, the requirement of written consent restricted paternal authority and widened women's options to express their will. Consent from parents and from the woman was a normal part of any marriage. But conflicts could ensue, and situations involving conflict disclose the limits of the norm and how social arrangements and customs superseded existing rules.

As do dispensations, issues of consent and dissent illustrate the extent of the church's entanglement in people's lives. In addition, a discussion of consent and dissent introduces a new element: an individual's right to decide. Issues of consent and dissent challenged the limits of patriarchal control. Premarital practices, to which consent and dissent belong, are an ideal analytical space from which to observe the many layers of individual and collective negotiations over intimacy, even in those cases in which marriage never took place. Although many people never married,[3] issues related to consent and dissent were a part of men's and women's daily concerns. Consent and dissent determined whether or not a marriage took place, unless rape or abduction was involved.[4]

Free consent to marry had been a long-standing ideal upheld by the church, an ideal that undercut the power of patriarchs as it gave marrying couples a means to assert their own marriage choices. Thus, consent meant two different things, depending on which generation invoked it: in the hands of the younger generation, escaping, avoiding, or challenging parental consent meant a questioning of patriarchal power and, eventually, the assertion of romantic and individual marriage decisions; in the hands of the parental generation, it meant the exercise of patriarchal prerogatives and, eventually, a recourse to subdue individual interests to family and wider class interests. Although the church never denied the benefits of parental consent, it also defended individuals' freedom to choose whom to marry.

According to some authors (Arrom 1985b, 93; Gutiérrez 1991), at the end of the colonial period in Mexico, patriarchal domains inherited from Roman law and colonial legislation had weakened and were gradually replaced by laws safeguarding women's rights. According to others (Seed 1988), throughout the colonial period civil society had moved to strengthen

---

3. McCaa (1983, 44) has calculated this percentage to be between 30 and 50 percent. Following our assertions concerning illegitimacy, high percentages of nonmarriage do not mean that nonmarried couples refrained from sexual relations and from having children. The social and moral consequences for women are discussed in Chapter 6.

4. For a discussion of rape and abduction, see Chapter 6.

parental consent, and with it, patriarchal control. In Peru no similar debate exists as yet. My own impression concerning the prevalence of either patriarchal control or individual free will is that in Peru (at least in Lima) patriarchal domains were continuously challenged in the course of the nineteenth century, especially by women resorting to the courts. At the same time, the church and the state reinforced patriarchal domains for the sake of social order. I will not attempt to show a definite trend in social norms, but rather to illustrate the visible tensions between women's arguments in court and the restricting forces of patriarchal rules. My story is a story of how patriarchal domains were disputed, not dismantled. Through these disputes, liberal notions concerning social relations in general, and women's rights in particular, gradually spread and took hold.

Although toward the end of the nineteenth century there was an increasing questioning of husbands' overarching powers, in Lima men still held most rights, and wives—considered to be "artists" and emotional creatures—were doomed to follow and obey their husbands.[5] However, in the course of the nineteenth century, paternal (or maternal) interference on marriage-related issues—including dissent—were increasingly ignored. At the other end of the spectrum, wives started using the free-consent arguments to underline their right to express their will, or at least to show how much their will, demands, and sufferings were ignored. Individual stories told by women seeking an annulment showcase the use of the lack-of-consent argument to thwart assumptions of parental authority and gender inequality. A look at the arguments raised concerning, first, sexual incompatibility, and later, character incompatibility, and the transition between both forms of incompatibility showcase women's reinterpretation of church regulations. As a result, wives often obtained annulments, which in turn showed women and everyone watching them that marriage was not as insoluble and sacred as assumed.

Dissenting Parents

As a rule, the church stood for equality of the generations in the eyes of God and stressed the importance of individual freedom to marry. In contrast, the

---

5. "Si el hombre á causa de su facultad é inteligencia más extensa, es más sabio, la mujer por su sentimiento es esencialmente artista." Or, more succinctly: "La mujer casada es una persona que depende de su marido; y como tal, el marido debe proteger á la mujer, y la mujer obedecer al marido" (García Calderón 1879, 1318 and 1319).

state (specifically in the 1776 Pragmática) stressed the requirement of paternal (father, mother, or guardian) consent for underage children. Although this requirement was addressed to whites and "distinguished Indians," all social groups complied with it. The Pragmática also allowed paternal dissent when the marriage threatened to damage the family's honor or there was some menace to the state's integrity (Rípodas Ardanaz 1977; Martínez Alier 1974, 11; Porro 1980, 361–92). Parental interference in marriage decisions was meant to discourage marriages among persons of unequal race or economic rank—in other words, those perceived to be ill-suited socially. Although both church and state were interested in safeguarding marriage and the family, the spheres of intervention were distinct, as were the reasons for which such intervention occurred. In contrast to civil regulations safeguarding social hierarchies by imposing parental will, the only impediments the church officially accepted were affinity and consanguinity up to the fourth degree, ritual kinship and sexual intercourse in the stipulated degrees of kinship, religious vows or chronic diseases, and coersion into marriage (see Chapter 3).

Beyond its selective support of parental authority, the church and the state, as well as society at large, shared the notion that women in general (not only underage girls) and the family had to be protected and controlled in order to defend their social image and the family's honor. Protection and control, however, should occur within acceptable confines and honor a child's wishes. Family and society were ideally governed by a natural law meant to benefit all. As expressed by one of Lima's lawyers around 1820:

> It is absurd to think that when God established paternal authority He would only have wished to benefit children, and not their parents and society at large. Where would we find a man willing to fulfill his parental duties if he could not expect to be respected, obeyed, and served by his children? Society is also interested in cementing this relationship in order to guarantee the security of its members. From there it follows that natural law does not impose on all of us anything that would not be compatible with our own well-understood interests.[6]

This interpretation of divine will, with all its implications for social organization, was translated into an ongoing fixation on matrimony and family

6. Ibid.

expressed by legislation, counseling, and even imprisonment. The church and the state recognized, however, that natural law had to be adjusted and reinterpreted to fit practical circumstances. In the same lawyers' words, there were limits imposed on parental authority: "The power of a father has, it is true, its limits and they are fixed in relation to what are the interests of the father, the son, and society, and depend on the status of the persons, on the nature of government, and the conditions in which society lives."[7]

Loosely translated, this meant that children, fathers, and society had distinct interests, and that the form this reconciliation of interests took depended on who the persons involved were, on state policies, and on customs. Behind such statements lay firm and well-entrenched convictions that had been upheld for centuries. The church stressed the general validity of the God-derived law; the state, its translation to fit social purposes. But both entities recognized the assiduous ties between godly will and social organization. At the same time, the generalities in both interpretations allowed for enormous leeway and much debate as to when, where, and how rules applied to whom.

Daily life—as seen earlier—saw the persistent display of class and race differences. In the context of dissent, class and race were also arguments parents used to oppose their children's marriages. As support, the parents might cite a child's "lack of experience" (that is, children's inability to recognize social differences). Colonial notions about purity of blood and illegitimacy continued to play an important role in the minds of Lima's parents throughout the nineteenth century.[8] No case was encountered in which "state security" was considered (at least at an explicit level). Dissent involved wider social issues, such as race and class, but it was handled as a "family matter."

Manuela Sánchez's baptism certificate stated that she was the daughter of an unknown father. When she wanted to marry Manuel Salinas, a *pardo* and musician in the Dragoons Squadron in Lima, a man named José Jimenes appeared claiming to be her natural father. He opposed her marriage to Manuel, using the Pragmática of 1776 as precedent. He claimed that he and his present wife were of Spanish origin (meaning that they had "clean

---

7. Ibid.
8. In his in-depth analysis of the parish of San Sebastián in Lima in the seventeenth century, Mazet (1976, 79) noticed that: "Il est remarquable que les marriages entre gens d'une meme ethnie de base (Blancs, Noirs, ou Indien) forment 86.48 % des 3,721 cas étudies. Malgré les efforts de l'Eglise, le concubinage était bien la forme normale des relations interethniques."

blood").[9] Manuela's lawyer refuted her father's pretenses by arguing that the Pragmática did not grant natural parents the right of dissent because natural fathers did not have a thorough knowledge of the situation nor had they taken part in a child's upbringing, and thus they could not know what was best for the child. Still, lawyer and father went on arguing for several months. Paper after paper was added to the file, discussing and trying to prove whether Manuela was whiter or socially better than her mixed-blood suitor.[10] The more intense the debates, the smaller the actual racial difference was likely to have been. If José was truthful about his relationship to Manuela, then he apparently forgot that in the judges' eyes illegitimacy was as great a taint as being dark-skinned. Because José had been absent during Manuela's life, his opposition was dismissed, and in 1813 the curia authorized the marriage between Manuela and Manuel.

It could happen that well-established prejudices did not necessarily determine the outcome of matrimonial disputes.[11] This, of course, does not mean that the church actually encouraged interracial or interclass marriages, only that it flattened minor differences when necessary. By siding with a couple and dismantling parental dissent based on race, the church unwittingly lessened social disparities. Transgressions of the intraracial marriage norm, on the other hand, reveal tendencies in social behavior, such as patterns of racial self-perception and the need to emphasize racial difference.

Another option to circumvent parental dissent was spatial mobility. Lima was a place where people from distant provinces could go to escape parental and ecclesiastical confinement. Letters from parents far away in the provinces petitioned the archbishop in Lima to help them prevent marriages of their children there. The parents knew that in Lima matters were easier for children escaping parental dissent "because its large population always allowed the discovery of somebody [a witness] willing to swear that they knew the spouses and that they had no impediment."[12] But no matter where dissent came from, parental opposition was actually successful in very few

---

9. Case 552, AGN, Cabildo, CCI, L 25, C 421, 1813, Sánchez vs. Jiménez.

10. The original racial reference was "contrallente sambaygo o collote," meant to disparage the man involved.

11. Rípodas Ardanaz (1977, 37) writes: "Cada vez hay . . . un mayor número de jóvenes de ambos sexos que se resisten a seguir los dictados paternos en la elección de estado y que, dentro del estado conyugal, se niegan a aceptar el parecer de sus mayores y, llegado el caso, prefieren arrastrar el sino de lo que, con presentimiento romántico, llaman 'nuestro trágico amor.' "

12. AA, LM, L 11 (1870–1903), Carta del Vicario foráneo y Párroco de la doctrina de Coracora al Provisor y Vicario General de Lima, 23 February 1906.

cases. By running away, by asking the church to intervene, by simply waiting until coming of legal age, or by foregoing an inheritance (something that did not harm the popular classes too much), children could, in the long run, marry whom they wanted.[13]

Nevertheless, throughout the nineteenth century parents continued to interfere when they believed that a marriage would damage the social standing of the family. Children could escape parental dissent; however, beyond the formal, written dissent, parents could use more subtle means to influence their children. Parents who did not agree to the choice of marriage partner could opt, for example, simply not to provide a written consent. Along with this passive demonstration of unwillingness, they could resort to the less tangible pressure of intrafamilial authority. In 1830 Don José Lino de la Barrera y Velarde suspected that "even if my father does not oppose it, surely no one will be able to get his signature showing his consent to my impending marriage."[14] After all, free will was something that could also be exerted by parents.

While parents lost ground in the court, control was being exerted in the domestic sphere in quiet, low-profile acts. Reiterating opposition to a marriage and commenting on "harmful" social differences during family lunches and dinners could weaken the most headstrong of children. This is illustrated in the cases of two upper-class fathers in Lima who dissented their sons' choices of socially "suspicious" women. One case occurred at the beginning of the nineteenth century and the other at the end. These cases also offer an illustration of the subtle changes in moral and social discourse pertaining to dissent.

The first case involved the Marquis de Villafuerte's family.[15] Don Pedro de la Puente y Querejazu, the marquis' son and a pupil at the Convictorio de San Carlos, had been in love for a long time with Doña Isabel Pando, and in 1809 he wanted to marry her. According to his father, it was public knowledge that Isabel had just given birth to a child, whose father was a second lieutenant in the Spanish Royal Navy. The identities of both the mother and father were registered as "unknown," but after a few days, the lieutenant offered to acknowledge the child by means of a royal and ecclesiastical decree.

---

13. Such general assertions can be found, for instance, in Case 813, AA, LM, L 10 (1850–69), 1856, Basañez vs. Villafuerte. According to Rípodas Ardanaz (1977, 42) theater pieces presented in this period underlined romanticism and love as the main reasons to marry.
14. Case s.n., AGN, Corte Superior, CCI, L 96, 1830, de la Torre de la Lama vs. de la Barrera y Velarde.
15. Case s.n., AA, Inmunidad Eclesiástica, L 18 (1777–1820), Pando vs. Fuente.

As a Spanish officer, he needed the king's and the church's permission to do so. The priest, however, asked that the mother's name be revealed. Trying to avoid a scandal, Don Pedro offered to recognize the child as his legitimate son. In the marquis's words, this was "a plan to make him [Don Pedro] put up with a child engendered by another man." In an attempt to prevent Don Pedro's marriage, the marquis and his wife had already moved to disinherit him, according to the Pragmática's provisions. But the marquis thought that this alone would not prevent Don Pedro's marriage, and that disinheriting him would not forestall Don Pedro's primogeniture and access to entailed estates, to many trusteeships and boards, and to the responsibility for memorial services (*aniversarios* and *capellanias*) that were part of the family's social and economic position. Thus, the lieutenant's offspring, whom Don Pedro was now recognizing as his legitimate son, would one day acquire all the titles and the property that should rightfully descend to the marquis's blood heirs.

In a society bound by honor codes and high moral expectations, Don Pedro's decision to legitimize a child who was not his own was very unusual. Perhaps Doña Isabel was the victim of hearsay, and the child had actually been fathered by Don Pedro? We will probably never know the real story. What rings true is that the marquis recognized that even among the rich, disinheritance would not prevent a marriage or enforce dissent, because it was impossible to "disinherit" the family's prestige.

Almost a hundred years later, Don Gregorio Guillén opened a dissent case against his son, Don Manuel Guillén, who wished to marry a widowed woman, Doña Delmira Mariluz. The father alleged that his son was born in Arequipa, not in Lima, and that he was underage. Church regulations stated that couples should be married in the parishes where they had been born, so marrying in Lima was contravening ecclesiastical rules and meant that the couple had something to hide. According to Don Gregorio, ever since her husband had died, Doña Delmira had been well known for her unbridled behavior and bad habits. It was even rumored that she was involved in criminal litigation and was betrothed to another man.[16]

In a completely different case, Don Manuel was accused by the mother of another girl, Manuela Rodríguez, of being engaged to her daughter, who had already borne him a son. Doña Rosa, Manuela's mother, for different

---

16. Case 0239, AA, LM, L 6 (1880–99), 1890, Mariluz vs. Guillén. The case brought against Don Manuel by Manuela Rodriguez was added at a later date to case 0223 to prove Don Manuel's immaturity.

reasons from those of Don Manuel's father, wanted to prevent Don Manuel's marriage to Doña Delmira (or possibly, Doña Rosa's accusation may have been trumped up by Don Gregorio?). In this second case, Don Manuel argued that there had been no engagement or marriage promise. In his response to his father, Don Manuel contended that he had "good moral reasons" for marrying Doña Delmira, and that his father did not know the "circumstances." In the end, he simply asserted his own adulthood: "I think that a man like myself, who has been working for a living for several years, is capable of making judgments and knowing what he is doing. Nor should such a man be considered a minor" (ibid.).

We do not know the outcome of the two cases. But both utilize views about loose women versus honest and pure women, and about parents' rights as a result of this image to interfere in a child's marriage. In contrasting these cases, we find that, at the beginning of the nineteenth century, the family's honor was a central argument for dissent. At the end of the century—when there were no more honorific titles—dissent resulted in a direct confrontation between father and son, in which the son's majority, or lack of it, and compliance with the church's requirements were core issues. Adulthood was by then defined by a person's profession or career and degree of financial independence. It was a new concept and was successfully used to stop paternal interference. By the end of the nineteenth century, a son could challenge parents' opposition with his own adulthood, not necessarily defined by age, but rather by economic independence.

In both cases, parents used the option of a written dissent to urge their sons to relinquish marriage. However, parents also took legal steps and investigated the women involved. Thus, dissent could involve more than just writing a letter to the *provisor;* it could demand months or even years to pursue matters. During this time, parental tenacity stifled family relations, and pressures on children grew.

Although in these two cases parents were alive when their sons married, low life expectancy limited parents' interference because it was likely that parents had passed on by the time their children married.[17] Guardians often took their place in this generational battlefield, but guardians seem to have been less successful in impeding "undesirable" marriages, in part because they were less able to resort to watchful family pressure.

Doña Josefa Torres had lost her parents and grandparents and was in the care of Don Antonio Albares de Villar, her guardian. In 1812, when she was

17. Such an argument is also made by Ferry (1989) for early colonial Caracas.

sixteen, she met a merchant from Galicia, Don Manuel José Domínguez, who "inspired me with the inclination and a decision to become his wife, after I had been assured through my own experiences with him, and from information gathered from other people, of his good disposition and mannerly behavior." Unlike some girls her age, Doña Josefa had not been blindly seduced, but had made efforts to obtain some references about the person whom she wanted to marry. This allowed her to present a strong case when Don Antonio opposed her marriage on the grounds that the merchant from Galicia was not an adequate match for Doña Josefa. In Doña Josefa's eyes, Don Manuel's lack of possessions (class differences) was no impediment. To the contrary, she thought her guardian's dissent was irrational, because "I have enough goods inherited from my grandfather for this young Domínguez to administer with his honesty and knowledge, and they are enough to sustain our marriage and gradually increase our belongings." In her written petitions, Josefa went so far as to state that no one (not the church, not the Juez de Menores) had a right to obstruct an individual's decision because neither the 1776 Pragmática nor the Real Cédula of 1803 conferred such a right on any party.[18] Behind these words, we recognize the hand of a lawyer who, in Doña Josefa's name, was a resolute defender of individual liberty. Witnesses, all of them Spaniards and merchants, were brought in, and Doña Josefa obtained permission to marry after only three months of negotiations.

In her petitions, Doña Josefa stressed the merchant's potential to administer her fortune. The story might have had a different outcome had the merchant Domínguez been a person of uncertain background and without witnesses (in this case, guild support) who were willing to vouch for his rank and status despite of his lack of property. In this case, social relations—among people who perceived themselves as equals—bridged economic distance, and thus gave "individual will" a decisive place and firmer footing in the matrimonial arena. Here again, the church helped to level social strata, which, in this scenario, were erected on economic reputation and standing.

Children, priests, and lawyers devised an array of arguments to contravene parental dissent, sometimes pushing ahead of social convention, sometimes retreating into traditional gender roles. Although some exceptional

---

18. "No es de razón que por los maxistrados inferiores al Principe se aumenten dependencias y trabas a la libertad de los Hombres para casarse, quando los Principes Legisladores no las han puesto en sus Leyes y Constituciones."

cases like Doña Josefa's were argued from the perspective of individual liberty, frequently the reasons used to counterattack parental dissent were embedded in widespread traditional perspectives on women. Women themselves accepted and used such arguments: "Have my father feed me or have him give his consent so that I can marry," María del Carmen told the *provisor* in 1810.[19] Both options were effective and left parents little legal ground on which to oppose marriage.

Overall, dissent cases show two general systematic features: dissent could be expressed in various ways—in writing, by resorting to family pressure, through investigation, or by resorting to public opinion—and dissent was gender-biased. It is interesting to observe that in the course of the century nothing changed in the gender-based arguments that expressed parental dissent or lack of consent. When parents or guardians opposed a marriage of their male heirs, the central argument was usually linked to concerns regarding the woman's moral qualities: widows were an inadequate match, and so were women engaged in criminal litigation or suspected of having affairs with other men. These women had a tainted public record and certainly were not virgins. When parents opposed the marriage of their female heirs, the argument was usually that the prospective husbands were neither rich nor white enough. These arguments reflect gender-specific expectations that went beyond other motivations for registering dissent, and they carried race and class discrimination acted out by her parents on one hand, and a bulk of moral pressure on women acted out by his parents on the other.

In dissent situations the church helped to level out minor class and race differences, often acting against prevalent self-perceptions of racial or class superiority. However, when social differences were obvious to everyone, the church remained ambivalent, often silent. Only in one instance did the church categorically endorse a woman's right to decide against her parents: when a daughter invoked religious calling, that is, when she preferred convent life to marriage. Many girls were sent to a convent or a *beaterio* at a very early age to learn to read and to pray. From the parents' perspective, this was meant to enhance the girl's social image, to allow her to find a "deserving" husband and thus guarantee her material well-being and happiness. A pure woman could be offered in marriage to a better-off man. Thus, to a certain degree, virtue could bestow social mobility. According to the church, the minimum marriageable age was twelve for girls and fourteen

19. AA, Expedientes Matrimoniales, July 1810, Chirinos vs. Mata Sotelo.

for boys. Thus, girls who were only twelve years old were able to challenge their parents' wishes when it came to marriage, and if they decided to remain in a convent, they could count on the church's full support. The church thought that there "was no parental authority that could impede a child's entrance into religion."[20] For some women this alternative offered an escape from an oppressive, mundane world, from parental impositions, and from "marital duties."

Lima's Santa Rosa stood as an example of an extreme case in which parents were disobeyed. The events, which took place in the sixteenth century, have been retold ever since. This saint's life story was (and is) part of popular culture. While still very young, Rosa decided to remain a virgin. When her parents set out to look for a suitable husband—a noble, honest, rich, and virtuous bachelor—she locked herself in her room and cut her hair. Her parents were appalled and beat her. Later, they came to accept their daughter's decision and religious passion.

The knowledge of this saint's opposition to her parents will was sometimes explicitly used as an argument to win the church's ear. Sometimes the pattern was the same, as when parents tried to "rescue" their daughters from a genuine calling to the religious life; and sometimes the pattern was reversed, as when daughters with no sincere religious calling used the saint's story to avoid parents' dissent. An intermediate alternative to escape parental dissent or to avoid a forced marriage was to seek a temporary seclusion in a convent. Parents, however, could also use a temporary seclusion to "help" daughters make up their minds, that is, to agree to *their* choice of a marriage partner.[21] In other words, a temporary seclusion could turn into a permanent seclusion when daughters either discovered their religious vocation while staying in the convent or used the convent to permanently escape parental control. The church helped either way, but it had its own priorities: for the church religious vocation came first, then parental authority.

The church, then, offered escape routes for couples who could prove that parental opposition was irrational and restrictive by generally accepted

20. For a case in 1815 where a young daughter opposed her worried parents, see AA, Beaterio de Santa Rosa, L 3 (1782–1829), Expediente seguido por Don José Zaldívar, padre de Doña Juana de Zaldíbar para sacarla del monasterio. In 1820, when Juana was seventeen years old, she became Sor Juana de Santa Rosa. There was no "Beaterio de Santa Rosa" in Lima. However, it seems significant that "monasterio" is mentioned in the title of this file, because it documents the monasteries' and *beaterios*' overlapping roles. See also Chapter 5.

21. Case 577, AGN, CCI, L 16, C 236 (6ff), Autos seguidos por Paula Silva sobre que su hija Gregoria Lobatón sea recluída en un convento hasta su mayoría de edad para impedirle contraiga matrimonio con persona inadecuada.

standards, when parents opposed a real or alleged religious calling, and when parents—as we will see next—forced very young daughters to marry.

Marriage Arrangements: Breaches of Consent

As a logical outcome of the hierarchical notions of a society based on natural law, parents, guardians, and even priests could talk women into marriage, especially if they were still very young. Unlike Santa Rosa, many children who resisted eventually agreed to marry, but if the marriage did not work out, they could turn their initial opposition or their parents' imposition into an argument to obtain an annulment. Yet many years of marital hardship could lie between the taking of the vows and the annulment.

Dolores Lloyd was the daughter of an Englishman. Her mother had died when she still was a small child, and she had been raised by an aunt. In 1847, when Dolores turned fifteen, her aunt insisted that she marry another Englishman, Jorge Rex. Dolores complied with her aunt's wishes. Soon after the marriage, Dolores complained to the ecclesiastical court that her husband had been beating her. In her desperation, she asked for an annulment. Her argument was that she had been forced into the marriage and that her father had not written a letter of consent for the matrimonial license file. Moreover, several witnesses confirmed her husband's abuse and the girl's misery. Initially, Dolores petitioned for annulment, but she ultimately asked for a temporal separation (a divorce). The suit started in 1847, and by May 1848 the judges had already decreed that Dolores had proven her case. Thus, she was divorced and returned to her father.[22]

Something similar happened to Carolina Agur.[23] Her maternal grandmother and her aunt, who took advantage of her "submissive attitude and lack of experience," had forced Carolina to marry Manuel Gavitano when she was only fifteen years old. In 1860, four years after she had obtained a divorce from Manuel, she reopened her case and petitioned for the annulment of her former marriage. To get her divorce, she had argued that she had not given her consent. Now, for the annulment, she added two new arguments: first, Manuel was her uncle, yet no dispensation had been placed in her marriage file; and second, although both spouses lived in the

---

22. Case 866, AA, CD, L 90 (1843–47), 1847, Lloyd vs. Rex.
23. Case 701, AA, NM, L 66 (1860–63), 1860, Agur vs. Gavitano.

Santa Ana parish, the marriage ceremony had occurred in the parish of San Sebastián, which contravened church stipulations. Each argument was strong enough on its own to warrant an annulment; furthermore, the lack of a dispensation was ruled a sin.

In the case of Carolina and Manuel, the *defensor de matrimonios* (church-appointed lawyer in charge of "rescuing" a marriage) argued that many spouses obtained dispensations that validated their marriages only after the fact. Nevertheless, in 1866 the court granted an annulment based on the omission of formalities, marrying outside one's parish, lack of a dispensation, and—surprisingly—bigamy. This last factor heavily influenced the outcome. When Carolina proved that (unbeknownst to her) Manuel's first wife was still alive when she had married him, even the *defensor de matrimonios* had to accept the ruling in favor of annulment.

According to my sample of matrimonial licenses, the average age at marriage for women of all racial groups in Lima in the first three decades of the nineteenth century was 23.2 years, and it climbed to 24.0 between 1840 and 1890. This may indicate that pressures on women to marry young decreased slightly in the course of the nineteenth century. For men the average age at marriage was around thirty years throughout the century. In the cases of both Carolina and of Dolores, the women were well below the average age when they were forced into marriage, and that was a central reason the church was willing to grant annulments.[24] So even if extreme pressure could force very young women into marriage, they could appeal to the church and obtain either a divorce or annulment after they matured or found someone to counsel them about their alternatives. If a woman was still underage, she would be returned to her parents' care. In a contradictory way, the church intervened temporarily on behalf of these minors against their parents or guardians, then returned these same children to parental authority in the hope that parents had learned their lesson. Thus, the church had—in individual cases—managed to reconcile the principle of free consent and parental authority.

Although the church defended its ideal of free consent, parish priests, supposedly immersed in Catholic doctrine, did not always uphold it conscientiously. Especially in rural parishes, they often contravened the church's position by imposing marriage on couples, perhaps as a response to the

---

24. Another case, in which the girl was only twelve years old, is registered in AA, NM, L 62 (1847), Carpio vs. Escobedo. In this case, Eulalia Carpio's aunt had threatened to throw her out of the house and to beat her if she resisted marriage.

high rate of illegitimacy, which also was a central concern of the church. However, this was not the only reason.

Procreation was supposed to take place within marriage, and thus the church fervently engaged in marrying people, even in disregard of its own rule of free consent. The higher cause was the avoidance of sin. Fighting against illegitimacy and sin required denying long-standing indigenous traditions, in which "marriage"[25] usually occurred only after the birth of one or more children. This practice contradicted the whole notion of virginity and reproduction within Christian marriage. Christian morality could be misused by priests to persecute peasants "in their care." A new couple also meant more income for the church, not only because marriage itself required the payment of fees and the arrangement of celebrations in which considerable money was spent, but also because a new household would be obliged to give shares of its produce to the local priest.[26]

In 1848 twenty-year-old María Méndez and her mother owned an *estancia* (small farm) in the Santa Eulalia valley, located about eighty kilometers from Lima. That year she wrote a letter to the ecclesiastical court in Lima describing what had happened to her. When she had reached her thirteenth birthday—that is, according to canon law one year after she had become "marriageable," the sacristan Fray José Sibante ordered her to an interview. Maria and her mother had to travel for many hours to see the priest. When they arrived and "with no further introduction, he told me that he had a husband for me, telling me also that this man had a lot of money and that it was not wise to lose this opportunity."[27] María rejected this offer, arguing that she did not know the man and that she did not love him at all. The priest insisted that María marry, and he proceeded against her will.[28] It was seven years after the marriage before María got up the courage to write a letter complaining about the priest's arbitrary behavior. Although this may be an extreme case of church interference in personal decisions concerning

---

25. The Quechua word for marriage is *servinacuy*, which has been translated as "marriage on probation" or "trial marriage."

26. In colonial times, peasants producing "Indian" crops were exonerated from *diezmo* payments (that is, 10 percent of their produce), but sometimes they had to pay the *veinteno* (5 percent). These payments had already been legally abolished in the 1812 Cádiz Constitution, and then again—because they still existed—in 1856 and well after this date. A new couple had its own land and animals, and thus became another unit liable for contributions in kind.

27. Case 887, AA, NM, L 63 (1848–49), Méndez vs. Barbieri.

28. Perhaps the priest was María's biological father, which could explain his aberrant behavior. Priests fathering children in rural communities were not uncommon, but there is no clear evidence for this particular case.

marriage, it is significant that it occurred at all and that María was expected to accept the husband selected by the priest.

Men also suffered interference. In 1814 Ignacio Simón, a resident in the town of San Domingo de los Olleros, forty kilometers south of Lima, filed a complaint against the local priest, Dr. Don Gregorio Bedoya, who, as Ignacio wrote to the archbishop, "had made me marry María Peta Blas from this same town, against my will and telling the *alcaldes* to lash me fifty times with a whip." When Ignacio later asked another priest about the validity of the marriage, he learned that it was invalid because Father Bedoya had proceeded against Ignacio's will. This second priest then made Ignacio pay 40 pesos to marry him to another woman. María Peta Blas, who had not wanted to marry Ignacio either, had left town.[29]

There is no sentence registered in the file; however, it may be safely assumed that the tacit separation of the couple after marriage, and the new marriage of Ignacio, led to an annulment of the first marriage based on a no-consent argument. These situations reflect a complete disregard of peoples' right to freely marry. Like parents forcing young girls into marriages, priests were assuming "parental" duties and rights to force people into unwanted unions instead of upholding the church's proclaimed requirement of free consent. Moreover, many priests were infamous for their sexual relations with women in their parishes. A priest could intimidate a woman by playing on her fear of offending God or of antagonizing a locally powerful individual.

Antonia Solís, in a letter written in 1817, stated that many years earlier she had gone from Yauricocha (a mining center) to the nearby town of Tusi to gather some potatoes for her children, whom she had born out of wedlock. When she arrived at Tusi, she met the *teniente de cura* (local priest assistant), Don Mariano Medrano. To her great surprise, this stranger generously offered to help her, even to the extent of giving her shelter in his house. Antonia felt suspicious about this strange behavior and declined the offer. A few hours later, the priest sent one of his servants to Antonia to ask her to come for dinner. She kindly thanked him for this invitation but rejected it. The priest was upset and offered yet another invitation, this time sending out the town's mayor and other local authorities to bring Antonia to him by force. The whole town was watching and wondering why a woman who had just arrived would be treated so badly. Antonia was led to the convent house where the priest was waiting. Drunk and angry, he

---

29. Case 91, AA, NM, L 59 (1810–19), Blas, Gutiérrez vs. Simón.

accused her of being a prostitute. He then threatened to marry her to the first bachelor coming along the road. He ordered the mayor to go out and grab the first available victim. Antonia protested and let the priest know that all that was happening was a violation of her rights. She refused to consent, arguing that no banns and other formalities had been carried out and that she had a family to care for. No tears were sufficient to stop the priest. Struck by fear, the mayor came back after a while with an Indian called Manuel Chagua, who also was a stranger in Tusi. Antonia and Manuel were obliged to hold hands while the priest read out the matrimonial liturgy.

Although Manuel insisted on his conjugal rights, and Antonia several times found herself in precarious situations, the marriage was never consummated. Antonia eventually bought her way out.[30] For years she had never had money or time to present her complaint in Lima, but in 1817 she was ready to fight for an annulment. In the meantime, the priest had died. The *defensor de matrimonios* found Antonia's story hard to believe. But Antonia's defense counsel was convincing: "It doesn't matter that the Defensor de Matrimonios says that the story is incredible; after all, he had to say something in order to fulfill his job. There is nothing unbelievable in this world beyond supernatural events. . . . Did the priest have to go out of his way? Who could prevent him from doing what he did? The priest, respected and feared by his parishioners, was the arbiter of the lives of these two miserable people."

And, he was. Antonia, being an Indian mother with children, probably already had a "husband," but the priest's maneuvers were an attempt to cast off Indian marriage practices and replace them with Christian moral standards. (He called Antonia a "prostitute"). Through his questions, Antonia's defense counsel eloquently signaled how frequent and widespread this kind of attitude was. The connection between Indian marriage and consent also raises the question of cultural tolerance. In other words, upholding free consent implied the tacit recognition of non-Christian marriages and morality. This, in turn, may help explain why so many priests, especially in rural parishes, resorted to violence to impose marriage according to Christian rules.

The priests' power, their firm entrenchment with local authorities, and the threat of scandal rendered many protests futile.[31] Under such direct

30. Case 576, AA, NM, L 59 (1810–19), 38ff, 1817, Solís vs. Chagua.
31. See, for example, the story told by María de la Cruz Yupari from Cerro de Pasco in 1868 in a long letter to the prefect in Huaraz (AA, n.d.).

pressure, many young and inexperienced Marías and Antonias were married to men they did not like or want. Only later in their lives would these women learn that there were some interstices in the church's matrimonial regulations that allowed them to challenge a priest, and that their consent was important to validate marriage.

The bulk of accusations against "misbehaving" priests came from rural areas (probably as a result of the greater leeway priests had because they were further removed from a bishop's or an archbishop's control). However, in Lima priests were also accused of being seducers and professional marriage procurers; they had been known to kidnap nubile girls[32] and were also guilty of "abuses of the confessional." In 1851 Tiburcio León wrote a letter to the archbishop accusing the priest from the San Francisco church, who acted as the confessor to the girls of the Colegio de la Caridad, of abusing his position. The priest had been telling the girls that in order to avoid future temptations from men, he had "to bless the hidden parts of their bodies." When the girls showed the priest their "hidden parts," he made the sign of the cross and told the girls not to mention the incident to anyone.[33] Although one may only guess how many more such blessings occurred in other confessionals, events in rural and urban parishes reveal the meddling of priests in people's private lives, a meddling that for moral, sexual, and cultural reasons countered the very definition of free consent attached to marriage. In their daily interaction with parishioners, priests often did not live up to church rules.[34]

It was the victims who reminded priests of the rules; the initiative lay in their hands. Transgressions of consent were used to morally discredit local

---

32. Case 581, AA, Esponsales 1802/1893/1907 *[sic]*. Toribia Solórzano's father presented a strong complaint and many witnesses against a priest in the Santa Ana parish in Lima. Toribia had been fighting with her father, and the priest offered shelter, clothes, and food. When she returned home after several days, she confessed to her father that she had been raped by the priest. Toribia was thirteen years old. The priest was found guilty, and all his possessions were confiscated to pay for the "damage."

33. Case 864a, AA, Comunicaciones Oficiales de Curas, L 13 (1830–49), 1851.

34. For a discussion of cases held in the AA under "Capítulos" (accusations against priests) see Hunefeldt (1983, 3–31). One particular case, in which a priest was the natural father of three girls and one boy, is found in case 774a, AA, Sección Comunicaciones, L 4 (1840–50), 1847, Carta suelta de Simona Cierra de Alvarez. When the mother of the children died, they were picked up by their priest-father, who—according to Simona, the nominated tutor—mistreated them, made them work like slaves, and did not even allow them to sit at the table to eat with him. The matter reached the court because the children ran away to look for their uncle, who then claimed maintenance payments from the father.

priests and thus challenge local power holders and also—at the end of the line—the consistency of church ordinances. Beyond the loss of economic assets, such inconsistencies eroded the church's power and became a powerful argument for secularization. The church was consistent in confronting dissenting parents or those who failed to take their children's free consent into consideration. Understandably, the church had much less motivation to uphold tenets of individual free will when it involved a perpetuation of cultural differences and illegitimacy. Cultural differences and natural children led to "disorder," and the church's control over these aberrations was widely supported by most of the empowered segments of society.

In more general terms, this also raises the question of what consent was and was not meant to be.

The Dubious Nature of Consent

Because it involves opinions and interpretations, consent is open to reinterpretation and appropriation. In the context of nineteenth-century Peruvian matrimonial issues, consent gradually lost its initial canonic meaning and was reinterpreted in broader social terms. In the course of the century, the moral aspects of consent were enlarged to incorporate interpretations of how race, class, and gender hampered the expressions of free consent.

In the highly illiterate society of the time, a written consent letter was not easy to procure; and even when a priest wrote and filed the letter, that did not necessarily mean that the person signing it understood its meaning. Quite frequently, consent letters were signed by third parties because the couple did not even know how to write their names. If no written consent was included in the marriage file because couples could not read nor write, because the priest forgot, or simply because things were done hastily or those involved thought it unnecessary, the couple, a lawyer, or the priest himself could use the argument of deceit to sue for an annulment. In such circumstances, ecclesiastical judges were forced to interpret actions as expressions of consent. Were, for example, holding hands or writing a love letter expressions of consent? No matter what the "consent signals" were, the church could interpret words or actions as expressing consent when they were not intended to do so and, consequently, force people to remain married against their will; and—vice versa—people could request that a word or action be incorporated into the church's "customarily" recognized expressions and, consequently, continuously enlarge the meaning of consent.

Nineteenth-century Lima was not the first place where the church and its parishioners faced uncertainties about consent. As early as twelfth-century Europe,[35] ecclesiastical authorities knew that the greater the absence of rules or the possibility of implementing them, the wider the leeway for personal will and communal authority (as opposed to institutional authority). Only gradually did the church create the rules to the game, and yet there never seemed to be enough rules to definitely settle "misunderstandings" or "misrepresentations."

The social consequences and the practical implications of interpretation are particularly well illustrated by a case that occurred in Arequipa, one of Peru's largest cities, in southern Peru. Agustina Olazábal was a singer and dancer; occasionally, she also survived by sewing. She lived in the *casatambo* that belonged to the powerful Goyeneche family. In her 1817 appeal to Lima's archbishopric, Agustina remembered the frenzied circumstances surrounding her wedding:

> We both lived in the same *barrio*, and this gentleman [Manuel Fernandes Pasqual] was fond of visiting me frequently. Being aware that such behavior would affect my honor, I told him several times not to come back. People were already talking. . . . Talking of love, not as a gentleman but as a villain, he told me that he intended to marry me. . . . I accepted gladly, but I was also worried about his caresses, to giving myself as his wife, fully convinced that there was no deceit. In

---

35. This meant that: (1) the union of the couple was fundamentally based on the agreement of the parties. With no rules, any practical success depended on personal will to fulfill certain commitments. Thus, rituals and consummation were much less important than individual willingness. (2) Consequently, family and feudal lord (read governmental agent) were essentially subject to the consent of the spouses if marriage was to be accomplished and maintained (which in turn meant a completely different version of "patriarchy"). (3) Couples preferred a public scene, which was not defined by family or seigneurial structures, but by the local community in its parochial and religious functions. As a result, it was society as a whole that validated a marriage, not the state or the church (Sheehan 1978, 7–8). These conclusions are derived from a reading of 1150s canonic and theological traditions (based, in turn, on records in the Decretum Gratiani and the Libri IV Sententiarum of Peter Lombard). Here the center of thought was the couple, whereas family, feudal lord, and children were basically left aside. The later preponderance of the church's decisions regarding matrimonial issues would be based on this separation.

this way, we celebrated our *sponsalia*,[36] and sensing that his parents' dissent would be insurmountable, he schemed so that we could go ahead without their permission. He showed me the route we would take to go to see one of the priests. And, indeed, everything happened as planned. We went to look for the priest, Don Esteban Villegas, and not finding him, we went directly to the Priests' School to look for the Señor Provisor. We were always guided by our objective of getting married. Witnesses, who had been hired by Don Manuel, were with us on this search. As the Señor Provisor was not at the school, we waited for him until after 10 at night. When he finally arrived, we entered the Sala Rectoral, holding our hands and expressing our wishes with the specific words: "Be you my witness how this Señora is my wife and this Señor my husband."[37]

After a few years, Manuel Fernándes abandoned her, and Agustina used the description of her wedding to prove the unconventional circumstances under which it had taken place. Such circumstances—she hoped—would cast doubt on the validity of her marriage and enable her to marry another man, Don Marcelino Carreño.[38] There was no written consent in her file from either her or his parents, no banns had been read, and the witnesses had been paid. Four years later—at a time when the wars of independence were well under way—a decision from the ecclesiastical court was still pending. In the proceedings, Manuel and Agustina made the "mistake" of admitting to having had sexual intercourse. Whatever the other circumstances, consummation—considered a decisive expression of consent and the existence of a marriage relationship—had taken place. This information made it even more difficult for the church to decide whether the wedding ceremony as described by Agustina could be considered a valid marriage or not. Given the circumstances recounted by Agustina, even the *defensor de matrimonios* wondered if a marriage had really occurred.

In 1825, eight years after Agustina filed her request in Lima, it was more or less arbitrarily decided that Agustina and Manuel had lawfully married. This decision was returned to Arequipa for an evaluation by yet another tribunal,

---

36. *Esponsales:* promise of marriage recorded with a notary. Normally *esponsales* implied a firm decision to marry later on, and the notarized registration was, many times, a first agreement on how assets would be distributed and managed. For a more detailed assessment on *esponsales*, see Chapter 6.
37. Case 417, AA, LM, L 8 (1810–19), 1817, Olaxábal vs. Fernández Pasqua, Carreño.
38. One of the guerrilla leaders in the central highlands during the wars of independence.

the Junta de Calificación, meaning that Agustina's file had moved back from Lima's archbishopric to the provincial ecclesiastical court in Arequipa, a court that presumably had a better and more direct understanding of the couple's intentions. In Arequipa, four facts led to the decision that a marriage had occurred. First, Manuel voluntarily sought the *provisor;* second, a priest had been present; third, by holding hands both parties had expressed their wish to marry; and fourth, during these events, the required witnesses had been present. Consent, priest, and witnesses were the triad that validated the marriage. The evidence of consent remained open to interpretation and challenge. Holding hands in the church was interpreted as symbolizing consent, even if no other marriage rituals had been carried out (such as banns or the written parental consent). The central argument of the *defensor de matrimonios* to validate the marriage under these very peculiar circumstances was the expressed will of the spouses, even if no written record of their consent existed. Such a generous understanding and interpretation of the nature of free will in some cases suited the needs and particular interests of individuals (above and beyond meeting the prescribed rituals of the church), but it could be used to force marriage on individuals as well. In this case, Agustina would have preferred less magnanimity on the part of the church in interpreting consent.

Moreover, social expectations cemented the existence of consent. People had been watching how Manuel had visited Agustina regularly. Agustina knew that the only way to justify Manuel's frequent visits was by letting neighbors know that these visits presaged marriage and thus implied her consent. It was the morally proper and expected outcome, even if everybody knew that the couple had to escape parental dissent, which in this case, as in most others, was based on "social inequality." Agustina was "only" a seamstress—and worse yet, a singer and a dancer. Thus, in addition to the ecclesiastical triad of consent, priest, and witnesses, social circumstances also indicated the likelihood of a valid marriage.

Nearly ten years after Agustina's initial request, this case again reached the ecclesiastical court in Lima. This time, Manuel and Agustina were fined equally for the costs of litigation, which meant that both parties were found guilty of violating "the rites and ceremonies" prescribed by the church. They were sent into seclusion, he to the Convento de los Recoletos, and she to the Casa de Educandas. But in the high-court decision nothing definite was said about the legality of the marriage. Thus, only a few months later, the *defensor de matrimonios* reopened the case and insisted that the marriage was valid and that Agustina and Manuel were not free to marry anyone else. By 1826, however, the wars of independence had ended with dramatic consequences. For Agustina and Manuel (and probably also for Marcelino, Agustina's patient suitor), economic problems were added to the uncertainty surrounding their marital status. Before independence, Manuel was in financially sound circumstances, which was the reason why his parents did not want him to marry Agustina. Several witnesses now confirmed that Manuel and his family had lost all their possessions and that he was obliged to work as a tenant on a small farm. His family's opposition had evaporated, but now Manuel was unable to support a family, and Agustina still wanted to marry Marcelino.

Throughout the ten years this case lasted, the spouses fell victim on the battlefield between parental authority and the church's defense of consent. At the same time, the absence of a court decision concerning the validity of the marriage showed that church regulations were open to question and reinterpretation. These regulations only became important when people tried to legitimize an existing marriage or to establish a new one with official backing. An ecclesiastical suit over the failure to fulfill a prescribed marriage ritual was meant to either validate or annul a marriage. Consent could be added when missing or used as a way out of an unhappy relationship.

This contradictory possibility illustrates both the weaknesses and strengths of the church in controlling people's lives. In general, people were deeply imbued with religious feelings and were afraid of sinning. After all, Agustina wanted to make sure she was not offending God, and she went to considerable trouble to find out. For ten years of her life (and one should add that these years were her "reproductive years"), Agustina was trapped while church authorities debated her case. The "sacramental belief" and the prescribed rituals were the church's strongest holds over peoples' lives. The main weakness was its permanent confrontation with social reality: people acted according to their desires, sometimes even in direct contravention of the church's stipulations and parental wishes. Manuel was not able to overcome his parents' dissent and fulfill his marital obligations. Agustina opted for a lover in spite of her neighbors' assumptions and pressures. Consent and dissent only became important when Agustina wanted to make sure her marriage to Manuel was invalid in order to marry Marcelino, a step that would allow her to better meet social expectations. The moral and social burden was on Manuel, Agustina, and Marcelino; but they—in spite of their temporal seclusion—carried on with their lives, and there was not much else the church could do.

In Agustina's case, she was punished and secluded in the Casa de Educandas in Arequipa. The ecclesiastical authorities perceived that as a mature woman she should have known the rules and complied with them. Carolina and Dolores—the two under-age girls forced into marriage by their parents and guardians—returned to their parental homes without punishment because the church understood that, as minors, they clearly had married against their will (or at least understanding) and were in need of protection. Here the parents were to blame for noncompliance with ecclesiastical rules, and one way of halting their interference was to expose their concealment of an impediment. Thus, penalties for transgressions varied according to age, social status, and circumstances. Penalties imposed on transgressors could include an obligation to listen to a certain number of masses and to receive communion, or to volunteer in one of Lima's hospitals.[39] Youth and high social status also combined to produce a more indulgent punishment. Although differences persisted, in the course of the nineteenth century the church softened punishment for everyone. Toward the end of the century, a typical punishment for noncompliance with church rituals was to have offenders fast "on two days convenient" to him or her.

While noncompliance with formalities, and especially consent, was a part of almost every annulment or divorce petition in the records, new arguments were gradually added. The relative importance of consent based on convenience declined as the importance of consent based on love increased. In the ecclesiastical courtrooms, wishes, expectations, and rights were gradually added to the consent argument.

When Matilde Sánchez was only thirteen years old, her mother and elder sister, who were both heads of the school Matilde attended, compelled her to marry a Frenchman, Oscar Rospigliosi. Recalling her suffering, she later wrote: "Still a child and not yet having felt in my heart any urge to love, nor in my nature the need to fulfill love through an intimate relationship with a person of the opposite sex, I was forced into marriage, first with promises and gifts, and later under duress and with violence."[40] To give her complaint a legal tone, she also mentioned that she had not given her consent, that her husband had abandoned her, and that he was not only French but also Jewish. These arguments helped Matilde to obtain an annulment in 1856.

Although consent remained an important feature of divorce or annulment arguments, it was always mentioned in combination with other reasons: noncompliance with church rituals, mistreatment and abuse, adultery, mismanagement of family funds, and, last but not least, cultural differences, such as being French, Chinese, or English, or not being a Catholic. The

39. Case 90, AA, NM, L 58 (1799–1809), 1800, Betancur vs. de Pro y Martínez.
40. Case 990, AA, NM, L 64 (1850–56), Sánchez vs. Rospigliosi.

church's rules, rituals, and principles were used as arguments in order to reach divorce or annulment without relying strictly on issues of consent—or to put it differently, consent became the formal and legal vehicle to widen the scope of accusations against parents and husbands. When used by women to obtain an annulment, consent was packaged with several layers of accusations that had little to do with consent and often—as in the case of family fund mismanagement (Chapters 7, 8, and 9)—were well beyond the realm of church influence. Over time, the relative importance of the consent argument decreased, and this decrease was paralleled by a move from ecclesiastical to civil court as more "material" claims became attached to it.

As in the case of prenuptial rituals and proceedings, which could be misunderstood or misread, the issue of what consent meant for individuals was ambiguous. Equally as important as the form in which "free will" was expressed (holding hands, writing love letters, or signing a statement) is the question of its definition. Even when a woman gave her formal written consent, other factors could be at work—for instance, her fear of social consequences. And it was the interpretation of the influence of such fears that gave the church latitude and subjectivity both to decide a case and to impose punishment. In a similar vein, it also gave women a wider social framework to denounce the pressures to which they were subjected. By the mid-nineteenth century a more liberal and socially oriented interpretation of consent had reached the courtrooms. In a case defending a female client who had filed a written consent in her matrimonial file and was now divorcing her husband, one of Lima's court lawyers reasoned:

> Sometimes it happens that fear restricts the liberty with which consent is given. There is consent, but not one freely given, as is required for marriage. In other situations, consent is just in appearance, just words uttered superficially and without conviction, something completely contrary to the notion of consent. The church does not evaluate what is hidden in the minds of people or the kind of fear they feel, but only addresses that which is explicitly stated and recorded. Based on the intensity of the fear, the church will then proceed to externally separate those who have never been intimately married.[41]

The notion of fear as a limitation to free consent was not new; it had already been made explicit during the Tridentine Concilium in Rome

---

41. Case 266, AA, NM, L 58 (1799–1809), Hurtado de Mendoza vs. Alcozer.

in 1546. From being a philosophical principle useful in explaining the intricacies of human will, it became, in Lima by the nineteenth century, a legal argument to rescue women from bad marriages. "Free consent" gradually (that is, over four hundred years!) was used to express personal anxieties and fears derived from social pressures. A philosophical principle once deduced from the observation of human behavior was brought back to challenge social structures.

There were, indeed, wide gaps between what was "explicitly stated and recorded" and what was "hidden in the minds of people." Behind every claim of fear and intimidation, women in Lima's courts identified a man, often the father or the guardian, sometimes the prospective husband, who had forced them to consent. Doña Simona Torres, for instance, was forced by a suitor to declare that it was her will to marry him, in spite of the fact that she had already opened a matrimonial file with Don Gaspar Jurado. According to Doña Simona, this was the result of the "panic and fear" she felt when this suitor threatened to kill her if she insisted on marrying Don Gaspar.[42] Doña Simona had experienced, and could prove, direct intimidation. Fears were "explicitly stated and recorded." Many more layers of fear surfaced from what was "hidden in people's minds." Such layers of fear, and their translation into consent arguments, were compounded in María Mercedes's afflictions, which she described in a letter to Guayaquil's bishop. In 1817 her letter and her file reached Lima's archbishopric to substantiate her depositions.

The prebendary Don Tomás Borrego, a subdelegate, was the guardian of María Mercedes and her sister. After the girls' parents had died, he had dutifully looked after their well-being. According to María Mercedes, it was her sister who insinuated to Don Tomás that María was ready and willing to marry. Soon afterward, a cousin of Don Tomás, Don Pedro Marcos Borrego, asked María to marry him. She commented: "It was in this situation that I found myself agitated by conflict; on one side because I felt no inclination to this man, and it was the first time I met him, and on the other side because I thought about the immediate kinship relationship of this gentlemen with Señor Borrego, who in turn would have been greatly disappointed had I responded negatively.... In these circumstances, I decided to answer the proposal, without compromising myself, using the words, 'Yes, we will see.' "[43]

42. AA, Expedientes Matrimoniales, 1805, Torres vs. Jurado.
43. Case 45, AA, NM, L 59 (1810–19), 1817, Arteaga vs. Borrego.

María Mercedes found herself in a matrimonial situation from which she could not easily withdraw. She owed obedience, gratitude, and submission to her guardian, which implied an acceptance of his cousin. When María's sister informed Don Tomás about the "good" news, he was pleased and agreed to the marriage. María Mercedes decided to try to explain to him that she was not as fond of her suitor as everyone thought. Out of fear of offending Don Tomás, she tried to soften her explanation by saying she might change her mind. Her story, when she eventually wrote to the bishop, was very different: she stated that her aim was to extricate herself from the engagement because she wanted to marry someone else, a marriage she had been arranging on her own. Events moved faster than she had anticipated. A few hours after her conversation with Don Tomás, he had contacted the vicar, who was willing to grant certificates of dispensation for marriage banns in order to accelerate the wedding. That same day at 6 p.m., the vicar arrived at Don Tomás's house. He noticed María Mercedes's wariness, but attributed it to "female mysteries." Circumstances accelerated still faster.

"And here Your Excellency has the whole picture of my conflict," María wrote in her letter. "If I annoyed [Don Tomás], it would seem that I was letting him down, and I would lose the protection on which my subsistence depended. The respect everybody felt for him at the same time insured my own honor. My repulsion increased and I found myself trapped."

María Mercedes could not rely on other relatives to help her because they were quarreling over inheritance issues. While Don Tomás called the bridegroom, María Mercedes for the last time asked the vicar to delay the marriage. This time the vicar reacted to her request with displeasure. Soon afterward Don Pedro Marcos Borrego arrived, and he and María were married. These events took place in a private house, not in the church.

María Mercedes tells us what happened next: "After the ceremony, I almost went crazy. Desperation made me want to disappear from among the living. That same night I resisted making love with my husband, and on the next day, which was July 23, I was unable to avoid insulting Don Pedro Marcos Borrego publicly. I could not bear having him near me. I could not stand him, and therefore conjugal life was impossible."

In her letter, María emphasized the violent circumstances in which her marriage took place, and she invoked the bishop's mercy: "Your Excellency will discover at first glance, through Your well-known wisdom and foresight, that this marriage did not take place in an environment of free decisions, which is what is required. My consent only came about because of the grave fears and respect of Señor Borrego, which were so tremendous that they were even bigger than the ones I would ever have felt should I have opposed my parents' wishes." Furthermore, she argued that the vicar was not the priest who should have married her, and when María Mercedes complained to him, he had even told her that no procedure whatsoever could reverse the situation. She was not satisfied by this answer, and this was the reason she carried her case to Lima's ecclesiastical courts. Given the combination of arguments used, including the nonconsummation of marriage, María was probably freed from her husband.

María's arguments illustrate the intricacies of consent. She was well aware of her debt to her guardian and the social conventions that restricted her openly opposing Don Tomas's wishes. These were reinforced by the reaction of the vicar, who dismissed her concerns as "womanly" attitudes. The chain of misunderstandings originated in her particular condition as a protected and well-treated white woman, and in her own acceptance of this role. María's honesty in her letter to Lima's archbishop discloses the many assumptions that underpinned "free consent." In raising these arguments, María unraveled the fictitiousness of consent in a social environment in which many sophisticated pressures were exerted on women. Thus, the whole notion of consent was expanded into very personal, subjective, and flexible realms. Although consent had been given, it was not an act of free will, and it would never be an act of free will as long as pressures existed.

Beyond merely being coerced by parental will, María Mercedes's and Doña Simona's cases demonstrate the other ways in which women could be forced into marriage. The boundaries were set by physical violence on one side, and by moral and social considerations on the other. In both cases (as in many others), women resorted to the ecclesiastical court's mediation, and by pulling together all arguments the church might listen to, they rescued their right and the possibility to define consent in their own terms. Each claim was carefully scrutinized; all claims together portray a nonconsent argument that had stretched to include the personal-concrete and the social-general anxieties to which women were exposed.

Finally, a third dubious consent scenario related to death. Generations of theologians had worried about marriages carried out on the deathbed. To what degree was a dying person able to express consent? And to what degree was the other person willing to be married for the sake of salvation and altruism rather than as a matter of free will? The deathbed was the court in which the church's moral and social subjugation directly confronted the question of free will.

Carmen Lusurriaga presented an annulment petition in the Sagrario parish in Lima in 1849. She explained that in 1830, when she was twelve years old, Domingo Manrique had seduced her into coming with him from Quito, her native city, to Lima. One day Domingo was brought home with a wound in his chest. The priest was called to administer the last sacraments. As a part of the procedures, and with the intent of providing eternal salvation, the priest married them on the spot without matrimonial formalities.[44] Domingo survived, however. Carmen's doubts about the validity of her marriage express some common theological questions:

> This comic act could not produce duties and obligations from the parties involved, because consent, which constitutes the essence of matrimony, was absent. There was no consent in Manrique's case because fever had driven him mad.... and there was none and could not be any consent on my part since I was acting out of moral coercion, which is, according to the spirit of civil and canonical law, a real force. I was overwhelmed with religious fear of the sort that weighs on the soul of an educated person following the maxims of the Catholic Apostolic Roman religion. This is enough to explain that an inexperienced person like myself acted with no will of her own on that unfortunate day.

Prior to writing her petition, Carmen had married another man, José Centeno. Thus a charge of bigamy was hanging over her. The court ruled that she was to separate from her second husband until it decided which marriage was valid. In the end she obtained the annulment of her first marriage, but the court took until 1860—eleven years after she first presented her petition—to reach its verdict.[45]

When death approached, many couples who had lived together "illicitly" for years were suddenly very interested in coming to terms with God. Salvation was the ultimate reason to marry. Nevertheless, death was not always imminent; in spite of real or faked illnesses, people recovered. Following the Bible, mankind's destiny was to worship God and reproduce humankind; reproduction was tied into marriage. Thus, marrying meant obeying God, and obedience to God assured a person's entrance into heaven. Priests would always ask a dying person whether he or she was married. If the answer was no, the priest would try to convince any single person who happened to be present to marry the dying person. This noble act would ingratiate both with God. When marriage occurred under these circumstances, it was

---

44. Case 869, AA, NM, L 63 (1848–49), 1849, Lusurriaga vs. Manrique.
45. Case 869, AA, NM, L 66 (1860–63), 1860, Lusurriaga vs. Manrique/Centeno.

particularly embarrassing if the sick person survived and later on claimed very earthly conjugal rights.

In 1860, after Agustín Salazar "had received a fatal prognosis," Natividad Flores married him to appease the priest's whinings. Agustín survived, and shortly afterward we find Natividad asking for an annulment because Agustín was refusing to feed her and was mistreating her in other ways.[46] Neither "deathbed consent" or mistreatment was considered sufficient to dissolve the marriage, however, probably because consummation had taken place.

Death could also become a tool for obtaining a yearned-for spouse. In 1818 Pedro Molero, a second lieutenant of the King's Dragoon Regiment, complained of having been victim of such manipulation:

> About four months ago, following my charitable feelings and my religious devotion, I married Doña Josefa Morales in the last days of her life when she was suffering from a disease unknown to the professionals. The reason for this decision was that I had earlier had an illicit relationship with her from which we had three children who still live. Her spiritual adviser persuaded me she was dying and that it was necessary to legitimize those children. So I agreed to marry her, which was the highest sacrifice I could make. In the middle of the night after the marriage, Doña Josefa had a miscarriage, and so I discovered that she had been pregnant because of immoral indiscretions during the time she was not with me.[47]

The lieutenant had a princely income of 60 pesos a month; only if Doña Josefa was married to him could she ask for a corresponding allowance for herself. Doña Josefa was deposited in the Copacabana *beaterio*, and Pedro was required to pay 20 pesos a month for her maintenance. Although it is hard not to make any moral judgments, it certainly was true that many women died in childbirth, so that the combination of the fear surrounding pregnancy and the belief that marriage was attractive in God's eyes explains many marriages under deathbed circumstances. But it also illustrates the desperation felt by women who faced the stigma of illegitimate pregnancy.

Sometimes, though, not even death was a convincing argument to marry, precisely because contemporaries knew that the timing of death could be

46. Case 810, AA, NM, L 66 (1860–63), Flores vs. Salazar.
47. Case 384, AA, CD, L 87 (1815–20), 1818, Morales vs. Molero.

uncertain. In 1890 Rafaela Mejía, an Indian woman living in Lima, explained that "for more than eight years I have lived intimately with Don Pascual García. We have had five children, of which two still live. Because I became gravely ill, I had to enter the Santa Ana hospital, where the doctors ordered that I be administered the last sacraments. My lover and consort García was called in order to go ahead with our marriage.... García asked for eight days, but when they passed, at the instigation of a woman named Serna with whom he has illicit relations, he did not fulfill his promise."[48] The existence of children and a long-term consensual union gave Rafaela a superior moral standing and allowed her to accuse another woman and her lover of having an "illicit relationship." But she knew that only marriage would validate her claim on Don Pascual.

People knew how to use such ploys as deathbed marriage simply as a means to manipulate an unwilling partner into marriage. The threat of death could bring about a violation of consent rules from the priest, from a man, from a woman. In a sense, then, death was the ultimate weapon to manipulate free will and consent.

The philosophical and social implications of consent and dissent were amply debated in ecclesiastical records. The impression that free will and love were an integral part of this debate has to be placed in perspective. Overall, there were relatively few cases in which parental dissent or a lack of consent were brought forward in the courtrooms. Even in hindsight, when a marriage was on the verge of divorce or annulment, most matrimonial files indicate that both parental consent and of the marrying individuals had been granted with no opposition. This may mean one of two things: either children complied with their parents' wishes, or parents knew that opposition was in vain; either most women had no complaints, or they had accepted their lot. Reality was probably a nearly equal combination of both. Still, in about 5 percent of the reviewed matrimonial files, some form of resistance was registered in the ways described above,[49] and only

---

48. Case 0183, AGN, Expedientes Judiciales, CCR, L s.n., 1890, Mejía vs. García.

49. Between 1574 and 1689, Seed (1988, 178) registered 6 percent of marriage cases in which parents expressed dissent and the church acted on the children's behalf in Mexico. (There is no comparable information available for this early colonial period for Lima.) In Mexico, parental interference became increasingly more successful as a result of the implementation of the 1776 Pragmática. Between 1574 and 1689 the parental "success rate" was 7 percent, whereas in 1715 it was 24 percent, and in 1779, 36 percent. In Lima few dissent cases presented at the ecclesiastical court register a final sentence. Thus, it is difficult to establish a comparable "success rate," for the final decades of the eighteenth century. Nevertheless,

small shifts in the arguments regarding either consent or dissent are visible in the course of the nineteenth century. Nevertheless, court conflict over the consent issue shows that tensions between rules and realities existed, and the records portray how the issue of free will was used to gain legal support when social pressures and expectations had influenced individual decisions, signaling a dramatic and conflict-ridden transition to some form of individualism amidst patriarchal pressures. The issue of consent was secularized as women from many different walks of life made their personal issues a matter of public debate. In the process they redefined the relationship between individuals, society, church, and state.

The Incompatibility Argument

The notion of character incompatibility evolved out of the recognition of sexual incompatibility, an argument the church accepted as a reason for divorce because it hampered biological reproduction, the essence of marriage. However, social constraints and the heightened moral discourse made women hesitate to bring bedroom intimacy into the courtroom, and husbands restrained them from doing so as well. Thus, marital conflicts involving sexuality were infrequent throughout the nineteenth century.[50] However, the few available court cases involving sexual problems provide a glimpse of how sexual incompatibility was expanded into a broader notion of character incompatibility. In a sense, the notion of character incompatibility brought the individual back to the divorce arena and forced litigants to rid their court arguments of the sweeping moral rhetoric. Incompatibility stands as a conclusion to accumulated experiences.

The church's reasoning ran as follows: Sexual incompatibility prevented the reproduction of the species and thus was a religious issue. However, incompatibility was never perceived as "only sexual," that is, biological; it also encompassed emotions and compassion. Sex had to "work" for reproduction

---

I suspect—based on a reading of cases—that in nineteenth-century Lima parents had little success in dissent cases. Some evidence of children's greater irreverence is discussed in cases in the following chapters.

50. Cases referring to "sexual problems" in Lima (3 percent of all conflict cases between 1800 and 1820, 5.5 percent between 1840 and 1860, and 4.7 percent between 1890 and 1910) mention "incompatibility" as the *primary* problem.

to occur and for children to be healthy after birth. According to widespread interpretations, only sexual pleasure allowed women to overcome the fear of childbirth. Similarly, health and sex were knit together psychologically. The absence of pleasure resulting from biological *and* character incompatibility threatened health and reproduction.[51] At the beginning of the nineteenth century, reproductive success was deemed to require a "correct" amount of male seed implanted by an appropriately rigid male genital. Too much or too little endangered health and life.[52] Thus, sexual incompatibility was used as an argument for divorce even when children existed. A woman could be forced by the rules of convention to argue sexual incompatibility, but often sexual incompatibility—legally accepted as grounds for divorce—really meant character incompatibility. Prostitution, in turn, was widespread but little talked about and was perceived as a "male need." So, when a woman could prove that her husband frequented prostitutes, she could argue that her husband was suffering from an "overabundance." "Moral transgression" became a "physical transgression," so even if the courts accepted the double standard, they could not deny the biological-overabundance argument. In contrast, venereal disease, a widespread consequence of prostitution, was not deemed a reason for divorce. If proven, the judges would only rule that a husband remain away from the bedroom until health was restored. The connection between prostitution and venereal disease was clear in people's minds.[53]

Everyone knew that venereal diseases were common among Lima's inhabitants, to a point that, as one person put it, "if these infections were

---

51. Such understandings were in line with what people knew about sex and reproduction in seventeenth-century England (Crawford 1994).

52. Wrote Tomasa Borda in 1810: "Consummation within marriage is indispensable, and its main goal is to have children. And it is well known that the lack of seed and more so the overabundance of seed and the virile member are an impediment when it hampers cohabitation." Mathias Sosa, her husband, countered the argument by stating that they had had three children: "During marriage Doña Tomasa has procreated three legitimate children, and unless she now wants to say that these children are adulterine children to prove her case, it can easily be verified that there is no such lack or overabundance of seed. If these defects exist now, they must also have existed at the beginning of our marriage." Tomasa had to undergo vaginal examination, and Mathias's "virile member" had to be measured. At the end, Tomasa—after bringing in eighty witnesses—was allowed to return to her mother in Nazca. Case 93, AA, CD, L 86 (1810–14), 1810, Borda vs. Sosa.

53. Case 201, AA, LM, L 8 (1810–19), 1818, Avalo vs. Leon. Confirming the relationship between sexuality and health/sin in the eyes of Manuela de Espíritu Santo Avalos, a daughter born to this couple after eight years of marriage died two months after birth.

reason enough to separate a couple, then Your Excellency would have to decree divorces every day."⁵⁴

Toward midcentury, women in Lima's courtrooms explicitly connected the reproduction argument with sexual pleasure. In 1847 Marina Cavero, married to the soldier Tiburcio Ulloa, wrote to the ecclesiastical judge: "I cannot have intercourse with this man without risking my life. . . . And when intercourse is not possible, procreation can not occur, and matrimony is not accomplishing its main goal. I find myself unable to have sex with a person more adequate for me. I would like to avoid this expression, but desire, which is the first law of nature to gain happiness, exists, so why should I renounce these rights [!] when there are laws that open the door to enjoy these rights?" Marina argued that Tiburcio's "virile member was monstruous" ("un hombre de físico abestiado"), and to document her case she stated that prostitutes too had complained "because they could not endure him." Marina's charges were carried further than Tomasa's, and a doctor's opinion was requested. He rejected Marina's reasons and argued that virgins—as Marina presumably was—tended to "magnify" and that "use" would bring elasticity. Time would solve the initial incompatibility problem.⁵⁵

It seems significant that two out of seven cases registered between 1840 and 1860 explicitly talked about female sexual desires, to the degree that in one case a husband accused his wife of "having abdicated the virtue and modesty inherent to a wife, telling with the utmost insolence about her sexual wishes."⁵⁶ In his eyes, modesty and virtue were incompatible with expressing sexuality. Talking about sex in the courtroom might publicize a husband's inadequacy, and one way to silence a blunt wife was to demand her compliance to standards of modesty and virtue. In a sense, arguments based on economic equality and on sexuality were both answered with the same rhetoric about virtue.

In most sexual incompatibility cases, it was women who declared that they were either too "narrow," too afraid, or impotent.⁵⁷ But this was not

---

54. Case 300, AA, LM, L 8 (1810–19), 1814, Espinoza vs. Sagredo.
55. Case 761, AA, NM, L 62, 1847, Cavero vs. Ulloa.
56. Case 747, AA, CD, L 93 (1857–59), 1859, 17ff, Burunda vs. Figueroa. Mercedes Burunda ended up leaving her husband. He accused her of adultery, but Mercedes never showed up in court.
57. "Valdez, my husband, wanted me to claim that impotence was on my side, and when I told the truth, he left Lima," wrote Isabel Loyola in 1857. Her husband was a lawyer, and Isabel obtained an annulment in 1860, after witnesses had been brought in. Case 868, AA, NM, L 65 (1857–59), Loyola vs. Valdés.

always true. A woman could claim that she was the one having sexual incompatibility problems, a way of rescuing her husband's deficiencies and thus safeguarding his masculinity. Consequently, a husband did not have to acknowledge sexual incompatibility, and both spouses had a case that would stand up in court. When both partners in a divorce case agreed that they were suffering from sexual incompatibility,[58] especially when they had had no sex for years and no children had been born, even the *defensor de matrimonios* easily came to the conclusion that a divorce was in order. Descriptions of intimate life are necessarily charged with subjectivity, and even if judges attempted to verify testimony by measuring and examining, no final "truth" could be gleaned from biological facts. Thus, no matter what doctors, judges, priests, and witnesses said, whatever spouses interpreted as "sexual incompatibility" *was* sexual incompatibility. And this argument became the ultimate intimate weapon to escape an unhappy marriage and the grip of the church. But it presupposed both partners' tacit agreement, a mutual consensus to argue the existence of irreconcilable differences.

Most cases that claimed "sexual incompatibility" included other charges.[59] However, it was the sexual-incompatibility argument that judges responded to, because it endangered health, life, and procreation. What had begun in the bedroom (sexual incompatibility) was taken to the ecclesiastical courtroom and then was turned over to the civil judges, where its interpretation was widened to create the notion of a character incompatibility. In the end, not only sexual problems but also domestic violence, abandonment, adultery, and frequenting prostitutes were used as proof of incompatibility rather than as moral imputations against men. Toward the end of the century, this more encompassing interpretation of incompatibility made it unnecessary to delve explicitly into sexual problems. Moreover, sexuality disappeared from divorce allegations altogether. Talking about sexual problems in court became unnecessary and undesirable: "No matter how strong the reasons are to keep up the social bonds born out of marriage, there are grave reasons, recognized by civil and canonic law, that demand the separation of the spouses and the preclusion of their reciprocal duties concerning the bed and the house. . . . It is better for couples to separate when marriage

---

58. Case 056, AA, NM, L 65 (1857–59), 1857, Vergara vs. Palacios. Maria Vergara and Miguel Palacios had been married for eight years. Miguel argued that they had never copulated because shortly after marriage María had told him that she suffered from a uterine disease that made it impossible for her to have sex. In court, María simply concurred with this.

59. In the Borda vs. Sosa case, it was debts; in the Avalo vs. Leon case, it was brutal beating; in the Loyola vs. Valdes case, it was abandonment and adultery.

is not and cannot be the focus of peace and domestic happiness."[60] Sexual incompatibility and domestic happiness had been equated, and the court needed no proof of unfulfilled marital obligations.

In the conflict cases analyzed, the arguments of domestic happiness and character incompatibility were used for the first time in 1892 to decree the separation of an Indian couple.[61] And this marked the appearance of new sounds in the courtroom: character incompatibility, not sexual incompatibility, led to mutual hatred that could result in homicide of a spouse or cruelty toward children.

That year Ismael Gao, a lawyer defending an Indian client, Braulia Pumacaja from Cocachacra, against adultery accusations by her husband, Juan Mamerto Cadillo, argued: "The incompatibility of characters, and the physical violence that results from it, very clearly show that for this couple it is impossible to remain together. And this is precisely when the law has to be brought in to dissolve a marriage that has become unworkable and may result in crimes provoked by mutual hate. . . . But it is not only the incompatibility of characters and the threat to my client's life that has forced her to petition for a divorce. Something more dramatic is involved: it is her wish to safeguard the threatened future of her [three] children."

The progress from claims of sexual incompatibility to claims of general unhappiness was a first step toward divorce by mutual consent. It was also a step away from church interference in intimate relationships, which led to couple-centered decisions brought before civil court. Couples began to gain autonomy in approaching the civil court and in shaping their cases in a way that focused on them as individuals (in the liberal sense) rather than as subjects of the church. The long-term evolution of courtroom arguments, which stretched from reproduction to sexual incompatibility to character incompatibility to mutual consensus resulted from a heightened moral climate in which the discussion of sex was made taboo, but which also allowed men and women to use their perception of their marital relationship to either continue or end their marriages. Individuals' bedroom stories and sentiments had been introduced into divorce arguments and the law, a development that paralleled—albeit at a different level of reasoning—the growing perception of women's economic hardships and the injustices inherent in double standards.

60. Case 0106, AA, CD, L 113, 1892, Amoretti vs. Osores.
61. AA, CD, L s.n., Pumacaja vs. Gao, 1892.

The church, being less monolithic than it might appear, harbored doubts about what was right, desirable, or attainable. Elements of arbitrariness were unavoidable in the ecclesiastical decision-making process. Cases expressed not only the church's evolving interpretations but also different interpretations by individual priests, theologians, and judges. In the final analysis, then, the church itself contributed to the many uncertainties surrounding consent, dissent, and incompatibility. People were aware of these minor, ongoing moral reformulations, and they—especially women—used them to find legal means to assert their individual rights. Concretely, women used the principle of consent and the notion of fear and unhappiness to describe moral and social wrongs done to them. By the middle of the nineteenth century, nonconsent was still considered a breach of canon law, but in most cases women argued that some other transgression had also occurred: the accused spouse was a Frenchman, an Englishman, or a non-Catholic (thus implying he was a foreigner estranged from prevailing cultural and religious norms); charges of bigamy and the existence of illegitimate children were interpreted as a social rather than a moral concern. In a parallel fashion, women had equated sexual incompatibility with character incompatibility. Thus, people's reasoning was moving away from strictly defined church proscriptions toward a reinterpretation of such proscriptions that incorporated a rapidly changing social context. Every change opened maneuvering space within institutional inadequacy.

Had the church wholeheartedly agreed to women's widened interpretation of the lack of consent and incompatibility, soon all marriages would have been liable to annulment. In the church's eyes, the proximity between a socially defined consent and free will and the move from sexual to character incompatibility was a dangerous liberal twist to its own theological discussions of consent and sexuality: it expanded women's leeway to bargain their way out of marriage—to become "loose" and "sly" creatures while undermining patriarchal assumptions and the holy sacrament of marriage. All imaginable situations could be interpreted as forced marriage, and the only real and definite expression of consent was the opposition to parents' dissent. All self-interpretations of sexual incompatibility turned divorce decisions over to the individuals involved.

Civil and ecclesiastical judges were aware of this potential breach of social and religious convention and therefore cautiously evaluated each particular situation and, whenever possible, rejected a more encompassing definition of consent and incompatibility. This explains why in most cases in which lawyers or women forwarded arguments in the "wrong direction," ecclesiastical judges and the *defensor de matrimonios* were unwilling to grant an annulment. Often consummation—even in cases of rape—took the place of consent; often physical examinations of women's bodies concluded with the denial of incompatibility. The body replaced the mind to save marriage and patriarchy.[62]

---

62. Cases of rape and how they were interpreted by men, women, and the church will be addressed in Chapter 6.

5

Guarding Marriage from Conflicts

Couples and *Beaterios*

Aside from the canonic interstices left open by prematrimonial church regulations, marital conflicts were seen not only as a threat to public order but also as a threat to the survival of the holy sacrament of matrimony. Conjugal quarrels had to be regulated and dealt with.

When Alberto Flores Galindo and Magdalena Chocano (1984) studied Lima's conjugal conflicts in the period between 1760 and 1810, they found that the socioeconomic tensions and conflicts experienced throughout Lima were reflected in daily interactions between spouses.[1] During these fifty years, conjugal conflict cases increased from 14 between 1760 and 1769, to 32 between 1770 and 1779, to 105 in the next decade, to 263 between 1790 and 1799, reaching 305 between 1800 and 1809. This count reveals a dramatic increase of domestic violence cases brought to court toward the end of the colonial period, at a time when population growth remained almost unchanged (1984, 403–23).

---

1. In a footnote, Flores Galindo and Chocano (1984, 419 n. 2) wrote: "En este ensayo nos emplazamos en el nivel de la práctica cotidiana. La ideología de la sociedad colonial ha sido estudiada de manera casi exclusiva como institución o como norma. El "deber ser" que se puede percibir en la legislación o la prédica religiosa. Nos alejamos de esos territorios trajinados para tratar de explorar los claroscuros de la vida cotidiana." This is analogous to my own critique.

By contrasting the total number of marriages in one year with the corresponding conflict cases for the same year, Flores Galindo and Chocano calculated that, at the beginning of the nineteenth century, 6 percent of Lima's married couples were engaged in a divorce suit, a percentage that persisted throughout the nineteenth century. According to my own findings, between 1800 and 1820, 4 percent of Lima's couples were involved in a lawsuit; between 1840 and 1860, this percentage rose slightly to 4.4 percent; and between 1890 and 1910, it reached 6.5 percent. Although this represents a small group of married couples, nevertheless—as mentioned by Flores Galindo and Chocano—it is higher than in Ruán (France) in 1792, but certainly much lower than present-day percentages in Europe or the United States. But in France (and elsewhere in Europe) at the end of the eighteenth century[2] and nowadays, requirements to pursue a divorce varied greatly from the conditions found in nineteenth-century Lima. France had experienced a revolution in the wake of which marriage and divorce had become a secular issue, a contract (Blasius 1985). In Lima, marriage and divorce were handled by the church until well into the twentieth century, which makes the higher percentage of marriage litigation in Lima even more astounding and reveals how much of the moral climate in the age of rising liberalism was aired in Lima's courtrooms. Francisco García Calderón, one of Peru's most prominent jurists at the turn of the twentieth century, commented:

> The similarities between the two civil codes [Napoleon's and the Peruvian civil code of 1852] are numerous. Definitions relied on the preciseness and the logic of the Napoleonic Code. The contract has the same verbal meaning in both codes, as well as the study of its conditions. Some literal translations can be found in several titles, especially in those referring to marriage, the rights and duties of the spouses, paternity, filiation, etc. . . . [However, T]here is a huge difference between both bodies of law in regard to marriage and divorce. The Peruvian code does not reach secularization. . . . Matrimony is a religious act. . . . Article 156 of the Peruvian civil code explicitly states that matrimony is ruled by the principles put forward by the Council of Trent. . . . In family issues, Catholicism commands civil law." (García Calderón Jr. 1954, 51–52)

Thus, the period between 1800 and 1820 is a point of departure to analyze

---

2. For England, see Stone (1990), and for Renaissance Italy, Kuehn (1991).

the change in arguments and litigation strategies over the century.[3] Between 1840 and 1860 many expressions of conflict took on new undertones in spite of unchanged legal assumptions. As was the case for Indians and slaves, the wars of independence did not bring about dramatic changes for women. Although visible early in the century, changes are much more defined and visible around 1870. It was then that urban masses and rural workers appeared on the political scene and the city's population grew substantially. These developments triggered radical responses from previously quiescent groups; and to deal with these responses, society more strictly enforced women's traditional roles and upheld men's prerogatives—as we will see—with uneven success, and not without increasingly more radical responses from women.

To a degree, somewhere between the *barrio* and the court, the outcome of conjugal conflicts also depended on actions taken by family members. Sometimes family members were also neighbors, sometimes they paid for a woman to enter a *beaterio*, oftentimes they offered shelter from a violent husband, and at times they even intervened with force in couples' physical aggressions. Mentions of intervention by family members appears in 24.2 percent of all suits presented at the ecclesiastical court between 1800 and 1820. Between 1840 and 1860 the figure dropped slightly to 23.4 percent, and between 1890 and 1910 family members appeared only in 12.5 percent of the cases (Table 5.1).[4] The declining intervention of family members in couples' quarrels is paralleled by a decreasing percentage of women who were living with a family member when a suit was presented at the ecclesiastical court: from 10.5 percent between 1800 and 1860 to 4.5 percent between 1890 and 1910 (Table 5.2). Although neighbors still provided a solid support network, family members were either playing a diminished role or were mentioned less frequently.

---

3. Data here and in Flores Galindo and Chocano's article was taken from three series in the Archbishopric Archive (AA) in Lima: Litigios Matrimoniales (LM), Causas de Divorcio (CD), Causas de Nulidad (NM).

4. For the first half of the nineteenth century in Mexico City, Arrom (1985b, 247–49) informs us that "the interference of relatives was the most frequently cited source of marital conflict." This seems to be another striking difference between Mexico City and Lima, although Arrom concedes that things were changing toward midcentury. In Lima, the intervention of family members included both their meddling in conflict and their being a source of conflict. In contrast to the percentages given, accusations of mistreatment, adultery, and abandonment ranked much higher than family intervention throughout the nineteenth century (see Tables 8.3, 8.4, and 8.5, appendix).

Table 5.1 Family intervention in matrimonial conflicts, 1800–1910

	1800–1820	%	1840–1860	%	1890–1910	%
Yes	99	24.2	50	23.5	56	12.5
No	298	72.9	143	67.1	379	84.6
Others	10	2.4	15	7.0	1	0.2
No data	2	0.5	5	2.4	12	2.7
Total	409	100.0	213	100.0	448	100.0

Source: AA, LM, CD, NM.

Without allies such as parents or siblings, a women's chances of success were low, making submissiveness an unfortunate but viable alternative to continuing a suit. However, the gradual retreat of family members from intervening in conjugal quarrels and lawsuits also fostered changes in the discourse women brought to court. Left on their own, divorcing women had to clearly state what they felt was wrong with gender inequality, especially when it came down to defending conjugal assets and earnings, that is, their own and their children's sheer survival when faced with a husband's abandonment and men's legally stipulated prerogative of controlling and administering all family earnings.

Although neighbors and family members proved to be effective in helping women, this was not always enough. Some husbands proved to be extremely vicious. A man might fight neighbors and family members, even when he had already been reprimanded and punished by *serenos, alcaldes,* and the police, and still have the nerve to come back to beat his wife and threaten to kill her: "He completely disregards court orders, and thinks he is especially tough."[5] When everything had failed to stop a murderous husband, a wife might be forced to leave home.[6] But if a married woman left home without church permission, she could be charged with abandonment and lose her right to alimony and acquest (her 50 percent of conjugal assets).

For married women, the "right" decision was to resort to the courts rather than just to walk out. According to Peru's 1852 Civil Code, a divorce suit could be opened for adultery, physical cruelty, or bad treatment (including attempted homicide), hatred ("odio capital"), incorrigible vices such as gambling or drinking, a husband's failure to meet the family's minimum

---

5. Case 941, AA, CD, L 93 (1857–59), 1857, Peres vs. Pisarro.
6. Case 0234, AGN, Expedientes Judiciales, CCR, L s.n., 1892, De oficio contra Manuel de la Asunción por lesiones.

Table 5.2 Women's location when filing a divorce and who opened the file, 1800–1910

Locations/ Periods[a]	Men	%	Women	%	Kin	%	Third Parties	%	Total
In Beaterio									
1800–1820	16	40.0	24	60.0	0	0.0	0	0.0	40
1840–1860	5	25.0	12	60.0	2	10.0	1	5.0	20
1890–1910	7	70.0	3	30.0	0	0.0	0	0.0	10
With kin									
1800–1820	18	41.9	22	51.2	3	6.9	0	0.0	43
1840–1860	7	31.8	15	68.2	0	0.0	0	0.0	22
1890–1910	9	45.0	11	55.0	0	0.0	0	0.0	20
Free[b]									
1800–1820	22	46.8	25	53.2	0	0.0	0	0.0	47
1840–1860	17	43.6	21	53.8	0	0.0	1	2.6	39
1890–1910	132	87.4	19	12.6	0	0.0	0	0.0	151
In conjugal home									
1800–1820	58	21.9	203	76.7	2	0.7	2	0.7	265
1840–1860	26	21.8	92	77.3	0	0.0	1	0.8	119
1890–1910	86	33.7	166	65.1	2	0.8	1	0.4	255
In master's home[c]									
1800–1820	4	66.7	2	33.3	0	0.0	0	0.0	6
1840–1860	1	100.0	0	0.0	0	0.0	0	0.0	1
No indication									
1800–1820	2	25.0	2	25.0	0	0.0	4[d]	50.0	8
1840–1860	3	25.0	5	41.7	0	0.0	4[d]	33.4	12
1890–1910	5		4		0		3[d]		12
Total cases									1,070

SOURCE: AA, LM, CD, NM.
[a] 1800–1820: 409 cases.
 1840–60: 213 cases.
 1890–1910: 448 cases.
[b] "Free" means that they were living on their own and working.
[c] These cases refer to slaves involved in divorce suits.
[d] To these numbers I have added those few cases in which it is not clear who opened the suit (as some files are incomplete) and there is also no indication as to where the woman was at the time the suit began.

budgetary needs, refusal by the wife to go anywhere her husband wanted to go, abandonment of conjugal residence or continued denial of marital obligations, unjustified absence for more than five years, madness, chronic contagious diseases, criminal sentence ("por pena infamante") of one of the spouses (García Calderón Sr., 1879, 780, cites art. 192 of the Civil Code).

The first step in ecclesiastical court was to petition to leave the conjugal home and move to a *beaterio* or to an "honorable" household. After listening to both sides, the *provisor* made the final decision as to where a wife should go.[7] *Beaterios* offered physical security for women victimized by their husbands. These women were called *refugiadas*, literally meaning refugees. More frequently, however, a husband petitioned to put his wife in a *beaterio* on the grounds that she needed to improve her behavior. These women in turn were called *depositadas* (depositees).[8] Both spouses could object to the final decision taken by the ecclesiastical judge, a strategy often used to hamper the continuation of a suit. As long as the residency of a wife was not resolved, a suit begun in the ecclesiastical court could not move on to civil court; and as long as no civil court action proceeded, a woman could not request alimony or claim acquest. Thus, husbands had a vested interest in delaying a suit to avoid alimony payments and to retain the administrative control of the couple's common property.

Beaterios were dependencies of Lima's archbishopric. At least until the 1880s, *beaterios* were located on the edges of a still quite small city. About five blocks from the Plaza Mayor, Lima's main square, was the Beaterio de Viterbo; about eight blocks from the Plaza across the Rimac River (already beyond the city walls) was the Beaterio de Copacabana, originally dedicated to helping Indian women; and three blocks down from Copacabana, close to the Jardín de los Descalzos, lay the Beaterio del Patrocinio or Amparadas. The Instituto del Buen Pastor was located in the extreme south of the city, close to the city wall (see the map on pages 46–47). Toward midcentury,

---

7. The legal stipulations to open a divorce file included: "Para que alguno de los cónyuges pueda entablar la acción de divorcio, en los casos permitidos en el código civil, es necesario que se presente al juez eclesiástico competente, ofreciendo por escrito información sumaria sobre los motivos que le asisten para intentar el divorcio. El juez ordenará la información con citación del otro cónyuge, y recibida en el modo dispuestos para el exámen de testigos, se dará traslado al otro cónyuge. Con la contestación, resultando mérito bastante, se declarará expedita la acción de divorcio, y se mandará citar á los cónyuges, señalándoles dia y hora para que comparezcan en el juzgado al acto de conciliación" (Código Penal de Enjuiciamientos, art. 372–74). "Llegado el día y la hora que señale el juez, tratará de conciliar á los cónyuges; y en el caso de no lograrlo, se acordarán los puntos siguientes: 1. La casa ó lugar en que debe permanecer la mujer durante el juicio, en clase de depósito; 2. La pensión que mensualmente debe dar el marido á la mujer durante la causa, y por via de alimentos, si ella no tiene como mantenerse; sirviendo de base la descripción y estimación, aunque sea aproximada, de los bienes que el marido está obligado á hacer, sea demandante ó demandado" (ibid., art. 375; García Calderón Sr. 1879, 780–81).

8. For an illustration of these distinctions during the colonial period, see Van Deusen (1987, 18–19).

there were still only haciendas and small plots of land for growing crops beyond the city wall.

Founded in the seventeenth century, Lima's *beaterios* fulfilled varied functions over the course of time and accommodated different kinds of women.[9] Some *beaterios* had been founded to admit only white or only Indian women. Gradually, they opened their doors to women from diverse ethnic groups, but inside the *beaterios*, hierarchies among inmates were not erased. Some women had more money than others; some had servants or slaves; some could count on benefactors; others could not.

In Peru,[10] the *beaterios'* initial and most important function was educating young girls under the tutelage of nuns in a secluded environment. In their confinement, girls learned appropriate behavior, moral values, and Christian doctrine; sometimes they even learned to read and write. In the course of the colonial period, some *beaterios* opened their doors to women who were separating from their husbands, to widows who sought to retire from the world, and to women who had "gone astray," that is, women who in one way or another were not adequately fulfilling their assigned social roles.[11] *Beaterios* also provided medical care or were close to hospitals. Moreover, as there were no special jails for women until the early 1860s, *beaterios* were used as prisons to punish minor transgressions and to redeem prostitutes, an option mother superiors resisted by all means, because inmates could eventually escape and because "criminals"—especially prostitutes—were a bad example for all other inmates.

At the end of the nineteenth century, another function was added to the *beaterios* in Lima. By then we find entire families asking for admission, alleging that they wanted to retreat from turbulent city life to pray to God. Husbands would ask that their wives and children be received in order to help them in a desperate struggle for survival.[12] Toward the century's end, the *beaterios'* multiple functions spread out among different institutions: the

---

9. Fuentes (n.d., 3:88–126) provides a history of Amparadas written by someone (no author is mentioned) toward the end of the eighteenth century. Interesting in this account is the confusion as to when the *beaterio*, the Casa Real, and the Casa de las Divorciadas were founded. It seems that toward the end of the seventeenth century all three occupied the same building. See especially pp. 124–26.

10. For a description of this institution in Mexico, see Muriel (1974).

11. Because *beaterios* took care of so many different "social problems," they were sometimes referred to as *casas de recogimiento* (houses of retirement).

12. AA, Beaterio de Copacabana, L 3 (1860–1921), Solicitud de Melchora Sagasti, 1877; Escrito de Antonio Tord casado con Adela Mendiguren al Arzobispo de Lima, 1896.

Beneficencia Pública took over social cases and hospitals, the Casa del Buen Pastor became the place in which divorcing women could seek refuge or were deposited by their husbands, and numerous schools and jails were built.

In the course of the nineteenth century, a decreasing number of women undergoing divorce could be found in *beaterios* (Table 5.2).[13] Between 1800 and 1820 and between 1840 and 1860, one out of ten women in the process of divorce had entered a *beaterio*. Between 1890 and 1910, however, the number had dropped to one out of forty-four women in a *beaterio* (including those residing in the new Instituto del Buen Pastor). A growing number of women either remained in the conjugal residence or simply abandoned their husbands rather than filing and then following up on a lawsuit. Some cases show that couples could live separately for many years before resorting to court intervention. Many more never went to court, choosing instead to rearrange their lives independently and away from public scrutiny.

When Dolores Trebejo filed suit in 1853, she had been living on her own for over four years. Her husband, Ascencio de la Cruz had abandoned her without reason, she claimed. Ascencio, to the contrary, claimed he had been forced to leave because of the dissolute behavior of his wife. He had taken her back to her family in the province of Corongo (in the northern highlands), and he continued to provide for her. Yet Dolores had returned to Lima with another man with whom she sold beer in the Alameda. Ascencio then had her secluded in a *beaterio*. Moved by her tears and promises, he allowed her to return home. But "her good will only lasted for one month. She became entangled in another relationship, and she has lived with this man for the last four years." In court Dolores refused to go back to her husband, and the *provisor* ruled that she be returned to the Beaterio de Amparadas. However, she ran away before the decree was carried out.[14]

Joaquina Aranda and Tomás Lizarsaburu had been separated for ten years. She had led a "scandalous life," while he, a soldier, took part in battles

---

13. Between 1800 and 1820, 45.5 percent of the couples were already physically separated when they filed a suit in the ecclesiastical court. Of the 45.5 percent, 11.5 percent lived on their own, 10.5 percent lived with an adult family member, 12.5 percent remained in their homes (the husband having left), and 10.0 percent were in a *beaterio*. Between 1840 and 1860, the percentage of couples separated when the suit began rose to 49.3 percent: 18.3 percent were on their own, 10.3 percent lived with a family member, 11.3 percent remained alone in their home, and 9.4 percent were in a *beaterio*. Between 1890 and 1910, 49.6 percent were separated by the time they went to court: only 4.5 percent lived with a family member and 2.2 percent in a *beaterio*, but 33.7 percent were on their own, while 9.2 percent remained at home.

14. Case 032, AA, CD, L 91 (1848–53), 1853, Trebejo vs. de la Cruz.

to earn a living for them. According to Tomás, she "had sunk into deep degradation." Tomás filed suit in 1852 because Joaquina was telling people that she was married to him, while everyone knew that she "behaved like a streetwalker" and had had several children by different men. In presenting his divorce suit, Tomás wanted to "cut off this cancer. With a legal divorce no one will any longer think I am related to her, and her scandalous behavior will no longer harm my reputation."[15]

Both of these couples lived separately for years, and they went to court only when the husbands felt their honor and reputation were threatened. The husbands initially raised no objection to the separation, but they sought a divorce when their wives publicly proclaimed their "liberty" through their immoral conduct. Although in the first case (Trebejos vs. de la Cruz) the husband resorted to a *beaterio*, it was a short-lived and unsuccessful seclusion. In the second case (Aranda vs. Lizarsaburu), neither spouse considered the possibility of going to a *beaterio*. Seclusion could—as the first case shows— be contravened by simply running away, but sometimes runaway wives were found and forced to enter a *beaterio*.[16] Sometimes women themselves chose, as a matter of honor, to join a *beaterio*: "I want liberty, but not in the streets, because it is not honorable to expose myself to sinister interpretations."[17] Although men and women had their own specific reasons to resort to a *beaterio*, and "good behavior" and honor continued to be crucial ingredients of gender relations, for different reasons both men and women used this form of seclusion less frequently. In spite of the gradual disappearance of the practice of seclusion, what happened in and with *beaterios* illustrates wider social processes and changing gender relations.

Beaterios and Allowances

The decreasing importance of *beaterios* to solve conjugal conflicts closely related to a growing hesitancy to socially expose oneself and to a changing occupational profile of couples resorting to the ecclesiastical court[18] (Tables 5.3 and 5.4). In the course of time, more lower-class couples were involved

15. Case 715, AA, LM, L 10 (1850–59), 1852, Aranda vs. Lizarsaburu.
16. Case 821, AA, LM, L 10 (1850–59), 1856, García vs. La Torre.
17. Case 049, AA, LM, L 10 (1850–59), 1852, Vásquez vs. Fabiani.
18. Because information on women's work is almost nonexistent, I had to consider male occupations. A reading considering racial indicators is even thinner. In most cases (from the

Table 5.3 Male ethnicity among quarreling couples, three periods, 1800–1910

	1800–1820	%	1840–1860	%	1890–1910	%
Spanish/Criollo	22	28	10	36	11	38
Castas	19	24	—	0	—	0
Asians	1	1	—	0	8	28
Blacks	7	9	1	3	—	0
Indians	25	31	17	61	10	34
Mestizos	5	6	—	0	—	0
Slaves	1	1	—	0	—	0
Total	80	100	28	100	29	100
No data	329		185		419	
Total cases	409		213		448	

SOURCE: AA, LM, CD, NM.

in lawsuits, and to enter and live in a *beaterio* cost money that husbands were less able to pay.

It seems that members of the military, merchants, artisans, state and private enterprise employees, and rural workers were by far the most quarrelsome groups in ecclesiastical court throughout the nineteenth century. In other words, most conflicts involved the middle and the lower classes.[19] In regard to class, the importance of the different groups relative to each other seems to follow general economic trends and the changing social structure in Lima. Some occupation-related changes can be inferred from Table 5.4: a sharp drop in artisans in the second period (1840–1860), probably

---

1,070 cases for our three periods), 87.2 percent make no explicit reference to the racial features of the couples. Taking these limitations into account, we find that among the remaining 137 cases, 31.4 percent refer to the Creole-Spanish group and European immigrants, 13.9 percent to *castas*, 38.0 percent to Indians, 3.6 percent to *mestizos*, 5.8 percent to blacks, and 6.6 percent to Asians. Counting together, on the one hand, "whites" (*criollos*, Spaniards, and Europeans) and supposing they represented the bulk of the upper and middle classes, and, on the other hand, all the "others" (*castas*, Indians, blacks, *mestizos* and Asians) representing, supposedly, the lower echelons of society, we perceive that marriage conflicts involving the upper and middle classes accounted for 31.4 percent of all conflicts, whereas those involving the lower classes accounted for 68.6 percent. The reading of the cases goes beyond these questionable statistics to provide a sense of the relationship between race/class and marital conflict.

19. Although the cases include rich merchants, high ranking military officers, and some men with more than one occupation, only a few cases involved Lima's elites. Arrom (1985b, 220) provides the class background of couples seeking divorce between 1800 and 1857 for Mexico City. However, well-known limitations on illustrating or comparing social classes apply here and render comparisons between both cities unviable.

related to the replacement of artisan work by imports; heightened conflicts related to merchants in the third period (1890–1900), reflecting—as we will see—not only the importance of mercantile activity but also wives' greater involvement in their husbands' businesses; the high number of marital conflicts among landowners throughout the century, reflects the continued migration to the city and women's participation in agrarian production and the sale of produce. More conflicts among employees and state employers reveal their increased numbers in the government and in commercial and industrial enterprises.[20] Also noticeable is the steadily high percentage of unemployed husbands, showing that approximately 10 percent of divorcing women were (and often had been before the filing of divorce) the sole family providers.

Unless a wife had resources of her own and was willing to use them to pay for her residence in a *beaterio*,[21] husbands were required to pay a monthly

Table 5.4 Male occupations among quarreling couples, three periods, 1800–1910

Occupation	1800–1820	1840–1860	1890–1910
Military	43	15	25
Artisans	58	5	22
State employees	12	4	7
Slaves or house servants	8	—	—
Landowners	17	8	17
Priests	2	1	—
Employees	11	7	16
Miners	2	—	1
Daily wage earners	3	—	2
Professionals	4	5	2
Merchants	42	11	45
Out of work	17	9	9
N.A.	190	148	302
Total	409	213	448

SOURCE: AA, LM, CD, NM.

20. Table 5.4 also reflects some more obvious conditions: slavery was abolished in 1854, so "slaves" disappeared from the records as a category of litigants; "priests" did not marry but could have children, thus they could also be subject to alimony claims for women and children.

21. Civil Code 1852, art. 205. A typical resource of women was paraphernalia, which—as will be seen in greater detail in Chapter 7—included such items as jewelry and furniture, and sometimes real estate that was not under a husband's management or control. For comments

allowance, no matter who had opened the court case. These payments were an essential requisite to seclusion in a *beaterio*, because these institutions did not have funds to provide food, clothing, furniture, and other necessities to their inmates.[22] The ecclesiastical judge would determine how much a husband had to pay for his wife's admittance to the *beaterio*, for her monthly maintenance, and for her legal expenses (*litis expensas*). Thus, a woman's comfort and success in pursuing a lawsuit greatly depended on her husband's income and his generosity. The simple matter of providing for a woman's basic necessities in the *beaterio* often became a stumbling block preventing the closure of a divorce case.

At the beginning of the nineteenth century, entrance fees fluctuated between 25 and 30 pesos, and monthly allowances between 4 and 200 pesos. Until the middle of the century, husbands were expected to provide for their wives according to their own level of income and to "what their wives had been used to before." A shoemaker, for example, could be asked to pay 20 pesos monthly,[23] a soldier 8 pesos, a landowner up to 200 pesos. However, a husband's income was not always easy to determine. Many men had no permanent work; others juggled several occupations. Merchants, the military, artisans, and people employed in the service sector were especially subject to such uncertainties. Soldiers, for example, frequently worked as artisans, private security guards, or musicians. The soldier Pedro Espinoza had been hired by the government mint, located in Santa Ana parish; at the same time, he worked as a musician. He expected his wife to live on 3 *reales* daily (approximately 11 pesos a month). When she dared to complain, he silenced her with a blow from a club and threatened to kill her. When Pedro asked the *provisor* to send his wife to a *beaterio*, he wanted to pay the same amount. To his surprise he found out that not only his wife but also the mother superior thought that this allowance was not enough,[24] which

---

on maintenance in a *beaterio* and paraphernalia more generally, see also García Calderón Sr. (1879, 781 and 274–75, respectively).

22. *Beaterios* had a longstanding history of financial problems. At the end of the eighteenth century, a proposal was forwarded suggesting that women in *beaterios* should sew and weave to clothe the army in return for the king's support (Fuentes 1861, 3:120).

23. AGN, RA, CCI, L 72, C 744, 1807, Guzman vs. Dávila. She was in the Viterbo *beaterio* because her husband had mistreated her. In her civil court lawsuit, she asserted that her husband was earning 20 reales (approximately 2.5 pesos) each day. He, in turn, argued that he worked so hard that he was spitting blood, for which reason he could no longer continue working.

24. AA, LM, L 7, 1805, Espinoza vs. Aranda. For her own security, the wife was asking to be separated from her husband and suggested that she be placed at her godfather's house.

meant that Pedro's wife received more in the *beaterio* than when living with her husband. In such cases, the *beaterio* provided a more adequate living place than a woman's own home. *Beaterio* support payments also became a measure of a "living wage." Mothers superiors who demanded a reasonable level of support for the women in their care sent an unequivocal message to husbands who thought that their wives could live on air and blows alone.

A wife's standard of living in the *beaterio* reflected her origins and her husband's status. Considerations of honor could help secure a better lifestyle for a woman in seclusion because as a matter of honor, husbands were willing to loosen their purse strings. Some voluntarily paid 40 pesos or more.[25] The wages of a husband could also be garnished. Spouses of high ranking members of the military or the state bureaucracy could speak to their husbands' superiors to ask that the Auditoría General de Guerra (highest military accounting office) or the corresponding state accounting office transfer a stipulated share of the husband's salary directly to the mother superior or the wife. Officers and soldiers were even incarcerated when they did not obey their superiors and continued to resist making payments. According to law, the allowance must be one third of a husband's salary; this meant 8 pesos a month in the case of a soldier and 12 pesos in case of a cadet or a middle-ranked bureaucrat. In the first decades of the nineteenth century, it was impossible to survive in a *beaterio*—or outside it—with 8 or even 12 pesos. Many wives thus had to seek supplemental income.

Unmarried women seeking to enter a *beaterio* encountered similar financial difficulties. The only viable alternative for a separation in a common-law marriage was, according to the prevailing social standards, an "immoral" option. Single mothers and extremely poor women relied on family members to provide monthly payments or earned a livelihood in the *beaterio*—often working for their better-off sisters[26]—or in some other morally acceptable institution, such as a monastery.

By 1890 fees had been standardized and categorized in the Instituto del Buen Pastor. Husbands paid 10, 20, or 30 soles. A woman whose husband

---

25. Case 470, AA, LM, L 8, 1812, Póbera vs. Moreno. Vicente Moreno, who paid more than 40 pesos, was a silversmith with a shop and, at the same time, a soldier in the militia of Lima's *Escuadrón de Dragones*.

26. There were few women who could survive on what they produced in the *beaterio*, and many women resisted working at all. Josefa Herrera had been living in Copacabana for ten years "serving all of [the nuns] just to get some food, under the worst imaginable conditions, without ever receiving the slightest human help, nor ever having acquired even half a penny from my husband in all these years." Case 265, AA, CD, L 83 (1802–4), N. vs. Herrera.

paid the lowest rate was obliged to work for the benefit of the institute, either sewing or washing. Other expenses, such as clothes, shoes, or drugs, had to be provided by the husband. The 1890s were an economically difficult period: the Beneficencia had ceased to pay its 200 soles subsidy for poor women to the Instituto, and job opportunities for unqualified women were always scarce. Such developments, according to the comments of the mother superior, made it impossible to transfer to the lowest category women who were paying either of the two higher rates. It was not the women who were asking to reduce the monthly allowance, however, but their husbands, who argued either that troubled years lay ahead and they would no longer be able to pay the higher rates or that their wives had incomes of their own, higher than the allowances they received.[27] To keep a wife in a *beaterio* became more difficult. Honor began to cost more money than an increasing number of lower-class husbands could afford, and this perhaps convinced some husbands that their wives' seclusion was an increasingly inconvenient solution. By standardizing rates, the Instituto not only created more homogeneous conditions among secular inmates but also took over a decision previously handled by ecclesiastical judges and husbands, a minor signal of an ongoing process of secularization.

Frequently, husbands refused to provide the stipulated allowances. In court, husbands' justified this by pleading poverty or repudiating the immoral behavior of their wives. If a husband had filed a suit accusing his wife of adultery, he would argue that he had no moral obligation to feed and dress her. The ecclesiastical curia usually agreed with this argument,[28] but this resulted in a reduction of income to the *beaterios*. State and church were unable to sustain the *beaterios* alone. Only occasionally could the archbishopric ensure the payment of a woman's admittance fee and perhaps her first month's allowance, to help safeguard "public morality." So public morality *and* honor cost money, which both the church and husbands were increasingly less willing or able to pay for.

27. AA, CD, L 113, 1892, Beltrán vs. Cerezo. Milagros Cerezos's mother had been paying 8 of the total of 17 soles paid by José Beltrán before he asked that this figure be reduced. Thanks to the combined payments of her mother and her husband, Milagros was at the top of the second-to-highest category. See also Case 0147, AGN, Expedientes Judiciales, L 389/RPJ 386, Expediente 386.8, 1900, Escolástica de Freyre con Augusto Freyre sobre aumento de pensión alimenticia. This case involved a sixty-year-old wife of a colonel. The colonel requested that his wife no longer receive one third of his salary because she owned property and that she be put into a *beaterio*. However, the civil authorities thought it was absurd to request her seclusion since she had already been receiving the money for several years without having been in a *beaterio*.

28. Case 443, AA, CD, L 83, 1804, Argomedo vs. de la Parra.

When monthly allowances went unpaid, the mother superior, in defending the economic interests of the institution, could ask the wife to leave, even if the *provisor* had dictated that she be kept under strict surveillance. As early as the beginning of the century, the mother superior of the Beaterio de Amparadas wrote: "It is custom here that if the husband does not come up with his due allowance after the third day, [his wife] would go out to the street . . . as the *beaterio* does not have the necessary funds to keep so many women."[29]

In an even more radical demand, the nuns in the Beaterio del Patrocinio asked Magdalena Espino to pay a monthly rent of 12 pesos for a room in the building as well as to provide four candles, soap, thread, and shoes. Magdalena reported that the mother superior told her that "if I did not deliver these items she would send me out to the street."[30] And so it happened. Out on the street, Magdalena did not find a job, and the estate she had inherited from her parents was withheld by her husband.

In spite of the recommended procedures to engage in a divorce suit, women could work outside of the *beaterio* ("on the streets"), seek refuge with friends, neighbors, or kin, or in some cases, live off public charity. Many women had never learned a trade and were facing a tight labor market. So leaving a *beaterio* made women dependent on others. In general, none of these options improved a woman's "moral purity," the ostensible purpose for sending a woman to a *beaterio*.

According to social convention, husbands who accused their wives of minor moral transgressions would be more likely to pay monthly allowances than husbands who felt that the transgressions were of such a magnitude that their wives did not merit any support. No matter what the reason (real or perceived), women more often than not experienced hard times in the *beaterio*. Many were soon convinced that it was better to return to marital life. "Marriage reconciliation" was interpreted as the result of the woman's moral improvement, and a husband gained social stature for his consummate generosity in taking her back. However, the motive may have fallen short of generosity. A wife's departure for a *beaterio* meant an increase of family expenditures because somebody had to be hired to do the domestic chores while the wife still had to be supported. Lower- and middle-class people found these expenditures onerous, and *beaterio* payments were often

---

29. Case 532, AA, NM, L 58 (1800–1809), Ruiz vs. Robledo.
30. Case 195, AA, LM, L 7, 1802, Alzado vs. Espino. The couple had been married for sixteen years. He was an Indian bureaucrat in his home town of Magdalena (one of Lima's suburbs). She had been accused of adultery.

withheld. On more than one ocassion, these financial constraints were the prime motivation for "reconciliation," or for letting a wife go off to live on her own.

In 1840 Casimira Valenza was living in the Beaterio de Recogidas with two of her children, both of whom were less than seven years old. Her husband, Manuel Servigon, and her two older children continued to live together. From the *beaterio,* Casimira wrote to the *provisor* telling him that neither she nor her children had anything to eat because Manuel was not paying the monthly allowance. Manuel responded that, in the first place, he had never wished to separate from his wife and that their quarrels had resulted from the interference of third parties. He also mentioned that if his wife would return to him, "the little I give her, added to what I spend on myself and my children, would be enough and more abundant; she would stay at home looking after those unfortunate children, and I would go out to the street to eke out a living."[31] It appears that material convenience could persuade couples to reconsider the benefits of a married life together.

In this scenario, children played a crucial role, not because of the possibility that they could be emotionally damaged (children's emotional necessities were scarcely mentioned), but because the family's economic survival was endangered and children could starve.[32] A woman could enter a *beaterio* with her daughters, but sons could accompany her only until they reached seven years of age, after which they were entrusted to their fathers. There were fathers who argued that neither girls nor boys should be exposed to their mother's bad influence, and sporadically they used this argument to gain custody of their children—also a tactic to oblige a wife to humbly return. In two extreme cases, fathers even asked to be the guardians of children who were still being nursed. These concerns about a child's "moral future" could go so far as to let a child become ill or die while parents quarreled over custody and allowances.[33] Furthermore, children who lived with their

---

31. Case 047, AA, LM, L 9, 1840, Servigon vs. Valenza. See also Case 0224, AA, CD, L 113, 1891, Parodi vs. Ravena. The woman was white, seventeen years old, and the marriage had lasted for five years. They had two daughters, and she was pregnant. Shortly after having been placed in the *beaterio,* the woman asked to leave because a smallpox epidemic had appeared in Lima, and the *beaterio* was located beyond the municipality's declared safe zone.

32. Chapters 9 and 10 provide a more detailed discussion of the role of children in cases of divorce.

33. Case 53a, AA, CD, L 83, 1803, Jayo vs. Balenzuela. Josefa Balenzuela had an eighteen-month-old daughter and was pregnant. She was nursing her daughter at the time she was sent to the *beaterio* because her husband accused her of adulterous behavior. Her husband was a *casta* (*quarterón*), a squadron commander (*cabo del regimiento de Dragones*), and had a hat shop.

mothers in a *beaterio* were subject to its rules: much prayer, isolation, and meager rations (if any). Fathers could force a separation between mother and children in a *beaterio* by refusing to support the child.

The moral goals of the *beaterio* were thus undercut by budgetary constraints. A mother superior was left with few options when faced with a woman who did not have resources to cover her own expenses (even if it was because the husband was failing to provide the residence fees). Many women had no choice but to go into the streets to fend for themselves and their children. In addition to the *beaterio's* structural budgetary problems, men and women both increasingly questioned the rationale for the institution itself. Men complained that *beaterios* no longer restrained licentious wives (the moral issue); women complained that seclusion made it impossible for them to pursue their rights in regard to management of their assets, and their obligations in regard to providing for their children (the economic issue).

The Moral Issue

Although *beaterios* might temporarily alleviate domestic violence, they were primarily—and increasingly—a device to secure a husband's honor. For a woman to seek a divorce was considered equivalent to denying marital responsibility and submission, and it left her open to charges of libertinism and promiscuity. An accepted solution to safeguard a man's honor when a divorce was pending was to isolate the wife from the evils of everyday life and thus rescue her purity in the hopes of returning her later to the safe harbor of marriage.[34] For men the *beaterios* were the place "where women who had abandoned their obligations and despised their husband's honor had to go."[35] "Bad women," who used increased mobility to cheat on their husbands, were feared.[36] Wrote a husband: "When women divorce their

---

The couple had been married for four years. When he failed to pay the monthly allowance, Josefa went to see her husband's military superior, the Marquis of Montemira. The marquis ordered that her husband be sent to jail, and that she could go to an "honest house," in other words, to the home of relatives or friends.

34. See, for example, AA, CD, L 84 and L 87, 1815, Masa vs. Cañedo: "La muger casada desde el momento en que se aparta del Marido, no puede recidir en otro lugar que no sea un depósito seguro, sin arbitrio para mantenerse en la calle."

35. Ibid.

36. Not even Segura, Lima's *costumbrista* writer—we may recall—had been completely sure about his wife's wanderings (Chapter 2).

husbands, they are to be deposited following orders from the court in one of the houses designated for such purposes. They are to be handed over to the mother superior to be isolated from every suspicious communication and to prevent their coming and going, which is so pernicious and odious and against a husband's honor, which these women scoff at under the pretext of seeking divorce."[37]

Many complaints coming from disappointed husbands reached the ears of the vicar general. These included accusations of an "unconstrained atmosphere" in the *beaterios*, where these husbands expected their wives to be morally improved. When Juana Masa and Manuel Cañedo began their divorce suit, Juana was sent to a *beaterio*.[38] Soon Manuel asked the *provisor* for permission to move his wife to a convent because he had no money to pay for her allowance, and he feared that in a *beaterio* she would have the same freedom of movement as she had when she had initially returned to her parents' house. A husband's suspicions grew when his wife had been educated in the *beaterio* in which she had been placed. These wives—husbands argued—were well acquainted with the nuns, who would protect them and allow them to do whatever they wanted.[39]

In principle, life in a *beaterio* was meant to separate women completely from the world, even to the point of occasionally forbidding visits with parents. But rules were frequently ignored, and both the nuns and the secular women enjoyed a great deal of what life had to offer. In complicity with the porch guard or one of the nuns, women managed to receive messages and visitors from the outside, including lovers. In not a few cases, surprised husbands found their wives walking at night on Lima's streets, sometimes alone, sometimes in entertaining company. In spite of the strict regulations regarding the organization of life in the *beaterios*, these institutions—according to judgments forwarded by church officials—failed to impose equality, avoid internal power struggles, or ensure the judicious and heedful dedication to educational and religious purposes. Promises to celebrate a mass or to pray for a deceased person's soul, for which *beaterios* had received donations, went unkept. By the 1820s, people complained that while in the past all the women living in a *beaterio* were obliged to attend mass daily, now

37. Case 53a, AA, CD, L 83, 1803, Jayo vs. Balenzuela.
38. AA, CD, L 84 and L 87, 1815, Masa vs. Cañedo.
39. AA, CD, L 83, 1803, Jayo vs. Balenzuela. Josefa Balenzuela had been reared and educated in the Amparadas *beaterio*. "En este Beaterio de las Recogidas se ha criado la dha. mi Muger desde sus primeros años y es tanta la familiaridad que tiene con la Prelada y religiosas que será dueña de la Puerta y Calles."

"each does as she pleases." The overall picture was one of great internal disorder.

In the early 1800s, husbands complained particularly about the Beaterio de Copacabana, frequently the site of public scandal. Rumor claimed that women entered the *beaterio* only to leave permanently[40] via the roof or even the irrigation channels.[41]

Priests were accused of involvement with secular inmates.[42] Some brief comments on the Copacabana at the end of the nineteenth century show that life within the walls had apparently returned to "normal." By then, the secular women had learned to "behave according to the rules of the house, leave the *beaterio* only in cases of some necessity and with the mother superior's permission, sing in the choir during the day, and at the night wear appropriate dresses."[43]

What was perceived as a return to normality in Copacabana toward the end of the nineteenth century was probably less a real change in behavior than the result of a shifting ethics. By then, it was taken for granted that leaving a *beaterio* in case of necessity was an acceptable option, while earlier it was seen as laxity. Perceptions of the *beaterio*'s functions and internal governance had gradually adapted to new social demands. By 1900 Copacabana's image had been rehabilitated, but Patrocinio took its place as the target of social criticism.[44] I suspect that the poorer the image that society had of a *beaterio*, the greater were the number and the intensity of feminine demands coming from within it and the stricter was a mother superior applying the no-allowance-no-residence rule. In spite of the social differences of *beaterios*' inmates, these institutions brought together women with similar complaints and demands, and experiences were exchanged. Women's shared fears and grievances had a homogenizing effect, which sometimes was expressed in actions of mutual aid among them.[45] Comfort and self-assertion were the

40. AA, LM, L 27 (1800–1809), Mendoza vs. Useda. The husband was asking that his wife be transferred to the Viterbo *beaterio*, and he promised to pay a 12 peso monthly allowance.
41. AGN, RA, CCI, L 68, C 689, N. vs. Ramos.
42. AA, Visita al Beaterio de Copacabana, 1811.
43. AA, L 3 (1860–1921), Razón de las costumbres que se observan en el Beaterio de Nuestra Madre de Copacabana, 1878.
44. AA, Beaterio del Patrocinio, 1857–1899. This document also contains a detailed account of the *beaterio*'s properties.
45. "Se ve obligada á mendigar," mentioned Gregoria García in 1805, "la piedad de las pobres compañeras, que llebadas de conmiseración cristiana la auxilian en lo que pueden, quitándose á las veces de la boca el pan diario de su alimentación." Case 220, AA, CD, L 87, 1805, Hernández vs. García.

result. It is perhaps not by chance that husbands complained about wives' lack of submission after a *beaterio* experience, quite in contrast to their own expectations of encountering a "morally corrected" (that is, more submissive) wife. *Beaterios* were a social battleground of diverging expectations and demands.

Some husbands trying to avoid *beaterio* payments tried to jail their wives. But, judges themselves thought that this was going too far. Women understandably opposed it even more strongly. Prisoners in jail had no legal or civil rights whatsoever.[46] In the course of time, it seems, people accepted the idea that the *beaterio* was not a jail and that women had to be free to leave if they wanted to take care of their worldly business, including their divorce suits. Through the accumulation of complaints, women demonstrated to the judges that seclusion was unjust when husbands used it as a tactic to deprive them of property rights, assets, and even food for themselves and their children. By not paying, husbands forced their wives to find income alternatives, and as this became more common, the *beaterio* option lost ground. The family's economic survival mattered even more than the cherished discourses on male honor.

The Economic Issue

Once women were in the *beaterio*, they could pursue an ecclesiastical suit petitioning for divorce, while at the same time beginning a civil suit in which they claimed their shares of marital assets. A woman's success or failure in her suits would determine the size of her maintenance allowance in the *beaterio*, and, more importantly, her alimony following the divorce. However, to push her demands in both courts, a woman needed help from someone outside of the *beaterio* to manage her affairs, and such a person

---

46. In 1815 Lucía Vega initiated a lawsuit against her husband, Pedro José Barba, a silversmith with a public shop, accusing him of "double adultery." In response, Pedro sued *her* for adulterous behavior. Nothing happened to him, but she was escorted to prison. Shortly afterward, Lucía complained to the *provisor*, describing how *beaterios* and jails were compared: "[Mi depósito . . .] debe verificarse en Casa honesta, como Beaterio, ó Monasterio, y nunca en Carceles, ó parecidas vejaminosas reclusiones, que mas tienen de pena, que de custodia de las personas, ofreciendo esto el inconveniente de frustrar qualquiera condescendencia, ó prestación de la Encarcelada á unirse, ó transar el Pleito, que nunca se concibe libre, sino estorsionada, y Coacta en quien sufre la Carcelería." Case 626, AA, CD, L 87 (1815–20), 1815, Barba vs. Vega.

was not easy to find. An independently wealthy woman (one who had at least rescued her jewelry from her husband's grip) could speed her legal proceedings by hiring a lawyer, but most women were dependent on the husband's support, and as a litigant in the suit, he clearly had little incentive to help forward her case. Lawyers and *litis expensas* were expensive, and the average woman could nearly starve if she attempted to meet these costs on her own. Each document and petition had a specified price.[47] Simply by not paying support, husbands could delay the conclusion of a suit to the point that even the most assertive of wives might give up and settle for a reconciliation. However, reconciliation did not necessarily mean that the couple lived together again.

Women—for their part—were less and less willing to go into seclusion. Although a *beaterio* could provide protection from a violent husband and (despite the best intentions of the church) often proved to be a relatively free environment for its residents, women recognized that they lost control over their material well-being while interned in the *beaterio*. Women in seclusion had little or no influence over what their husbands did with their common property. Maria Basurto, an Arequipa resident, came to Lima to defend her rights. In a letter to Lima's archbishop she wrote: "It is not fair, Your Excellency, to send me to a jail [she was referring to the Instituto del Buen Pastor] that will deprive me from pursuing my defense and impede that I make use of my rights."[48] This forthright notion of unfairness gradually spread and became a prevalent argument by 1900.

Of the women who presented a lawsuit in the ecclesiastical court between 1800 and 1820, 38 (13.7 percent) continued their legal quarrels in the ecclesiastical curia, and 9 (2.3 percent) in the civil courts; between 1840 and 1860, 25 (17.2 percent) went to the ecclesiastical curia and 8 (5.5 percent) to civil courts; and between 1890 and 1910, 5 (2.4 percent) continued their fight in the curia, and 5 (2.4 percent) in civil courts. The combined effects of the decay of *beaterios* as a secluding device and women's greater capacity to solve their problems on their own instead of using the courts explain the sharp drop of second and third trials later in the century. Women had learned that they were on their own.

---

47. Contrary to what happened in Mexico, where legal services were free to the poor, in Lima no one was exempt from paying. Filing fees were: decree, 4 reales; *auto,* 7 reales; declaration, 3 pesos; notification, 1 peso; presenting a document, 4 reales; an appraisal (*derechos de tasación*), 3 pesos and 5 reales. See, for example, AA, CD, L 86 (1802–4), Villar vs. Olivera.

48. Case 0335, AA, CD (1890–1910). L 113 1891–2. Basurto vs. Lopez.

By law men had the right and obligation to administer a family's wealth. The underlying "philosophical principle" stated that "the administration of marital goods needs to be in a husband's hands, and women are to be in charge of the children and the family; marital power [that is, husbands' power over their wives] can not be ignored: men's and women's spheres are different, but if women were given more rights to make the same decisions as their husbands, and not obliged to obey their husbands, both heads of household [!] will fight over their respective prerogatives and, as a consequence, both will suffer" (García Calderón Sr. 1879, 1317–19).[49] This did not change when a woman entered a *beaterio*. The husband retained control of wealth until the courts decided otherwise, the couple obtained a divorce, or one of the spouses died. As long as no resolution was reached, husbands were entrusted with everything. Thus, husbands tended to prolong lawsuits as long as possible, and wives in the *beaterio* had to file claims against them for squandering marital goods. Women of all backgrounds were victims of husbands who delayed the legal procedures and profligately wasted the family's assets.

The families of Doña Josefa Encalada and Don Francisco Zárate had arranged their marriage. When their marital conflict started, Doña Josefa valued her assets at 100,000 pesos, in addition to several *fincas* that produced a 6,000 peso annual rent. In a letter written in the *beaterio*, she argued that her husband was living off these funds while she had to content herself with a 200 peso monthly allowance.[50] This extremely unjust situation led her to petition that someone else be put in charge of administering the family assets. Don Francisco was obliged to come quickly to terms with Doña Josefa, which he did. He declared his willingness to leave the administration of her assets in her hands if he, in turn, received an indemnity for the opportunities he had lost because of marrying Doña Josefa in the first place, such as losing *patronatos* and *capellanías* (rents and interests on landed property) to other male members of his family. He asked for a 1,200 peso annual pension from his wife's landed properties. She accepted this trade-off, and shortly afterward, in 1831, the civil suit was dropped by mutual agreement.[51]

Around the same time, but at a much lower level in the social hierarchy, Petronila Velasco accused her husband, Justo Anglade, of adultery

---

49. García Calderón (1879, 1317–19) shows how these principles were translated and are represented in Peru's 1852 civil code, and how the "philosophical climate" of the day simply restated men's prerogatives.

50. This is the highest alimony requested at any point in the century.

51. AGN, CS, CCI, L 104, 1831, Zarate vs. Encalada.

and mistreatment, and demanded alimony. Petronila claimed two slaves as her own property, which her husband was now using for himself. "This small income constitutes all I have and, thus, I cannot allow Don Justo to administer it," she wrote. "His squandering and all the pressures he exerted on me while we were still together to sell this slim means of earning a living are more than enough reasons to deny him the control, which is only given to husbands who don't have Don Justo's vices and who behave quite differently."[52] Petronila accepted the legal and social rules of the game (that other wiser and more prudent husbands should be allowed to administer conjugal assets) but claimed that *her* husband could not be trusted because of his lack of character and dependability. If enough witnesses corroborated the husband's incompetence, the court would ask him to return the goods—unless, of course, they had already been squandered.

Such attitudes were not exclusive to Lima's white or *mestizo* population. María del Rosario Soriano, a black woman, accused her husband, Juan Ramos, who was also black, of adultery and mistreatment. He had threatened her life, and she asked to be admitted to the Beaterio de Amparadas. Her husband kept a slave that she claimed was her own. María del Rosario argued that if the slave were given to her, she would be able to stay in the *beaterio* without requiring her husband to pay any allowance, "because the wages the slave could earn would be enough money for a decent monthly allowance."[53] In this case, however, the *provisor* did not agree to the divorce, and he decreed that the couple should reunite. Whenever there was the slightest sign that a marriage could be reconciled, property rights became a secondary priority. The ecclesiastical curia understood that María was looking for economic independence from her husband, an act endangering the bond of holy matrimony. In addition, "only" mistreatment and adultery were involved—occurrences too common to be taken seriously—no mismanagement on Juan's part could be proven.

Two cases involving Indian women, one who had inherited land from her parents and another who worked in a liquor shop, help us complete the picture across the social spectrum of the struggles that occurred over common property in the *beaterio*. In 1809 Estefanía Quispilloc had been in the

---

52. Case 628, AGN, Cabildo, CCI, L 8, C 82, Anglade vs. Velasco. A similar case was presented by Juana Gómez in 1860. She had been married to Andrés Zaya for thirteen years, during which time she had suffered from beatings and mistreatment and the humiliation of seeing her husband's concubines. All her witnesses were peasants and supported her accusations against her husband. The court granted the divorce and returned her cattle.

53. Case 585, AA, NM, L 58 (1799–1809), Ramos vs. Soriano.

Copacabana *beaterio* for two months, during which time her husband gave her 8 pesos per month for her maintenance. She claimed that this was not enough money to buy soap, shoes, and other essential items. Moreover, she argued that these monthly payments came not from her husband's income but from money he received from rents on her land, and he was keeping for himself the difference between the 8 pesos and what the rents actually brought in.[54] With great perspicacity, Estefanía asked that the amount she received be adjusted to equal the rents. If this increase was granted, she would be able to file a civil suit to regain her inherited possessions. She did not run the risk of being returned to her husband, and by asking that her allowance be increased to a fair share, she was also creating a precedent as to the value of this land as well as establishing that it belonged to her.

Evarista Francia, an Indian woman, had been forced as a very young girl to marry Francisco Baca.[55] She, too, challenged the legitimacy of her seclusion during the divorce proceedings. Around 1850, after ten years of marriage, she was accused of treating her husband as a "domestic and a servant." They jointly owned a liquor shop, where she worked side by side with him. According to Evarista, she was in charge of selling the liquor and managing the shop, whereas Francisco frittered away their earnings and was drunk most of the time. Her anger increased when he accused her of adultery and put her in the Beaterio de Amparadas. While there, she learned that her husband had been selling liquor behind her back and then spending the profits. Evarista's case was particularly difficult because her father was convinced of her adultery and sided with her husband. Evarista argued that "this imprisonment is not fair given the character of the suit [because Amparadas is the *beaterio* for] criminal prostitutes." She insisted that her husband had not proven his accusations and that her assets must be taken care of. In other words, she offset all moral claims by asserting her economic rights. However, she lost the case.

All these women were afraid that a husband's dishonest behavior would be their ruin. Even when a woman's daily sustenance was guaranteed, she could still lose access to her inheritance or the property gained through

54. Case 490, AA, CD, L 87 (1815–20), Dávalos vs. Quispilloc.
55. Case 814, AA, CD L 91 (1848–53), Francia vs. Baca. She wrote: "[a] espenzas de mi padre no se asía otra cosa que sacrificarme con ponerme en el duro caso de sobrellevar la fuerza con que se me obligó a contraher un matrimonio, que la opinión pública sensora de los prosedimientos lo rechazaba". Pero agregaba "como el deber de un hijo es consagrar el respeto de sus padres, tube que desprenderme de algunas iluciones."

her own work.[56] "Work" was an "abstract asset" difficult to quantify and recover because it left no visible traces or tangible value. Women without any verifiable property could only ask for alimony and thus were largely at the mercy of their husbands.

Toward midcentury women's resistance to seclusion grew, especially among those earning a wage. Women sought alternatives to the *beaterio*, such as taking up residence in a godmother's house, the parental home, or homes of friends who had positive social reputations. But increasingly, as shown earlier, more women remained on their own. By now, a woman knew that by accepting seclusion in a *beaterio* she risked losing her economic contribution to the marriage. Seclusion meant waiving her right to work and her control of conjugal property and usually led to poverty.

Remarried widows were somewhat better off. They were wiser, but more important, they could use children from previous marriages to negotiate the intervention of third parties to guarantee the safety of the assets belonging to the offspring. Very few remarried widows secluded themselves, or were secluded, in *beaterios*, but when they did, they already had an intermediary to administer their assets directly. Even then some husbands managed to evade an intermediary's actions simply by hiding assets or claiming poverty.[57]

Sometimes a temporary seclusion in a *beaterio* could have unexpected outcomes, especially when assets and income were involved. In 1854 Manuela Carvajal and Salvador Palavicino had been married for eight years. For seven years prior to the marriage, Manuela had earned a livelihood for herself and a daughter from her first marriage. Her guardian, who had raised her and had treated her like a daughter, would occasionally lend her money to plant beans on a plot owned by the Count de la Torre. Because Manuela had been receiving money from "another man," Salvador prosecuted her for adultery, stating that "although I am a poor man living from my labor, I will, by God's law and in order to live in peace with my conscience, sacrifice a part of my earnings to put this wretched woman in a *beaterio*."[58]

---

56. "Si abraso el depósito y dexo la Tienda de mi labor, quedo yo y mis hijas solo á las expensas de Don Diego, y si este no me ministra los sufragios precisos para llenar estos deberes, como asi sucederá por su indolencia, y por su desvaratada conducta, quedaremos todas expuestas á la mendicidad." Case 532 was followed up in several court cases: AA, NM, L 58, 1805, Ruiz vs. Robledo; AA, LM, L 7 (1800–1809); LM, L 8, 1811; CD, L 87, 1816; CD, L 84, 1805; AGN, Cabildo, CCI, L 14, C 209, 1808.
57. Case 953, AA, CD, L 90, 1845, Porras vs. Quirós.
58. Case 772, AA, CD, L 92, 1854, Carvajal vs. Palavicino.

In 1854 the *provisor* ruled that Salvador would have to pay 17 pesos per month to his wife in the *beaterio*. This represented slightly less than 75 percent of his income as a *mayordomo* (administrator) at the *hacienda* Chuquitanta (where he earned about 25 pesos per month). But the judges knew that the couple's income was much higher and included income from an *almidonería* (a shop in which clothes were starched), which they had established and operated together, and from land the couple jointly cultivated.

Salvador's arguments to justify secluding his wife were based on principles of honor and conscience. Manuela resisted entering a *beaterio* by showing how she was kept on the short leash: "It is hard to understand how I could feed myself, rear a daughter, and pay for the legal proceedings with seventeen pesos, and all this while hidden in a *beaterio*, unable to engage in judicial action on my own and dependent on others to seek out sewing work for me.... Seventeen pesos are not elastic, nor do I have Jesus Christ's virtues of being able to divide up five loaves." Her comments reveal that she knew that in the *beaterio* her independence would end and that she would have to rely on others to help her find work as a seamstress (the desired occupational alternative for "honest women"). Without her own resources, she would never be able to pay legal expenses to defend herself. Her future depended on how well she fared in her divorce suit, and on how her labor would be recognized by the civil authorities and by her husband.

Because the joint income was necessary for their survival, Manuela and Salvador ultimately resorted to an intermediate solution: Salvador dropped his initial charges of adultery; Manuela left the *beaterio* but did not return to live with her husband. If they had separated legally, both would have experienced severe hardship. An agreed-upon separation, negotiated outside the court, was a better solution financially. The more a woman participated in the family economy, the less viable it was to send her to a *beaterio*. A tacit divorce came into being, which diminished the role of *beaterios* (and the ecclesiastical court and the church as well).

Men also found ways to reconcile the nonpayment of allowances with their wives' continued seclusion by voluntarily adjudicating a portion of (often uncertain) family rents to pay for a wife's maintenance in a *beaterio*. This was a means to disentangle oneself from a ongoing commitment to support a wife, transfer the risks of an uncertain future to her, and, last but not least, perpetuate the existence of *beaterios*. The conflict in 1846 between Doña Juana Enríquez and her husband, Don Esteban Jiménez, a *diputado* (deputy) from the province of Huarochirí and a landowner, illustrates the perceptions and implications of this alternative.[59]

For ten years Don Esteban failed to pay the monthly allowance of 50 pesos that the court had decreed when he first placed his wife in the Beaterio del Patrocinio. Within her first eleven months in the *beaterio*, the mother superior had already indicated that Doña Juana did not have any other alternative but to leave and find work in the streets. Between then and 1856, according to Doña Juana, "he has decided to play the angel by pretending to comply with the law. However, this is just a tactic to delay the proceedings, and he stands there waiting to see whether he will have to pay. He gains time and paralyzes the legal course of action. By always waiting until the last moment, he seeks to perpetuate my horrifying needs, my hunger, and my deplorable situation."

Confronted with the threat of his wife leaving the *beaterio*, Don Esteban assigned half the rents from a house to support his wife, an amount—he argued—higher than the 50 peso monthly allowance. When Doña Juana claimed that he owed her 3,500 pesos for overdue support, Don Esteban responded that this "was one of the cases in which the obligation to provide for food ceases to exist, because the person receiving [this rent] has now an enhanced position according to article 261 of the Civil Code and article 1423 of the Code of Proceedings."

The house had been bought during their marriage, thus, according to law, half of the house would be her acquest after divorce. By delaying the divorce proceedings and prolonging Doña Juana's stay in the *beaterio*, Don Esteban perpetuated his right to administer the property. Whether the tenants paid or not, or the rent went up or down, was Doña Juana's problem; *he* had fulfilled his obligation toward her. Initiated in the ecclesiastical court in 1846, this lawsuit was reopened in the same court two years later, and then again in civil court in 1856. It was only then, in 1856, that the acquest issue was set straight. The court decreed that Don Esteban pay the outstanding 3,500 pesos, and even threatened him with confiscating his belongings if he were found guilty of further delaying the proceedings.

This case shows the enormous bargaining ground in which husbands could maneuver to circumvent allowance responsibilities and also how

---

59. Case 796. Between 1846 and 1856, this case was presented in several trials: AA, CD, L 90, 1846, Jiménez vs. Enriquez; AA, NM, L 63, 1848; AGN, CS, CCI, L 617, 1856 (Juicio de alimentos); AGN, CS, CCI, L 613, 1856 (Juicio sobre posesión de una finca).

moral assumptions (honor and seclusion) undermined women's economic rights. The time gap between the ecclesiastical court action and the civil court proceedings also illustrate how long a wife could find herself trapped in the church-marriage-honor triangle before asserting her rights. The ten-years duration of this case—and we do not know if Don Esteban actually paid the outstanding amount to his wife in 1856—represented a quarter of a lifetime in midcentury Peru.

Women of very unequal social backgrounds and very different ethnicities, struggled to take back control. However, only in exceptionally well-documented cases—such as the one above—did the civil courts side with a wife. Only if a woman could prove her husband's irresponsibility or was rich enough to satisfy her husband's demand for monetary compensation could she prevail. The lower a woman's social status and the fewer "exceptional" proofs she could offer, the higher the probability of the court dismissing a claim for self-management, especially if it could be argued that something more precious—the marriage—was at stake. Nevertheless, in all cases, women revealed a clear notion of their property rights and of the dangers of seclusion in a *beaterio*.

In short, the institutionalized control of marital conflict marginalized women still further from access to common property. Only a few legal opportunities existed to rescue at least something, even if it was only a claim for support that in reality would never be paid. Such struggles sent a message: something was terribly unfair about how the law, the judges, and the system dealt with women's hunger and women's property rights. In the long run, women's insistence on justice for themselves and their children, both in the *beaterios* and—as will be discussed in subsequent chapters—outside of them, led to a rethinking of prevailing rules.

Some Final Thoughts

Barrios, ecclesiastical regulations, and *beaterios* were an integral part of people's lives and an arena for the expression and handling of marital conflicts. In some sense, *beaterios* were an extension of the *barrios* and church regulations: *barrios* applied popular rules and perceptions, *beaterios* represented institutionalized morality. Both "regulated" marital behavior and by doing so underlined how Lima's society envisaged marriage, honor, and moral conflicts and their possible solutions. In the role of mediators, neighbors, ecclesiastical courts, and, specifically, *beaterios* played a crucial role in defining gender roles and in shielding marriages against conflict and disruption. Over time, people continued to air opinions on neighbors' domestic problems, whereas *beaterios* lost influence.

Until midcentury, *beaterios* were primarily a refuge for women; thereafter, they became institutions through which husbands sought to preserve morality and to counter women's defense of their economic rights and their evasion of marital control. Throughout the second half of the nineteenth century, couples resorted less to *beaterios*, signaling husbands' difficulties in dealing with the arguments brought forward by their wives, who had begun to replace moral rules and notions of honor with denunciations against the injustice of seclusion, arbitrary dependence on a husband's allowance, and the mismanagement and squandering of women's common-property assets.

The gradual decline of the *beaterios* signals a changing perception of divorce and conjugal life and illustrates a decreasing capacity to control marital conflict through institutional means. Women living in *beaterios* created new ways to approach these domestic conflicts, but women who lived outside the *beaterios* noticed the changes too. Because *beaterios* were basically a "female issue," what happened within them was discussed widely in Lima. Such talk based on shared experiences lay at the heart of women's increasing resistance to entering a *beaterio*. Women understood that seclusion in the name of their own or their husbands' honor weakened their capacity to control what happened to their assets. Fewer husbands were willing or able to pay the costs for maintaining a wife in a *beaterio*, either because they really did not have the means to do so or because they came to distrust the beaterios' suitability as a means to improve their wives' morality.

Thus, in the course of the century, the existence of *beaterios* helped to bring forward ideas regarding the consequences of inequality between the sexes. Those women who by virtue of their poverty, race, or insertion into the labor market did not figure in men's struggle to maintain their honor reacted to this injustice as much as did better-off women. More and more, the resolution of conflict became secularized, leading to the growing importance of the legal aspects involving conjugal assets. It is also true that among the lower classes other types of "economic arrangements" were increasingly pursued, such as the handing over of rents or a de facto separation. In spite of the fact that the *beaterio* reflected in miniature the social differences of society at large, women from different social strata had shared problems, and they eventually engaged in a common struggle while in the *beaterio* together. Once they returned to life outside the walls, there was little an Indian shoemaker's wife had in common with a white merchant's wife.

In spite of the increasing success of the arguments put forward by women, certain social structures, including *beaterios*, had surprising longevity. This may be because they were modest stores of wealth in which the church had invested some moral authority. With the decay of *beaterios*, the church lost an important institution to safeguard marriages and families and to control female morality. However, *beaterios* and conjugal conflict resolution were but two of the church's many trenches. On much broader grounds, the church impelled almost all aspects of female/male and intergenerational relationships in the premarital arena and in marriage itself.

PART II

Couples and Everyday Life

Beyond the institutional means to control, foment, and establish family life and marriage, liberal ideas also found their way into the even more subtle workings of everyday life, of family life, of gender relations. The neighborhoods, the church, and the state—as seen in the previous chapters—had a definite say in how people thought and behaved. With many drawbacks, and confronting many levels of individual and collective resistance, some more liberal forms of thinking began to permeate life in the city. Neighbors intervened to help women and families in need, no matter if they were married or not, and thus helped shape a gender ethic that restrained abusive husbands and adulterous wives. The mechanisms the church used to maintain influence in peoples' lives (dispensations, consent, dissent, incompatibility) were reformulated and adapted to changing living conditions and were expanded to encompass more life situations that in some way reflected a heterogenous multiethnic reality. The redefinition of institutional means also meant a shift toward more secular outlooks. It was not a one blow secularization project. To the contrary, it was a secularization that resulted from the accumulation of arguments in many different realms of life as the content of dispensations shifted toward worldly consideration beyond the confines of the church's definition of impediments, consent and dissent. Interpretations were expanded to encompass social pressures as hampering the expressions of free will, and in doing so, revealed the way in which these social pressures were at work. In nineteenth-century Lima, sexual incompatibility was reinterpreted as character incompatibility while at the same time making sex taboo. And *beaterios*, traditionally under the aegis of the church, became state-regulated entities to shelter women, albeit still under the internal rule of nuns.

Such subtle changes were the result of decades of legal argumentation in the ecclesiastical, and increasingly, civil courtrooms, especially through arguments brought forward by women who argued their cases, their humanity, and their rights (or rather the injustices they suffered because of existing rulings and expectations). These trends in the institutional background became even more visible when women argued in civil court for their very earthly belongings, earnings, and assets. Such economic arguments transversed the prematrimonial arena (Chapter 6), affected the way in which dowries were conceived, understood, and readapted (Chapter 7), and shaped the way in which women used moral contradictions to enhance their access to property, to finally being heard by grudging judges and resilient husbands (Chapters 8 and 9).

This second part deals with the arguments brought forward by very different kinds of women in civil matters and with how such matters, in turn, signal a process of adaptation to liberal ideals: personal rights and freedom, equal opportunities, and civil rights.

6

Women and the Dangers of Premarital Sex

Since the Council of Trent in 1563, the Roman Catholic Church had incessantly tried to impose on society restrictive moral codes, especially concerning sex. In contrast to the leniency afforded dispensations, and consent and dissent issues, society viewed sexual transgression as an alarming instigator of moral and social disorder, notwithstanding the central involvement of priests in moral scandal as was seen in Chapter 4. According to the church, sex should take place within marriage; premarital and extramarital sex were condemned. However, illegitimacy rates in Lima remained high throughout the nineteenth century, indicating a serious weakness in the church's control over this intimate sphere of life.[1] A high percentage of Lima's inhabitants did not comply with the church's sexual and courtship rules—or at least failed to follow the dictated schedule for rites of sexual passage—instead marrying after having had sexual relations, and even after having one or more children, or not marrying at all.

In ecclesiastical and civil courts, men and women defended having engaged in premarital sex. Their justifications reveal important perceptions

---

1. For a detailed account of illegitimacy rates, see Chapter 1. Here it is important to note that illegitimacy registers in matrimonial licenses represent illegitimacy rates among people who, having been born illegitimate, later married legally (thus leaving a record of illegitimacy in the marriage file). Thus, these percentages represent the "lower boundaries" of illegitimacy rates in Lima.

of sexuality and gender relations, including the central role of virginity. Supremely important in law, family life, and interpersonal relationships, virginity was a central issue both before and after marriage. Its social weight was perpetuated in order to disqualify many women—like the ones we will encounter here—as "serious" contenders for matrimony. Once virginity was lost, a woman was worth less because she also lost her social standing and perhaps even the support of her family.

This chapter's central aim is to discuss the social and personal character of premarital sex in nineteenth-century Lima. Such an analysis helps to explain the growing number of children born out of wedlock and to understand the plight of "natural mothers." Premarital sex (especially in the form of rape or elopement) was a way of escaping social predicaments. Rape or elopement could erode race and class boundaries; and sexual relations and the notion of "corrupted" virginity were bargaining chips used by lower-class women to challenge the elites' and the church's moral proscriptions. Social hierarchy was undermined, and with it, the way in which Lima's elites had envisioned a new world dominated by liberal ideas. Moreover, elites themselves often had much to hide.

Escaping Social Predicaments

Elopement and rape were transgressions of both the moral code and civil law. They represent extreme instances of illicit premarital sexual relations and a distortion of the normal course of courtship. In some cases, these acts functioned as techniques to circumvent family expectations or ecclesiastical surveillance.[2] In spite of the flexible handling of consent and dissent issues, elopement and rape could force an unwilling consent from either a woman or her parents. Abduction could circumvent the impediments of affinity, consanguinity, or religious vows. It also leveled social hierarchy. In a multi-ethnic setting such as Lima, deviations signal a mechanism used to bypass "inequality." Convincing a woman to leave her parents' house or raping her, particularly if she was of a higher social class than the seducer or rapist, could occasionally win a man marriage into a family of better social standing.

---

2. In Europe since at least the twelfth century, elopement has been understood as a way to diminish parental authority (Sheehan 1978, 13).

Although courts often did not reprimand rapists, imprisonment or an indemnity could be mandated. When the rapist was willing to marry his victim and she consented to the marriage, all charges were dropped.[3] Punishment depended on the conditions under which rape had taken place, and even more on who the victim and the victimizer were. Cultural traditions also made it difficult to clearly delineate what constituted rape. During popular festivities (such as carnivals),[4] crowds allowed for anonymity. In many Indian peasant villages, there were (and still are) fiestas in which "rape" is a ritualized communal affair.[5]

Law and society made provisions to compensate victims rather than to punish offenders of sexual transgressions. The reasoning behind this was that by losing her virginity a raped *doncella* (virgin) became less marriageable. Lost virginity by itself was an insufficient argument to obtain monetary compensation or to make a suitor marry his victim. Lima's judges were more inclined to favor a case in which the issue of "lost virginity" was seconded by a proven accusation of rape. If the rapist was willing to marry the woman and she freely consented, the cause for punishment had vanished. Rape was understood as a moral and social offense rather than as a violation of a woman's body or a physical attack. Punishment was most severe when the victim and the rapist were of a similar social standing or when the victim was under twelve years of age. When men resorted to drugs, the law also considered women victims, even if they had consented to have intercourse (García Calderón Sr. 1879, 923–24).

In 1800 Pablo Núñez y Ansures, a descendant of Spanish parents, claimed that his daughter Manuela had been abducted and raped by Severino de los Santos, a black man.[6] Severino responded that Manuela was a willing participant: "She told me she wanted to marry me even if I was black, and she

---

3. AGN, Corte Superior, CCR, L 64, 1840, Causa seguida contra Don José Oriamuno por estupro a joven doncella en noche de Carnaval. "Los desfloradores de muger virjen ó doncella por la fuerza y la violencia son verdaderos estupradores, y estan comprendidos en la cuarta clase de los delitos públicos. La Ley 1ra. del referido Título y Partida le imponen la pena de dotar a la Desflorada o casarse con ella, con otras que las LL. Recopiladas, dejan al arbitrio del Juez." How the notion of dowry in exchange for virginity was handled will be discussed in Chapter 7.

4. See, for example, AGN, Corte Superior, CCR, L 64, 1840, Causa seguida contra Don José Oriamuno por estupro a joven doncella en noche de Carnaval.

5. For a case in Matucana, a small town in Lima's outskirts, in 1809, see Case 295, AA, NM, L 58 (1799–1809), Llacsayauri vs. de Ochoa.

6. Case 412, AGN, RA, CCR, L 91, C 1127, 1800, Causa seguida por Pablo Nuñez y Ansures contra Severino de los Santos por estupro de Manuela Nuñez, su hija.

also assured me that if she did not go ahead with her plans, her parents would bury her in a monastery, cut her hair, and dress her in a bag for her whole life." Manuela confirmed the kidnapper's assertions. Soon afterward, the church called for an explanation for the father's "irrational opposition." At the outset, the dissenting argument focused on race. However, the church's representatives failed to perceive a great racial disparity between Manuela and Severino, and they asked for proof. No evidence was presented, but a new argument subsequently appeared in the records. Race was replaced by a new dichotomy: "undistinguished family" versus "distinguished family." Severino's pride was at stake. He had been willing to acknowledge his darker skin, but not his less distinguished ancestry. He contended that he was the grandson of a *cacique*, an ethnic leader of an Indian community, and as such he had to be considered a *mestizo* and not a black person. "And because I am a *mestizo*, it cannot be said I am humble and of low origin, as Don Pablo [Manuela's father] says, because neither *mestizos* nor those descending from them are perceived to be of low status. To the contrary, many have achieved honorable positions in the civil and ecclesiastical professions and Your Majesty does not hesitate to engage them."[7]

Multiple layers of racial and ethnic perceptions intertwine in this quote, and we find a rare demonstration of ethnic self-perception by a nonwhite person. Aggressiveness and self-assertion were necessary weapons in an ethnically endogamous society. Manuela's fears of seclusion, a long-standing relationship between both partners, including a *sponsalia*, and the racial prejudices of Manuela's father left few doubts about the probity of this marriage. In spite of the good arguments in favor of this union, elopement was a necessary vehicle to gain social acceptance and, perhaps, individual catharsis that would ameliorate mutually perceived racial differences. Individuals might be successful in circumventing prejudices, but in society at large many people tended to magnify racial disparity to stress their own whiteness: a *mestizo* became a black person. Fear of social change led those classified as "white" to scapegoat darker-skinned people; and they took aim at blacks, *castas, mestizos,* and Indians. Disputes were expressed in racially derogatory terms: "The *castas*'s insolence makes Spanish people, be they Spaniards or Creoles, the victims of their sanguine audacity," said Doña Antonia Rivera in 1805.[8] People who held such prejudices were very unwilling

---

7. See also Case 4, AGN, RA, CCR, L 7, C 70, 1800, Abril/Damasco Tirado.
8. Case 259, AGN, RA, CCR, L 104, C 1264, 1805, Autos criminales seguidos por Doña Antonia Rivera contra Marcelina Seminario (samba), por las graves injurias en agravio de su

to give their daughters away in marriage to somebody perceived as racially inferior. Increasingly, the practice of miscegenation and an emerging pride in being a *mestizo* made it difficult for parents to find arguments against an unwanted marriage, especially if their daughters gave their consent. In this sense, elopement, abduction, or rape, and the consequent loss of virginity, were a complicated way to undermine entrenched racial hierarchies.

Aware of the limits of dissent arguments based on increasingly blurred racial and economic boundaries, parents would sometimes pretend they knew nothing of their daughters' schemes. An elopement allowed parents to avoid formally dissenting, which would amount to publicly acknowledging their impotence in preventing a marriage they should have opposed according to public opinion. After elopement, moral sanctions ranked higher than racial fears, and this absolved parents' of social criticism. Now they were expected to actively encourage marriage to avoid illegitimacy, unless the disparity between the eloped lovers was too great. Ideally, after elopement each spouse performed his or her respective vows, duties, and promises, leading to family reconciliation. Thus, elopement and consummation created space for negotiation in a society where racial hierarchies were otherwise rigidly fixed.

As in Agustina Olazabal's case (Chapter 4),[9] elopement was a relatively simple and straightforward arrangement: both partners agreed to a plan of escape, trusting that a wedding would follow soon after. But this was not always what happened; marriage after elopement could be postponed— sometimes forever. At the outset, romance could prevail, but more often, romantic notions crumbled in the face of harsh daily reality. Love was not always a central motive. Rapists, as well as occasional and career seducers of women, used elopement to obtain immediate sexual triumph or satisfaction. One way of socially disparaging a woman was to dishonor her, and the most effective way to do that was to sexually assault her, either through seduction or rape, and then make it public.

Women knew that men's intentions could be ambivalent, a thought that was threatening to them, and that may be a reason why they let priests bless their "hidden parts." All women who had surrendered their virginity before marriage were immoral, even in the eyes of the seducer. Distrust of men's real intentions was especially acute among women who engaged

---

persona, hecho ocurrido el día 25 de junio de 1805 en la vía pública, para la que solicita una sanción de acuerdo a su delito.

9. Case 417, AA, LM, L 8 (1810–17), Olaxábal vs. Fernándes Pasqua/Carreño; see pp. 128ff.

in sexual relations with men of higher social standing. The consequences of premarital sex, especially if no marriage followed, were class specific. Rich women married downward, but usually married; poor women usually remained single, bore illegitimate children, and occasionally obtained some compensation for their lost virginity or for their children. A woman of good social and economic status who had had premarital intercourse, had eloped, or had been raped or abducted had to be content with a husband who was beneath her because, or so ran the argument, he was willing to forget his pride to save her reputation and more corruption and mischief. He thus became her savior and was entitled to a dowry, together with her loyalty and eternal submission. However, if marriage did not follow elopement or rape, it was better for both the victim and her family to make as little commotion as possible. Once a trial began and witnesses were called, a woman's honor and aura of chastity could be lost forever. This would happen even when a woman could at least win compassion by portraying herself as the victim of male violence.

Between Rape and Seduction

The hazy line between gentility and villainy led many women to disaster. Women could cry rape, but few of them publicly accused their seducers. One of the few brave women who dared to take her case to the courts was Matilde Costa.[10] She had been born in Lima and, in 1890, was seventeen years old. The man she accused of rape had lived with her mother and was the father of Matilde's four half-siblings. In her deposition, Matilde described what had happened:

> For two years, Brondi [the rapist] tried to win me over with affectionate words, and he finally obtained what he wanted; but when he knew that I would go back to the school of Señora Isabel Suárez de Scaramone, he told me that it would be a shame and scandal to appear in my present state (referring to the fact that I was to be a mother). It was my mother who two years before [when Matilde was thirteen years old] had taken me to the house of the Brondi family, leaving

10. Case 0107, AGN, Expedientes Judiciales, CCR, L s.n., 1890, Querella instaurada por Doña Martha Andrade contra Don José Brondi por seducción, rapto y estupro.

me there while she went to work on the land. I entered this house pure and innocent . . . and this was how I remained for the next two years. On June 28, 1890, my mother took me away from there, but a month before I had already lost my virginity. Brondi used violence to disgrace me. I was ashamed and did not tell my mother. . . . It was daytime when he attacked me, but nobody saw him do it; there were other people in the house, but I did not scream, fearing everyone would know.

Since then, "He took me to the Padre Gerónimo street . . . where he installed me in an interior room, and immediately left. He did not come back until the next day between seven and eight at night. At around ten he left again and in this way continued to visit me daily, sometimes during the day, sometimes during the night. I remained in this situation until November 13 [approximately one month]."

Brondi's sister, who acted as a witness on her brother's behalf, tried to prove that Matilde had agreed to continue having sex with her brother. But, curiously enough, she also claimed that Matilde was pregnant before she lost her virginity, a blasphemy to ecclesiastical ears—after all, only Mary the mother of Jesus could conceive a child while being a virgin.[11] This may explain why, in spite of the absence of eyewitnesses, Brondi was condemned to a three-year prison term and required to provide support payments for the unborn child. In an environment in which institutions were unsympathetic to this kind of plight of women, it was a drastic punishment. The harshness might also be because of Matilde's very young age and because Matilde and Brondi were of similar social standing, white and lower-middle class. In cases of greater social disparity, judges were much less inclined to penalize rape and seduction. They were convinced that accusations against socially superior men were used by lower-class women to obtain financial benefits or even a husband of higher class standing. If admitted, these accusations would undermine social order. Judges also knew that often the dividing line between rape and "voluntary rape" was vague. This was especially true for rape accusations against men who lived close to their victims.

Although men and women managed to find room for intimate encounters, opportunities were limited by the physical availability of a place and

---

11. For a discussion of the biblical underpinnings of virginity, sodomy, and pregnancy, see Bishop (1995).

by the watchful eyes of parents, neighbors, and priests. Brondi had enough money to rent a room where he could "visit" his victim, even though Matilde was not a stranger but a woman with whom he was in close physical proximity, both in the domestic sphere and in his workplace as a teacher in Matilde's school. As in Buenos Aires (Socolow 1980, 43–44) and in colonial Mexico (Scardaville 1977, 160ff, 196; Pescador 1994, 220ff), violence against women in Lima usually originated among people who had a close relationship with their victims.[12] Sexual captivity and dependence demonstrate the way in which a young girl could be "trapped" by someone she and her family relied upon. The accused rapist was almost invariably a teacher, the mother's lover, or a deceived or rejected suitor.

Familiarity and dependence were also factors in a case registered in 1891. For several years, Felix Aybar had been supporting a woman and her daughter, María Ester. When she was thirteen years old, María Ester claimed that Felix had raped her. Felix denied the charges even though the medical examination showed recent vaginal injuries. Although María Ester never retracted her accusations, Felix received no punishment.[13] In this case, both mother and daughter depended on Felix for their livelihood in the context of the common-law arrangement. In contrast to the Brondi case, however, María, her mother, and Felix were "unequal" partners. The women were of lower social standing than Felix and were economically dependent on him.

In spite of the significance of virginity, rapists were not always successful in bending the will of either the victim or her parents. In 1809 Don Nicolás Gonzales, a soldier, accused another soldier, Manuel Carbajal, of raping his daughter, Dolores de Gonzales. Manuel had courted Dolores, but she had rejected him. Angered by her refusal, he hit her and then raped her in the middle of the street. Neither she nor her parents wanted the marriage, so they asked Manuel for pecuniary reparation for her lost virginity and social

---

12. A similar case is registered in 1815 when Francisco Polo, asking to obtain a license to marry Doña Manuela Herrera, found that her mother was strongly opposed to this marriage. Manuela's mother argued that her daughter was only fifteen years old and that Francisco was a vagabond who by pretending to be a "*maestro de escribir*" (teacher) had seduced Manuela and taken her from her mother's side. Francisco brought Manuela to an "honorable house," in contrast to Brondi, who rented a room. Case 265a, BN, D 9856, 1815, Expediente seguido por Don Francisco Polo sobre que se le libre Licencia para contraer matrimonio con Doña Manuela Herrera.

13. AGN, Expedientes Judiciales, CCR, L s.n., 1891, 14ff., Expediente de oficio contra Felix Arturo Aybar por estupro de la menor Maria Ester por quien se ha querellado su padre Don Enrique Pomar.

status. Shortly afterward it became evident that Dolores was pregnant, and Manuel—of equal social standing to the girl—went to jail.[14]

In spite of legal provisions, rape has always been hard to prove, given that the victim is often unable to face making a public declaration in the courtroom. To convict on a charge of rape, it had to be demonstrated that force had been used. "The burden of proof was placed on the victim, and punishment was rarely meted out to the offender" (Socolow 1980, 48; see also Lavrin 1989, 71). With few exceptions, there were no witnesses. Men usually were stronger or carried arms, and women might not scream or resist because of social inhibitions, including their perception of the racial or class superiority of their assailant and their fear of disgrace, or even because they failed to grasp what was happening to them. Beyond fears and ignorance, the legal proceedings to substantiate a case of rape were cumbersome. Rape lawsuits always began with a written accusation presented by the victim or her representative. The judge then requested a medical report, an examination many women apparently shunned. Then it was the victim again who had to name witnesses and present the questions these witnesses had to answer in court. Finally, the judge forwarded the accusation to the rapist and eventually an interrogation took place. At this stage, the file could go back and forth several times between rapist and victim before the judge— following the evaluation of the case by the prosecutor—passed sentence. Often trials never reached the witness stage, instead ending abruptly with the victim's deposition, a clear sign of how difficult it was to substantiate a case, and of how much victims shunned medical and public exposure.[15]

---

14. Case 239, AGN, AGG, Causas Penales, L 4, C 90, 18ff, 1809.
15. Other similar rape cases: Case 936, AGN, Corte Superior, CCR, L 110, 1850, Petronila Pantoja, chacarera yanacona indígena demanda a José Alvarez por violación de su sobrina Juana Pantoja a quien ha criado desde la infancia hasta la edad de 12 años que tiene; Case 055, AGN, Corte Superior, CCR, L 112, 1850, Vera vs. Flores; Case 0207, AGN, Expedientes Judiciales, CCR, L s.n., 1891, Marchería; Case 0165, AGN, Expedientes Judiciales, CCR, L s.n., 1891, De oficio contra Pedro Morante por estupro a Josefina Lara, menor de edad (11 años) en hacienda Cacapongo. Lurigancho; Case 0134, AGN, Expedientes Judiciales, CCR, L s.n., 1891, Denuncia interpuesta por el Dr. Don Manuel E. Patrón por Doña Manuela Chumpitaz contra Miguel Montellanos por falsedad; Case 913, AGN, Corte Superior, CCR, L 126, 1853, Contra Calisto Berrio, soltero, carpintero de Huaral de 14 años, por estupro a Dolores N. de 10 años; Case 849, AGN, Corte Superior, CCR, L 116, 1851, Demanda contra Fernando Miranda, español, soltero, platero, por estupro contra Isidora Infrangui, sirvienta menor de 16 años; Case 601, AGN, RA, CCR, L 102, C 1244, 1804, Demanda de José Mariano Toro contra Fernando Durán por rapto y violación de su hija.

Cases of elopement (sometimes involving rape): Case 866a, AGN, Corte Suprema de Justicia, PJ 81 (1856/1861), 1856, Expediente contra Don Manuel Lorenzo de las Casas por Doña

Even in seemingly clear-cut cases, when rapist and victim were social equals or when the victim was clearly underage, rapists often went unpunished. It is very possible that redress and/or compensation occurred more often outside the courtroom, by means of social pressure and intimidation, when neighbors, parents, or brothers took justice into their own hands. What court cases show, however, is how people translated rape accusations into monetary requests.

When Dolores Samudio's father learned that Juan Iginio, the man who had raped his daughter several years earlier, was planning to marry someone else, he rushed to the court and asked for payment from the rapist. The father claimed that his daughter was a virgin when she met Juan, and for that reason she had to be compensated. In his statement, he also asserted that Juan was notorious in his home parish of Chorrillos for raping several women. After the passage of so many years, however, it was the father's word against Juan's. Nothing could be proven at such a late date. For Juan, things were easy. "I found her," he averred, "as used as any public woman and without the virginity one would expect."[16] Apparently, after rape had occurred, Dolores continued her sexual relationship with Juan Iginio for many years and had received occasional gifts and some money to buy food from him. As long as there was no rival for Juan's favors, father and daughter could count on at least some compensation; when Juan decided to marry another woman, whatever support Dolores was receiving would likely disappear. However, after so many years, virginity could not be recaptured, and rape had been invalidated by consent. There was nothing Dolores could do to prevent Juan Iginio's marriage to another woman.

As in Dolores's case, many rapists evaded an accusation of rape by alleging that the victim had not been a virgin. Tarnishing a woman's social image and creating suspicions about her honor and good behavior made men look less guilty. It even enhanced their manliness. When judging rape, a woman's previous behavior was taken into consideration. If she showed the slightest signs of "public" life, she would be considered morally unworthy. Dolores had accepted the loss of her virginity and had continued having sex with

---

Andrea Lobatón por rapto y fuerza; Case 0124, AA, LicM, L 6 (1880–89), 1895, Francisco Ronceros por Don Juan de M. Camacho; Case 0222, AA, LicM, L 6 (1880–89), 1896, Ramírez vs. Aranda; Case 06, AGN, CCR, 1854, Estupro, N. vs. Silva.

16. Case 989, AA, NM, L 61 (1836–46), 1844, Expediente promovido por Felipe Samudio con Juan Iginio sobre anular su matrimonio por relaciones anteriores con su hija Dolores Samudio.

the accused seducer. For the judges, a rape verdict was out of the question, and her complaint, rather than winning her monetary compensation, was used against her as evidence of her immoral behavior.

A similar case happened in 1851[17] when Francisca Solonia's aunt accused Manuel Vera, a fifty-seven-year-old bread delivery man, of convincing her nineteen-year-old niece to leave her parental home. In contrast to Dolores' father, Francisca's aunt reacted promptly, but when she found the couple two hours later, "rape had already been committed." She asked the ecclesiastical authorities to take her niece into custody and to require Manuel to pay a monthly allowance to support her in a convent where honor could be restored. But Manuel answered these accusations by arguing that when he met Francisca two years earlier, she had already lost her virginity at the hands of a cousin of his. To strengthen his argument, Manuel mentioned that everybody, even Francisca's aunt, knew this. Maybe it was a showcase for male solidarity; the cousins backed each other. Maybe Manuel was not lying; after all, unlike the other cases, there was no medical report attached to the file.

If Juan Iginio and Manuel were telling the truth, the question arises whether virginity, elopement, abduction, and even rape could be social bargaining chips by which a woman could obtain money or a maintenance allowance in the name of honor. The degree to which these "chips" became part of a calculated strategy is hard to determine. No one would freely confess to such a "crime." However, under circumstances different from those experienced by Dolores and Francisca, the loss of virginity could provide a woman with a lifetime income.

Before Colonel Francisco Vásquez married, he had been a boarder in the house of his future spouse, Mercedes Badani, who was twenty-five when he first met her: "When she lived with her mother, I first had illicit relations with her mother; we, that is, Mercedes, her mother, and I have lived together; I paid for the expenses of the house. It was her mother who encouraged me to engage in this relationship with her daughter."

The church considered such relationships to be an impediment to marriage (second-degree affinity). But in more down-to-the-earth terms, a colonel was a partner worth some feminine risks, especially if he was willing to support the whole family. Given that women were widely considered to be "sly creatures," it was plausible in the eyes of the court that Mercedes's

---

17. Case 07, AGN, Corte Superior, CCR, L 114, 1851, Solonia vs. Vera.

mother had encouraged the colonel's intimacy with her daughter in order to continue receiving daily maintenance. Mercedes and Francisco had had sexual relations while living in the same house before marriage. Eventually they married, but around 1856 they decided to separate, and the colonel was obliged to grant an allowance to Mercedes. He countered by raising her past history and pled that the court should send his wife to a *beaterio*. His experience—he argued—had shown him that Mercedes's mother was morally unfit, and thus his wife should not be allowed to stay with her mother. "What kind of esteem may a person inspire who knew of her daughter's immoral behavior when she was single and then encouraged her running away from the house when married? It is impossible for me to conceive that, while I am paying for her subsistence, she lives in the streets, and even less in her mother's house."[18]

Several witnesses verified that all three had been living together prior to the marriage, but in spite of the colonel's allegations, Mercedes won the case because she was the colonel's wife. The question behind the verdict: How could the colonel have married someone who was morally unworthy? His behavior contradicted his arguments. Mercedes secured, as the law required, one third of his salary, which would be deducted directly and turned over to her each month. However, three years elapsed before this deal was set. In the meantime, Mercedes was allowed to live with her mother, but in poverty.

Elopement, abduction, and consensual situations—as in this case—often overlapped. Virginity had been gambled for security, or as Shorter (1973, 52) put it, we are facing "manipulative sexuality."[19] Government bureaucrats and military officers like the colonel had a fixed salary and a stable job. Had there been no marriage, Mercedes would not have gotten any money. Had her mother not encouraged the couple's relationship, they might never have married. This was a case in which "honor" was successfully safeguarded, although the neighborhood knew what was going on. In part, Mercedes's economic success was a consequence of her mother's manipulation, but we know little about the feelings of either woman. As in other cases, physical closeness provided an opportunity for a calculated seduction. However, it was the marriage that followed seduction that enhanced Mercedes's ability to win a stipend from the colonel. The "immorality" of double

18. Case 725, AA, LM, L 10 (1850–59), 1856, Badani vs. Vásquez.
19. Shorter's definition of "manipulative sexuality" is the use of sexuality "as a tool for achieving some ulterior external objective" (Shorter 1971, 54ff.). A similar idea is also voiced by Kuznesof (1991, 213) for Sao Paulo around 1836.

seduction (the mother and the daughter) had been cleansed through marriage.[20]

Once parents agreed to a daughter's marriage, the suitor was allowed closer contact with her, and the couple interacted with less surveillance. This made premarital sexual relationships more likely and rape less frequent and credible. Usually, but not always, the gradual rapprochement led to marriage.[21] From the parents' perspective, ignoring or permitting premarital sexual relationships meant accepting immoral behavior by their daughter, something for which they too would be censured, especially if the couple did not marry. Accusing a man of rape—that is, turning what was a "permitted seduction" into "unwilling intercourse"—at least recouped some of the girl's damaged dignity, purity, and honor. The seriousness of a rape accusation involved a higher degree of intimidation, which girls and their parents could use to persuade the seducer to marry. Thus, there were family, social, legal, and economic incentives that accounted for rape accusations. Nevertheless, there were also many reasons to silence a rape. When rape (or premarital sex more generally) was not recognized publicly, a daughter might still eventually be married off and under more advantageous circumstances.

Whether or not legal entanglements ensued, the loss of virginity always resulted in social reproach against the woman. Although virginity was a valued part of the prevailing social creed, some were willing to gamble with it. Lost virginity could be recaptured with marriage, but to some extent also with money—that is, with an adequate payment. So, especially among the less well-off, virginity was a commodity that could be traded for money to pave a daughter's way into marriage. The compensation for lost

---

20. As Lavrin (1989, 72) put it: "Here, the assimilation of socioreligious values is betrayed by the vernacular forms of speech."

21. Only if either the daughter or the parents later wanted to break the engagement, would the suitor possibly resort to rape to overcome their resistance. Case 839, AGN, Corte Superior, CCR, L 111, 1850, Don Tomás Guerra contra Andrés Peñaranda, dependiente de la huerta de California por rapto y estupro amalgamados con el robo de Apolinaria Guerra, su doméstica. The sixteen-year-old Apolinaria had been reared as a servant by Don Tomás since she was six years old. After he abducted her, Andrés wrote a letter to Don Tomás stating that he wanted to marry Apolinaria. In his answer, Don Tomás agreed to the marriage, "because I have no other intention than to recover my servant's honor." Very much in line with Guy's (1985) assertion that the extension of patriarchal control on domestics was a way to gain access to cheap labor and, in a more general sense, to implement "order and progress," this case in Lima at midcentury shows that here too such paternalistic-patriarchal notions were prevalent. For a similar assessment for Buenos Aires, see Szuchman (1988).

virginity became her self-apportioned dowry to a future marriage. Thus, a rich seducer was to be preferred to a poor one. A "conventional" price to compensate for lost virginity in nineteenth-century Lima lay between 2,000 and 3,000 pesos among the lower and middle classes.[22]

There is no instance of a case pursued by a victim on her own behalf; parents or a close relative always participated in the lawsuit. And in a few cases, one gets the impression that when an appropriate partner was at hand, premarital sexual relations were encouraged by either parents or their daughters as a controlling technique.

Elopement, abduction, and maybe even "voluntary rape" can be understood as strategies not only for a child to force parents to give their consent but also for parents to compel a partner—who did not have marriage on his mind—to marry their child. Thus, virginity could become a weapon in conflicts over marriage and an issue in intergenerational and social battles.

Conditions under which elopement and rape occurred, the social status of the people involved, and the issue of volition opened these acts to interpretation and manipulation. Biologically, virginity was irreplaceable. Socially, it could be "reconstructed" at some personal or monetary cost; that is, those involved negotiated and agreed upon either a sum of money or marriage. Both possibilities expressed—beyond honor codes—mutual perceptions. If disparities were too great, money was the better alternative. Because all women (rich and poor; black, white, and Indian) were at some point virgins, loss of virginity was an encompassing argument against men who used their education, class, or racial superiority to gain sexual access to women of lower social status. These women could use the loss-of-virginity argument to obtain some compensation, and in doing so they imperiled a man's reputation. When, in contrast to a man's self-perception, the differences between the aggressor and his victim were not great in the eyes of the judges, aggressors not only risked damage to their reputations but also to their wealth, because virginity weighed more among social equals.

It was impossible to foresee the outcome of a trial involving loss of virginity, seduction, abduction, or rape. As with all moral issues, rules were never applied consistently. Cultural background, class issues, and many

22. Following Pescador's analysis of similar cases at the end of the eighteenth century in Mexico, it seems that the "virginity price" was lower in Mexico than in Peru. Prices mentioned by Pescador fluctuated between 6 and 300 pesos (1994, 199). Lavrin mentions a range between 100 and 1,000 pesos (1989, 63). There was, of course, a difference in what was petitioned as a compensation for lost virginity and what was actually awarded and then paid.

subjective interpretations found their way into the arguments leading to court and ecclesiastical decisions. Social appearances were always a central concern. The innate haziness of moral issues allowed for a high degree of manipulation to include or exclude certain people from participating in the honor game. Without honor, there was no social mobility. And not much about this changed during the nineteenth century, although it seems— if a general tendency may be detected based on the available cases and the blurred dividing line between "voluntary and involuntary rape"—that toward the end of the nineteenth century more lower-class women were involved in rape accusations to obtain monetary compensation. In other words, women, subjected to toughening moral codes, retorted by wagering men's social reputation. Men and women bargained over virginity in court. But for men it was a device to question, humiliate, and subordinate women; and for women it was a device to question men's intentions and object to moral double standards. Where institutional rules governing marriage and virginity were invoked, men had patriarchal rationalizations against women—and often racist arguments as well.

Talking Women Into It

Many cases of seduction, elopement, and rape probably developed following a promise of matrimony whispered into female ears eager to believe that it would come true. But only if a betrothal had been formally registered with a notary were the parties legally bound to fulfill a marriage promise. Since colonial times, people had resorted to notarially recorded betrothals to express their readiness and wish to marry. It was an option, not a requirement. These *sponsalia*[23] recorded why marriages had to be postponed: an impending trip, the death of a close relative, or hounding creditors. More

23. Rípodas Ardanaz (1977, 63–65) provides a description of *sponsalia*: "Los esponsales constituyen una preparación voluntaria para el matrimonio, como que suelen precederlo sin ser necesarios para su validez. Consisten en la promesa y aceptación mutua del futuro matrimonio. Para contraerlos basta el solo consentimiento de las partes, si bien se acompañan a veces con otras solemnidades que van desde la bendición sacerdotal hasta su protocolización en el registro de un escribano. A menos que se disuelvan por alguna de las causas previstas por el derecho canónico, obligan en conciencia bajo culpa grave, y la parte afectada por el incumplimiento de la promesa tiene derecho a introducir demanda al respecto ante el juez eclesiástico—único al que corresponde conocer en estos casos—el cual puede, con penas espirituales, llegar a compeler al matrimonio a la parte renuente.... El deseo de que los

often than not, the couple admitted to having had sexual intercourse and declared their willingness to recognize their offspring. In these declarations, the date of the wedding was set, and sometimes a man would agree to pay an allowance to the woman if for any reason the marriage did not take place by that time. Legally recorded betrothals appeared sporadically in notarial records (*protocolos*) throughout the nineteenth century[24] then almost disappeared in the 1890s. This occurred partly because *sponsalia*—as I will show—were subject to abuse and misunderstandings. Over time, the *sponsalia* became a family concern, and today it is celebrated by a family party (resembling today's engagement ceremony) in which rings are exchanged.

When a notarial instrument could be produced, the church readily intervened to impede a man's marriage to another woman. No further evidence was necessary, something that was not the case in elopements and rapes. Although *sponsalia* were registered with a civil notary, only the church could enforce them. Men accused of breaking an engagement could not be prosecuted in civil court. A letter would go to the appropriate priest, who called the transgressor into confession.

Doña Petronila Thompson used ecclesiastical legal channels to interfere in her suitor's marriage to another woman. In 1899 she wrote a long letter to the *provisor* telling him that her fiancé, José del Carmen Gallardo, had emigrated to Cajamarca to marry another woman. Petronila was asking for church intervention, having at hand the legal instrument verifying her betrothal to him.[25] Success depended on speed and expediency: communications in Peru were not the best—although they had improved somewhat by the time Doña Petronila wrote her letter—and more often than not a letter reached its destination too late. To be successful, a woman had to know well in advance where the impending marriage would take place. Although a great deal of gossip as well as more formal channels of information existed, Peru's large size still enabled a fleeing suitor to slip away. So even if *sponsalia*

---

esponsales se ciñan a determinadas formalidades marca, paradójicamente, una tendencia a minusvalorar—y aun a desestimar—en aras de conveniencias sociales, la obligación de conciencia nacida de una mutua promesa privada. . . . Ciertos abusos, erróneas creencias o fraudes en torno a los esponsales parecían abonar la necesidad de esos recaudos. A veces se invocaban, de buena o mala fe, esponsales inexistentes. . . . solía estimarse que los verdaderos esponsales eran rescindibles por uno de los espondentes en caso de notoria desigualdad entre familias, y esto aunque la doncella se hubiera entregado en vista de la promesa."

24. Some representative examples of the language used and the promises forwarded may be found in AGN, Protocolos, José Cubillas (PR 173: f 58v, 1850); Eduardo Huerta (PR 279: f 139v, 1850); Francisco Palacios (PR 593:f 195, 1880); Juan Cosío (PR 161: f 109, 1850).

25. Case 0255, AA, LicM, L 6 (1880–99), 1899, Thompson vs. Gallardo.

existed, there were loopholes. Ultimately, Doña Petronila did not prevent her fiancé's marriage to another woman. The letter failed to arrive in time to stop José del Carmen, but at least the new spouse learned that Petronila existed.

As in the case of consent, a whole set of external conditions could be interpreted as proving a marriage proposal had been made, in spite of regulations (Civil Code 1852) requiring a notarial record to make it legally binding. The informal proposal, and sometimes even the written record, were tactics men used to get women into bed. Many women were unaware of the legal requirement for a notarial registration, and when a woman's lover decided to marry someone else, there was often no legal recourse. In my series of records on marriage conflict, the notarized *sponsalia* was produced in only four cases, although many more women claimed that a promise had been made to them by their suitors. Particularly in Lima's outskirts and in the rural areas, there were no notaries, even in the late nineteenth century, which of course made this source of (relative) protection unavailable to most Peruvian women.

In 1896 Jesús Huapaya, a woman from Mala, a small town south of Lima, accused Guillermo Fontana of reneging on his marriage proposal and of having "abused my innocence to the extreme of making me the mother of his son."[26] Guillermo declared that he had never made such a promise, and if it were true, Jesús should present the notarized document. Obviously, none existed. Jesús testified: "To present a written record is impossible, because in Mala there are no notaries where one could do such a thing and people are not used to doing it. Above all, my reputation and the son I had with Fontana should not be harmed. To allow this to happen would be a crime and a blow against morality, which should be protected from all such seduction. If no credence be given to the gravity of my complaint, in any case, I have a right to ask that the said Fontana recognize that I carried his child and also that I merit some compensation and monthly payments to feed this child."

The only evidence Jesús was able to present in court was a ring Guillermo had given her in front of her parents and the argument that in Mala—as in other rural areas—people were unaccustomed and unable to ask for notarial registration of betrothals. This was not enough to convince the judges, and thus she was in no position to impede Guillermo's marriage to another woman. Jesús also failed to obtain financial support for the child, and she was barred from appealing the verdict. Instead of acknowledging that lack

26. Case 0140, AA, LicM, L 6 (1880–99), 1896, Huapaya vs. Fontana.

of bureaucratic infrastructure was an obstacle, the judges demanded that the law be strictly followed. As justification, the defense lawyer took up the widely held argument that women were sly creatures from which men must be safeguarded:

> The experiences of many centuries have given proof of female shrewdness, by which undiscerning youngsters and virile men are trapped into dreadful and unplanned marriages and *sponsalia*, which increase public disorder and whose consequences are a plethora of sins, unhappy families, adulterous children, prostituted women, and an infinite variety of ailments. Thus, the problem has to be attacked at its very roots, through use of the *sponsalia*. Legislators' wisdom made it a requirement to write marriage proposals down in order to prevent a less than sagacious young man or an old man in love from falling prey to an astute girl or a malicious mother.[27]

Closer to reality were experiences such as that of Jesús. Jesús had a ring and a pregnancy; other women had several children. Still the courts at least until midcentury were inclined to declare unmarried fathers free of legal obligation. By the 1850s paternal support for legitimate and natural children—as will be discussed in later sections and in Chapters 7 and 8—was enforced more frequently. Even then, however, nothing could force a man to marry the children's mother. In McCaa's apt wording, Charles IV's 1803 decree that only written and notarized promises of marriage counted "tied the unmarried woman's hand in courtship and in the courts" (1994, 23).

Occasionally women resorted to their love letters to prove their suitors' vows to marry them. Although judges strongly insisted on the existence of a betrothal document—increasingly so toward the century's end—and women learned there was not much they could achieve without it, some credit was also given to letters, which were perceived to be less questionable than the stories a person or a lawyer might tell. In 1860 Doña Adela Punchar stated that "Don Jacinto Aguilar [her suitor, a thirty-two-year-old bank employee from Trujillo] solicited me under the pretense that he would marry me, and he used all kinds of artifice and reiterated that he would fulfill his promise as soon as his circumstances changed; that is, when he would have the means sufficient to meet his obligations. . . . Thus, he obliged himself formally, and I gave myself away entirely, leaving my honor and my future

---

27. Case 476, AA, Esponsales, 1809, 18ff., Pozo vs. Ruiz.

in his hands. At his side, I suffered deprivation and poverty for seven years. Nevertheless, I withstood all these hardships with resignation, even the loss of the two children born out of this ill-fated liaison."[28]

For seven years Don Jacinto had been paying one-third of his 54 peso monthly salary to Doña Adela. During this time, two children were born. Don Jacinto's payment of support to Doña Adela was a tacit recognition of his paternity. When the children died and payments stopped, Doña Adela asked the court that they be continued to compensate for her "corrupted virginity" and "voluntary rape." Don Jacinto refused, claiming they had agreed that payments would be made on the condition that Doña Adela live an honest and moral life, which, he argued, she had not done. Happily, witnesses confirmed Doña Adela's decorous and pious behavior. They told the judges that the real reason behind Don Jacinto's refusal to continue support payments was his marriage to another woman, which entailed the maintenance of their children. The final judgment, given in 1864, was favorable to Doña Adela. The existence of the love letters she had presented in court that proved that even after her children had died Don Jacinto continued to talk about marriage, her pregnancies, and her decency superseded the requirement for a written *sponsalia*. I suspect that the central reason for her success was others' perception of her social behavior. Her suitor knew that this would become an important argument, and he attempted to circumvent it by accusing Doña Adela of scandalous and immoral conduct. Both were playing the same game skillfully, but social credit was on *her* side.

As in most other cases, everyone in the neighborhood knew about Doña Adela's longstanding relationship to Don Jacinto. This knowledge, including the payments offered to Doña Adela, helped her to vindicate her honor. She had shown that her suitor had demonstrated his good intentions to marry, and marriage would cleanse earlier sexual wrongs. Many disputes over breach of promise probably ended in extrajudicial arrangements, behind which lay an array of private social pressures and the patent sense—as in Doña Adela's case—of the terrible injustice of dismissing abundant proof of an intention to marry. It was a way in which society—or "the anonymous hand"—could contest and override the law as laid out in the Civil Code. But success could never be guaranteed. Some women waited their whole lives to settle matters, and even when witnesses and documentation provided evidence of paternity and long-outstanding marriage promises, the outcome was still unsure.

28. Case 951, AGN, Corte Superior, CCI, L 769, 1860, Punchar vs. Aguilar.

Talking Men Out of It

From our discussion so far, one would conclude that women were almost exclusively the ones who were cheated. This is not entirely true. Women in some way were more prone to be cheated and had more to lose; but men also had at stake their emotions, financial well-being, and reputation. Basically there were three scenarios that greatly enhanced a woman's ability to escape a marriage or to change her marriage partner: by rescinding a marriage contract (a legal possibility), by resorting to family support, or by resorting to communal support (both social possibilities).

The opening of a matrimonial file, even more than registering a betrothal with a notary, was a demonstration of a willingness to be married. Instituted as early as 1614 and delineated more clearly in 1670, the objective of a matrimonial file was to find out whether a couple was freely entering a marriage and whether impediments existed (Rípodas Ardanaz 1977, 69). Before a matrimonial file could be approved, consent and dissent issues would have to have been resolved. If marriage did not take place within six months after opening the file, then each of the partners had the right to withdraw from their bond. In 1889 Emilia Paredes was in such a situation. She had made up her mind to marry Manuel Napurí, a younger man, instead of Luis Boza, a widower, thirty-nine years of age living in the San Lázaro parish. Luis moved to block Emilia's marriage. Emilia's father, as advocate for his daughter, told the ecclesiastical judges that six months had elapsed since Luis first discussed marriage and that there was no written notarial promise of marriage.[29] Emilia and her father were successful, and Luis Boza's petition to impede the marriage was decreed inadmissible. Women too could change their minds, and time erased prior commitment.

In the cases reviewed, legal mechanisms and arguments differed according to sex, but there were at least as many men as women who insisted on marrying. Some suitors resorted to violence or even rape.[30] Others transferred their belongings to their in-laws' house before marriage, which was a way of assuring the marriage would take place while securing the suitor. Physical violence, spatial proximity, the handing over of personal items and furniture, and legal demands and queries were part of the strategies, especially those of men, to get married. Women, mostly helped by parents, could successfully reject a suitor (in contrast to those cases where parents

---

29. Case 0209, AA, LicM, L 6 (1880–99), 1889, Paredes vs. Boza.
30. Case 742, AGN, Corte Superior, CCR, L 114, 1851, Bicabarra vs. N.

registered their dissent or forced their daughters to marry against their will). Proximity could provide parents with first-hand knowledge of their future son in-law, and if he did not come up to expectations, he ran the risk of being dismissed. His household goods would be returned to him, sometimes with an appropriate discount to pay for the damage to the woman's reputation, including a presumed or real loss of virginity.[31]

Indian women in Lima's rural provinces particularly relied on communal support when it came to resisting a suitor. In such cases, not only her parents but a whole town stood behind her.

> I am five month pregnant. I—a poor deceived woman—am ashamed and repentant. Men pretend to be good and in good standing [here, the man in the case called himself a *compadre* to the subprefect], and with tricky sophisms spur on the deadly poison of incontinency to give free reign to their passions .... Fernández says that I am influenced by my kinfolk and the false community, implying that they should not stop me from joining him, and he does not want me to see them. *I cannot live with him as mandated by our Holy Catholic Church, and, if church officials ask me to join him, I have resolved that I will flee to unknown countries, leaving behind my possessions, and I'll never return. In my conscience, I know that I am not married"* [emphasis added].[32]

These words, from María Ifinia Dávila in the town of Tupicocha (in the province of Huarochirí) in 1828, demonstrate her firm determination not to marry Fernández in spite of her pregnancy. As a concubine, María Ifinia recognized that she could not live "as mandated by our Holy Catholic Church." Pregnancy did not deter her from leaving her lover; her "conscience" was stronger. Here individual decision is contrasted to moral and social prescriptions, and communal support counteracted ecclesiastical wishes. Unlike rape and seduction—events with few if any witnesses—common-law marriage, especially in rural areas, involved a broad social network. As in the many cases in which neighbors intervened on behalf of wives, a whole community could side with a woman. Even if she was unmarried, like Maria Ifinia, she could count on her community's support to escape ecclesiastical

---

31. Case 0170, AGN, RPJ, L 377.1, 1898, Juzgado de Primera Instancia, Juicio ordinario iniciado por Don Santiago B. Dodero contra Don Juan P. Limas y esposa sobre devolución de especies.
32. Case 172a, AA, Comunicaciones Oficiales de Curas, L 1, 1828.

rules. Obviously, decisions such as that taken by María Ifinia had a high cost, particularly if they antagonized a powerful priest, or when a woman—unlike Maria Ifinia—did not have a means of survival.

To get married or to get rid of an unwanted suitor (or husband) women would even resort to witchcraft or accuse others of witchcraft.[33] Juana Rosa Tagle's case was one of extreme desperation. She had waited twenty-six years for Don Ignacio Iguaguirre to fulfill his promise of marriage. Throughout that time—she told the judges—her hopes were kept alive by his spectacular gifts, including nothing less than two houses, each with twenty-five servants. By 1840, however, "without my having given him any reasons whatsoever, he changed his preference and has abandoned me because he prefers a witch called Angela Carasa, born in Chancay [a town north of Lima]."

According to Juana Rosa, Don Ignacio had abandoned her several times in the last years and the new concubine was to blame for it. In a letter to Lima's archbishop, Juana Rosa asked the ecclesiastical authorities to incarcerate her contender and submit her to the Inquisition, because for "these kinds of people the Inquisition is the appropriate place. She has scorned me several times by turning into a mouse, a dog-falcon, a hen, and a fox. Every day she enters my room and does not leave me in peace, she hits me continually and I am fed up so that I don't know what to do."[34]

It is possible that Juana was mentally ill, but her insanity may be an expression of the tensions arising in her situation between marriage and nonmarriage. Juana's accusation did not provoke further investigation of Angela, but one wonders to what degree the feelings Juana put on paper were part of a common female language and attitude to deal with perceived male dishonesty and marriage deceit and fraud. Even today when a woman discovers her husband's adultery, she may refer to "the other" (*la otra*) as a *bruja* (witch), who has no respect for matrimonial rights. Similarly, women who have disentangled themselves from a suitor will call the new girlfriend a *bruja*, because she can stand this horrible man. Whatever the psychological reasons behind such expressions, their existence shows female avenues to deal with marriage pressures and marriage cheaters.

---

33. For a broader assessment of the meaning of sexual witchcraft in colonial Mexico, see Behar (1989, 178–206). In only one case (see below) such arguments were brought forward, not necessarily indicating the disappearance of witchcraft, but the increased limitations to express these "female powers" in a male-dominated system.

34. Case 018, AA, Particulares, L 2 (1840–1922). n.d. (approximately 1840).

Women used the mechanisms of witchcraft, communal or neighborhood backing, and parental support to gain some control over the matrimonial arena. Whereas a man could allege that a woman was not a virgin or lacked moral virtue, women had to build wider social networks to make their case. In the course of time, women became more conscious of this and resorted to it with increasing success.

Silence Became a Habit, Precaution a Necessity

Lost virginity or the birth of natural children was a stigma that could prevent a woman from marrying. Some women and their parents were successful in disguising the problem until after the marriage. However, it was difficult to continue fooling a deceived husband once the ceremony was over. Doña Maria Lama's story illustrates how one such situation was handled.[35] She had given birth to a daughter, who then was reared in the house of the Count of San Isidro. To hide the pregnancy, Doña Maria went away under the pretense that she was suffering from gout. Her parents then began to search for a suitable husband, that is, somebody from a similar social background and, if possible, somebody far enough away from Lima to ensure that he would not have the faintest idea of what his fiancée had been through.

Six months after the birth of the child, that is, "when there were no more shadows around her eyes, or weaknesses or other symptoms that could have made the husband object to the bride or become suspicious of her disease," they found just such a man. His name was Peragalo, a corregidor from the Lucanas mining province in the highlands. Peragalo—who curiously is not referred to as "Don" Peragalo—did not even travel to Lima to see his bride; the marriage took place in 1772 by proxy. When the couple finally took up residence together, the husband "noted the corruption [lack of virginity] of his spouse by observing the precautions [referring to some strategy to fake virginity] the beautiful sex uses to hide its frailties; but his good name made him remain silent. By revealing the indiscretion, he would have dishonored

---

35. Case 298, AGN, Cabildo, CCI, L 38, C 629, 1818; and RA, CCI, L 162, C 1671, 1819, Autos seguidos por Doña Mónica Lombera, hija de Doña María Lama contra la testamentaría de su madre, sobre su filiación y su consiguiente derecho a sus bienes.

himself and his wife to no gain. Although gossip later exposed the mystery, he himself acted in good faith."

Peragalo conveniently died soon after his marriage. To protect his wife's social image, before he died he made an *arras propter nuptias*,[36] in which he praised her virginity. Either immense generosity or a gift of a great deal of money—before he was aware he would die—account for Peragalo's behavior. Don Antonio García—the husband of Doña Maria's daughter, who had set out to prove that his wife had a right to her mother's share of the inheritance—explained it in the following terms: "The *arras propter nuptias* given to a woman who is not a widow invariably praises a wife's ethical virtues, her virginity, and other attributes she possibly lacks, but which are supposed to exist, in order to enhance one's own and one's family's social standing, and it also serves to leave an honorable document for posterity."

Given this argument, the *arras propter nuptias* could not be used to prove Doña Maria's virginity at the time she married the corregidor; a natural daughter or son could have been born prior to their marriage. Don Antonio's account concludes with some important generic remarks: "The world knows little if it ignores women's vagaries, their extravagances and strange ways of thinking. Even those linked through holy marriage every day deny the existence of their children because they hate their husbands or for other reasons. [Doña Maria's silence] was there from her youth until her death. Silence became a habit and precaution, a necessity. The honor of widows is not less delicate than the honor of virgins. Not everyone knows that a natural child is a legitimate heir to his or her mother. On this are based a thousand worries and prejudices."

Having said this, his wife could claim her maternal inheritance. The executor of the will, of course, accused Don Antonio of inventing the whole story. But this only pushed Don Antonio to forward new and revealing arguments: "No one hides frailties more than high-class people. These people ignore what the midwife, the wet nurse, the black confidant and servant, the provincial *chola*, the boy from the corner, or the neighborhood know; our gentlemen and potentates in their magnificent houses only know what respectability allows them to know without offending their high

---

36. *Arras propter nuptias*, or 'gift after marriage,' referred to a transfer of money from the husband to his wife in compensation for the dowry he had received. In most cases, it was also stated that this transfer was made to her because of her good moral qualities and her virginity. As dowries, *arras propter nuptias* were notarially recorded. This issue will be dealt with in more detail in Chapter 7.

status. I don't need to remind Your Excellency of the many perjuries by means of which those of 80 or 90 years of age pretend to be 50, and the overall unrealistic attitudes of those people." In this final argument, he conjured up the well-known behavior of the upper classes, and a portrait of daily interaction between them and those beneath them. As in other filiation cases,[37] an array of witnesses were called; but it was, above all, the declarations of the servants which were decisive to the trial's outcome. Even if Peragalo obeyed the honor codes to safeguard his wife's (and his own) reputation, house servants, midwives, wet nurses, and neighbors remembered her shortcomings. Elites told their dependents how to behave, but now dependents had an opportunity to use those rules to measure their masters against the elites' own accepted norms of proper behavior. In March 1820 the court declared Don Antonio's wife to be the natural daughter of Doña Maria Lama and a Don Francisco, allowing the daughter to receive her share of the inheritance. Filiation was hard to prove because these cases were handled with such caution and secrecy, but on the other hand, everyone in the city and beyond knew that illegitimacy was part of daily life, occasionally even among upper classes. Claims could take a long time to surface: "Silence became a habit and precaution, a necessity." In this case it took a whole generation, in part because the "cheated" husband neither wanted nor had the opportunity to do otherwise.

Family honor had been safeguarded until the mother died, but the significant inheritance finally overrode the need for silence. When money or assets were involved, people—especially if they had been the victims or the "result" of frailties—were very willing to expose "moral corruption," even if it pertained to their own kin. Because married women were allowed to appear in ecclesiastical but not in civil court, husbands stepped in, especially when an inheritance could offset a meager dowry. However, fewer natural children belonged to the upper classes; most either did not know who their parents were or simply had little or nothing to inherit. Moreover, Lima's wills show that—in contrast to Don Antonio's assertions—natural children were often acknowledged and obtained their share of the inheritance.

37. See, for example, Case 447, AGN, RA, CCI, L 93, C 965, 1810, Autos seguidos por Pascual Zambrano Albacea y uno de los herederos de Doña María del Carmen Cabrera o Pereda solicitando se le reciba Información en el juicio sumarísimo de amparo de filiación.

This case was similar to Doña Maria's. In 1810 María del Carmen lived on a hacienda near the town of Ica. Both of María's "natural parents" had been dead since 1797. María's husband petitioned for a monthly pension for his wife and received a payment of 700 pesos from María del Carmen Pereda's grandaunt.

Not all husbands were as genteel and silent as the corregidor from Lucanas. Sometimes honor was set aside by a deceived husband who openly denounced his unchaste wife. But as described earlier, Lima was a city in which it was difficult to hide. Therefore, there was more than one reason to remain silent after discovering that one's bride was not a virgin. The church did not recognize a "virginity impediment," so a marriage could not be annulled on the grounds of the bride's lack of chastity. If others knew, the only way to vindicate one's honor was by leaving the girl, or, if already married, by divorce. The *arras-propter-nuptias* solution, the paid-for reassertion of a wife's chastity, was mostly a strategy of the upper classes. Even among upper classes, however, this only worked when not too many people knew or in any case were discreet enough. Lower-class husbands would be exposed to mockery and to ongoing suspicions about their wives' whereabouts. Social ridicule and uncertainty about the paternity of the family's children were men's main concerns.

Such painful ethical problems affected a husband and *vecino* (citizen) from Huaraz, a northern highland city, in 1819. His responses were common among *vecinos*, the better-off city dwellers. In this case, as in earlier ones, it had been the girl's parents who had been looking for a husband for their daughter: "Following repeated petitions from her parents, I married under pressure, . . . firmly convinced that my wife was a virgin. I even told them that I would only marry her if she was a virgin." After he had talked to the local priest and the parents, and both had assured him that his future wife was a virtuous woman, he found out that she "had given her heart to the most wretched and despicable man in town . . . who strolled on plazas and streets telling everybody [about her indiscretion]."

Life and honor for this unfortunate husband were one thing: "I am a man who views life and honor as being equally important,"[38] thus his "education and principles did not allow [him] to see [his] honor humbled." His future also was forlorn, because "public opinion can dishonor a husband of a vicious wife. Now public opinion criticizes my wife and scorns my ingenuousness, but these same people will condemn me to disgrace for generations to come; my children's legitimacy will be suspicious in the public eye. I myself, if I had children, would be worrying and thinking whether they were a result of my wife's impure and illegitimate love affairs. And then, how could I devote care and love to these children I suspected were not mine?"[39]

38. "Soy hombre que miro la vida, y el honor en igual Balanza."
39. Case 549, AA, NM, L 59 (1810–19), 1819, Salirrosas y Gonzales vs. Roxas.

For this husband, suspicions arose from the very beginning. Only when consummating the marriage did he realize that he had been cheated, that she had had sex with the town's well-known seducer, and that everyone but him was aware of the situation. When a lack of virginity was exposed, the way the public responded depended on the social status of the people involved, which implied that people in society had class attitudes about virginity. When parents and women searched for a husband, they knew that after marriage the truth could surface. They trusted—as Doña Maria Lama's parents did—in the husband's silence or forgiveness. However, no matter what a husband's intentions were after his disappointment, there was little he could do when people started talking. In a society where status was an important attribute for economic success, virginity became a bargaining chip even after marriage. A wife's lack of virginity could be used by others to defame a husband and destroy his career and reputation.

Even in the midst of a pregnancy, some women and their parents were bold enough to claim virginity to be intact. If the child's father was unwilling to marry to the mother, then another man had to be found to avoid the stain of illegitimacy. But some candidates could not easily ignore a pregnancy in its sixth or seventh month. Still other men had their own, often quite peculiar, ways of noticing that something was wrong even before pregnancy became visible.

In 1816 José Mimbela, a barber with his own shop and a militiaman in the Sixth Dragoon Company, described how Petronila Barraza's parents tried to convince him she was a virgin.[40] The parents' insistence on the perfection of the match created suspicions, and he was even more cautious than the corregidor from Lucanas and the *vecino* from Huaraz. José was a mulatto who lived in Lima and knew his way around the town. He set out to observe his future wife "as it was necessary for me to find the flavor of this woman." In order not to raise suspicion, nobody resisted José's attempts to approach Petronila. But when "she extended her hand to me, I felt her irregular pulse and I noticed a slight pregnancy fever. Right then and there I told her what I thought. In later conversations, I told her that she should not expect to menstruate as all women do. My prediction came true, nothing happened to her that month, and so my suspicions grew. . . . Moreover (and speaking to Your Excellency with the appropriate decorum), I then decided

---

40. "Me la intentaban meter por donzella." Case 66, AGN, Auditoría General de Guerra, CCI, L 21, C 347, Barraza vs. Mimbela.

to make love to her and found her as sleazy as any public woman."[41] José Mimbela's diagnosis had little to do with medical scrutiny.[42] He used popular tactics by which men tested women. Sexual intercourse afterward confirmed he was right, thus perpetuating the "correctness" of the test. José did not marry Petronila, and when she later initiated a legal proceeding to obtain an allowance for her son, José refused to assume any responsibility.

Petronila's reasoning ran differently in a direction we have already seen. She argued that, with "furtive and surreptitious maneuverings," José had seduced her. The court's final decision said the son should be handed over to José for him to "fulfill his parental duties, to rear and educate him." It was very difficult for a woman to prove paternity, but it was equally difficult for a man to demonstrate that he was *not* the father. More than biology, society ascribed paternity. And society was represented by witnesses and neighbors, who were willing to describe in detail a person's background, how reputable and upright a woman and her parents were, and the behavior of the couple.

Frequently, the line between true and faked virginity was deliberately blurred. Although society in nineteenth-century Lima heavily emphasized the value of virginity, people displayed few scruples about disguising lack of chastity. It was important that a woman was a virgin, but if she was not, there were several reasons to be silent and pretend. Consequences multiplied according to how much people knew and gossiped. The cases discussed here range from the elite (the corregidor and the *vecino* from Huaraz) to barbers. Women were both victims and participants in the widely shared social hypocrisy. Nevertheless, there are some striking differences in the handling of the virginity issue. Peragalo was silent, and even offered an *arras propter nuptias* by which he "rescued" his honor and the image of purity of standards. The man from the highlands in Huaraz exposed himself to social criticism, something that probably had to do with the socially narrower confines of a small city. Regional elites were under close scrutiny, hence

---

41. In original Spanish version: "Como me fue preciso, el saver el gusto, de la Muger, que se me comprometía para saver su gusto, en ello no encontré el menor embarazo, y a tiempo de darme la mano, le encontré el Pulso, con una calenturilla de preñez, y en el mismo instante, le hise patente. Y como se entregó enteramente a mi boluntad, fue advertida por mi al desengaño de Esperar la Luna del mes, en la que efectúa toda muger. Viendo pues que ha ésta, por el menor assomo, le vertía el un apize fue mi primer recelo. . . . Lo segundo (y ablando con la veneración devida) por sólo salir de la duda, y dar curso al Matrimonio tube Cópula con la sitada Muger donde la encontré como qualesquiera mundana." See note 40.

42. Such strategies as "feeling the pulse" were harshly criticized by more scientific opinion as being the strategies of charlatans and *curanderos* (popular healers) (Fuentes 1861, 4:20).

his insistence on the honor argument. He was irrevocably trapped. The barber, a person of dark skin, knew the "popular" ways. He did not trust, as the man from Huaraz did, what priests and parents had to say about his future wife's virtues. He found out for himself; he knew "how to read" the pulse, and he did not hesitate to take her to bed. Virginity was important for all men. For some, however, concerns about honor and virginity drove their behavior, and the absence of virginity created suspicions about paternity; for others, virginity or rather the lack of virginity (without the equation to honor) was an expeditious argument to circumvent marriage and paternal responsibilities.

The Consequences

After engaging in premarital sex, a woman was enormously vulnerable and almost completely dependent on the good will of her suitor or her (or her parents') ability to cover the deed with a veil of secrecy. Such ongoing dependency surfaces in the stories told by women about what happened to them in the days, weeks, and years after seduction, elopement, or rape. These stories almost invariably came to light only when divorce or annulment threatened. They represent the worst-case scenario; for these women, everything had gone wrong.

In 1808 María Mercedes Santiago de Ulloa, who characterized herself as a "poor *mestiza*," petitioned for the annulment of her marriage to Eugenio on the grounds that she had been abducted, that her marriage had taken place in a foreign parish, and that her family had not been asked for their consent.[43] She left Lima with her seducer to marry in Yanahuanca, a town located on the route to the central Andean highlands. Yanahuanca's priest refused to marry them and sent them off to a nearby parish in Oyón (in the province of Cajatambo). During this trip, María Mercedes began to fear that

---

43. Case 566, AA, NM, L 58 (1799–1809), 1808, Santiago de Ulloa vs. Vera. "Considerada en clase de una infeliz mestiza, o chola sorprehendio mi inocencia Eugenio Vera persuadiéndome a que casase con él para conseguir un enlace [she had a five year-old daughter], en que no desmintiendo nuestra calidad lograría los desahogos de comodidad que proporcionaría su trabajo y afecto. Mi poca edad, la ignorancia de mi clase y la eficacia del pretendiente forzaron mi condescendencia. Propuesto el contrato a mi Nutriz lo repugno con seriedad penetrando su irregularidad; pero más empeñado Eugenio me insistió a la fuga franqueándome la ocasión de verificarlo."

she had made a terrible mistake: "I understood my wrongdoing and started to despise this man whose few talents and lack of regard toward me made me perceive that the way I was treated was not according to the way I had been reared. There I ended up amidst the miseries of a highland hacienda. He, not having anything, went to his mother's house, where misery made me even more aware of my thoughtless misstep."

Eugenio, for his part, argued that María Mercedes was pregnant by another man when he met her, and that they had not run away together. To the contrary, he implied, her coming with him was a way of escaping social and familial reproach. Both stories sound plausible and are similar to arguments in other cases. Regardless of who the father was, María Mercedes's description eloquently reveals a woman's extreme dependency once having left the parental home. Moving to another town where she had no social ties to compensate for her lost virginity weakened her position even further.

In 1810 Petronila Alvarado described a similarly dramatic story. She was born in Lima, and her husband, Don Manuel Tafur, was from Huánuco, a city in the central highlands, where he took her: "Having tried hard and insistently, even with illegal means, Don Manuel Tafur gained my submission in Lima, and I gave him my hand as a wife. Like all women, I was responsive to his charm and, consequently, exposed to deceit by following his generous offers. Once he succeeded in seducing me, he convinced me to come to this town, where, as he told me, he supposedly had a lot of money and where we would live according to the manner I was used to and even much better." Petronila sold all her possessions in Lima because Don Manuel convinced her that everything would be better in Huánuco. When they arrived, however, she realized that his father owned only a few small properties, which Don Manuel was supposed to administer; but he preferred "pastimes, games, and diversions." They were poor and survived only thanks to her father-in-law, who provided them with 4 reales each day.[44]

Conjugal quarrels and beatings added to Petronila's economic disenchantment. Don Manuel even left her out in the streets. Finally, he went on a trip without arranging for her maintenance, and when her father-in-law died, Petronila's situation grew desperate. She sold her last pieces of jewelry and began borrowing money from her neighbors. She had lost all her belongings—worth 1,815 pesos and 27 reales—and she asked the ecclesiastical authorities to help her to get them back. In this manner, she

44. Case 268, AGN, RA, CCI, L 93, C 976, 1810, Autos seguidos por Doña Petronila Hurtado contra Don Manuel Tafur, su marido sobre la devolución de sus bienes.

placed a price on her misfortune. Petronila lost her honor and her fortune; she never saw her jewelry again.

Different reactions are discernible in the cases of María Mercedes and Petronila. María Mercedes was a *mestiza*, who claimed to be pure and innocent. Petronila, in contrast, had a small fortune. María Mercedes, who had no resources, petitioned for a continuation of support from her former husband. Petronila did not claim virginity or ask for maintenance. The issue of virginity was solved by the marriage that followed. She just wanted to recover what rightfully had belonged to her and what had been used up by her husband. Both of these women had been seduced by promises, although under slightly different circumstances, and they lived with considerable sorrow and disappointment afterward. Their mechanisms of defense and their arguments represent two extremes of a spectrum of many possible situations and outcomes. Seduction and conflict were confronted in different ways according to the woman's background and resources, although they both belonged to what at the beginning of the century was identified as the lower-middle class.

Dependency intensified with children, of course. With the presence of children, the search for material support overrode all other considerations, even virginity. Ultimately, being without children, María Mercedes and Petronila were, in a short-term economic sense, more fortunate than many of their Peruvian sisters.

When Children Were Born

Virginity could be redeemed, but a pregnancy out of wedlock—particularly if the child survived the dreadful social and hygienic circumstances—was more difficult to overlook. Natural children had inheritance rights, and judges required that fathers provide for both natural and legitimate children.[45]

45. According to paragraph 235 of Peru's 1852 Civil Code: "Son hijos ilegítimos los que no nacen de matrimonio ni están legitimados . . . La palabra ilegítimos tiene dos acepciones distintas. Cuando se le considera en oposición á la palabra legítimos, denota á todos los hijos que no han nacido de matrimonio; pero considerada en si misma se puede decir que con respecto al padre los hijos ilegítimos se dividen en naturales é ilegítimos; y con respecto á la madre, en ilegítimos y adulterinos. Se llama hijo natural el concebido en tiempo en que el padre y la madre no tenian impedimento legal para casarse. Para que estos hijos naturales se distingan de los demas ilegítimos del padre, es necesario que estén reconocidos" (García Calderón Sr. 1879, 1069).

Out-of-wedlock pregnancy led to social and personal tragedies—leaving children on church porches or in orphanages, allowing them to die, giving them away, and occasionally even selling them.[46] Between 1796 and 1801, 1,109 children were left in Lima's orphanage.[47] Toward midcentury, Fuentes (1861, 3:208) revealed that eighty-five to ninety wetnurses had to be hired each year at 6 pesos per month. They took children home with them until they were at least twelve months old, and some kept them until they were three years old. According to Macera (1977, 324), in a society in which people believed that unbaptized children went to heaven and became angels, there existed a "psychological gap" to justify abortion and infanticide. Moreover, according to law, abandoned children (*niños expósitos*) were legally "legitimate children." Psychological attitudes as well as legal stipulations created incentives for child abandonment.[48]

Illegitimacy, in spite of its frequency, merited "social condemnation." Had it not been for testamentary rights given to natural children, we would probably never have learned how disgraceful "illegitimate birth" could be, particularly among those whose honor and social status greatly depended on the behavior of their daughters. Emotional portraits of the past such as the one given by Doña Maria Lama are rare. Let us recall that in 1818, her

46. See AGN, CS, CCI, L 572, 1854, Jacoba Oré. Jacoba's father signed a document in which he transferred his daughter to Don Francisco Carrera alleging he was too poor to keep her. The *síndico procurador* stated that "this procedure is completely illegal, because parents do not have the right to take such decisions. Accepting this procedure would be to install a personal serfdom contrary to all universal precepts. If poverty would be a reason to go ahead with such attitudes, we would be close to allowing parents to kill their children, and then we would be back to the savageries of the twelfth century." See also AGN, CS, CCI, L 720, 1859, Doña Inés Belaunde de Mendiburu con el Señor Don José de Mendiburu para que le devuelva una muchacha que le obsequió. Often such "transfers" were made possible because parochial registers were avoided, or dealt with with such negligence that birth and baptism records were lost or never entered: "Los interesados por una costumbre inveterada cuando se les presenta un bautismo anotan en la primera tira que tienen a la vista el nombre del niño que se ba á bautisar, el de sus padres, padrinos, etc. para despues estamparlo todo en el libro parroquial." AGN, PR 279, Notario E. Huerta (1850–51).

47. Here we need to remember that only about 2,000 children were born in Lima each year at the beginning of the nineteenth century (see Chapter 1). McCaa (1991a, 212) states that child abandonment was "an acceptable form of infanticide" in Europe. Similar attitudes are documented for rural Chile around midcentury (Cavieres and Salinas 1991), Buenos Aires, Sao Paulo, and Guadalajara (respectively: Little 1978; Mesgravis 1977; Brennan 1978).

48. José Méndez Lachica, a lawyer in the Real Audiencia in Lima, argued that honorable people and priests had a right to abandon their offspring when threatened by social condemnation or a death penalty (Macera 1977, 316).

daughter initiated a filiation trial against the executor of her mother's will to prove that she was her mother's natural daughter. Behind her stood her husband, Don Antonio García, who outlined the moral quandary: "When a woman of high standing gives birth out of wedlock, even parents are often unaware of their daughter's grief. . . . If after birth the mother marries a man different from the child's father; and if this marriage is followed by still another marriage that lasts until the mother's old age, one must recognize that the birth that had taken place so far back in time, and was the fruit of juvenile thoughtlessness, has to be dug up from under a triple zeal of bashfulness, fear, and the parents' and husband's claims of virginity; that is, in the obscure chaos of a secrecy, which has kept things hidden for such a long time."[49]

The daughter, Doña Monica Lombera, who had been born under the "veil of secrecy," had immediately been handed over to a wet nurse, then to another, and another, and finally was reared in the Count of San Isidro's house, where she was provided for by her father. Later her mother married and had two children. At the trial these individuals willingly declared that their mother—on the pretext of having the gout—had left her parents' home to give birth to her first child "in order to hide away from her parents' watchful eyes and from others who frequented the household." Don Antonio García wrote:

> This young mother thought differently from other mothers, who decide to abandon their children, out of necessity, or due to their parents' ignorance, or because they, who created the child, have an impediment to ordinary marriage. . . . Doña Monica [Lombera] was a natural daughter of Don Francisco Lombera, a person of merit who had affection for the woman he wanted to marry. This marriage did not take place because her parents expressed their dissent. Don Francisco was poor, and only later did he make his fortune. Faith and Don Francisco's resilience prevented their daughter from being abandoned on the porch of a church, to join other poor and disgraced children. He kept the secret and supported his daughter until Doña Monica was old enough to start a family and become a respectable mother herself. Such concerns make her clearly something different from other desperate mothers, who, when confronted with

---

49. Case 298, AGN, Cabildo, Cci, L 38, 1818; and RA, Cci, L 162, C 1671, 1819.

similar impairments, abandon their children, condemning them to be orphans.

This story exposes an unconventional option among the upper classes in a society so prejudiced against illegitimate birth. Most illegitimate children had to be hidden, or more frequently abandoned, according to available statistics and to Doña Monica's husband. Doña Monica's father was willing and able to support her, especially when his fortune later improved. But the case presents clear evidence of prevailing social perceptions, linked both to the issue of parental opposition to marriage and to the social treatment of natural children and the lack of virginity. Don Antonio focused on the mistreatment of natural children and the ruin caused by defilement. To that picture, he contrasted the actions of Don Francisco, who steadfastly met his parental obligations. The trial was a showcase for the positive effects of paternal responsibility. The combination of arguments was an intelligent one in an environment that was extremely sensitive to matters of illegitimacy, because it promoted an implicit acceptance of paternal responsibility to offspring.

Because most natural children were not as lucky as Doña Monica, more frequent scenarios included the desperate search for acknowledgment of paternity and for financial support. Neighbors, midwives, friends, and *compadres* knew details about a couple's life; and many opinions could thus be called upon in the courtroom to attest to a man's day-to-day behavior toward and involvement with a woman and her children. In Cipriana Parra's case, the father himself had admitted his paternity. She wrote:

> In my youth, when I was still inexperienced and did not know that promises for the future should not be believed, I accepted Don Joaquín Moscoso's promise to marry me. I lived with him for some time, during which I lost my virginity and bore a natural child, Juan del Carmen. Don Joaquín has recently died. Before he passed away, to corroborate the *sponsalia* for our future marriage, he arranged that the godfather, Don Fernando Silva, who was chosen by Moscoso, should recognize Juan in baptism, thus carrying on his marriage promises. When I first met Moscoso, he was a poor street vendor, and we both worked together to rear our son. Later on he earned more money and started separating from me, after causing me many pains and troubles. That's when I told him to leave me, to go away, but to pay an allowance for his son. That's what he did, until a friend of

his, Don Ramón, with whom he lived until his death, told him stories about me, and since then I have no longer received his support.[50]

Moscoso had made marriage promises to Cipriana on several occasions, and there were many witnesses to their long-standing relationship. She and Moscoso had worked together, yet once he (not she!) became rich, he left her, continuing to pay for his son until somebody convinced him he had no obligation to continue. Only when Moscoso was dying and his conscience troubled him, did he call upon a godfather to set right his relationship with his son. After his death, Cipriana was still trying to prove that payments to their son were a tacit recognition of paternity and his initial willingness to marry her. Inheritance and allowances explain why "natural mothers" were so eager to have the fathers of their children sign baptismal records.[51] These written records made paternity "legal."

Cipriana claimed her son's one-fifth share of the inheritance, which by law was the right of natural children. Cipriana had not been defeated by her problems with Moscoso: she had married another man, who now presented her petition "with the license she gave me." In this case, inheritance rights were added to the broken marriage promise. Thus, the lawyer defending Joaquín Moscoso's patrimony attempted to show that "Don" Joaquín had no natural children. First, he noted, no child was mentioned in Moscoso's will. Second, Don Joaquín "had not been known in society simply with the name of Joaquín Moscoso, as one designates a black or any other person of low social extraction. To the contrary, he has always been called 'Don' Joaquín Moscoso." The lawyer thus slyly implied that *another* Joaquín Moscoso was the father of Cipriana's child. After his client's death, Moscoso's lawyer tried to deny paternity. Because Moscoso had started out as a simple street vendor but later became rich, his lawyer and his legitimate heirs had to secure his good social standing and reputation, which meant denying any "moral transgressions" (such as having had an illegitimate child) to "cleanse" his public record. However, so many witnesses were on Cipriana's side that Don Joaquín's lawyer failed to win the case. Her relationship with Moscoso had been public knowledge, and this was the way she fought the argument that she was "just another woman trying to find a father for her children."

50. Case 937, AGN, Corte Superior, CCI, L 587, 1855, Autos seguidos por Cipriana Parra en representación de su hijo Juan del Carmen Moscoso contra la testamentaría de Don Joaquín Moscoso sobre filiación de dicho su hijo.
51. For example, see Case 08, AGN, CS, CCI, L 652, 1857, Soria vs. Moreno. This case involved a sergeant who had a natural daughter and three legitimate children.

In another case, registered in 1857, a lawyer argued that it was "not the first time that the unhappy children of unknown fathers just go ahead and choose a father they think is most convenient to them from among the many who could have been their progenitors.... Everyone in town is convinced that baptismal records state what mothers declare or what godfathers claim to be true; and for this reason they do not prove anything but age and devotion, unless a natural father has registered his signature."[52]

On the other hand, Cipriana's story demonstrates the surprising ease with which women accepted, and lived with, broken marriage proposals. When children had been born in these circumstances, the woman's main interest became the children's welfare and, eventually, the defense of their inheritance rights. Once the issues of maintenance and inheritance were settled, women usually refrained from pursuing further arguments based on a betrothal, particularly if written proof did not exist.

Poverty frequently explains the diverse arrangements that men and women used to live together outside wedlock. When economic circumstances improved, a man might accuse his wife of lack of chastity to disentangle himself from his "marriage agreements," despite previous pledges. Whereas society and the church disapproved of common-law marriages and expected unmarried couples to hide their liaison, the more people who knew about an extramarital arrangement, the greater the options that existed for a woman to retain respectability, to obtain recognition for her children, and eventually, to gain a share of the children's paternal inheritance. In other words, forcing women to be silent was also a way of pretending that public morale was "right," and of safeguarding men from accusations of moral transgressions and monetary compensations.

Similar circumstances benefited Doña Nicolasa Rodríguez in 1840,[53] when she presented to the court a love letter from Don José Asca in an attempt to prevent his impending marriage to another woman. When Nicolasa and Don José had first met, he was seventeen years old. In his letter to her, he lamented that he could not marry her. During the following eight years, however, they lived together and had three children. Although the judge admitted her complaint into court, she eventually recognized that it

---

52. Case 932, AGN, Expedientes Judiciales, CCI, L 664, 1857, 38ff, Doña María Josefa Palomino pretende esclarecer su filiación, mediante una sumaria información de testigos previa citación de las Señoras Mujica y Prunas, escrito de las citadas señoras al Juez de Primera Instancia, fs. 5.

53. Case 967, AA, LM, L 9 (1820–49), 1840, Robles vs. Figueroa; and AA, CD, 1840, Rodriguez vs. Asca.

made no sense to oppose Don José's new marriage: "Since I first initiated this suit, more than four years have elapsed, and I have not received any benefit from my opposition; I am now convinced that it is of no use to continue this quarrel. I am also certain that my whim harms my three children. If I let him marry, I hope that he will at least treat the children well. Therefore I want to stop this battle."

Perhaps Don José and his family were pressuring Nicolasa so that in the end she wished only that he would treat the children well, which included providing support for her and them. Even if legal efforts could establish that there had been a promise of marriage and could thus prevent Don José's marriage, this was not necessarily the desired outcome. The initial "consensual" situation had changed, and it seemed wiser to just let go. It was important for women, though, to go to court, even if at the end they accepted the marriage of their suitors to another woman. When fathers did not pay, women—as Nicolasa did—went back to court and reactivated rather than began a lawsuit. There was a legal antecedent women could call upon. By having shown how "reasonable" she had once been, the rights of her children had already been tacitly recognized, and this exempted her from presenting further proofs of paternity. Usually a quick sentence followed.

It is noteworthy that in most cases in which natural children were born, it was the man who married another, not the woman. Thus, men left behind children from the first liaison. Although some women also married other men after giving birth to one or several children, overall, the moral climate of the day narrowed women's options. Thus, above all, it was men engaging in premarital (or parallel) sexual relationships who were "accountable" for high illegitimacy rates.

Lieutenant Colonel Don Juan Manuel Ugarte, an artist of seduction and a conqueror of virgins, had many natural children. His story reveals how a man could have several parallel relationships with women from varied backgrounds, and how women linked to each other only through their relationship with one man perceived each other.

In 1855 the lieutenant colonel lodged in Lambayeque at the home of Don Miguel Navarrete and Doña Andrea Castillo, who were considered *vecinos*, that is, respected citizens of this northern coastal city.[54] "After he had been there for a few days," wrote their daughter, Doña Manuela, "he began pressuring me to get married, and to achieve this he used the most

---

54. Case 919, AGN, Corte Superior, CCI, L 633, 1856; and L 726, 1859, Navarrete vs. Ugarte.

exquisite resources and tricks so that I would give him the *yes* he so much desired." She continued:

> Being young and inexperienced, and without knowing the world, isolated in a town and without understanding anything beyond the domestic horizon, a daughter of my family and younger than 17, I must confess that I was fascinated, believing that his propositions were sincere and came from an honest and well-intentioned heart. I agreed to marry him and gave myself away to him. When I went to my father to tell him about my decision, he was filled with indignation, arguing that Ugarte was no proper spouse for me, because his social position did not match my own and because he was well-known for his immoral customs, something I was not aware of due to my inexperience. I had only come to know Ugarte during the time he stayed with us. When he sensed my father's opposition, he doubled his efforts and asked me to leave my parent's house and move with him to Lima."

And this was exactly what she did. From that day on, she "was completely subdued and doomed to wait for Juan Manuel to fulfill his promise of marriage."

For a year she believed he was preparing the necessary paperwork to get married. In the meantime, she had a daughter and not much more time passed until one day

> Ugarte was bold enough to bring three children he had had with a *mestiza* to our house, telling me to take care of them now that I was going to be his wife; that this was the only alternative for me if I wanted to prevent him from returning to his former relationship and avoid more expenses, which money should be saved for the family we would be starting. From my point of view, I repeat, I suffered all this with resignation, angelical patience, humility, yes, even candor, resigning myself to a situation which up to a certain point hurt the feelings of a seventeen-year-old girl of good family, who had been a virgin and for whom the world once was full of flattery . . . . Now I found myself in some dirty and miserable rooms, without the least comfort. Ugarte did not want me to have friends or go out into the street and even less that men come to visit me. He was afraid I would be aware of his wanderings and wrongdoings, or maybe he was naturally jealous. I lived in a prison, waiting for my master to come back, and he

expected me to be kind. . . . Recently he demonstrated total iniquity by marrying, about a month ago, a young woman called Carmen N., whom he probably also cheated. . . . This man, who absolutely lacks any decency and morality, had been out conquering other women at the cost of my sacrifice. That is why he insisted that I remain at home.

To convince Carmen N. of his devotion to her, Ugarte even gave her some of Doña Manuela's jewelry and clothes. With no remorse whatsoever, he confessed that he "had married, not out of love but out of convenience, because this woman was rich and that later the new wife would help to satisfy her [Doña Manuela's] needs."

A sentence was handed down in this case, and Doña Manuela received a monthly allowance of 25 pesos to rear her daughter. This—she argued—was not enough even to eat: "How is it possible, Your Excellency, that I should pay for all our needs with only twenty-five pesos? The least one must spend each day for food is one peso. This accounts for thirty pesos a month. Suppose I were a black woman and not a Señora, that I should not live in a house but in a coach house. Even this would cost not less than five pesos a month. Suppose that I myself do the cooking, that I myself do my daughter's and my own laundry; but still there is no way I could cure diseases, and I do not know how to make shoes either." She asked for 40 pesos per month, which represented one-third of the lieutenant colonel's income. Her request was denied on the grounds that the other offspring also had to be fed.

This narrative illustrates what coming to Lima meant for a provincial white woman, and the many perils faced once away from the parental shelter. It also reveals how men "conquered" women by taking advantage of their traditional seclusion. Young women of good family often remained ignorant about men and received no real counseling about sex and marriage until disaster had struck.

In this case, three different classes of women participated in Ugarte's matrimonial history. As a military man with a regular income, he was a desirable spouse. One of "his" women was a *mestiza*, who bore him three children and never claimed anything in court; the other was white, apparently a middle-class woman from a northern province, who bore him a daughter and told the whole story to the judges. And the third was a rich white woman in Lima, probably a virgin, and the one he finally decided to marry. Clearly it was the seclusion of these women that prevented them from piecing together a more accurate picture of Ugarte's world, which made his philandering possible. In the end, there were four children born out of wedlock and one marriage.

The account provides at least some insight into the roots of Lima's high illegitimacy rate and also demonstrates how women and society accepted and lived in these settings.[55]

Of the three women involved with Ugarte, only one was able to expand her consciousness to recognize the inconsistencies of her relationship. Yet in every context in which Doña Manuela criticized Ugarte, she blamed her own inexperience and argued that she was treated as being beneath her social status. She never offered a defense of womanhood against treacherous treatment by men, as men frequently did against women. But she did present the "bill." As seen earlier, transgressions between social equals often proved to be the most costly. The *mestiza's* silence may be interpreted as acceptance of her inequality. Through her silence, Carmen N. (not even her last name is mentioned in the file), Ugarte's spouse, won both protection and material goods—Manuela's jewels and clothes—even though this silent acquiescence might have arisen from ignorance about the other women. In short, we see one man and three very different women living intertwined lives. The lieutenant colonel manipulated and charmed; money, children, and gifts were interchangeable while he held the monopoly (and thus the control) over each woman's life.

In regard to the colonial period, Luis Martin (1983, 150–51) argues: "What makes [this period] peculiar is that the illicit sexual relations between the sexes were perceived and reported by the Church, by civil authorities, and by many European observers as a widespread social disease, which was so common and habitual that it was accepted as normal by a large segment of society."

But as seen, "social disease" implied many different experiences, and not everyone in the game was willing to accept the rules silently. As the nineteenth century progressed, natural children became one more argument used to discriminate against the popular classes, among which, presumably, illegitimacy was most widespread. Although popular classes reacted in their own terms to ideals of honor and moral expectations, pressures to conform to the ideal were increasing.

55. It is remarkable how the actual sexual behavior in Lima resembles the accepted and legislated behavior among Germanic tribes. Writes Teichman (1982, 55): "Among the Germanic tribes in pre-Christian times legitimacy was partly a matter of race and class, so that a child could not be legitimate if its parents were unequal in rank or of different races." And "a legitimate child should be defined as one born as the result not of any sanctioned sexual act but of a sexual act which is sanctioned precisely because it accords with the rules governing reproduction" (88).

At the same time, women began to speak out against the double standard of morality. Their complaints reveal a strong desire to see men fulfill their promises of marriage, and above all, take care of their offspring. Women knew that it was difficult to force a man to marry, but natural children were a compelling argument because these children evoked broader social issues, and this, in turn, strengthened the claims of unmarried women. Not even Peru's president in 1854 was exempt from these claims.[56] As a consequence, discussions involving these issues—natural children and public attitudes about single mothers—sounded quite different toward the end of the century. Such arguments were summarized by Adriana Pastor in 1896. In her case, as in so many others, her suitor, Don Emilio García Pacheco, had announced his intention to marry another woman: "Moral law, conscience, and even the church itself cannot allow an individual who has natural children . . . to marry a woman who is not the mother of those children without providing for their future, because this is a duty of all fathers; and it is not possible that a marriage can take place with another woman, who at the same time is unaware that there are children, and who, later on, will suffer the problems and the conflicts which unfailingly arise because the father did not formally recognize his children. There are different rights for recognized and unrecognized children."[57]

Even more blunt were the writings in 1903 of Petronila Tapia, who had several children with José Sebastián Piana: "As I do not have a written record, I do not oppose his marriage to another woman, but I do ask Your Excellency not to forward a marriage permit until the civil judge has decided how much he will have to pay for the maintenance of my children."[58] Ugarte's *mestiza* and his white provincial mistress could have made the very same plea. They did not, at least not in court.

The Pastor vs. García case in 1896 is one of the few at the end of nineteenth century in which a concern for the "other woman" was taken into account, and it indicates how a more inclusive way of thinking about these issues developed when children were added to the mix. In a more direct way, as in the Tapia vs. Piana case in 1903, women began to demand social support in their suits against irresponsible fathers. Natural children were part of everyday life, and mothers expected the church and the state to recognize their needs and fathers' maintenance obligations. They accomplished this by

56. Case 949, AGN, CS, CCI, L 574, 1854, Polison vs. Castilla.
57. Case 0210, AA, LM, L 11 (1870–1903), 1896, Pastor vs. García.
58. Case 253a, AA, LM, L 11 (1870–1903), 1899, Tapia vs. Piana.

eventually accepting a father's marriage to another woman and by defending their children's rights. This was not only in their own interest but also in the interest of society at large, at a moment when positivism underlined the virtues and responsibilities of motherhood. Abandoned children were a threat to scarce municipal and ecclesiastical resources and to public morality. Because individuals were coming to be seen as responsible for their own actions, a reasonable solution to illegitimacy was to urge fathers to accept their duties and (what was perhaps more effective) to make them support their natural children. From a female perspective, a delicate blackmail was involved: society dictated that women remain in the home, avoid public appearances, and if possible, not work at all. So who would support the children?

Doña Manuela claimed that her allowance was too little to meet daily needs and the increasing cost of living. Adriana went farther. She criticized moral standards and legislation, above all the way laws relating to natural children were applied. Even more radical comments came from women who were unsuccessful in either marrying or obtaining financial support for their children.[59]

The honor code could be manipulated by the audacious of both sexes. Social fragmentation along class and race lines encumbered the emergence of an ideal bourgeois family. Something was terribly wrong about how gender relations were defined. In the course of the nineteenth century, women learned that promises for the future should not be trusted; men learned that promises of virtuous behavior in the past were underhanded, in part as a result of their own doings.

59. Other cases in which opposition to marriage is registered, either by parents or the woman involved are: Case 0262, AA, LM, L 11 (1870–1903), 1896, Valenzuela vs. Eyzaguirre; Case 0253, AA, LicM, L 6 (1880–99), 1894, Casaña vs. García; Case 0247, AA, LicM, L 6 (1880–99), 1899, Sotomayor vs. Forja; Case 0240, AA, LM, L 11 (1870–1903), 1899, Sánchez vs. Coronel; Case 0217, AA, LM, L 11 (1870–1903), 1905, Puntriano vs. Puntriano; Case 213, Comunicaciones Oficiales de Curas, L 1, 1808, Fuentes vs. Guapalla; Case 483, AA, LM, L 7 (1800–1809), 1809, Puente vs. León; Case 636, AA, Esponsales, 1812, Vilchez vs. Abregu; Case 723, AGN, Corte Superior, CCI, L 567, 1854, Ballesteros vs. Exelmes; Case 835, AGN, Expedientes Judiciales, CCI, L 749, 1859, Grillo vs. Zevallos; Case 0214, AA, LM, L 11 (1870–1903), 1917, Poma vs. Chanca; Case 0195, AA, LicM, L 6 (1880–99), 1892, Jordán vs. Stagnano; Case 0105, AA, LM, L 11 (1870–1903), 1892, Alvares vs. Escalante y Viteri; Case 0111, AA, LM, L 11 (1870–1903), 1896, Balcázar vs. Estrada; Case 0142, AA, LM, L 11 (1870–1903), 1896, Espinoza vs. Paucarchuco; Case 0175, AA, LM, L 11 (1870–1903), 1890, Luján vs. Céspedes; Case 939, AGN, Corte Superior, CCI, L 284, 1841, Predasa vs. Olavegoya; Case 113, AGN, RA, CCI, L 17, C 194, 1802, Campos vs. Vergara. And, foreigners were no exception: see Case 925, AGN, Corte Superior, CCR, L 124, 1853, Oliva vs. Ray.

The Messages

The issue of sex and the dependence of women is a core element in how society produces and reproduces its fundamental characteristics. Throughout the nineteenth century, much of marriage and premarital life revolved around virginity. This chapter showed sex and virginity as essential ingredients in the cultural manipulation of marriage that included the creation of a space for bargaining and negotiation in a highly fragmented society. Men and women had different issues at stake, and as they bargained across the decades minor changes in moral perceptions appeared.

In a society in which blacks, whites, Indians, and others coexisted, different moral qualities were attributed to different sectors of the population. Virginity had a price among the middle and lower classes, and premarital sex was perceived as a social disaster among upper classes because nothing but utmost secrecy could prevent the loss of honor. But even then, elites were often at the mercy of their lower-class servants. Behind these differences lies the understanding that virginity had different prices depending on who owned it. This assumption, in turn, greatly influenced gender relations. As a one-time bargaining chip, virginity was subjected to abuse. From men's point of view, virginity was something to be "taken" by degrees of violence, from seduction and elopement to abduction and rape. Taking a virgin was a measure of manliness among men; it could be used to humiliate an opponent for economic, social and/or political reasons; it could be used to get an otherwise unattainable wife. From a woman's point of view, the loss of virginity could become a legal weapon to demand reparation and support, if not marriage. Once children were born, the maintenance request was stronger if the woman had been a virgin when she first had sex with the child's father. For many women the loss of virginity was—eventually—a romantic event. However, deception often followed, and marriage was not always the outcome. Especially among the lower classes, the loss of virginity did not necessarily lead to marriage. To the contrary, there is evidence that with the backing of a community and the family, women could and would resist marrying in spite of having lost their "honor."

Diverse strategies and objectives played out on the bargaining ground lie at the base of "irregular" family settings. The high rates of illegitimate birth are the single most significant expression of these manifold familial arrangements, even if for many couples marriage was the sought-after option. To a great extent "irregularity" was made possible by racial diversity, that is, by men's perception that not all women merited the same recognition or treatment under the same honor codes. There were women a man would marry (virgins of higher social standing, greater wealth, and whiter skin), and there were women with whom he could have children without entering into the responsibilities of marriage (lower-standing, mostly Indian or colored women who were willing, or who believed they could surpass social barriers by giving up their sexual virtues).

There existed very dissimilar virtue and honor benchmarks. Society's overall expectations of adequate and decent behavior were jeopardized daily under different class- and race-based scenarios. In the realm of unfulfilled expectations women measured their own situations and their husbands' or lovers' attitudes, comparing them against the ideal. Then they asked the courts (both civil and ecclesiastical) to do something in the name of these societal and religious ideals. In the course of time, moral ideals expounded to women became more stringent; at the same time, women denounced more insistently the double standard and the implicit racism underlying such duplicity, and they demanded that civil judges intervene to rescue their children from starvation. The gap between moral ideals and women's claims widened as women moved their claims from ecclesiastical courts and moral concerns to civil courts and pecuniary demands. As we will see in the following chapter, this gap is even more palpable in the realms of legal bargaining when dowries, subsistence, and marital obligations were tied into the moral arguments surrounding marriage.

7

Dowries and Marriage in Civil Court

The practice of dowry exchange had a bearing on how inheritance was distributed, whom one should or could marry, and how a new family's economic and social life was organized. As such, it connected kinship structure to the economy. Dowries transferred assets within a social group or among different social groups, and in so doing altered the character of these relationships. In the multiethnic world of nineteenth-century Lima, the mechanisms of transfer blended cultural traditions, social perceptions, and intergenerational relationships. In contrast to the moral issues attached to virginity, consent, and natural children; the triad of dowry, *arras propter nuptias,* and alimony represent explicitly economic aspects of intergenerational and marital bargaining. Significantly, marriage and divorce were dealt with in ecclesiastical court, but dowries were a civil court problem addressed only after a divorce file had been opened in ecclesiastical court. Although honor and morality were vital ingredients in both judicial arenas, the economic aspect of marital life—money for survival—was also a critical point of contention.

Defining Dowries: The Legal Context

The giving of a dowry began a cycle of exchange between two families. It was not a single event involving a unilinear exchange; in many cases it represented the knitting together of the first threads of what would become long-term entanglements. The manifold meanings and implications of dowry exchange required complex legal rules, involving stipulations on inheritance, marriage, and divorce. The decay of the dowry system during the nineteenth century resulted in a widening of possible marriage choices, a weakening of intergenerational manipulation, and increased male control on marital assets and women's income. In the face of its disintegration, however, women found it possible to manipulate the *definition* of the dowry to further their struggle for economic survival in the face of abandonment or divorce.

A central definition of dowries—at least in modern occidental societies— was the endowment of a daughter by her parents when she married. According to Peruvian legislation, a dowry was "everything a woman brings into her marriage to make marital life possible" (*"Se llama dote todo lo que lleva la mujer para sostener las cargas del matrimonio"*). However, parents were not always alive when their children married, nor was the full dowry necessarily transferred to the new couple on their wedding day. By deferring the payment of a woman's dowry, parents could buttress dependency while reinforcing generational interaction (and sometimes conflict). In some cases, parents simply did not have liquid or portable assets with which to endow their daughter.

Influenced by Spanish legislation, the Peruvian civil code until the end of the nineteenth century recognized that there were different kinds of dowry, depending on when the dowry was handed out, who apportioned it, and whether the individual items listed as being part of a dowry were appraised or not.[1] Spanish law and Peruvian codes restricted parents' leeway to dispose of their wealth. Parents were induced to treat their children as equitably as possible. Although legally imposed restrictions on inheritance were a device to slash patriarchal control, parents still had much leeway to interfere and control their children's lives.

When parents died, their executors established *hijuelas* (inventories) prior to the division of the estate. In these inventories, dowries were considered an inheritance given in advance to daughters. For that reason, execu-

---

1. Definitions included: *adventicia* (consisting of items owned by a woman) or *profecticia* (consisting of items given to a daughter by her father or other male paternal relative); *voluntaria* (given by someone who was not obliged by law to do so) or *necesaria* (given by those who by law are obliged to endow a woman); and *estimada* (when the dowry items were specified and priced) or *inestimada* (when no value is given for the items involved).

tors had to make an accounting of the dowries, even those given years earlier. Following the inventory, the executor appraised the dowry and allocated its equivalent value to the heirs, striving for equity and fairness among all. If at the time of death the parents' wealth had increased, daughters could receive further allotments over and above the amount they had been given as a dowry. If the reverse was true, the son-in-law was required to return an amount corresponding to the loss. This was added to the *hijuela* to be redistributed in equal shares to all heirs. Regardless of when it was originally given, it was not until an inheritance from the wife's parents had definitely been settled that a dowry could be considered finalized. By making a son-in-law responsible for the dowry, he and his wife remained linked to *her* natal family. When parents-in-law enjoyed a long life span, the dowry relationship could mean that a husband remained entangled with his wife's family for decades. By tying a husband to his wife's family, a dowry weakened the preeminence of the paternal family and, at the family-cluster level, the typical superiority of "wife-receivers" in a patriarchal society.

The 1852 Civil Code tended to attach similar meaning and weight to dowries and *arras propter nuptias*. However, a reading of wills shows that there were class distinctions in how dowries and *arras propter nuptias* were handled. Among the middle and upper classes, the exchange occurred shortly after marriage by means of a notarized transfer of the dowry reciprocated with a tenth of the husband's total wealth to his wife in the form of an *arras propter nuptias*. This followed Spanish custom very closely. Ideally, the *arras* was equal to the value of the wife's dowry, and its receipt was registered in the dowry instrument.[2] Among middle- and lower-class people, the gift of the *arras* sometimes had to be postponed until long after the wedding, when the wife's dowry had been used to earn the money to make the donation. Among the lower classes—as will be discussed—the practice of exchanging dowries and *arras* became blurred during the nineteenth century. Objects and transactions defined as a dowry or as an *arras* no longer matched either elite traditions or legal expectations.

As documented elsewhere in Latin America (Couturier and Lavrin 1979; Nazzari 1991), parents used dowries to ensure their daughter's upward

---

2. The amount of a man's wealth apportioned in the form of *arras* varied from society to society, as did the timing at which a woman had access to it. In Barcelona in the thirteenth and fourteenth centuries, women received half of their husband's belongings and could freely manage them. In Genoa in the twelfth century, the *arras* also comprised half of a man's wealth (Owen-Hughes 1978, 277–78).

social mobility by attracting the "right" spouse. The dowry was also a social mechanism providing the foundation for the creation of a new household. Because the giving of a dowry presupposed a postnuptial "donation" of the *arras propter nuptias*, the institution had the character of a transaction, a financial exchange of sorts. It could be used to exclude social inferiors and newcomers from marrying into the elite because, in principle, the *arras* had to match the dowry in value. Parents wished to marry their daughters to suitors of equal or better social standing, and a dowry was the means to achieve this ideal. In line with the stipulations of the 1776 Pragmática, a dowry was a parental mechanism to manipulate the choice of a marriage partner. Although parents were obliged to hand down equal shares to their children, they could withhold a dowry (as they could an inheritance) when they disagreed with a daughter's choice of a husband. Thus, it also was a means to reproduce class and race segregation (Mariluz Urquijo 1960). For the seventeenth and eighteenth centuries, Martin (1983, 104, 139–40), in his portrait of social relations in Lima, describes marriage as a social and public deal, usually based on family interests. Dowries were an instrument to bribe people, to alter their will and desire, as well as a way to uphold class interests and "racial purity." Underage children who contravened parental wishes could not only be disinherited, but in the case of daughters, could also be "disdowried."[3] In Lima, throughout the nineteenth century, civil codes kept this threat alive.[4]

In colonial times, once a dowry or portions of it had been transferred to a new couple,[5] earnings derived from investing dowries became acquest (*gananciales*). The use of a dowry and its investment required the

---

3. The *mejoras* represented a positive enforcement of parental authority. In colonial Spanish law, parents could grant *mejoras* of between one-fifth and one-third of the total inheritance; Peruvian civil codes indicated that only the one-third *mejora* was applicable and that it could not exceed double the amount of what the other heirs received as their share of the inheritance.

4. "Estas dos disposiciones declaran en general que la hija menor que se casa contra la voluntad de sus padres, no puede exigir dote; y es de notar que para este caso no se requiere que el ascendiente alegue causa: por solo el hecho de haberse contrariado la voluntad paternal, cesa la obligación de dotar, y por consiguiente el derecho de exigir dote" (García Calderón Sr. 1879, 789).

5. No pattern concerning when the timing of the transfer of the dowry and the *arras propter nuptias* is discernible in Lima's nineteenth-century notarial records. It was bequeathed before, after, or during marriage, even though the law mandated that *arras* could only be handed over to a wife *before* marriage. The law did not mean to restrict marital generosity but to ensure that husbands did not use this device to escape creditors, because according to law when a husband died, dowry and *arras* had to be paid ahead of all other debts. If, nevertheless, the law was not strictly observed, this reveals a high degree of flexibility, which perhaps indicates that

woman's (or her family's) approval. Modifications to the basic intent of the Pragmática of 1776 gradually appeared. In the 1852 Civil Code, everything obtained from dowry investments, or—when there was no dowry—half of the paraphernalia, became part of commonly held assets of the marriage. Only clothes, the marital bed, basic household furniture and supplies, and capital given as *arras* and dowry (not including any interest or profits earned from the use of that money) were excluded. A woman's control over these items was protected. Even when prosecution over inheritance was pending or creditors were claiming debt payments, the dowry or half of the paraphernalia and the *arras propter nuptias* legally remained a woman's property that had to be protected from any other claims. (Regulations governing merchants' families varied from the norm. A merchant could use his wife's dowry as security for a loan[6]). As a result, the conflict arising from the existence of a dowry and the special rights attached to it, and the claims of creditors became a "liberal controversy": special property rights for women were incompatible with an open market economy (see Chapter 9).

Even when spouses contributed unmatched portions to the marriage, acquest (in money and in kind) was divided equally. If a woman deserted her home, she could not claim an acquest for the period of time she had been absent. In the 1891 code, men were subjected to the same pecuniary punishment.[7] As a widow, a woman was entitled to receive the full amount of her dowry, the paraphernalia, and the *arras propter nuptias*. In addition, she had a right to receive half of the earnings accumulated during her marriage (the acquest). In other words, a husband had a right to half of the earnings derived from his wife's property, but the dowry itself and the groom's gift to the bride remained the property of the woman.

Until 1852, if a woman brought nothing into the marriage, when widowed she could ask for one-fourth of her husband's personal property (the *cuarta marital*), defined as items notarized as being his prior to the marriage. After 1852, the *cuarta marital* rule was extended to the husband. The widowers of rich wives now received one-fourth of their deceased wife's property. In this

---

the decision to give the *arras* was based on personal interaction rather than strict compliance with existing rules.

6. Civil Code Arts. 979ff. For a general presentation on dowries in Peru's civil code, see also García Calderón Sr. (1879, 789–93).

7. Valverde 1942, Título VII De los deberes y Derechos que nacen del Matrimonio: 366ff.; also 43–44; and *Actas de las Sesiones de la Comisión Reformadora del Código Civil Peruano*, D.S. 26/81922, con registro de las sesiones a partir de 1928, particularly fascicle 6, títulos III–X: 256–73.

way, the Spanish *cuarta marital* was renamed and became the *cuarta conyugal*. Thus, the *cuarta* was insurance for the widow (and later also for widowers) in cases when no common property (acquest) had accumulated during the marriage or when a woman had married without a dowry. Notably, the *cuarta conyugal* rule assumed that a husband or a wife had some personal wealth. The 1852 Civil Code explicitly regulated which kind of expenditures (funeral and clothing costs, the temporary allowance given to a widow until the *hijuelas* were set, and so forth) had to be paid from which kind of goods.[8]

In short, there existed two kinds of wealth, defined by who made the contribution and when: personal goods, designated as either the man's or the woman's individual contribution to the marriage; and commonly held assets, defined as acquest, including earnings from the investment of dowries, *arras*, and paraphernalia.

The *instrumento dotal* (notarized dowry document) formally recognized a woman's right to her dowry and required a husband not to misspend or use it to his sole advantage. The *instrumento* involved a moral promise as well as a written statement. In case the husband died or divorce ensued, both *arras* and dowry went to the woman. If the woman died or a separation ensued and there were no children, her dowry and the *arras* had to be returned to her family.[9] If children existed, a woman's dowry and the *arras* became a part of the children's maternal inheritance after her death, which their father could use toward their support and education.

A married woman retained her property rights to the dowry, but it was her husband who was in charge of administering it. The sole exception

---

8. If no notarial register detailing what each of the spouses had brought into a marriage existed, the entire estate at the time of death was considered to be part of the acquest. If there were children from a previous marriage, a dowry acknowledgment or a notarized *capital de bienes* (a prenuptial agreement specifying individual allotments) limited what would not be inherited by the children of the second marriage. Any inheritance a woman received from her parents after marriage and in addition to her dowry was administered by her husband, and both spouses had acquest rights to the profits obtained from inheritance investments. This was true for a husband's inheritance as well as for a wife's.

9. This was a feature that Spanish colonies and Mediterranean societies had in common (Kirshner 1978; Klapish-Zuber 1985). Apportioning a dowry involved many immediate purposes, such as the display of status and the public announcement of a new or renewed family alliance. It was a way to compensate monetarily for a lack of nobility and virginity and to establish hierarchies between two families and the spouses themselves. Because dowries could comprise many different items, these hierarchies were charged with subjectivity and thus expressed generally accepted norms. Given the subjectivity involved in the assessment of the value of the items included in a dowry, returning a dowry was a delicate matter. Class alignments and family clusters could wither and lead to legal action.

to a husband's overall control was the paraphernalia, a woman's personal belongings, typically including her jewelry and furniture. Spanish colonial law and the 1852 and 1891 Civil Codes, protected paraphernalia extremely well against the onslaught of creditors or a husband's arbitrary misuse. In the case of a husband's mishandling of his wife's paraphernalia, she had legal means to seek redress. Of all her property, jewelry was perhaps the most protected. Heirloom jewelry represented tradition, deep generational links, and an expression of the female line of accumulation within the extended family in a bilateral inheritance system. A woman's jewelry, together with a trunk of clothes (which were relatively expensive and more often than not were also heirlooms), were the material representation of "womanhood." Jewelry could also be a family's last resource to free itself from painful debts or hunger. A mother willed jewelry to a daughter so she would have a "life raft" in case her husband failed to provide for her or abandoned her outright. A husband's gift of jewelry augmented a wife's personal belongings and was a measure of how well she fared in her marriage.

In exchange for a woman's contribution to marriage (the dowry and since 1852, eventually half of the paraphernalia), a husband was expected to fulfill his marital duties, which basically were to feed, shelter, and clothe his wife and their children. If a husband failed to meet these duties after he received the dowry, his wife could use—and we will see that wives actually did use—this fact in building a court case against her husband. In court, proof of a dowry transfer created a strong case for alimony and thus opened the doors of civil courtrooms to women. In all other legal entanglements, women needed a husband's permission to file in court.

On occasion, women without a dowry received an *arras* following their marriage. The notarial record addressed why the woman did not have a dowry or why the husband chose to make a donation. These *arras* praised the wife's virtues (even if it had no basis in fact, as was the case with Peragalo recounted earlier). For widows who remarried, the *arras* was meant to buy her chastity even though she was no longer a virgin. Thus, especially when an *arras* was notarized shortly after marriage or was given without the precedent of a dowry, it was a public demonstration of a wife's sexual purity and/or future chastity. A delay in apportioning an *arras* could create suspicions about a wife's virginity among parents, neighbors, and friends awaiting its public recording. In this sense, a wife's virginity had a "public component." Although meant as a reward for receiving a pure wife, the *arras* remained under the husband's control. A wife could only use her *arras,* and the family's resources in general, with her husband's written consent or after divorce, declared mental illness, or death. Whatever its intention, the *arras* was a compensation with no definite rules. In Lima most husbands did not hand over an *arras propter nuptias* when there was no dowry,[10] which signals the essentially economic character of this exchange rather than its virtue-virginity component. Grooms often promised a postnuptial contribution based on anticipated future earnings. Throughout the entire century, only two cases, both in 1820, show that the *arras* was equivalent to the dowry received and represented approximately one-tenth of the husband's total fortune. Surprisingly, in most cases the *arras* was considerably larger than the dowry.[11] Such distortions signal important deviations from the norm. People from various social backgrounds mentioned dowries and *arras* in conjugal conflict cases and in wills; often, however, these exchanges were used as an abstract idea or a device to express honor codes and eventually gain some economic benefits.

The unofficial nature of *arras* also allowed a husband freedom to choose when and how much he would hand over to his wife. The anticipation of a promised *arras* gave husbands considerable leverage after marriage and became a continuing influence on a wife's behavior. It could be used to punish a woman's "bad behavior" or disobedience, such as refusing sex. The social association between virginity and *arras propter nuptias*[12] was thus expanded to mean a widened control on women's moral behavior in general. However, according to the law, only if a husband had transferred an *arras* immediately following the wedding could the funds be safeguarded from creditors. It was not possible to make a quick *arras* transfer to escape financial responsibilities. Thus, the law granted creditors protection against the rights attached to a bilateral inheritance system, or, to put it differently, the risks of the market—a very fluctuating one in the nineteenth century—enhanced women's prospects to have their dowries augmented and limited the ability of husbands to use an *arras* as a moral whipping device.

Each social group had different stakes in the dowry system. Whereas for upper-class families dowries were essentially a demonstration of social status

---

10. A postnuptial "countergift" occurred only in seven wills in 1810, in three in 1820, in two in 1830, in one in 1840, in four in 1850, in one in 1860, in none in 1870, in one in 1880, and none in 1890 and 1900.

11. This, in turn, was so in four cases in 1810, in one case in 1820, in two cases in 1830, in none in 1840, in two in 1850, in one in 1860, in none in 1870, in one in 1880, and in none in 1890 and 1900.

12. In this case the *arras* very closely resembled the Teutonic *Morgengabe* (morning-gift), a reward for virginity that formally established control of women's sexuality and was not bound to the existence of a dowry. See also Owen-Hughes (1978, 275).

and prestige and a way to block social mobility, for middle-class men they were a means of financing commerce or establishing a business. Using a dowry as start-up capital involved great risk. Many families were successful with this strategy, but others witnessed disaster when their investments failed; and after the disaster could come divorce and claims to recover dowries. Among the lower classes, the new family often depended on dowries as the immediate monetary reserve in order to survive; and in most cases, they were distributed by the marrying woman or a relative, rather than by her parents.

Many agents, including women themselves, recognized the "social usefulness" of the dowry system. Some dowries were handed out by guardians and others belonging to the wider kinship network. Masters endowed their female slaves. People with money, no heirs, and charitable ideals would leave rents or money to institutions such as the Buenas Memorias de Dotes y Obras Pías, and the Colegio de Niñas Expósitas (Fuentes 1861, 3:194), and from 1837 on, the Beneficencia Pública de Lima provided dowries for "honest," poor or orphan girls upon their marriage or entrance into a convent. Husbands who received these dowries were usually members of the lower classes. If the couple did not have children at the time the woman died, they were obliged to return the amount received. In case of separation, both partners were obliged to return the dowry money, which would then be allocated to the next girl on the waiting list. The size of these dowries was comparatively low, fluctuating between 300 and 1,000 pesos, in contrast to upper-class dowries, which fluctuated between 20,000 and 40,000 pesos. The institutional granting of dowries was subject to rules somewhat different than those for society in general, but the basic intention was the same, that is, sponsoring marriage as the desired form for reproduction—both sexual and cultural—as well as an incentive to Lima's much-needed population growth and "moral improvement."[13]

In summary, then, understanding the social roles of dowries and inheritance is problematic because their definition and use changed according to the class of the litigants and the time when the suit was brought. By the

---

13. From very early on in New Mexico—and also in Lima—dowries given out by the Crown were meant to enhance a *mestiza's* social standing to make her attractive to a Spanish spouse. Early in the colonial period, such a dowry was a device intended to compensate for the lack of Spanish women who emigrated to the colony (Marshall 1939, 169–70). For an in-depth discussion of the laws and stipulations concerning institutional dowries (*dotes de patronato*) in the nineteenth century, see García Calderón Sr. (1879, 791–93). Until very late in the nineteenth century, dowries were subject to new rulings as to how, when, and who could or should receive them. Thus, although the importance of the dowry practice decreased throughout the century, there still was much ink used to refine their allocation.

nineteenth century, dowries had more functions and meanings in Lima's multiethnic environment than in the societies of the Mediterranean where the practice originated.

Dowries in Numbers

In industrial societies, dowries tended to disappear in the course of the nineteenth century (Goody 1983, 241). In Europe, the working class began to drop the practice early in the century; the middle and upper classes gave it up only toward the end of the century. These changes were related to the emergence of liberalism and the changes in gender relations within the family. In São Paulo, the best studied site in Latin America concerning dowries, the nineteenth century witnessed a drastic change and decay of the dowry system (Nazzari 1991; 1994, 401–13).[14] Nineteenth-century Lima was not an industrial society, and its social composition was different from São Paulo. An examination of inheritance records shows how frequently dowries were a part of matrimonial transactions in nineteenth-century Lima.[15]

The general trend is quite clear: by 1870 the number of wills mentioning a dowry drops to less than half the number at the beginning of the century. A sample across the century (Tables 7.1 and 7.2) shows that not only the absolute number of dowries but also the average total value decreased, dropping from 9,269 to 5,166 pesos.[16]

---

14. Nazzari (1994, 402) states: "Hacia mediados del siglo XIX, la situación había cambiado por completo: las hijas ya no obtenían mayores privilegios que los hijos. Se hacían pocos legados a las hijas solteras, y menos de un tercio de las familias acaudaladas [in contrast to 90 percent during the seventeenth century] otorgaba dotes; las que lo hacían, otorgaban legados comparativamente menores con un contenido diferente que no servía grandemente para que los recién casados se mantuvieran. En fin, los esposos acabaron por mantener a sus esposas, en lugar de que éstas proveyeran la mayoría de los medios para el sostenimiento inicial del matrimonio, como había sido el caso durante el siglo XVII."

15. All dowries mentioned in the wills are considered, whether they were handed out at the beginning of marriage or later. Some female testators mentioned that they had received a dowry, others that they had given dowries to their offspring, and in some cases both kinds of transaction were mentioned. Thus, a single dowry could involve two generations but was registered as one case with two occurrences. Not considered are cases mentioning an "inheritance" given to a woman, even if the transfer took place at the time of marriage.

16. This decay in the value of dowries is even more notable when the devaluation of the peso since 1885 is taken into account.

Table 7.1 Dowries mentioned in wills, 1810–1900

Year	Total No. of Wills	No. of Married and Widowed Testators	No. of Wills Mentioning Dowries	%
1810	192	132	33	25.0
1820	174	133	25	18.8
1830	154	105	21	20.0
1840	122	88	16	18.1
1850	125	84	18	21.4
1860	91	63	12	12.7
1870	151	102	10	9.8
1880	159	106	14	13.2
1890	102	73	7	9.6
1900	124	90	8	8.9

SOURCE: AGN, Notarial Records, Wills.

Table 7.2 Average dowry, 1810–1900 (in pesos)

Year	Average Value of Dowries	Range: Lowest / Highest
1810	9,269	500 / 47,744
1820	8,787	500 / 33,000
1830	4,042	450 / 14,000
1840	5,755	200 / 27,750
1850	8,175	500 / 45,000
1860	7,940	200 / 60,000
1870	5,157	600 / 20,000
1880	5,400	700 / 25,000
1890	4,875	1,500 / 10,000
1900	5,166	200 / 13,000

SOURCE: AGN, Notarial Records, Wills.

Dowry composition was also mentioned in another type of notarial record: the dowry acknowledgment. Although records exist for 1800–1820 and 1840–60, no acknowledgments appear between 1890–1910. For 1800–1820, dowries ranged between 200 and 114,000 pesos. Between 1840 and 1860, the range ran from 300 pesos to 100,000 pesos. Dowries at the lower end (200 to 3,000 pesos) were registered in the families of artisans and small merchants. In the range between 3,000 to 10,000 pesos, we find bureaucrats, lawyers, and members of the military. The last and smallest group, those endowing daughters with 10,000 pesos or more, included *hacendados* (estate owners), military officers, prominent merchants, and the nobility. Neither period exhibits a clear tendency in regard to the timing of the exchange. Although some dowries were given at the time of marriage, records indicate that many exchanges occurred years after the wedding, although most fall within a range between one and nine years.

Between 1800 and 1820, the average amount transferred was 14,135 pesos. Between 1840 and 1860 the average had declined to 9,450 pesos.[17] In wills, amounts registered are lower than in the dowry acknowledgments. Thus, the average size of a dowry varied according to which kind of document is examined. The difference can be accounted for. Poorer people did not bother to register the dowry exchange and assumed that a declaration in the will was enough. Some wills even make this explicit. Thus, dowry acknowledgments are less representative of the existence of dowries than are wills, because wills also reflect dowry practices among the less well off. Although there is a difference in the range of the amounts transferred, in both wills and dowry acknowledgments we observe the same decline. This finding is underlined by a comparison of our data with research on Lima's nobility in an earlier period. At the end of the eighteenth century the average dowry for government ministers (*ministros* and *regidores*) was about 40,000 pesos (Lohmann 1974), three to eight times greater than the average only fifty to one hundred years later. Between 1810 and 1850, a few dowries in amounts close to 40,000 pesos were registered, and similar amounts also appear in 1860, probably reflecting the guano boom. But by 1890 these large amounts had vanished completely. The highest amount registered that year was 10,000 pesos in a dowry for the daughter of a German immigrant whose fiancé was a local merchant. Thus, dowries had become much less important for Lima's inhabitants, especially the elites, than they had been at the beginning of the century and earlier.

Leaving aside potential problems with averages, dowries on average were much smaller in Mexico City and Buenos Aires than in Lima (Bronner 1978; Kicza 1983; Ladd 1976; Socolow 1978). Because Mexico City and Buenos Aires were economically strong—especially their merchant classes—it may be that dowries as a social institution among elites were more important in societies dealing with financial crisis. (Could this indicate that elites used the dowry to tighten bonds? Or, maybe a hurried transfer of money from Spanish fathers to Creole sons-in-law shortly before they had to leave for

17. The samples for each period were gathered from wills in notarial records. In a few cases, the dowry acknowledgment refers to a point in time earlier or later than the period mentioned.

Spain after 1825?) If we compare Mexico City, Buenos Aires, São Paolo, and Lima a few decades later (Ladd 1976; Socolow 1978; Nazzari 1991) we find that the size of dowries in Lima dropped the fastest. The economic crisis preceding and following the War of the Pacific (1879–85) cancelled a rapid transfer option. The Chilean occupation drained liquid resources out of the country. The landed elite was forced to pay *cupos* to avoid damages to their properties; Lima was plundered several times, both by the Chilean army and by Lima's inhabitants. The intensity of the economic crisis made it impossible to make dowry payments as large as earlier in the century, in contrast to the more stable and dynamic economies in Mexico City, Buenos Aires, and São Paulo toward the 1870s.

In spite of the equality stipulations concerning dowry and inheritance, there were differences between daughters and sons, not necessarily in terms of how much each received, but in terms of the items passed down. For the most part, male heirs received property (houses, *haciendas*, *solares* (urban lots), *callejones* (alleys), *chacras* (vegetable gardens), and *fincas* (small landed property), whereas women received dowries consisting of money and paraphernalia. Of the eighty-eight dowry acknowledgments (for 1810, 1850, and 1890), only thirteen (14.8 percent), all valued at more than 3,000 pesos, contained landed property; and even then, in terms of the total value of the dowry, the real estate was not the most important share. Real estate went to sons; male status was measured in land. Women were rated by their marriage partners and the money and other valuables they contributed. A gender-differentiated transmission of assets helped avoid the dispersal of a family's real estate.[18] Endowing women with money and consumption items—which had a notarially recorded "price"—made transfers between families more transparent and easier to handle in case of marital conflict or death. Although endowed daughters were not completely excluded from land ownership, productivity and transparency worked against them. For most elite families, land was an essential resource: it granted prestige, security, and often the collateral for loans. By restricting a daughter's access to land, parents could postpone the fragmentation of their agrarian enterprises, at least until death made partition unavoidable.[19] It was also a device

---

18. Lima was not the only place registering such trends, as noted by Owen-Hughes for Sienna in the thirteenth and fourteenth centuries and Toulouse in the fourteenth and fifteenth centuries (1978, 281).

19. In the case of Medieval Europe, this system has been interpreted as a mechanism to prevent women from owning land or property and thus to "disinherit" them since, after

to reinforce a husband's status and power within the new family. Daughters were temporarily "paid off" to keep the estate together. Husbands, in turn, obtained money they could use more easily at their own discretion. Thus, across family-clusters, patriarchal convenience in both generations account for an item-differentiated inheritance pattern.

Overall, dowries and inheritance were most frequently mentioned in merchants' and agrarian producers' wills, and the same is true for acquest. Throughout the century, merchants and estate owners account for 62.5 percent of all dowry transactions (37.4 and 25.1 percent respectively), and 67.2 percent of all mentions of acquest (28.3 and 38.9 percent respectively). The next two social groups resorting to dowries and acquest were artisans and the military. Artisans accounted for 6.8 percent, and the military for 6.1 percent of the wills mentioning a dowry; and the corresponding percentages for acquest were 6.2 and 1.8 percent. Such tendencies, as will become clear in the following sections, are also reflected in the cases revolving around conflicts over dowry, inheritance, and acquest.

In the course of the century, dowry composition changed: the relative weight of traditional dowry items shifted, and more nontraditional items became a part of dowries. As was the case in São Paulo (Nazzari 1991), money, furniture, and clothing increased proportionally to property. Wills and court cases involving lower-class people list as dowry items only clothes and small amounts of money (200 to 300 pesos). In regard to *arras*, these records mention only occupational skills or educational level as the man's contribution to the marriage. Jewelry continued to be an important part of a woman's paraphernalia. Toward the end of the century, some completely new items appeared, such as shares in a business enterprise or government bonds, reflecting economic developments and the ways in which people, especially women, adapted the content of dowries to new economic schemes.

In Lima we observe a shift in the way in which property circulated, with an evolution from dowries to the predominance of inheritance and common property shares. The nomination of a spouse either as a will's executor or its beneficiary reveals changes in inheritance patterns and the degree to which spouses were trusted and became entrusted with property and money (see Table 7.3).

After 1880 the practice of dowry exchange fades just as the use of acquest increases. Around 1860, a period of economic growth for Lima, the number

---

marriage, they would no longer participate in their family's efforts to strengthen itself through reproduction and monetary increase (Owen-Hughes 1978, 284ff).

Dowries and Marriage in Civil Court 237

Table 7.3 Dowries, acquest, and will executors, Lima, 1810–1900

Year	(1) Total Married and Widowed Testators	(2) Dowries in (1)	%	(3) Acquest in (1)	%	(4) Wife or Husband Is Will Executor[a]	(5) Others Are Involved
1810	132	33	25.0	13	9.8	43.1	17.0
1820	133	25	18.8	11	8.3	31.3	26.5
1830	105	21	20.0	3	2.9	27.5	34.8
1840	88	16	18.1	10	11.4	58.0	22.0
1850	84	18	21.4	8	9.5	41.5	32.0
1860	63	12	12.7	8	12.7	40.5	35.1
1870	102	10	9.8	14	13.7	37.0	27.8
1880	106	14	13.2	13	12.7	48.6	24.3
1890	73	7	9.6	20	27.4	34.4	18.8
1900	90	8	8.9	28	31.1	50.9	16.4

SOURCE: AGN, Notarial Records, Wills.
[a] These precentages refer only to married testators. In the case of a widowed partner, obviously, there had to be a "third" person.

of recorded dowries and acquest is, for the first time, equal. In absolute terms, the number of recorded dowries tended to decline from 1860 to 1880, when there was a slight increase, caused perhaps by a demographic gender imbalance due to the War of the Pacific. After the 1880s the declining tendency continued. In the long run, the dowry system was replaced by inheritance and the procurement by men and women of acquest generated from marital assets. What was earned by the man and the woman as a couple became more important than what was passed down by the woman's parents.[20] The heightened importance of acquest reflects the recognition of

20. However, a combined reading of inheritance patterns and dowry transfers shows differences among social groups. By examining occupations mentioned in wills, an approximate classification by social standing can be developed. Although wills frequently fail to mention occupation, a testator's occupation can be inferred by looking at the composition of the estate. Based on wills, the following occupational categories were developed: housewives, wage laborers, bureaucrats, artisans, employees, agrarian producers, members of the military, professionals, industrialists, merchants, miners, priests, moneylenders, and the unemployed. Of the twenty-one dowries registered in 1820, eleven record an occupation, and of those, seven indicate participation in some kind of mercantile activity. The remaining four records indicate agrarian producers, artisans, and members of the military. In twenty-one records reviewed for 1830, merchants account for fifteen dowry registers. Between 1860 and 1890, the merchants' participation diminished to half of the 1830 figure. In 1890 participation increased among

a shared contribution to marriage in the course of a whole life, a recognition that is also reflected in an increasing tendency to entrust wives and husbands with the execution of a will, in contrast to nominating a third party to establish *hijuelas*. These facts together show a concentration in the transmission of wealth toward the nuclear family: wives became their husbands' heiresses, and the wider family's meddling ebbed. Evolution from dowry to acquest centered property rights in the nuclear family and reduced dependency on the extended family, a tendency that parallels the diminution of family involvement in marriage conflicts (Chapter 5). The transmission of wealth moved from a patriarchal pattern, or a pattern shaped by gender—women receiving jewelry, household items, and money; men receiving real estate— to one where gender was less of a factor in determining the allocation of goods. However, it is surprising that in spite of increased trust expressed by the growth in use of acquest and of spouses as executors of wills, the "distrust percentage" remained high, above 50 percent roughly. In wills, husbands recognized the nondowry contributions of their wives (domestic chores, childbearing, and often work in the market) but still viewed them as sly and incapable of managing economic affairs. And, as will be shown later (Chapters 8–9), wives' contributions recognized by husbands in wills were fervently disputed when conjugal conflicts arose.

---

agrarian producers, who represented 40 percent of the dowries. This reflects the expansion of *haciendas* in Lima's outlying areas. It may also reflect the arrival of Italian immigrants, a group that largely became agrarian producers and that traditionally practiced dowry exchange. Symptomatically, use of dowries among the military proves to be stronger in years of political unrest (9.1 percent in 1820, 16.7 percent in both 1870 and 1880). A similar pattern is not present in peacetime. Among agrarian producers, the percentage of participation in inheritance tends to diminish in 1830 and 1840 (with 16.7 percent and 11.1 percent respectively), but it reappears in 1860 (33.3 percent) and continues strong in 1870 (43.8 percent), 1880 (42.9 percent) and 1890 (25.0 percent). This indicates a pattern of accumulation of wealth that we would expect in an agrarian export economy. Those living from interest earned on loans remained throughout the century at around 34 percent, whereas there was an almost nonexistent reference to acquest. For artisans inheritance was insignificant, probably indicating a decay in their overall economic performance. In only two years (1820 and 1860) did artisans account for around 10 percent of all the cases where inheritance and occupation are mentioned (38.9 percent in 1820 and 70.6 percent in 1860). In the first two decades, whose unrest made mercantile activity difficult, merchants became imperceptible. They regained a presence after 1860, when they reached 25 percent (of the 87.5 percent of the cases mentioning acquest and occupations); in 1870, they accounted for 40 percent (of 71.4 percent of the cases), 50.0 percent in 1880 (of 46.2 percent), and 38.9 percent in 1890 (of 90 percent). The parallel sequence for agrarian producers was 16.7 percent in 1820 (of 54.5 percent), and a perceptible increase toward the end of the nineteenth century: 37.5 percent in 1860 (of 87.5 percent), 40 percent in 1870 (of 71.4 percent), 50 percent (equaling merchants) in 1880, and 27.8 percent in 1890.

Elites and the Decay of the Dowry, 1800–1860

In the course of the nineteenth century, the huge sums for dowries faded away. In the wake of the wars of independence, the nobility (though not the Creole elite) was stripped of its traditional bulwarks of social, political, and economic privileges, making enormous dowries and inheritances unattainable. Still, Lima's elites struggled to continue the practice of dowry exchange.

Some couples were more successful than others in using the dowry as a start-up capital. Great fortunes could disappear in the turmoil of political unrest and economic uncertainty. This was particularly true in the first half of the nineteenth century, when, as seen earlier, dowries in the 40,000 peso range still existed. Don Gerónimo Boza, the heir to an entailed estate, had received a dowry worth 40,000 pesos on his marriage to Doña Josefa Mendoza. Albeit exaggerating his insolvency for legal purposes, his complaints echoed those of other elites:

> I have been reduced to a frugal and sober life and have felt more than others the consequences of the general unrest and the specific disgraces of my house. Since my father died on June 14, 1826, I have not stopped filing suits against different people, with the [female] will executor, with my siblings, and with some creditors of my deceased father. This has been the reason for the disappearance of the fortune I had in cash from the dowry of my wife, for the decay of the estate, and why the business ventures I have embarked on have failed. In spite of economic failure, my conscience rests in peace. Not so my tormented soul.[21]

Spiritual torment and "general unrest" were important ingredients of life in Lima in 1830. Such complaints coincided with a decay of the dowry between 1820 and 1830, in terms of both frequency and values (Tables 7.1 and 7.2). The number of recorded dowries dropped from thirty-three in 1810 to twenty-five in 1820, and to twenty-one in 1830; similarly, the average size dropped from 9,269 pesos in 1810 to 8,787 in 1820, and to 4,042 in 1830. Moreover, transfers that had been promised prior to the outbreak of the war could not be executed later on, even if one's social image was at stake. Since dowries sustained not only marriage but also social networks and

---

21. Case 889, AGN, CS, CCI, L 253, 1840, Boza vs. Mendoza.

future investments, failure to pay a dowry could lead to a family's social and economic breakdown. Lawsuits seeking to recover lost money and prestige became common after the war. Many noble families became generationally and collaterally split as a result of these broken promises.

In 1809 Don Eduardo José de Arrescurrenaga, a captain and the owner of the *hacienda* La Cieneguilla in the Lurín valley, opened a case against his father-in-law, Don Ignacio de Orué y Mirones. Don Ignacio was one of the perpetual councilman of Lima's city government. Don Eduardo José claimed that he had never received the dowry that had been promised to him when he married Doña Rosa, Don Ignacio's only daughter. Before the marriage, Doña Rosa's mother had offered to transfer a *finca* worth 10,000 pesos that belonged to her family but that had been leased to a third party. During the trial, Don Ignacio retorted that this could not be true because his wife had no right to dispose of any family properties. Because these families had a high social profile, the accusations against his parents-in-law had become common gossip in Lima and had hurt their social image.[22] His father-in-law insisted, however, that during the marriage negotiations, Don Eduardo José had agreed to his modest offer of the *principal*, that is, the couple could live in the best rooms in Don Ignacio's home and he would feed them. Scarce resources, he explained, limited his ability to help the couple.

Don Eduardo José retaliated by asking that he be allowed to declare the goods and money he was contributing to the marriage, so that when his wife died, his parents-in-law could not claim what did not belong to them. Throughout this litigation, Doña Rosa apparently remained silent. Only at the end did she mediate by waiving her right to any acquest. She made certain, however, that any dowry or inheritance she received would be considered her personal property.

Contrary to custom, but following the letter of the law, the husband registered his financial contribution to the marriage so that it could not be claimed afterward as part of the acquest. Because there was no dowry in its customary meaning, Doña Rosa would be unable to claim any share of the goods and money accumulated during the marriage. Here again dowry and inheritance overlapped. Even though a formal dowry had not been given, Doña Rosa and her family sought to have any future inheritance be considered a dowry, with all the special legal protection provided for dowries. This

---

22. AGN, RA, CCI, L 88, C 908, 19ff., 23, 1809, Arrescurrenaga/Orué y Mirones. This was "un asunto de que ya en la Ciudad se hablaba: principalmente en ciertas Casas, en las que tenia Don Eduardo interes, en que se viese, que su persona y nombre no era olvidado para una alianza de 1a. distinción."

case shows how, in spite of increased "poverty," elites managed—at least temporarily—to rescue the dowry system, even if the delivery of a dowry was postponed to an uncertain future. In the meantime, the prospect of a dowry secured the husband's obligations toward his wife. Renouncing her share of the acquest was the "guarantee" required to maintain the "patriarchal link" based on the exchange of a dowry from the father for the fulfillment of marital obligations by the husband. A new arrangement emerged in which intraclass conflicts arose and in which women had riskier prospects. A woman's economic leverage within marriage was weakened, and this rendered her vulnerable to the vagaries of life.

Doña Rosa lost on all accounts: if her parents could not escape financial ruin and the dowry was never given to her husband, she would have nothing with which to support herself in case of divorce or his death. Women who received neither acquest, dowries, nor inheritance faced poverty. The security that a dowry had provided was replaced by good luck (and eventually the *cuarta conyugal*). As dowries diminished in importance, elite women, especially, were left with no tangible argument (in court and in the bedroom) to oblige their husbands to feed and clothe them. Now, the only argument women could evoke was that their husbands should comply with the sacramental duties imposed on them by marriage. At the same time, when no dowry was forthcoming, a husband could still refer to his customary right to receive a dowry as a justification for denying his wife's right to acquest. As the dowry system weakened, a contractual element of marriage was lost; and with its loss, women were detached from their own families and from the protection the expanded kinship network provided against unscrupulous husbands. There was no dowry argument left to control a husband's behavior, women became more dependent on their husbands,[23] and men had even stricter control over family resources and female behavior.

As in the above case, among elites many dowries were promised as a declaration of good intentions. But many good intentions were devoured by economic circumstances. When a wife's family fortune decreased after the transfer of her dowry, her brothers could, at the time the family estate was divided, ask her husband to pay back that portion of the dowry that had exceeded their sister's equal share of the inheritance set by the *hijuelas*.[24]

---

23. The relationship between the decay of the dowry system and increased dependency has also been registered for Mexico (Couturier and Lavrin 1979) and São Paulo (Nazzari 1991, 402).

24. Case 837, AGN, CS, CCI, L 644, 1857, Corbalán vs. Granados. Here brothers-in-law in 1857 were asking for the devolution of a 20,000 pesos dowry following the instructions in

Such claims put heavy strains on in-law relationships. Many wills could not be carried out, meaning that the flow of wealth between generations within elite families was interrupted. This oftentimes led to lawsuits, a break of intraclass alliances, and city gossip. For elite families, it was hard to measure the consequences, but by the middle of the century it was clear that a major change had occurred.

Doña Ana María de Ulloa, the widow of Colonel Don Juan de Echevarría y Bengoa, wrote her testament in 1828. She had three daughters and a son. When Doña Ana María married, her parents had provided a dowry worth 14,000 pesos. The family's revenues came from the *partido* of Huamalíes, where they owned the Quivilla *obraje*. A fire in the *obraje* destroyed the dowry acknowledgment signed by her husband. Doña Ana María left Don Juan 4,000 pesos (in silverware, jewelry, and slaves), which equaled the value of Doña Ana María's inheritance. From her father, Doña Ana María inherited one third of the family's land in the Huamalíes *corregimiento* (real estate with a significant assignment of Indian labor) worth 13,000 pesos. This land was sold to her brother-in-law, and the funds were then used by her husband to buy a house, which had belonged to the marquis of Montemira, for 28,000 pesos. Doña Ana María and Don Juan promised each of their two surviving daughters a dowry worth 50,000 pesos. But the girls too were victims of the war and its aftermath, because the parents had to pay in installments, including 3 percent annual interest. They lost their cattle and their slaves, considerably reducing their earnings from land ownership.

The *instrumentos dotales* that the couple signed for their two daughters had a special characteristic: they were called *adpompan*, that is, especially bombastic, and involved a great display of wealth. They were notarially recorded "for the sake of maintaining the general opinion about our wealth and fortune, and to provide for the best recommendations for our daughters and sons-in-law." This kind of dowry insured that everyone in Lima and beyond was aware of its existence. Doña Ana María and her husband shared their house with their daughters and their sons-in-law. When the daughters gave birth, the mother presented them with trousseaux "always treating them in equal terms and with demonstrations of the love I feel toward them and my grandchildren." In her will, Doña Ana María explained that these gifts should be considered as part of the 3 percent interest payment on the 50,000 peso dowry promised to each girl.

Don Santiago Corbalán's will. They intended to use their sister's dowry to repay their father's outstanding debts.

In 1841 a copy of Doña Ana Maria's will was requested by her two granddaughters. Both had been minors when their grandparents died. Since then, changing political and economic conditions had diminished the family's fortune even further. The family still owned a *hacienda* and a house, and the granddaughters received revenue from the lease of these properties as payment on their dowries, which in turn were a nonspecified share of the still partially outstanding payment of the dowries of their mothers. The granddaughters claimed that the house and the hacienda should rightfully be given to them as part of their dowries, but instead the property had become "the object of greediness on the part of others."[25]

What is striking is that the dowry became a central argument to regain access to their inheritance (an inheritance that in the course of time had fallen to pieces) and to resist creditors. By equating inheritance and dowry, the two girls could prevent seizure, because dowries had a special legal status. The dowry argument in this case represented a final recourse to save what little was left of the family's estate. It was almost 1870 by the time an astute lawyer convinced the two girls to assemble family records from as far back as 1800 and present their claims to the court. The dowry still appeared as a legal argument at that time, but its effectiveness had dwindled. After many years of litigation, the granddaughters lost the case, partially because family relations and the concomitant dowry and inheritance issues had become so tangled that there were no viable solutions without confronting or alienating vested interests of many other people, including family members. For the judges and everyone else involved, it was easier to sacrifice the vestiges of a large family fortune and the economic future of two women who had lost their status as members of the elite.

Economic decay made dowry transactions less transparent and conflict more probable. Relinquishing acquest or paying interest were devices to prolong the life of the dowry system. But more and more, the dowry became a "paper-dowry"; that is, it only existed on paper, as a future promise. As a paper-dowry, the system still provided an income and kept the memory of female inheritance and privileges alive. Gradually, as these cases foreshadow, the dowry lost its special position. Creditors gained the upper hand; the "contract" replaced the "special rights" (see also Chapter 8).

Dowry and acquest were closely associated in people's minds and in the law. Earnings from the dowry and the *arras* became common property in the course of marriage. If this mental and legal connection was to prevail

25. Case 036, AGN, CS, CCI, L 266, 1841, Echevarría vs. Ulloa.

in the face of a declining dowry system, women would have to redefine what a dowry consisted of, and with it, its meaning. This redefinition was a pivotal transition to the recognition of women's domestic chores, labor, and contributions to marriage more generally, as women began to claim these contributions as equivalent to a dowry. This, in turn, underlined their rights to acquest in their own feminine terms. And it was especially among lower-class women that this redefinition took place.

Redefining Dowries' Content: 1800–1820

As the dowry practice was manipulated in courtroom settings, the rules and traditions surrounding it were obscured and even misrepresented. Less well-off women used the dowry system to challenge all-encompassing male rights over marital property. The goods and actions these women defined as part of the dowry practice (including compensation for seduction or rape) were not included in wills or dowry instruments but do appear in litigations. Women created these definitions as they brought suit in ecclesiastical court cases to justify and solicit a husband's fulfillment of his marital duties or his payment of alimony, and in civil court cases to gain or regain access to assets they claimed belonged to them. An inheritance might be redefined as a dowry (as in the case of Doña Rosa's granddaughters) and was also confused with acquest and alimony. Women defined money they brought to the marriage as a dowry in order to bargain over noncompliance with spousal duties and obligations. Last but not least, women argued that their labor be recognized as equivalent to a dowry. As the confusion grew and compounded, it made it easier for desperate women to construct arguments centered on the dowry to gain a payment of financial support from former husbands. Such cases refer to very small dowries (even smaller than those considered for "corrupted virginity"), implying that by stretching the original definition of the dowry to include exchanges of everyday household items and minuscule amounts of money, women gained recourse to laws that originally had been used to protect fortunes being exchanged among elites.

The redefinition of dowries in the arguments brought forward by lower-class women gradually helped to convince judges about the dangers involved in the continued practice of dowry exchange. As dowry arguments became less credited, they disappeared as an argument used in marital conflict cases toward the end of the century. In the meantime, however, lower-class women were quite successful in furthering their own purposes through a redefinition of the dowry system.

Some of the confusion in the definition of dowries can be traced back to legal stipulations that originated in colonial times in the *Ley de Real Partida*. The lack of precision in this set of rules in establishing at what point dowries were to be handed out, the relationship between those giving and those receiving a dowry, the kind of goods that could be considered a dowry, and the formalities required to define apportionment as a dowry, enabled Aniceta Montero in 1803 to claim that start-up capital for mercantile activity lent to her husband, Mariano Baldeón, by her uncle should be considered a dowry. Mariano did not agree with this interpretation, and resorting to the law he argued:

> When my wife tried to sue me for alimony, she tried to make everyone believe that I had received a dowry from Carranza, her dead uncle. She tried to distort things and confuse the judges . . . , without realizing that according to the *Ley de Real Partida* a dowry is what a woman gives to her husband when she marries him. . . . In no place in this *Ley* is it said that a civil contract should or may be considered a dowry, which is especially true in this case because this contract was signed with her uncle after the marriage had taken place. . . . These were private agreements in which both shareholders invested their money and, I, my own labor buying and selling produce. The profits from this enterprise can never be interpreted as having resulted from a dowry, nor does it correspond to the essence of what a dowry is.[26]

It was quite convenient for Aniceta to assume that her uncle's loan to her husband be considered her dowry. As such, her share of the acquest increased because she was entitled to half the proceeds earned from her dowry's initial investment. It also let her emphasize the importance of her family's contribution to the marriage. On several occasions in the suit, she mentioned that prior to marriage her husband had been only a poor tailor and that she had agreed to marry him to follow her family's wishes. Litigation went on in several different courts[27] where each side repeated the initial arguments. Mariano continued to point out that the "dowry" had been built "by the sweat of his brow," while his wife dedicated herself to promenades and

26. Case 376, AA, LM, L 7, 1803; and CD, L 83, 1804.
27. LM, CD, and CCI.

other amusements. Aniceta's was an argument based on legal speculation, in which a business contract at the time of marriage could eventually be perceived as a dowry payment because the wife's relatives were involved. Following legal stipulations, a payment had been received from a paternal relative close to the wedding day. The "civil contract" appeared to be a "dowry" because the circumstances surrounding the transfer of money were similar to those of a dowry transfer. Moreover, it was an amount of money successfully invested to turn a poor tailor into a small merchant. Thus, it was Aniceta's contribution that had enhanced their social standing, exactly the purpose of a dowry. She constructed all indicators to point to a dowry transaction that could not be dismantled by a "sweat-of-the-brow" argument or by claiming that the "essence" of a dowry was lacking. Presumably, the judge had to endorse Aniceta's arguments because they reflected the law.

For the less well-off, giving a dowry entailed a formidable family burden, even if it contained only the most basic household supplies. Such items were frequently listed in wills; but if marital conflict arose, these wills were not considered legal documents and so could not be used to safeguard the woman's right to the dowry, or more precisely, her paraphernalia. In contrast, the official dowry instruments (found mostly among the well-off) list basic household goods as *appendices* to transfers of sums of money, jewelry, and other valuable heirlooms. Consequently, the claim by lower-class women that basic household items were a dowry had no legal backing and depended on how the spouses themselves recognized them. Not surprisingly, spouses did not always share the same interpretation.

In 1819, after five years of marriage, Maria Moña, a Spaniard's daughter, asked the ecclesiastical court in Lima for a divorce from her husband, Marcelino Ramírez, because he frequently beat her and had not provided her with food and clothing. In a letter to the vicar general, she described her widowed mother's sacrifice to provide her with clothing, furniture, and even monthly allowances when she first married:

> I have now been married for five years, one month, and some days, and I am not able to count even minutes of happiness. It is true that I did not bring a dowry to the marriage because my father had no other goods than his honesty and work, and my mother had only her virtue and peacefulness. Nevertheless, in order to provide something, she gave me everything she had: more than twenty garments without counting the mourning dresses, the corresponding shirts, two new

sayas, in sum two full trunks of rich clothes, a silver table setting and a candelabra, a good bed, a shelf full of fine china and glasses, a new sofa, and a table. In sum, she equipped me for several years. She also bought clothes for the groom, paid the ecclesiastical fees and all other expenses for the marriage. My lost honor and my blindness compelled this poor woman to make such an enormous sacrifice. In spite of being a widow, she also paid for our rent during the first months of our marriage, and on top of this provided us with a daily allowance of six reales. When her own needs increased, she had to stop these payments. And it was then that calamities came upon us. One day a fork or a spoon was sold, another day a shirt or a dress, until all my belongings disappeared.[28]

When the couple had nothing left to sell or pawn, Marcelino, claiming that he had not received a dowry, asked his wife to go out to work, thus implying that there was no obligation on his side to provide for her. María herself admitted not having a dowry, but the items provided by her mother clearly were a part of what was generally perceived as paraphernalia, the portion of a woman's property that unquestionably belonged to her alone.[29] It is noteworthy that Maria's husband only dared to ask her to look for work after all her belongings had been sold. As long as some traces of a dowry existed (and unless he was a fool), he probably sensed that he was obliged to provide food and shelter for his wife. In this case—unlike the Montero vs. Baldeón case—things did not work out for María, in part because she had admitted that there had been no dowry. A sharper lawyer would probably have suggested that her paraphernalia should have fallen under the law protecting dowries. But even then, her mother's gifts did not appear in any register, and it would have been difficult to prove they ever existed.

Money, in contrast to items for everyday use, had a better chance of being recognized as a part of a dowry, because financial transactions were more commonly recorded. Paraphernalia—clothes, jewelry, and furniture—had a practical value but were much harder to appraise. Among the lower classes, the dowry transfers involved either money or goods, but only in very few cases did they involve both. Women who could claim dowry used by their

---

28. Case 380, AA, CD, L 87, 1819, Ramírez vs. Moña.
29. In the 1852 Civil Code, half of a woman's paraphernalia became a dowry when a woman did not apportion a dowry to the marriage. See this chapter, sec. 1.

husbands as an investment fared much better than those who had been endowed with the basic household goods. The meaning of this difference becomes clear in the Sotelo vs. Irrarasabal case.

When María married Manuel Irrarasabal, she received 200 pesos and a slave from her sister. Immediately after their marriage, Manuel sold the slave for 120 pesos. With the total, 320 pesos, he bought a tobacco shop at the Esquina de los Gallos in the city. This investment established his family financially. After ten years of marriage, a conflict developed, and María contended that the tobacco shop was part of her paraphernalia because the initial capital used to buy the shop was a wedding gift from her sister.[30] In this case, the expenditure of money could be traced back to the contract for the purchase of the shop shortly after the marriage. A slave represented something in between a monetary asset (because a slave was commonly bought and sold or rented out to third parties) and an "object" (because they rendered services). María's husband had used the slave as money, which prevented including the slave as part of María's paraphernalia. However, because of this dual definition of "slave," María could claim that the funds used to buy the tobacco shop were part of a dowry. Here we see how, depending on the items involved, a dowry argument could be turned into an acquest issue. In other words, if both money and everyday objects were involved, the "money argument" prevailed.

The definitions of dowries and paraphernalia overlapped, but so did those for civil contracts and gifts when they involved both dowries and paraphernalia. Matters became even more confusing when nonmaterial items were involved. Help from a wife's parents enabling her husband to obtain a position or a trade is a good example. Husbands resisted recognizing such help as a dowry, but poor parents sometimes insisted this was their endowment.

This was particularly true for smaller merchants working on commission. Baltasara Cárdenas, a merchant's daughter, in a letter dated in 1801, explained: "My father, for certain reasons, accepted my marriage, but told Domingo [her husband] that he would not receive a dowry, because my father was in debt and had only credit. To this Don Domingo answered on several occasions that the only thing he was interested in was in enjoying my father's credit and protection, and that he [Domingo] was able to keep up with his obligations."[31]

30. Case 010, AA, CD, L 92, 1856, Irrasabal vs. Sotelo.
31. Case 153, AA, LM, L 7, 1801, León y Otoya vs. Cárdenas.

Domingo worked as a merchant for one year in his father-in-law's *cajón* (store) located in Lima's Plaza Mayor. After his probationary year, his father-in-law took a risk and arranged an 8,000 peso loan of merchandise and another *cajón* for Domingo. Both men agreed to share the profits. The father-in-law's good standing with the merchants' guild gave him the credit to obtain the start-up capital. Domingo's contribution was his labor. Together they were very successful, having transactions totaling more than 55,000 pesos soon after opening. However, according to Baltasara, "Domingo's haughtiness grew with this success, and now he wanted to stand on his own feet. He dismissed all good advice from father, who was his main lender, and consequently ruined my father's good name and those of other merchants who participated in these transactions. A suit was brought to the Tribunal del Consulado (the highest merchant guild) and around 1793 or 1794 it came out that Domingo had a debt of more than 5,000 pesos. As if it had been my or my parents' fault, he abandoned our home, leaving me behind with two children we had at that time."

Domingo ran off to Ica, a coastal city south of Lima, and reopened a business on his own. After just two years, he again went bankrupt and had to flee. This time Domingo settled down in the town of Lurín, located in one of Lima's coastal valleys, until a friend of his father-in-law hired him as administrator of his *hacienda* in the Pisco Valley, at an annual salary of 800 pesos. His wife rejoined him, but their happiness was short-lived. Soon afterward, he lost his job and again deserted Baltasara. He had two responses when confronted with the accusation of abandoning his wife and children. He replied that he had no means to take care of them, but even if he could, he was under no obligation to help them because he had received no dowry.

Baltasara's answer to this demonstrates the distortion of the notion of dowry. She asserted how timeworn her husband's explanations sounded, stating that "if in the case of a wife without a dowry the common practice would be to expel her from the home and her husband's company and to send her back to her parents' house, other husbands then would argue that the same reasoning should apply to a woman who became old, ugly, or sick. And then marriage would be worth less than trash."

In this case, no money or other tangible items were involved, only "social links," but these were crucial to mercantile activity (the pace-setting economic activity of the period that was one of the few avenues to social advancement and financial success). Social prestige and commercial soundness were recognized to be more important than actual money; they were the means to obtain money. The husbands were right: intangible items were not part of traditional dowry transactions. In Domingo's view, credit and social connections—intangible items similar to the "sweat of one's brow"—could not be interpreted as being part of a dowry no matter how concrete a role they played in commercial success. Consequently, whenever his business failed or when he did not need to rely on his father-in-law's credit, he believed himself to be free of marital obligations. Conversely, the father-in-law's credit had made Baltasara a more attractive marriage partner. Merchants in Lima recruited newcomers—particularly if they were white or even of noble ancestry—by granting social and monetary support to start a new, or expand an old, business. The best way to cement the relationship was through a marriage alliance. This was also common practice among less powerful merchants who sought to expand their mercantile networks. But Domingo ruined his prospects by fulfilling neither his marriage obligations nor his commercial responsibilities.

This case demonstrates the weaknesses of the dowry system among merchants, particularly those who could not provide their daughters with tangible and traditionally recognized dowry items. In this milieu an expansion of one's social network and credit was equivalent to a dowry consisting of everyday household items. While the institution of dowries persisted among merchants, this mercantile variation twisted the meaning and the interpretation of what a dowry was and what it represented.

Dowries also became bargaining chips with which to overcome constraints of age and race. In 1815 the counselor to Manuel de Córdoba Nestares sent a letter from Ica to Lima's ecclesiastical authorities that vividly illustrates manipulation of the dowry to overcome the age issue:

> Doña Martina Mexía had been a widow of two husbands when she married Manuel. Her former husbands died of old age, which means that she was, to say the least, very unpleasant to the sight of men. Her marriage to Don Manuel was a big social event because of the great disparity in age between the two. She was a worn-out old woman, he a flourishing youth. This marriage could not have taken place without a substantial dowry. Nobody can believe that Don Manuel received Doña Martina's wrecked hands out of a ravaging passion or because of her great beauty. Doña Martina has never been beautiful, least of all now when she is 80 years old. One can only imagine the many sacrifices of his liberty and passion Don Manuel had to suffer when he embraced this disaster. No matter how insensitive one may expect

Don Manuel to be, it is unconceivable that he agreed to this marriage without an juicy indemnity.[32]

If a woman had enough money, a dowry could offset her old age. Here a woman, not her male kin, used a dowry to make a bargain that for different reasons benefited both partners: Doña Martina was one step closer to heaven through the holy sacrament of marriage, Don Manuel was one step higher in the social ladder. Although it may well be that the counselor exaggerated the disparities between the spouses (Don Manuel's age and the years they were married were never mentioned in the file), his argument illustrates a commonly held assumption about the link between age and money. Dowries made unequal marriages possible: women could "buy" a husband, and men used dowries for self-promotion. Thus, dowries disfigured the ideal of (romantic) marriage. The holy sacrament of marriage was an ideal assailed not only by extramarital love and lust but also by calculated marriages.

In slaves' hands, a dowry was a bargaining chip played against race to gain upward mobility. It was probably affection that motivated Doña Josefa de Irarrasabal to endow her former mulatto slave, Gertrudis Irarrasabal, with a dowry of cash, jewelry, *plata labrada* (silverware), slaves, and furniture valued at 3,849 pesos and 2 reales.[33] Doña Josefa wished to arrange a marriage for Gertrudis that would allow her to enjoy a life similar to the one she had had while living with Doña Josefa.[34] So she arranged Gertrudis's marriage to a silversmith, Mariano Morales. Doña Josefa's intentions were made explicit in a dowry instrument signed by the silversmith.

Class, racial, and age constraints had a price, as did virginity. Social differences could be diminished and sentiments be expressed. It is striking to see that this also holds true at the very bottom of the social ladder. Across the range of social groups, dowries were manipulated in different and sometimes colorful ways. No single behavior holds true throughout all the sectors of Lima's inhabitants. The social function and the meaning of the dowry itself were readapted to the particular requirements of a multiethnic society, playing apparently contradictory roles. Dowries deepened stratification by

---

32. Case 351, AGN, RA, CCI, L 132, C 1354, 1815, Córdova vs. Mejía.
33. AGN, Ignacio Ayllón Salazar, 1810, PR 14, f. 1199.
34. Ibid.: "Elebando adelante sus buenas y santas ideas por el amor que le ha tenido y tiene, aproporcionarle una dote capas de que pudiese servirle de apoyo para su casamiento si encontrase un Marido honrado con oficio Público conocido, que la pudiese sostener con el lustre que la exigia su propio amor."

keeping the circulation of wealth within class boundaries, but it also leveled social distances.

The Meanings of Dowry in Marriage

The point of departure for a new couple was established by what each partner contributed to the marriage. As *real* transfers of goods or money, the dowry determined the couple's standing in society as well as a hierarchy between the spouses. In the ideal case, the shares contributed by both spouses were of approximately equivalent value, expressing their racial and economic proximity. Information in wills, however, provides some surprising evidence about which partner normally brought the most goods or money into the marriage.

In the course of the nineteenth century, initial contributions to marriage for both men and women tended to decrease (Table 7.4). The number of

Table 7.4 Contributions to marriage by sex, 1810 and 1900

	1810	%a[a]	%r[b]	1900	%a	%r
A[c]	43	32.6	43.9	14	15.6	17.5
B	25	18.9	25.5	14	15.6	17.5
C	9	6.8	9.2	6	6.6	7.5
D	9	6.8	9.2	10	11.1	12.5
E	12	9.1	12.2	36	40.0	45.0
n.d.	34	25.8		10		11.1
	132	100.0	100.0	90	100.0	100.0

SOURCE: AGN, Notarial Records, Wills.
[a] Percentage on total wills from married and widowed men and women.
[b] Percentage as above, but resting those cases in which no information was given (s.i.).
[c] A: A woman brings goods/money into marriage. Only wills made by people declared to be widowd or married were taken into the sample. Dowries are included as apportionments brought in by women; *arras* as the counterpart brought in by men. If dowries and *arras* were declared, the case was included in C.
  B: A man brings goods/money into marriage.
  C: Man and woman bring goods/money into marriage.
  D: Neither man nor woman bring goods/money into marriage, and there are no delared goods or money in the will.
  E: The will mentions goods acquired throughout marriage, but none of the spouses has brought anything into marriage.

marriages where the wife contributed money or goods but the husband contributed nothing dropped from 43.9 percent at the beginning of the nineteenth century to 17.5 percent by its close, indicating once again a decline in the institution of the dowry. The number of marriages where the man contributed something and the wife nothing dropped from 25.5 percent to 17.5 percent over the same period. A slight decrease in the number of cases in which both partners contributed goods or money (9.2 percent in 1810, and 7.5 percent in 1900) hints that most couples were starting married life with less capital, a situation requiring greater self-reliance and less reliance on the extended family.

In 1810 marriages where neither spouse contributed goods or money accounted for 21.4 percent of all cases. By 1900, this percentage had climbed to 57.5 percent.[35] A relatively high percentage of these couples were able to accumulate some wealth, as indicated by their declaration of assets at the time of the writing of the last will (12.2 percent in 1810 versus 45.0 percent in 1900). Accumulation of wealth increasingly tended to take place after the formation of the nuclear family, and not as a result of initial allocations from the extended family. New couples had to rely more and more on their own resources, at least until they eventually received an inheritance. Toward the end of the nineteenth century, the recognition of assets acquired during marriage (rather than brought to it) coincides with the emerging predominance of acquest (Tables 7.1, 7.2, and 7.3). Between 1880 and 1890, there was a dramatic increase in the number of married testators mentioning acquest, and this parallels an increase in the number of couples who did not bring any assets into the marriage.

A woman's standing in the family largely depended on what she contributed to the marriage. In marital lawsuits where a husband had failed to provide for a wife who had a dowry, the woman prevailed. In a divorce action, a woman would declare the value of the goods in her dowry in order to justify her claim to the right to have her husband provide food, clothing, shelter, and alimony. In popular perception, women requesting alimony almost invariably had contributed a dowry or something they perceived (or insisted) was the equivalent of a dowry. In these arguments, women emphasized that their husbands had enjoyed a better life as a result of the existence of a dowry. This notion was deeply entrenched in people's minds

---

35. Such percentages clearly show that wills were not only written by rich people, but, to the contrary, and maybe increasingly so, by people who had started their married life with close to nothing.

and represented the basis of a very subtle, if unspoken, bargain between husband and wife. The marriage began with a contribution from the bride, but its acceptance entailed an obligation on the part of the groom.

When a new couple married with no dowry and there were no allotments made by the husband (such as *arras*), the outlook was not only bleak but support obligations were jeopardized as well. Dowries were defined as a supplement to help toward "the burdens of marriage." By reversing the definition, some husbands argued that they were not obliged to provide for a wife with no dowry. In very crude terms, this meant that parents could be blamed for starving their daughters. Such arguments not only double-crossed romantic love but also betrayed the sacramental nature of marriage proclaimed by the church and by existing laws.

Couples from all walks of life used the dowry—support obligation as shared integers in the equation—to justify complaints and suits. These mental calculations were fully demonstrated in the arguments put forward by José Rodríguez, a militia captain in Santa province, and his wife, María Cabrera. They had no children of their own, but José's natural daughter lived with them. After years of marriage, José infected his wife with a venereal disease. After repeatedly asking him to pay for a doctor, but with no success, Maria had to resort to legal action to get medical attention: "I cannot go on suffering so much hard-heartedness from my husband, and having heard him say several times that he did not want to spend money to cure me, because I did not have a dowry, and that I was only a burden to him, I decided to make his monstrous cruelty known to everybody."[36] Her husband's argument was that the lack of a dowry freed him from his obligation to pay for treatment.

A similar argument was brought forward by Don Domingo León y Otoya, the husband of Doña Baltasara Cárdenas: "In this case there can be no dispute about a father's obligation to endow his daughters. Without a dowry, a husband has no obligation to feed his wife, or to help her in any way in his house and company, or away from it. What's more, if a husband has not received a dowry, he is free to return her to her parents' house so that they feed her, because when no dowry is handed over to fulfill such obligations a woman does not have any right to participate in the family's wealth or to be fed."[37]

36. Case 107, AA, CD, L 83, 1803, Cabrera vs. Rodríguez.
37. Case 153, AA, LM, L 7, 1801, León y Otoya vs. Cárdenas.

How prevalent such notions were even among the lower classes is made particularly evident by similar expressions by husbands whose marriages had very limited economic resources. Some refused to pay their wives monthly allowances when, after a divorce petition had been filed, they were secluded in a *beaterio*.[38] Although these allowances were stipulated by law, lack of a dowry could be used as an argument to avoid making payments.[39] Soldiers' wives filing support claims were common in the courtrooms. Manuel Córdova was a militia soldier whose wife filed a claim against him at the military court (the Auditoría General de Guerra).[40] She had left Manuel, taking their children and household items with her, and Manuel's lawyer argued that the wife had no right to take the items (he did not mention the children) because she had had no dowry: "This woman has not contributed any dowry whatsoever. Although he had been promised 200 pesos, he never received them. In this way, the furniture she took with her, the dowries he gave to his three daughters, 400 pesos to each in addition to clothes and brand-new household items, all has been bought with his hard work that has now damaged his health and made him unable to obtain the same amounts of money."[41]

Because he had never received the 200 pesos dowry promised to him, the soldier felt that everything that had been accumulated during the marriage belonged to him alone. Here the lack of a dowry is extended to deny access to acquest, an argument that again went beyond legal stipulations.[42]

From the captain to the soldier, from the merchant to the storekeeper, from the artisan to the estate owner, husbands used a woman's lack of a dowry as an excuse to exempt themselves from financial responsibility, either because of real poverty or (more frequently) because they were simply not willing to accept that responsibility. Judges, both civil and ecclesiastical, did not necessarily approve of this interpretation of marital responsibilities, however. Law and custom, they argued, did not endorse such callousness. They recognized that dowries could easily become a negative asset and an "exquisite alibi for husbands, because it would allow them to bypass

38. Details for such cases are discussed in Chapter 2.
39. Case 220, AA, CD, L 84, 1805, Hernández vs. García.
40. Military personnel had to use military courts even for matters concerning their private or family lives.
41. Case 353, AGN, AGG, CCI, L 22, C 379, Córdova vs. Mena.
42. As mentioned earlier, women who abandoned their husbands lost their right to acquest only for the time they had been away without ecclesiastical approval.

such essential obligations" (as Doña Baltasara also noted). Thus, although dowries were intended to help a new couple and were considered a parental duty, husbands and wives were expected to assist each other mutually even when a dowry was lacking.

Household goods were the focus of another case. In 1806 Juan de Ubiñas, the owner of a warehouse, accused his wife of moving everything they had to her parents' house. Coach, servants, silverware, jewelry, and even his clothes had disappeared. Juan assumed that his wife's personal assets were subject to his administration and that her jewelry was his, because he had bought it: "This extraordinary occurrence is a grave crime. Because Doña Juana has not brought any dowry or other items into marriage but herself, in substance, I am the victim of looting or a violent robbery of all the possessions I have paid for with my money."[43]

Juana opted for pragmatism, even to the point of breaking the law. She may have justified her illegal maneuvering by means of an equation that placed men who did not fulfill their marital obligations in the category of "criminals." Men's administrative responsibilities over wives' property, as well as the misunderstandings concerning dowries, paraphernalia, and acquest, made it difficult to distinguish between legitimate property rights and common burglary. Given the difficult task of defining what kinds of assets belonged to whom and why, suits could last for years. More than alleged moral concerns, fear of legal complications may have motivated husbands to keep a watchful eye on their wives' "public wanderings." Women, in turn, oftentimes took the initiative, and thus placed the burden of proof of ownership on their husbands.

Although law and Christian morality prescribed spouses' mutual support with or without a dowry, there was a strong notion of a contract between marriage partners based on the existence of a dowry. In extreme cases this notion was pushed to the point of contravening the ideal of marital love. It could happen that a husband who was trying to disentangle himself from marriage would pay back (even with interest) the dowry his wife originally brought into the marriage.

Juan Gutiérrez Prio was an *encomendero* (a wholesale supplier) married to Manuela de las Bárcenas. The dowry she brought into the marriage had been worth 10,000 pesos. After five years of marriage and several children, Manuela accused Juan of mistreatment, adultery, and failing to provide for the family's support. It came as a shock to both his wife and her parents when

43. Case 284, AGN, RA, CCI, L 60, C 612, 1806, Ubiña vs. Lamas.

Juan announced that he was willing to pay 14,000 pesos to his in-laws if they agreed to take their daughter back. This new contract, a "reverse dowry," was meant to free him from further obligations toward his wife and their offspring.[44] Significant to our discussion is the answer Juan received from the *procurador del número*, the attorney of the Real Audiencia: "It has helped her little or nothing to have a rich husband and a 10,000 pesos dowry. The parents bought a rat for their daughter."

The use of the term *bought* ("comprar un verdugo") underlines the contractual characteristics of dowries. Women were as aware as men that a close relationship existed between dowry and daily maintenance and support. Neither a claim nor even a proven right, however, could replace food on the table if there was an unwillingness on the part of the husband to pay for his wife's support. Dowries did not preclude daily hardships.

In 1817, after fifteen years of marriage, Magdalena Vega, filed a divorce suit at the ecclesiastical curia against her husband Pasqual Ospina. She lamented:

> Fifteen years have elapsed since I married the said Ospina in *facie ecclesie* [complying to Catholic requirements], when I was but eleven years and six months old and following my parents' wishes. Throughout this whole time I have suffered ceaselessly due to my husband's vices and base behavior; I only managed to live in peace for one and a half years, after which he traded balm for poison. He began gambling, drinking, and having concubines, and never remembered to provide for me in spite of the fact that he had received a 400 to 500 peso dowry. Had it not been for a sister to whom I fled and who is married to Don Francisco Cairo, a miner in that parish, I would long ago have perished.[45]

Both men and women viewed the dowry as a valuable addition to their marriage. But even when a strong legal argument for alimony could be made based on the existence of a dowry, this in itself did not guarantee a favorable judgment to the wife.

44. Case 62, AA, CD, L 87, 1819, Gutiérrez Prio vs. de las Bárcenas.
45. Case 622, AA, CD, L 87 (1815–20), Ospina vs. Vega. Also see Case 261, AA, CD, L 86, 1812, Rodríguez vs. Hernández. After twenty-three years of marriage, the wife presented a divorce suit accusing her husband of adultery. In both cases, women used their dowries as an argument to obtain alimony from their husbands.

It is easy to imagine how dowries, alimony, and support were an important element in the definition of gender roles within the family. Bargaining—more subtle than any taking place in courts—was (and is) a daily reality of marital life. Behind economic survival strategies lay the idea of a contract established between the spouses. As dowry exchange began to decay and disappear, the subjectivity of these contracts increased. Ultimately, the contract involved the emotional life of a marriage rather than just its legal nature.

Married life was unpredictable even for those women with the dowry bargaining chip. Economic problems in the family had much to do with the "general troubles in society," but they also arose in the private sphere when husbands misused their wives dowries. Dowries consisting of cash intended as starting capital for merchants were particularly open to misuse. Merchants are often the first to suffer economic problems, and not all merchants were successful in circumventing economic fluctuations. The legal fallout from the loss of a dowry could go beyond the grave and turn into family financial disaster, with especially dire consequences for the woman trapped in the marriage.

In 1781 Bernarda Tello married Bartolomé Mesa, an Indian. Bartolomé had huge debts and faced several lawsuits because he had misused borrowed capital.[46] There was not a person in Lima willing to loan him a cent. He was a merchant and a sergeant in the Indian militia. When Bernarda married him, *she* contributed a dowry of more than 26,000 pesos with which Bartolomé was to restart his commercial enterprises. After twelve years, he had 86,904 pesos. Around this time, he abandoned his wife and went to Quito to continue business. In 1801 Bernarda initiated one lawsuit at the ecclesiastical curia, demanding alimony, and another at the civil court asking for the return of her dowry as well as an acquest. In response to the first suit, Bartolomé offered to return 13,000 pesos, half of the dowry money, in exchange for her withdrawal of alimony claims. Bernarda rejected this offer and continued her suit to regain the total amount of her dowry and an additional acquest. As revealed in her will, she had good business sense. She had lent thousands of pesos, including a loan to the highest merchant guild, the Real Tribunal del Consulado.

Bernarda described how—in spite of her commercial acumen—her husband had succeeded in defrauding her: "A husband who was completely bankrupt when I gave him a dowry, that owes all his fortune to this money,

---

46. Case 595. This case has been reconstructed from several sources: AGN, RA, CCI, L 15, C 161, 1801, (143ff.) and AA, CD, L 84, 1807, Mesa vs. Tello; AGN, RA, CCI, L 72, C 745 (30ff.), 1807; AGN, PR 15, Ignacio Ayllón Salazar, 1811 (last will of Bernarda Tello de Gusman).

now wants to 'reward' me by taking away half of what is rightfully mine; he does not want to contribute to my support, which driven by his conscience he has been willing to pay for in the past."

In 1807 Bernarda won the alimony suit, but the dowry and acquest issues remained unsolved. By 1811, when she wrote her will, Bartolomé had died, and the claim disappeared from the books. The husband used his wife's capital to rebuild his credit and his social prestige as a merchant, but he was not willing to repay the initial "loan." Creditors other than his wife would have been less merciful with Bartolomé. Simple calculations show she would have been better off financially had she lent her money to others. For Bernarda, marriage proved to be her worst business deal.[47]

Through their personal and legal struggles over property rights, women gradually constructed new arguments to gain economic justice. The cumulative social effect was particularly visible among women like Bernarda, who participated in the labor market. These women belonged by race to the lower echelons of society. For them, marriage was based on a free decision, at least in the sense that, within class-based restrictions, husbands were selected for emotional reasons. It was more difficult for these women to subject a husband to legal claims in the absence of the sociocultural expectations embedded in the web of relationships that traditionally existed among the elite. More freedom also meant that parents' interference ebbed because there was no blackmail over dowry. Gregoria García posed some intricate questions in 1805: "It is true that I did not bring a dowry into marriage, but it is also true that a husband has an obligation to care for his wife even if she has no dowry. If he wanted a dowry, why did he not then search for a wife with a dowry? Who obliged him or advised him to marry a poor woman?"[48]

Something radical was emerging among these women. The dowry issue had become a tool to gain justice in the legal system. The idea of a contract still existed, but it was no longer a contract in which a dowry and a husband's marital obligations balanced, but one in which mutual obligation tipped the balance.

Women also began to perceive their work (particularly work carried out alongside the male head of family) as "dowry" as good as parents could provide. In 1816 Justa Renay began a divorce suit against her husband,

---

47. The initial capital of 26,000 pesos invested at an annual interest rate of 12 percent would, after 12 years, have been worth approximately 101,295 pesos, or almost 30 percent more than the 86,904 she was claiming as a repayment of her dowry plus acquest.

48. In this case, the archbishop himself intervened on behalf of Gregoria and obliged her husband to pay a 25 peso alimony to her in one of Lima's *beaterios*.

Francisco Ayllon, accusing him of adultery, abandonment, and of selling the house she had inherited as a dowry from her father. In her accusation, she not only mentioned her husband's obligation to provide for her because he had received a dowry, but she also highlighted her labor:

> The justice I am entitled to demands that Don Francisco should confess that he sold my house, that he demonstrate how much money he received from it, and how, with these 400 pesos, he engaged in business. Because my father gave this house to me as a dowry, Don Francisco should not be allowed to use this money for his public concubines and immoral behavior while I find myself without what justly belongs to me. Even if he assumes that he has spent this money in taking care of me while we were together, I have to say that during this time I served him and bore a son to him. My poor resources now do not allow me to pay for my son's support, for his education, or for him to learn a trade. In the time my son has spent with his father, Don Francisco did not look after him as a father because the boy was already old enough to observe his father's immoral behavior.[49]

While all social classes identified a dowry with a husband's obligation to support his wife, lower-class women created new equations with which to interpret marital obligations. For some, support became an obligation because the wife had provided her husband with start-up capital; for others, having given birth to children, performed household chores, and provided sex justified a compensation; for still others, claims were based on the wife's participation in the husband's business, her work in the "public sphere." All these quite different arrangements were considered equivalent to a dowry comprising goods or money handed down by parents, although parents were no longer involved in the equation. The trade-off between a dowry and corresponding support was transmuted into the idea of a contract in a wider sense. In other words, women's resources were being viewed as capital. These shifts were translated back into how marriage was perceived. Women had begun to argue that marriage was not an unlimited contract in which they were totally subjected to a husband's arbitrary wishes.

María Moña, whose case was introduced above, made a vibrant argument against her husband's mistreatment that went well beyond her personal grievances and the recovery of her goods. She compared her life to the life

---

49. Case 501, AA, CD, L 87 (1815–20), Ayllón vs. Renay.

of a slave. In fact, in her eyes any women who lacked a dowry was doomed to lead a life worse than a slave: "Is it perchance a felony for an unhappy woman to have been born poor with no dowry to bring into marriage that she should be so severely punished? Isn't she worse off than a slave who gets paid and fed for her services? What? Is marriage a leonine contract in which a husband can get by however he pleases? No, it is a contract like all others: obligations are reciprocal, and any time one of the partners fails to fulfill his part, the other is not obliged to fulfill his."[50]

Mutual obligations, not individual benefits, were the essence of marriage, and with or without a dowry, that rule held. Even slaves had a right to be fed, clothed, and paid; so women, it was argued, should rethink their own "contract" with society. María answered her own rhetorical questions: "No, it is not sheer force that should impose rules on us, but reason and justice. Weakness must always be protected, particularly the weakness of a woman who has become the victim of a bad husband and who does not have any other resource but her voice against injustice."[51]

In this argument, women are not intrinsically weak, but are weakened by a "bad husband." The liberal notions of reason and justice were invoked as the guiding principles of gender relations, in contrast to "sheer force" sustained by "unreason and injustice." This was an equation that translated liberal ideals into real action in women's lives.

People mounted counterarguments, of course, and reshaped old arguments. The case of Don Domingo vs. Doña María summed up some common ones. As indicated above, he resisted recognizing his wife's right to alimony because she had no dowry. In addition to the "old" argument, he now argued that the dowry obligation trade-off was universally accepted by all societies, including Indians, which was meant to imply that in some way he was "universally right": "Among Indians, women are repudiated because they are ugly, and among Christians, the same happens when a dowry is offered and then not paid."

But as Baltasara pointed out above, this argument "trashes" the concepts of marriage and family. Dowries retained their importance in marriage in spite of their declining numbers in notarial records. They were part of legal disputes, discussions, and, more important, of social and gender perceptions. In several cases discussed above, the value of the dowry mentioned was less than 500 pesos; that is, the amount was miniscule when one

50. Case 380, AA, CD, L 87 (1815–20), 1819 Moña vs. Ramírez.
51. Ibid.

considers that its existence was being used to justify the right to a lifetime alimony.

At the beginning of the nineteenth century, arguments using dowries diverged widely according to who made them, a husband or a wife, a poor husband or a poor wife. Either the laws had to be changed or other mechanisms had to be established if marital relationships were to be regulated. Changes in the institution of the dowry had led to changes in relations within the family. A lack of dowry had become the legal reason by which governmental intervention was requested to protect women's weaknesses when confronted with bad husbands. It was not the "lack of a dowry" but the ability to prove that the notion of dowry was wider than its traditional meaning that enabled women to sue for support.

However, there were different paths that led to the formulation of these new defenses. The equation of dowries with female labor was a lower-class notion and represents a first step toward more women-centered defenses. Among middle- and upper-class women, we do not find similar arguments, largely because those women did not work. What prevailed for lower-class women was the equation of dowries with the obligation of support, a notion much like the one prevalent among husbands of all classes. Women found a legal vocabulary to claim support: dowries were legally defined, but their content was not; and it was the content that was reformulated to encompass female labor, childbirth, and housework. Only if this content were recognized and widely accepted would women be considered to be more than slaves. In the end, these new defenses followed a conservative course, they put new wine—the right of wives to reciprocity in a marriage—into old bottles, the statutes governing dowries. In the following decades, we see old bottles with new tags—some minor institutional changes—with soured wines.

One Generation Later

Around 1855, about the time when Baltasara was a grandmother, another case involving merchants illustrates the growing difficulties of dowry exchange. Credit held by merchants was not equivalent to liquidity; money existed largely on paper only, and had already either been spent or awaited collection. Thus, a merchant's economic standing was hard to evaluate, more so because only ongoing backing (that is, credit and social relations) could guarantee continued growth of a business enterprise. Risk was part of a merchant's life, but a faltering business could be mitigated through adequate social connections. Often it was hard for a merchant to know exactly how much he would earn by the end of a business cycle. Parents could easily misevaluate the true financial standing of a merchant being considered as a marriage partner for their daughter.

When the merchant Luis Torchello married his fifteen-year-old bride in 1857, the new couple received a 4,000 peso dowry from her uncle in addition to jewelry. Only a few weeks after the marriage, however, the girl's mother realized that her son-in-law was not what he had pretended to be, a rich and prosperous merchant. He had started selling her daughter's jewelry. This mother-in-law did not passively accept this outrageous news. Instead, she went to her daughter's new home and took back the remaining jewelry to avoid further misconduct. Later, in court, she justified her action by pointing out that her daughter was too lovesick to even being aware of what was going on, much less to do anything about it. And the mother's worries went further: her daughter was the sole heiress to the family fortune. Enraged at his mother-in-law's accusations, Luis argued that his wife's grandmother and stepfather, and his mother-in-law had abused his wife and that the stepfather had repeatedly tried to hit him.[52]

Perhaps Luis was a well-intentioned husband trying to build a life for himself and his wife by using the dowry as a supplement to his trade, but he made use not only of the dowry's cash allotment but also of the girl's paraphernalia. Family interference may have been the only way to prevent total loss of the dowry. As a merchant, Luis was involved in multiple business deals, which provided excellent cover to obscure where money came from and where it went. As long as money was the only element of a dowry for a new couple—as among the poorer segments of society—it was easy to demonstrate how the money was invested. Among merchants, however, the line between dowry and investment capital was not clear, and meddling by in-laws—in this case including the wife's grandmother—was common. Jewelry represented the female line of accumulation across generations, and in this case women from three generations joined to rescue the dowry from what at least two of them perceived as a husband's squandering. The generational alliance portrayed here reveals a sense of gendered control over a couple's assets, especially when it came to jewelry.

52. Case 934, AGN, CS, CCI, L 642, 1857, Torchello vs. Pando.

Middle-class peasants saw dowries and acquest in yet a different light. Celedonia and Mariano,[53] both Indians, were among those couples who could contribute equal shares to their marriage because each had livestock. Soon after marriage they began to quarrel, and the division of property became an issue between the respective families. In 1852 Mariano claimed that he had received fifteen cows as a dowry and that this transaction had been recorded with a notary. Prior to the marriage, he had been a muleteer and owned mule trains, but following the wedding he became a cowherd. The herd of cows had grown, and now he was claiming an acquest. He also argued that no one, not even his wife's family, could deprive him of his right as a husband to manage Celedonia's dowry. He agreed to separate from his wife if half the calves were given to him. Celedonia, in response, tried to prove that her dowry had eroded under her husband's care. She accused him of being a lazy drunkard, which was—according to witnesses—apparently true. She claimed that it was through her work that the herd had grown, adding to the conjugal wealth. When the conflict began, Mariano took the cows and tried to sell them. Celedonia was worried such an action would seriously damage her interests and her future. Mariano continued arguing that it was his right to administer the dowry, at least as long as Celedonia did not initiate divorce proceedings. (I have not found a final verdict in this case, but there is no lawsuit involving this couple in the Archivo Arzobispal, indicating that no divorce was filed and reconciliation may have followed or some agreement may have been reached).

Cows, goats, and other animals could be seen as a dowry, and their offspring as part of an acquest. When Mariano decided to administer the dowry and drop muleteering, he became completely dependent upon his wife and her family. No money or investments derived from selling his mules were mentioned. Either there were very few mules and the money resulting from selling them was insignificant, or—following Celedonia's argument—he had managed to spend it very quickly by and for himself. So after marriage, the couple was left with "her" cows and Mariano with a claim for an acquest. In the ongoing negotiations, Celedonia had strong footing, which was further reinforced by her family's backing. Mariano's claim for

---

53. Case 820, AGN, CS, CCR, L 118, 1852, Yaucán vs. Garcí: "Ha hecho extraer mi ganado con el objeto de venderlo, y en esto se hace un mal y me lo hace a mí, porque me deja reducida a la miseria, y no tengo con que alimentarlo a él ni a mi misma." A similar case pitted Mercedes Silvestre de Quilcamachay against her husband Hipólito Gimenes. But in this case, she was in the process of selling 100 goats she had received from her father as a dowry when matrimonial conflict arose (Case 0246, AGN, Expedientes Judiciales, CCI, L 1, 1891).

an acquest was based on the legal stipulation that he—as a husband—was entitled to administer the dowry. According to Celedonia, she had done the work, and he had wasted the earnings. Celedonia's concerns were not enough to outweigh her husband's legal rights. But then again, as among merchants, this peasant woman had a clear perception that "this is my jewelry, this is my dowry, this is my work, and it belongs to me, no matter what the law says."

The meaning and everyday use of dowries changed over time, and was class-specific. People developed different ways of using a dowry. In the early nineteenth century, women used dowry laws to safeguard many different kinds of property and fought for their rights in court. This tendency continued into the middle of the century, although women resorted less to court intervention. However, women themselves, their mothers, and their grandmothers resorted to direct intervention to save female assets from husbands' misuse. Laws concerning dowries did not change, but women's reactions did, and so did judicial verdicts. Women reasserted *their* contributions to marriage and in doing so—directly or through the courts—reduced a husband's leeway in managing conjugal property. Judges increasingly perceived the connections women were making between dowries, labor, and personal rights; and they retaliated by dismissing the legal privileges attached to the dowry, thus furthering the disappearance of the dowry system for reasons quite different from the ones that convinced elites that dowry exchange was no longer a viable institution.

Grudging Judges

Attitudes within institutions and state agencies also reflected a blurring of the definition of dowry. Especially in the case of public assistance agencies, dowries were no longer subject to the meticulous scrutiny of the colonial period, when authorities carefully watched when and to whom dowries were given, strictly following the order of names on the waiting lists. By midcentury poor and orphan girls who wished to marry were no longer a priority, and the dowries began to go to those with good connections to the bureaucrats in charge of managing the dowry funds. When a new director took over the Beneficencia Pública in 1854, the corruption inside the institution surfaced. For years the former directors had misused the funds by misrepresenting the last testaments of those who had donated money for the specific purpose of helping poor girls. It was revealed that even long-married women received shares, just because they or their husbands were *comadres* or *compadres* to the director. When lawsuits followed, the defendant's only justification was the hardship of the politically unstable times, which had left many married women poor.[54]

Another way of "misuse" was the dowry-argument to evade debts. When Doña Petronila Taramona married José de Alzamora Uncino in 1826, she received a dowry of 500 pesos in cash from the Archicofradía de Nuestra Señora del Rosario. That same year José, "because of my wife's honor, virtue, and other good characteristics," signed a dowry acknowledgment and gave her 10,000 pesos as *arras propter nuptias*, an amount representing a tenth of his total wealth. He promised that even if his financial situation declined, she should receive the same amount although it would under those circumstances represent more than one-tenth of his estate. When José died in 1858, Doña Petronila forwarded a petition claiming 10,500 pesos (dowry plus *arras*). In addition, she asked for the earned interest on this money. Their son-in-law, Don Gerónimo Fernández, was the executor of Don José's will. He responded that the estate was completely bankrupt and that Doña Petronila herself was to blame because she had mismanaged everything after her husband's death. Doña Petronila, of course, denied the charge. Her lawyer wrote:

> According to art. 3 of the December 29, 1851 code, my defendant has the right to ask for the deposit of the goods corresponding to her dowry and the assignment of alimonies. . . . Women's fate would indeed be sad if the payment of their dowries would be enmeshed with the demands of common creditors and had to run the same long and costly course through civil suits, without in the interim providing her at least something to eat. If this were so, it would not matter how large a woman's dowry was. She would be exposed to sudden starvation if her husband's estate has undergone bankruptcy. No legislation can or should permit such an atrocity. To the contrary, laws tend to protect a woman's property, whatever her husband's debts may be. This is the only way to safeguard women and to ease a woman's bad luck and unhappiness in marriage.[55]

54. Case 816, AGN, CS, CCI, L 574, 1854, Muñoz vs. de la Fuente: "Los sucesos políticos entorpecieron todo, ya no fue posible ver a la Señora que culpa tengo yo."
55. Case 021, AGN, CS, CCI, L 694, 1858, Alzamora vs. Taramona.

Many debts had been left behind by José, and what Doña Petronila's lawyer was arguing was that her portion of the estate, corresponding to dowry and *arras*, should be exempted from the claims of his creditors because of the legal privileges attached to them. In spite of such legalistic interpretation, the judge declared that all of the couple's property was to be entered into the bankruptcy proceedings after the meeting of creditors took place in November 1859.

This illustrates the changes surrounding the dowry practice. Because of the huge disparity between the original dowry and the *arras*, it can be assumed that the couple came from disparate social backgrounds. Don José may have merely been demonstrating his immense love through a gift of a large sum of money; in the dowry acknowledgment he praised the fine qualities of his wife. But the difference is still striking if we remember that *arras* were no longer widely given. This raises a suspicion that the laws governing the dowry and the *arras* were being manipulated to elude creditors. Although not much time had elapsed between Don José's death and the creditors' meeting, Doña Petronila's son-in-law accused her of squandering (or, implicit in his argument, of hiding) the family fortune before there was time to ascertain the family's true financial situation. In the interim, we may argue (and the judge who handled this case may have perceived) that she would have been able to skim off money equivalent to, or greater than, her claim. Therefore the judge was unwilling to accept her claims for *arras* and dowry. Despite legal requirements to the contrary, priority was given to the creditors' claims. The fact that the judge's final ruling was against Doña Petronila seems to indicate a familiarity with similar cases in which laws concerning dowries and *arras* had been brought forward to preserve family wealth.

A shared family responsibility, which included dowries, replaced the defense of women's properties and rights. Even though laws to protect dowries existed, it became clear that the law would not always be applied. Dowry issues were lifted out of the private sphere and interjected into judicial proceedings. In that setting, they were used to address "bigger" issues that involved all of a family's wealth accumulated over many years. This was possible because dowries were blended into the family estate from the moment of marriage, invested by husbands, and integrated into a family's resources. This reality reduced a woman's capacity to control her interest in the money, something that could threaten her sheer survival (especially when those resources were used to pay debts).

Throughout the century, the dowry in all its social settings became more and more a part of a widening network of monetary transfers and transactions. My quantitative analysis showed this plainly. As dowries became more broadly defined, both men and women resorted to the manipulation of the dowry as a legal entity in order to retake money from creditors, gain an inheritance, or receive support from public institutions. Even within the wider kinship network, the legal character of the dowry institution was used to build arguments for economic entitlement. For example, women, related only remotely to parents who long ago endowed a daughter, would come to claim a right to portions of these dowries once the initial beneficiaries had passed away. A childless woman might will her dowry to a favorite relative, thereby precipitating a furious dispute among all those who felt they had been closer to the departed and thus more deserving of her generosity.[56] The widening scope of dowry claims may explain why judges were less and less willing to make decisions that involved an acceptance of the protection of the dowry mandated by the letter of the law. As "dowries" came to comprise new items and situations, the definition of a dowry was diluted, and as a consequence, judicial quarrels increased. This was true for all dowry transactions, whether involving meager resources or in the case of *adpompam* endowments. It is also mainly for this reason that dowries and *arras* disappeared from the notarial records but continued to appear in lawsuits.

The increasing use of dowries as financial instruments is perhaps best illustrated by a 1902 newspaper advertisement.[57] It appears that the dowry was a business in itself, very much along the lines of an insurance company. If we can believe the advertisement, the world's first privately held company to provide dowries was founded in Lima. The Peruvian government granted *La Dotal* (the company's name) permission to engage in business. It issued dowry instruments for women ranging from 10 to 5,000 pounds sterling, which were purchased through regular monthly contributions to an account that could be opened at the time a girl was born. The corresponding amount could be redeemed when the woman married or when the period for which a dowry had been programmed elapsed, whichever came first. This, in turn,

---

56. Case 035a, AGN, CS, CCI, L 714, 1859, Ugarte. This suit lasted seven years, until finally they agreed to organize a drawing. The amount of the dowry involved was 3,000 pesos.

57. *El Eco de Puno,* Puno, 6 July 1904. Following the same organizing principle, this company also offered *títulos de previsión* to men and women for old age or disability, for establishment of a profession, and for military conscripts.

depended on the beneficiary's age and when the amounts paid ended. The monthly installments could be paid by anyone, including a woman herself. A new business had emerged out of old and long-standing traditions.

A Synthesis

Throughout the colonial period, Indian, black, and *casta* populations increased. Ethnic biases restricted the pool of available spouses, and dowries—imported from overseas—helped to uphold racial and class segregation. These restrictions applied, above all, to women, who seldom wanted to marry husbands considered to be "less white" than themselves. Whereas men would consider a marriage to a "less white" woman (especially if she offered a good dowry), white women and their families preferred spinsterhood if they failed to entice a white suitor.

Thus, among the upper classes at the end of the colonial period, the dowry was an expression of competing family interests among those with daughters to offer. Cause and consequence of this competition were, on one side, the parental control of marriage; that is, parents could force a daughter to marry a husband of their choice by offering a lucrative dowry. On the other side, young white women belonging to the same age-group had a difficult time finding suitable mates, which provided impetus to antagonize parents and express disobedience through romantic rebellion.

Conversely, men did not need to marry in order to have sex but could turn to women of "lesser" racial status for sexual activity and even reproduction. This not only weakened marriage as an institution but also made the dowry, in its traditional form, unnecessary. As dowries became a compensation for lost virginity, middle- and lower-class women redefined the practice in their efforts to obtain indemnity for "moral transgressions" by men. In this form, dowries helped to perpetuate class and ethnic divisions within an established legal framework for women and to bolster a moral double standard.

In spite of its declining importance, the dowry system was important to Lima's inhabitants, both in relation to marriage and to less sacramental sexual and moral behavior. Although usually parents gave a dowry to their daughter's husband, less-common variations existed. There were cases in which women did not bring a dowry into marriage but received an *arras propter nuptias*, which fulfilled functions similar to those of the dowry. There also were cases in which women gave dowries to their husbands.

The transformation of the dowry system in the course of the nineteenth century could be interpreted as the slow softening of patriarchal control and ethnic boundaries. As the nineteenth century progressed, dowries became more and more an issue involving husbands and wives, men and women. This was represented in the changing functions and appreciation of dowries, and at the same time in the characteristics of conjugal conflict that involved dowries.

It is quite clear (and this is a phenomenon, as far as we know, unique to Lima) that dowry exchange virtually disappeared among the upper classes in the first decades of the nineteenth century, while lower-class women insistently continued to use the dowry to forward their claims in Lima's ecclesiastical and civil courts in the name of their work and their childbearing. Thus in the course of the nineteenth century, if not earlier, dowries were descending socially, perpetuated primarily among lower-class women.

In the aftermath of the wars of independence, new political and economic conditions strongly influenced this change. Titles of nobility were abolished in 1828, and many Creoles and Spaniards left the country with their remaining belongings. The economic crisis undercut the viability of dowries; husbands and wives could not count on receiving the monies parents' had promised. This led to property disputes and a general distrust of dowry promises as well as a growing desire to avoid the encumbrance of dowry obligations. But since dowries were essential to the colonial legacy of women's support in marriage, the decline of dowries undercut women's rights within marriage and in the event of any separation.

Statistics show that the values of dowries declined consistently over time. Those cases not notarially recorded—in which payments for lost virginity were made or paraphernalia was simply handed to a new household—indicate that the popular classes used the dowry system, and that dowries in a changed version were much more frequent than wills and formal dowry instruments lead us to assume. Dowries increasingly became a part of wider, more complex civil transactions. Simultaneously, dowries and *arras* became means and ways to preserve family wealth from creditors. Dowries retained their privileged legal standing, but judges were increasingly hesitant to grant special considerations to arguments based on laws governing dowries. This, in turn, signals that judicial authorities were aware of the tricks played on men by lower class women and on creditors through what they classified as the misuse of dowries and *arras*. Thus, before dowries were dismissed, they fulfilled a vital role in transforming the legal arguments of lower- and middle-class women in ecclesiastical and civil court.

A simultaneous consideration of dowries, acquest, and inheritance shows that these mechanisms were important, above all, for two occupational groups: merchants and landowners. In both cases we observe the gradual replacement of dowries by acquest and inheritance, thus signaling patterns of change according to social (occupational) status. Cases of conflict—which basically refer to these two social groups—further reinforce the dowry's importance for such groups. It comes as no surprise that it was, above all, women from these two groups who injected radical thought into the discourse on dowries and started using them for many alternative purposes, thus departing from its traditional definition.

Money lent or donated by relatives, or contacts given for the purposes of improving one's social and business relations, broadened the definition of the contents of dowries, and in so doing inspired new legal strategies by women that had social ramifications. The increasing "civil-financial content" of dowries is obvious in the practice of making interest payments on a nominally promised dowry amount, as well as in the mistrust that ensued among people when bankruptcy struck. This broadened interpretation of dowries led to a widening of the scope of conflicts that were argued before civil judges, perceptibly diminishing church intervention in marital conflicts. Parallel to the church's lessening control on moral issues concerning the family, women's bargaining within their families shows a change in emphasis. When those changes spilled over the barriers of domestic life, the state—that is, the court and judges—were compelled to rethink the legal parameters on which they based their decisions. Dowries had always been a civil issue, but now women were using dowries to redefine the content of marriage and, by implication, their own situation within marriage. This led to hardened and more drastically gendered arguments both in the courtroom and in the bedroom.

Conflicting options developed. Women were entrusted with more responsibilities (as they increasingly became testamentary executors, heiresses, and guardians), but increased responsibility resulted in a loss of the "special" status attributed to women by society. The dowry (which had by now become the portion of an estate "reserved" for the wife) tended to be subject to creditors. Whereas women expanded their access to family resources, this same access diminished their legal protection.

The displacement of dowries by acquest and inheritance also had implications for gender relations. Dowries, in case of conjugal conflict, could be appraised for their monetary value more easily than an inheritance or acquest. The first was very much under parental control, and the second, under a husband's control. Thus, an increasing emphasis on acquest and inheritance magnified women's dependency on husbands. Because acquest usually began a process of family accumulation that preceded the handing over of an inheritance, this change also meant (if no conflicts ensued) the reinforcement of the nuclear family as opposed to the involvement of the wider kinship network.

A deterioration of the dowry system also occurred elsewhere, and has been described for Mexico (Couturier 1985; Arrom 1985b) and Brazil (Nazzari 1991). In both countries the decay of the dowry system has been linked to "dramatic changes" of family dynamics in the eighteenth and nineteenth centuries (Kuznesof and Oppenheimer 1985). Beyond these assertions, the persistence of dowries and their reinterpretation according to class show changes in gender relations over time within the family. These changes have to be considered in explaining how the use of dowries evolved, especially among lower classes. As instruments for developing economic and status differences, dowries were both tools *and* products of social stratification (Goody 1983, 257).

It is important to underline, however, that this development was not caused by economic growth and liberalism—it is possible to imagine a situation of economic recovery having refinanced the dowry system—but it did reinforce a general move away from traditional, religious obligations, which liberalism supported.

There is no doubt that dowries were an important aspect in the shaping of gender, family, and social relations more generally in Lima. However, it is also true that many people did not talk about dowries. Often they had no cows, no cash, no credit. As shown above, couples increasingly had to rely on their own resources as distributions from kin dwindled. What, then, were the arguments brought forward by women who could not and did not count on a legal argument based on the dowry? What were the common strategies for survival within the family beyond the dowry? In the absence of the dowry-maintenance trade-off, would women ask to have their childbearing and domestic chores contribution recognized, and challenge a husband's right to govern the family's income and expenditures?

8

Strategies for Survival

Struggles over Assets and Earnings

In nineteenth-century Lima, as in most other places in the world, women were in charge of the household and were held responsible for putting food on the table day after day, whether or not they had contributed a dowry to the marriage. Men were supposed to secure the money or the resources necessary to make this possible. Most women married, firmly trusting that a loving husband would care for them always. In the wedding ceremony husbands swore to do so, and many believed what they said. Socioeconomic conditions and people's proclivities, however, prevented the triumph of promises and universal ideals. Rare was the family[1] that could ensure its economic survival without experiencing tension. Despite the well-defined

---

1. Before we can analyze the methods used to maintain families, we must define *family*. This can be done spatially; that is, it refers to kin and nonkin residing in one household. Or it may be based on who contributes monetarily to the support of the household. However, no matter what definition one chooses, other problems arise. For instance, what is a "contribution" to the household unit in a setting where nonmonetary transfers were frequent? How do we account for contributions, such as social relations, through which other forms of income may be distributed? How can "income pooling" (Wallerstein 1984), and female domestic duties (cooking, mending, caring for the elderly and for children, etc.) be accounted for? In other words, do those activities that "informally" perpetuate physical and social reproduction fit into our definition of the family? One may restrict the definition of a family to the existence of a father, a mother, and children in the varying phases of the life cycle or regard the mother-child bond (the dyadic relationship) as the minimal expression of family life. In the latter case, the

division of labor within the family, spouses quarreled over the control of assets and income. The next day's bread, not sharing love, became the subject matter for intimate conversations.

Deprivation and poverty could be especially extreme for women. Social convention discouraged them from working, and husbands—following bourgeois understandings of honor—often opposed a wife's economic involvement. Even if a woman and her husband could agree that she should work, skin color created another barrier. The whiter a woman's skin, the more society resisted her entrance into the public sphere. As illustrated in Chapter 1, when she did find employment, a woman was inevitably relegated to marginal jobs. Even toward the end of the century, when nearly 70 percent of Lima's female population was employed, women remained largely excluded from the formal labor market.

According to law, only in extreme situations—such as prolonged absence or mental disease—could a woman be granted a court decree allowing her to circumvent her husband's control over her. This was the only legitimate way a woman could act on her own without first seeking her husband's permission to engage in "public dealings."[2] But she had to prove that her husband was ill-suited or incapable of taking care of family matters; only if such proof was deemed adequate would a judge decide to hand family decision making over to a wife. Of course, when a woman sued for a divorce or annulment, no one expected the husband to approve. But when a wife wanted to file a *civil* lawsuit, the attorney asked for her husband's written

---

definition of a family would rely on emotional bonds rather than on the "structure" or the living arrangements of the family.

Given these difficulties, added to the absence of household statistics for the later part of the century, the main accent in this study lies on the interacting couple. A society characterized by high illegitimacy rates and spatial mobility requires a broad definition of what a family is, and thus how to envision strategies of survival. Relying on our nineteenth-century documents, we gain the impression that more often than not the center of action, decision making, and conflict was the husband-wife dyad. Although sometimes parents were either directly or indirectly involved, their economic role was more passive than active, and their presence tended to diminish in the course of the nineteenth century. Similarly, only rarely did children appear on the stage. They were mute heirs, and only slowly—as will be seen in Chapter 9—did they become an added "bargaining chip" to women's claims for support. As long as there is no possibility of reconstructing changing household structures and internal family dynamics, I have had to assume that the basic unit of action was the couple, and that couples' behavior shaped the family.

2. Case 313, AGN, Cci, L 42, C 678, 1820, Muños vs. de la Fuente and Murga; Muños vs. Argumanis.

permission.[3] Because it was more complicated to begin a civil lawsuit, women were first pushed into the church's arms, with the expectation that the ecclesiastical authorities would calm them down so that, eventually, they would accept that their lot was one of endurance and forgiveness. If, in spite of this covert restraint, women resorted to civil courts after opening a divorce file in ecclesiastical court, they were probably among a minority firmly committed to confronting their spouses rather than being comforted by moral recommendations.

The outcome of a woman's attempt to challenge her husband depended on who she was and what she did. The fate of women and the results of their legal efforts differed according to whether they "had" assets or "made" money. Implied in this distinction are the levels of women's participation in the family economy and their social backgrounds. This distinction also encompasses women's attitudes toward marriage. All women—whether they had, made, or both had and made money—needed to be careful not to trespass the boundaries of "acceptable" public involvement and exposure. A woman who defended her right to income and assets was perceived as challenging the accepted division between the private and public spheres; and was, moreover, seen as questioning her husband's prerogative to administer family assets. Husbands feared the expanding economic involvement of their wives because they sensed that they were losing control over them. From this terrain of conflict emerged a revision of women's role in society.

When a Woman "Has" Money

Women who had money generally belonged to the better-off segments of society. Peruvian law—the Siete Partidas, the 1852 Civil Code, and the ACR (1923)—safeguarded a man's right to manage and dispose of marital and family assets, including money his wife brought to the marriage. With such unlimited economic prerogatives, a man's imagination could run wild thinking of ways to get hold of a woman's assets. As illustrated in

3. Case 899, AGN, CS, CCI, L 574, 1854, Mesinas vs. Morote. Doña Carmen Mesinas had initiated a civil lawsuit to demand that she be given the rent from her house, but for her petition to proceed, the court's lawyer required her to present her husband's written authorization to engage in this lawsuit. These issues will be dealt with in greater detail in Chapter 9. For a detailed reading of wives' legal options and limitations in Mexico, see Arrom (1985b, 65–92).

the preceding chapters, mercenary men would court women for the sole purpose of gaining access to their wealth. Such occurrences were hard to avoid in spite of the strict enforcement of the reading of the banns, a precaution intended to call upon the community's wisdom about the bride and groom. The gamut of calculated spousal cheating ran all the way from selling a wife's jewelry, managing her business enterprise, or hiding profits,[4] to bigamy and extortion. Dowries and paraphernalia—the "reserved" property of women—were not exempt. Legally, jewelry was a woman's paraphernalia; but if a woman had no dowry, her jewelry could be substituted, and half of it could fall under the law allowing a husband to manage it. Even when this was not the case, many husbands did not hesitate to sell or pawn their wives' jewels. Even the watchful eyes of in-laws could not always protect a daughter's assets.

In 1800 Isabel Dávila, a resident of the mining town of Cerro de Pasco, filed a complaint on behalf of her daughter, Francisca Novoa. After only four years of marriage, jewelry worth 7,000 to 8,000 pesos mysteriously disappeared from the daughter's chest. Shortly after the discovery, the husband began mistreating the girl so severely that she ran away. Her mother claimed that "had I not had him arrested in one of those mines following a decree from the subdelegate (provincial political authority) of Pasco, he would undoubtedly have killed my daughter because this is the only thing one can expect from a man whose design is to extort a woman's wealth and then run off wherever he pleases."[5] Although he was caught trying to escape arrest, the jewelry was never found. In the suit, mother and daughter accused him of being a womanizer. The ecclesiastical judge did not accept these charges, however, and he required Francisca to prove she had had legitimate reason to abandon her husband and home. She brought in witnesses who attested to her propriety, but her complaint was turned against her: she was accused of leaving her husband without court permission. The disappearance of her jewelry was not considered worthy of attention.

Bigamy, or even polygamy, was an extreme expression of calculated deceit: "Every day we see frauds of this sort, and there has never been a man stupid enough to engage in several marriages without changing his first name, his

---

4. For a case in which all these accusations merged, see Case 501, AA, CD, L 87, 1815, Renay vs. Ayllón. The couple had lived together only eight years, but had been married for twenty-two. They had an eighteen-year-old son. She came all the way to Lima from Carhuaz in the northern highlands, where she was living, and her husband had gone back to his native town Chiquián.

5. Case 411, AA, LM, L 7, 1800, Novoa vs. Larrañaga.

last name, his origins, or other personal characteristics to ensure the success of his irreligious behavior. Thus, for example, Cayo, who is married to Juana, would then appear to be Sempronio."[6]

Financial incentives often lay at the heart of calculated deceit, bigamy, or polygamy. At the beginning of the nineteenth century, the widely charged 12 percent annual interest rate would, for example, earn on 8,000 pesos (the value of Francisca's jewelry) an annual sum far exceeding the cost of supporting a wife.[7] A crafty husband could view his marriage as a source of interest-free capital.

Few women were accused of bigamy, and when it happened, it was not from malice but because a woman believed her first husband was dead. Given the turmoil of the times, it is not surprising that, after not having been heard of for many years, a husband might suddenly appear to reclaim his home.[8] The percentage of bigamy and polygamy accusations against both men and women rose from 1.7 percent between 1800 and 1820, to 3.8 percent between 1840 and 1860, and 4.2 percent between 1890 and 1910.[9]

Leaving aside less-than-honorable intentions, we find that reaching old age could also provide a man the opportunity to live off his wife's assets. In this situation, outwitting death replaced deceit as a strategy for survival. A man had only to live long enough, marry several times, and manage resources carefully. Between 1810 and 1900, 15.3 percent of those men who wrote wills had remarried, and 2.4 percent had ventured into a third marriage (see Table 8.1).

The case of an 82-year-old man who had married three times and had nine legitimate and three natural children illustrates the point. In 1890 Mariano Valderrama y Torres, a middle-class veteran, wrote his will. During his first marriage shortly after the wars of independence, the couple had lived with Mariano's mother. He had not received a dowry, and at the time of his first wife's death, the couple had not accumulated any jointly held assets. In 1852 Mariano married for a second time, and it was he who gave

---

6. Case 418, AA, NM, L 59, 1812, de Oleas vs. Gastelumendi. Petronila de Oleas came to know about her husband's wanderings after seven years of marriage and through information provided by several initially unrelated people. Her husband, who had originally come from Vizcaya in Spain, was married to (and had ruined before her) a woman living in the Trujillo Archbishopric.

7. An annual interest rate on 7,000 pesos was the equivalent of 840 pesos, that is, 70 pesos a month. The minimum monthly allowance for a wife in a *beaterio* was between 12 and 16 pesos.

8. Revealing in this respect is what happened to Bernardina Chaves between 1820 and 1858. See Chapter 1.

9. From AA, Series LM, CD, NM.

Table 8.1 Marriage and remarriage, men, 1800–1910

	Once-Married	Twice-Married	Thrice-Married
1810	82.1	13.7	4.1
1820	88.7	9.9	1.4
1830	72.3	21.3	6.4
1840	86.0	14.0	0.0
1850	70.0	25.0	5.0
1860	80.0	17.5	2.5
1870	87.9	12.1	0.0
1880	78.4	20.0	1.5
1890	78.9	21.1	0.0
1900	90.3	6.5	3.2
Century average		15.3	2.4

SOURCE: AGN, Notarial Records, Wills.

an *arras propter nuptias*, which included jewelry and 1,000 pesos, to his wife. In return, he received 1,076 pesos and half a *real* from his wife's mother. These items represented his wife's inheritance from her father. The couple also received an allowance of 180 pesos monthly. When the second wife died only three years after their marriage, her jewelry had to be sold to cover the funeral expenses. Just two years later, around 1858, Mariano married his second wife's sister, Rosa Pérez. Before the marriage, he had given Rosa 1,000 pesos in the form of an *arras*. This transfer was part of a family agreement in which Mariano's brother-in-law provided—as acquest on his wives' paternal inheritance—a monthly allowance. This was invested to pay for the family's sustenance. After 1860 the allowances stopped because the brother no longer administered the estate. Rosa received one distribution of 535 pesos, from which 172 pesos and 6½ *reales* (one-third) were handed over to Mariano. In addition, she received some valuables that were kept outside of Mariano's control. Together, the couple bought a little piece of land in the Villa de Chorrillos and invested money to improve it, selling it at a profit in 1864. The income from the sale became acquest.[10] In his will, Mariano wrote that his third wife had "brought with her a little jewelry, which, added to some I had given her, then had to be almost entirely sold to pay for our daily food and the food for our children at the time of the fateful Chilean occupation [during the War of the Pacific, 1880–81]."

Mariano was a typical colonial survivor. He lived on his salaries from the colonial and the republican states (which more often than not went unpaid),

10. AGN, CCI, L 336.6, 1890, Meléndez vs. Pérez; Pérez vs. Valderrama y Torres.

family inheritance, and marital arrangements; even sororate (marrying a wife's sister) was part of his multilayered survival strategy. The inventory of his many *capellanías* (in this case, the masses paid for on behalf of his ancestors) and several unresolved situations in which the state and even the merchant's guild owed him money, portray well the implications of "colonial heritage" in an individual's life. He had many assets but no money, even to pay for his wife's funeral. Jewelry was the "last resort" for liquidity, especially when war came about. The way in which he managed his daily survival and family business shows how people did not easily dismiss deeply entrenched *rentier* ideologies involving family, even within the rapidly changing broader social setting of the nineteenth century. To the contrary, it discloses how Lima's inhabitants depended for survival on dealings with family members. Mariano, being an old man with no family of his own, lived from his successive wives' inheritances and dowries, and he had to continuously bargain over these assets with his brothers-in-law. The intricate transactions and money transfers involved made sororate almost necessary because it made it easier to keep track over time of the many bargaining levels concerning dowries, acquest, inheritances, funeral costs, and so on.

Women venturing into a second or third marriage usually did not fare as well as men, but they had one advantage over women marrying for the first time: experience. Between 1810 and 1900 women remarried more frequently than men: 17.1 percent married twice, and 3.6 percent three times (Table 8.2). These rates may indicate women's social and legal need to have a husband at their side. Given that Lima presented a highly restricted "marriage market" and a society that placed great value on virginity, assets or money accumulated during a first marriage may have been the only reason widows were attractive enough to find another husband.

María Gonzales de Troya was widowed in 1792. Shortly afterward, Juan de Dios Landaeta insistently asked to marry her. She was the owner and operator of a bakery, and even though he had little experience with this line of work, he agreed to help expand her enterprise. Disaster followed: "Believing in a muddled way that I had a good husband, I traveled with him to the highlands to instruct him in the commerce of imported and locally produced goods. When I thought that he had learned something, I sent him off on his own with a small amount of money. For one year he did not come back and, when he did, he came with a *mestiza* and two children."[11] He subsequently made a second trip, only to return with yet another woman,

11. Case 237, AA, CD, L 83, 1804, Troya vs. Landaeta.

Table 8.2 Marriage and remarriage, women, 1800–1910

	Once-Married	Twice-Married	Thrice-Married
1810	80.6	16.1	3.2
1820	84.1	12.7	1.6
1830	70.9	19.4	9.7
1840	85.7	11.9	2.4
1850	77.2	15.9	6.8
1860	89.2	7.1	3.6
1870	68.6	31.4	0.0
1880	77.0	18.8	4.2
1890	83.7	16.2	0.0
1900	80.6	16.1	3.2
Century average		17.1	3.6

SOURCE: AGN, Notarial Records, Wills.

who, according to María, pocketed everything Juan earned. Consequently, "there was nothing left to sell . . . nothing of any value." María's assets had been used to the upkeep of her husband's concubines and *their* children, making marriage a bad bargain indeed.

Even when they were highly practiced and successful businesswomen, widows were restricted by social convention and the law from running their own businesses when they remarried. As property owners, they were favorite targets for men who sought through marriage to gain the entitlement to administer, spend, and take advantage of a business enterprise. The experience that came with a second or third marriage did not necessarily save these women from fraud. If we contrast Maria's and Mariano's multiple marriages, it is easy to see along which lines wealth within the family accumulated. A husband engaging in successive marriages became a point of capital concentration; while a woman doing the same became a point of capital dispersion. The only difference in this synthesis of economic performance in the course of two lives is gender.

Sociocultural expectations lay at the heart of different outcomes. Women, by definition, were unprepared to administer a business. Men like Maria's husband could resort to an argument that the family's economic future would be much bleaker without a man to oversee it. A longstanding and inculcated inferiority could become a source of abuse, a convenient set of mental conditionings to be exploited. In the courtroom, when a husband set out to prove what everyone already believed, he had won his case beforehand. Male support was not only a female wish but also a legally determined option. People justified these social and legal standards with blunt moral arguments.

The story of Simona Comin is very similar to that of María de Gonzales. Simona had inherited one of Lima's forty-nine bakeries from her husband. In his will, he had designated María as the guardian of their four children and the legatee of all marital goods. Simona's bakery was worth an estimated 70,000 pesos. Only a few months after her husband's death, she married a cavalry captain from the Carabayllo militia. Throughout the first years of her new marriage, Simona continued to work in the bakery, and she also spent its profits. But around 1812 she wrote, "I started receiving the cruelest treatment from my husband, and the money I had controlled until now was taken away from me."[12] Several witnesses testified on Simona's behalf, confirming her good management of the bakery as well as her proper social conduct. To save her life, the lives of her children, and her possessions, she sought refuge in a *beaterio*.

Gregorio, the cavalry captain, counterattacked in court by alleging that it had been he, who through efficient management had saved the bakery from bankruptcy. What is more, he claimed he had transformed his wife into a lady by removing her from a crude working life and daily contact with the slaves laboring in the bakery. Now, thanks to him, she was able to enjoy lavish summers in Chorrillos. Reading between the lines, we see that by being a "good husband" and shaping Simona to fit the ideal of an exemplary wife, he had "saved" her from managing her own business. What he did not say, but what everyone knew, was that as a military man his financial well-being entirely depended on his making a good marriage, and Simona was a very good catch. Against her explicit will, Simona fell into the trap of marriage and social expectations that forced her into a situation of economic dependency, exclusion, and seclusion.

Some husbands took over a wife's assets by sheer violence, and European immigrants were no exception. Although they brought new ideas to Peru, these did not change gender patterns in nineteenth-century Lima. White immigrants quickly found their way into the ranks of the elite classes by marrying upper- and middle-class women. In addition to an advantage based on skin color, European immigrants used conventional strategies to acquire goods and money through marriage, which in turn influenced

---

12. Case 158, AA, CD, L 86, 1812, Comín vs. Lamas; NM, L 59, 1813; see also AGN, RA, CCR, L 102, C 1247, 1804, Acusación de una esclava contra Gregorio Lamas por maltratos en la panadería.

their patterns of social mobility. How these immigrants handled marital and economic situations similar to those we have already discussed, and their behavior within their marriages, reveals much about the degree to which they assimilated the culture of nineteenth-century Lima or about cultural similarities.

In 1813 María Lemuz revealed some disturbing qualities of her English husband of three years: "When he arrived in this city, he had nothing; I, firmly convinced that he was an honest man, protected him and even became his wife after he converted to Catholicism. Consequently, I made him the owner of my few belongings, jewelry, and slaves. We have been working together in the wheat mill my former husband gave me . . . but now my new husband has completely taken over the administration of the business, he has the confidence and esteem of all my friends, and they have even extended him credit. He has become a distinguished man because of my help and commendable life."[13]

Conde Rojer (perhaps a Spanish version of Count Roger?), her husband, owed everything to her, yet when he took over her mill, he began to insult and beat her. In the records, María's complaints as a dependent wife—no food, no clothes, no attention—echo other stories. Not even her husband's non-Catholic and foreign background, however, helped María make a case for herself. She had managed an efficient enterprise, earned the "social connections," and brought her husband into the business. But all this together still did not suffice to convince the judge of her right to a divorce, which would have enabled her to retake her business.

Women reacted to what they increasingly recognized was appalling injustice. Often they struggled to come to grips with an inequitable situation through their letters and petitions to Lima's judges, which graphically portray the consequences of the unfair discrimination of the period. Even some of Lima's aristocratic daughters could not escape abuse, notwithstanding watchful parents concerned about the family assets.

In 1816 the marquise of Santa María, in a confidential letter to Archbishop Las Heras, complained: "Having tried all prudent means to convince Don Fernando Carrillo Márquez de Santa María [her husband], I still have not achieved a standard of living that matches the promises and obligations we agreed to through the holy sacrament of marriage."[14] Several times she had sought refuge in Lima's monasteries in the hope that this drastic action

---

13. Case 292, AA, LM, L 8, 1813, Lemuz vs. Conde Rojer.
14. Case 564, AA, Comunicaciones Oficiales de Curas, L 1, 1816, Marquesa de Santa María vs. Carrillo. She admitted that her worst fate ["peores contrastes"] began since the time "her

would improve her husband's conduct. It did not. Her husband openly "amused" himself with "*cholas* and *sambas*," their Indian and black domestic servants. Finally, she fled to the home of a female relative, where "I find myself in a room living as a sad woman, without any comfort, whereas my husband . . . is enjoying my properties. . . . I am living, but on very scarce resources, in spite of the fact that providence has endowed me with wealth." All the riches were of no use to her now; everything was in her husband's hands. Neither her noble origin nor her husband's moral trespasses were enough to regain her property. The archbishop turned her letter over to the courts, and the courts scrupulously enforced the law, dismissing the marquise's queries and upholding her husband's rights. But as we shall see, even women who worked and had few or no assets at all suffered similar injustices.

When Women Made Money

To support their families, lower-class women had to work. Sewing, selling at the market, lending money (if they had some), and domestic service were the most common livelihoods. (Only gradually during the century did women become bureaucrats, secretaries, and educators.) Women in desperate financial circumstances would turn to these traditional means of earning a living. When widespread economic crises arose—that is, when competition in the labor market reduced even further the already limited domain of female employment—women's desperation grew.

Dowries among the lower classes were either nonexistent or of little pecuniary value. Consequently, the notion of bartering a dowry for a husband's acceptance of the responsibility to care materially for his family did not fit the facts, especially among the poor. The gap between ideal and reality led to unfulfilled expectations that created a bargaining ground for men and women. The haggling that began in the bedroom was, in many cases, over something very basic—money for food:

> More often than not it was midnight when he came home, and he never got up before half the morning was gone. Sometimes angry, sometimes with tears and begging, I asked him why he didn't bring

---

uncle's support had vanished" ["desde que me faltó la sombra de mi Tío el marqués de Casa-Dávila"].

home at least some money for bread. "God will provide," was always his answer before he fell asleep. I would tell him to roll cigars, at least, or to do something, just so we could buy a little food. His answer was to ask what people would think when they saw him. Finally, when I pushed him harder, he told me that since I had not brought any dowry to go out myself; and he followed this with other insults. When he would finally get out of bed, he was unfailingly grouchy and insulting. Then he would disappear again until night, never giving a thought to whether his wife had eaten something. This has been going on not for one or two days, or for one or two weeks, but for months and years. Since I married, with a few exceptions, I have fasted continuously. Beating and slashing are indeed mistreatment, but nothing is as gruesome as hunger.[15]

Piece by piece, this woman pawned her jewelry. Neighbors occasionally helped her with a few *reales* or a bite to eat. Rent had to be paid, but her husband was never at home when the creditors banging at the door insulted her,[16] and she lived with the constant fear that they would throw her out on the street. This woman, the wife of a ship clerk whose income depended on being occasionally hired, and many like her, felt like "a straw in the wind, not knowing where to fall," while their husbands were often seen enjoying themselves in Lima's cafes. Her only option was to return to her mother's house, something she was able to do only after obtaining the necessary authorization from ecclesiastical authority.

When husbands did not provide for their wives, adultery was often the cause. One woman, who had been married only six months, explained: "This morning he told me that he was going out to work, and when I left my room, I accidentally encountered him at the Pescaderia corner strolling with his concubine. I told him where I was going, and then asked him, 'Didn't you tell me you were going to work?' He grabbed me, and she hit me. Even now I am spitting blood. If I ask him for money to buy food, he hits me and tells me he hasn't anything. He has money to pay for his concubine's room, but he doesn't pay for mine, yet if I want to work, he won't let me."[17]

This husband blocked one possible solution to his wife's predicament by refusing to allow her to look for work. Restrictions imposed on women's

---

15. Case 380, AA, CD, L 87, 1819, Moña vs. Ramírez.
16. Case 610, AA, LM, L 7, 1807; and CD, L 87, 1807, Mendoza vs. Useda. The only income the couple had was provided through the day labor of a slave girl they owned.
17. Case 638, AA, CD, L 86, 1812, Villachica vs. Villasanta.

participation in the labor market may have been more than just the consequence of the idealization of virtue and the lack of jobs. At times, obstinate male pride appears to have flourished by opposing the responsibility to meet the family's material needs. Beyond reflecting the mentality of the day, this strategy to restrict the wife from leaving the household also ensured that public confrontations, such as the one described above, might be averted.

In 1806 María Vellón described a similar episode; however, something more was involved this time: "On the many different occasions I have begged him to do something, he has always responded with insults. He sends me away saying, 'Leave me alone, don't you have anybody to embrace you? If you don't have anybody, that means that you have nobody who cares about you. If you had somebody, you would have left me long ago. I don't have the means to keep you. I intend to look for work after you are gone. In the meantime, I will do nothing because I don't want to capitulate to your wishes.' "[18]

Specifically to annoy her, Maria Vellón's husband refused to work. In a near reversal of the moral codes of nineteenth-century Lima, he expected his wife to dispense sexual favors to others for sustenance.

Class, age, and race inequalities between spouses, as well as material necessity, were at the root of some "moral transgressions." After one year of marriage, Rafael Ponse, an octogenarian wine producer, urged his wife, Petronila Chávez, to trade sex for money. She worked on a plot of land, share-cropping for the female owner. Her husband, she explained, "insisted on several occasions, telling me, 'Go, you stupid highland woman, look, I will not be sad . . . rub elbows with men. Take what they give you. Everywhere one has to look for ways to survive, and, look, I am telling you this and I am a person with a lot of experience. . . .' Finally, he opened the door, as he was telling me he was an open-minded, straightforward man who knew women very well and that from 'the profession' one could earn considerable amounts of money without losing one's reputation. [But I didn't do it] because I knew that my husband alone has a right to my body within the bounds of our marriage, but he has no right to oblige me to seek another man."[19]

This woman must have been much younger than her husband, who seemed willing to relinquish his sexual rights. Moreover, a *serrana sonsa* (stupid highlander) was subject to different moral rules, and this was true not only for Indians but also for *castas*.[20] The arguments brought forward

18. Case 631, AA, CD, L 84, 1806, Vellón vs. Robles.
19. Case 167, AA, CD, L 83, 1803, Chávez vs. Ponse.
20. Case 258, AA, LM, L 8, 1813, Heredia vs. Aguilar.

when racial and/or age disparity existed greatly contrast with the fierce accusations and moral outrage drummed up by husbands accusing their wives of adultery.

Here is evidence that despite prevailing mores, providing for one's wife was not always seen as a marital obligation. Instead, matters of daily life were subject to negotiation, including the possibility of selling a wife's body. Wives, especially those without dowries, had few options: tears, searching for employment, or finding someone (explicitly another man) who would care for them. All three options, in turn, spilled over into the realm of how women should or could act and react to their husbands.

Few women in nineteenth-century Lima knew what their husbands did for a living or what they earned. Lower wages and higher prices were pushing women into the labor market, and husbands often had to resort to multiple jobs to earn an adequate living. This helped obscure a husband's financial situation, making it possible to hide assets from a wife.

A gunsmith who owned his own shop and was also a militiaman illustrates this strategy. For fifteen years, this man had spent 33 pesos and 4 *reales* a month to support his wife and two children. This money had to be rigorously divided into 6 *reales* daily for food, in addition to 1.5 *reales* for bread, and 8 pesos for rent.[21] This was approximately the minimum monthly expenditure for a lower-middle-class household of four at the beginning of the nineteenth century. On a monthly basis, the gunsmith's family spent 22 pesos and 4 *reales* on food (38 percent) plus 1 peso and 4 *reales* for bread (3 percent), and 8 pesos for rent (14 percent). Shelter and food thus accounted for 55 percent and clothing accounted for upwards of 40 percent of the average monthly budget, that is, approximately 25 pesos a month according to our calculations based on this case.[22] Prices increased during the nineteenth century: between 1830 and 1920, the cost of meat, lard, butter, and rice more than tripled.[23] According to many testimonies, few people in Lima could make ends meet. As prices increased, heads of household resorted to diversifying their occupation by working multiple jobs or by including more members of the family (women and occasionally children) in income-generating activities. To be both a regular militiaman

---

21. Case 220, AA, CD, L 87, 1805, García vs. Hernández; AGN, Cabildo, CCI, L 10C 113, 1805.

22. These calculations broadly coincide with Gootenberg's (1990) calculations on prices in Lima in the first half of the nineteenth century.

23. Statistics on prices were only recorded officially since 1913. For information on prices for basic consumption items between 1913 and 1933, see Extracto Estadístico del Perú, published by the Ministerio de Hacienda y Comercio.

and own an artisan shop was such a strategy. Many alternative jobs were in what today is called the "informal sector" of the economy.

The example of the gunsmith also shows how this strategy could be put to use deceiving a wife. When conflict developed in the gunsmith's household, the wife and several witnesses declared that he was actually earning much more money than he spent on his family. He had never been called to account for this. Instead, by restricting the household accounts, he strictly controlled the activities of his wife and children, leaving them with little power to shape their lives. Husbands paid basic costs and sometimes demonstrated generosity, thus reinforcing male authority and extorting "good behavior" from women and children. Even today in Latin America, women expect to receive the *diario* (their daily allowance), after which they go to the market, cook, and then wait for the next day, when they hope their husbands will bring home enough money to repeat the cycle.

Failure to support the family ranked high among divorcing women. A large percentage of married wives protested abandonment and the lack of financial support. Between 1800 and 1820, 39.9 percent (111 out of 278) married women who presented a complaint in the ecclesiastical or civil courts claimed they received insufficient or no support; between 1840 and 1860, the percentage rose to 46.2 percent (67 out of 145); and was 41.8 percent (85 out of 203) between 1890 and 1910 (see Tables 8.3, 8.4, and 8.5). Unlike unwed mothers, married women could more easily resort to legal action because the law defined the responsibilities of husbands and fathers.

A woman's success in exerting some control over family finances also depended on a husband's occupation. Bureaucrats and military men had fixed incomes that were public knowledge. Artisans had variable earnings, but the nature of their occupation required that they maintain a fixed place of residence. Peddlers and day laborers, in contrast, had both variable incomes and no fixed place of work. Merchants, perhaps the most lucrative occupation in nineteenth-century Lima, were away from home for long periods of time, had irregular incomes, and asked friends (or, on occasion, the wife) to administer the household finances during their absence.[24]

It was advantageous for a wife to know where her husband worked and how much he earned, but men with steady incomes were in the minority.

---

24. Case 224, AA, LM, L 7, 1808, García vs. Cárdenas. Nicolás Cárdenas worked at the plaza del Real Presidio del Callao, and while living in the port city, he had asked a shopkeeper to sell food to his wife on credit, and at the end of each month, he would pay the bill. But this always resulted in arguments and abuse because, according to him, his wife always overspent.

Table 8.3 Demand reason and who presents the demand, 1800–1820

Main demand reason	Total	%	Man	%	Woman	%	Family	%	Others	%	Unidentified	%
Abandonment	125	30.6	12	9.6	111	88.8	1	0.8	1	0.8	—	—
Goods	49	12.0	9	18.4	40	81.6	—	—	—	—	—	—
Adultery	171	41.8	72	42.1	97	56.7	2	1.2	—	—	—	—
Children	4	1.0	3	75.0	1	25.0	—	—	—	—	—	—
Sex	7	1.7	1	14.3	6	85.7	—	—	—	—	—	—
Other	34	8.3	17	50.0	12	35.3	2	5.9	2	5.9	1	2.9
No data	19	4.6	6	31.6	11	57.9	—	—	—	—	2	10.5
Total	409	100.0	120	29.3	278	68.0	5	1.3	3	0.7	3	0.7

Source: AA, LM, CD, NM.

Table 8.4 Demand reason and who presents the demand, 1840–1860

Main demand reason	Total	%	Man	%	Woman	%	Family	%	Others	%	Unidentified	%
Abandonment	75	35.2	4	5.3	67	89.3	2	2.7	1	1.3	1	1.3
Goods	23	10.8	2	8.7	21	9.3	—	—	—	—	—	—
Adultery	72	33.8	41	56.9	31	43.1	—	—	—	—	—	—
Sex	5	2.3	2	40.0	3	60.0	—	—	—	—	—	—
Other	17	8.0	3	17.6	14	82.4	—	—	—	—	—	—
No data	21	9.9	7	33.3	9	42.9	—	—	3	14.3	2	9.5
Total	213	100.0	69	27.7	145	68.1	2	0.9	4	1.9	3	1.4

Source: AA, LM, CD, NM.

Table 8.5 Demand reason and who presents the demand, 1890–1910

Main demand reason	Total	%	Man	%	Woman	%	Family	%	Others	%	Unidentified	%
Abandonment	109	24.3	24	22.0	85	78.0	—	—	—	—	—	—
Goods	26	5.8	8	30.8	18	69.2	—	—	—	—	—	—
Adultery	232	51.8	170	73.3	59	25.4	2	0.9	1	0.4	—	—
Children	2	0.4	—	—	2	100.0	—	—	—	—	—	—
Sex	10	2.2	4	40.0	6	60.0	—	—	—	—	—	—
Other	50	11.2	24	48.0	26	52.0	—	—	—	—	—	—
No data	19	4.3	9	47.4	7	36.8	—	—	—	—	3	15.8
Total	448	100.0	239	53.3	203	45.3	2	0.4	1	0.2	3	0.8

SOURCE: AA, LM, CD, NM.

Getting one-third of the husband's income (the legally stipulated allowance to which a divorced woman and her children were entitled) was a dream in most cases. Even doctors, lawyers, musicians, along with merchants, peddlers, artisans, and day-laborers—about 90 percent of Lima's male population according to the 1876 census—did not have regular, predictable incomes. Thus for most men, hiding income from a wife was easy. This, in turn, meant that wives who went to court often did not know how much they should ask for alimony. When women formulated alimony requests, husbands could argue that their occupations simply did not produce enough or, if their history made that claim unlikely, they could declare they were experiencing bad luck in their finances. With the assistance of observant neighbors, a wife might estimate how much her husband earned by determining how much he spent on mistresses, or by calculating the costs of his promenades and visits to the bullfight arena.[25] But engaging in this guesswork was yet another expression of her ignorance about her husband's real income situation.

When a woman managed to find her way into the public sphere to seek work, there was a clear tendency to engage in typically female occupations, including wet-nursing and prostitution. Whatever the occupation, husbands retained the right to control a wife's earnings (that is, until the divorce was final). After giving birth, a woman could become an important income source for the whole family. In the first decade of the nineteenth century, Vicenta Ampuero went to see the *provisor* because her husband, a blacksmith, was mistreating her. They had one child and were so heavily in debt that even their kitchen utensils and furniture had been seized to pay the rent. "Seven days after giving birth," she recounted, "I went out to search for a child in need of milk, which would allow me to get some money and food for myself. I was lucky to find a position, and I even got a two-month advance payment." When Vicenta took the money to her husband to reestablish his blacksmith business "in order to honestly earn our living," her good intentions were betrayed. "This hope was in vain, because the little he made went right to the gambling house and, subsequently, the same happened to his tools, although he tried to make me believe they had been stolen."

Vicenta had no resources left with which to obtain money. Desperate and deceived, she sought shelter in a *beaterio* and tried without success to obtain a monthly alimony from her husband. He sought instead to revive their

---

25. Casc 557, AA, LM, L 8, 1812, Sánchez vs. Garavito. The marriage had lasted for eight years, and conflict arose when she came to know of Ambrosio's "public adultery" in the Chorrillos summer resorts.

marriage. Vicenta guessed what this meant, and what her husband would ask her to do next. "He tries to come back, but Your Excellency should ask what he has in mind. . . . He will sexually assault me, and then suggest that I cheat men, putting my dignity and life at risk (talking with respect) and offending God, without giving one thought to the one who belongs to him as his legitimate wife."[26]

First wet-nursing, then prostitution was a sequence that, beyond marriage's holy sacrament and mutual obligations, described facets of the division of labor. As another woman recounted, "Although my good husband asked somebody to tell me that I should become a prostitute to pay for my own food, I can't possibly do this, because I have never entangled myself in such a lascivious trade."[27] Obviously, women resorting to the ecclesiastical court had rejected such offensive and scandalous alternatives, but probably many more surrendered to necessity and a husband's impositions. On several occasions, Calistra Sierra had heard her husband scream at her that she was only good for black men ("que yo estoy buena para los negros con que estoy echa a volar"); he had also thrown her out of the house while he spent the time amusing himself with a concubine and had forced her to borrow money from others, which she had to repay later with her own earnings. "Women of better status work and hand their money over to men," her husband argued.[28] Lower-class women, in short, were seen as income-earners for their husbands. By withholding his earnings, a husband could force his wife to be the family provider, even if it meant selling her body.

The observation made by Calistra's husband was accurate: women in better economic conditions were also subjected to such pressures. Options such as wet-nursing were not limited to the very poor but were also found among small merchants and artisans. Wives from these social backgrounds were generally not prepared to work outside the home. When asked to find employment, they felt utterly offended and often retorted with the argument that they should not work because they were not of African origin or slaves.[29]

---

26. Case 23, AA, LM, L 7 (1800–1809); CD, L 87 (1815–20), Ampuero vs. Abarca.
27. Case 487, AA, CD, L 86, 1813, Quiroga vs. Gil. The husband was a small merchant, and the couple had a three-year-old daughter. At the time this case was brought to court, the wife was pregnant. They were both called in by the *provisor*, and he "obliged them to return to matrimonial life."
28. AA, CD, L 93 (1857–58), 1858, Sierra vs. Isaguirre.
29. When Doña Mercedes Heredia—who defined herself as a parents' daughter—complained about her husband, she arrogantly avowed she could not possibly be expected to perform menial tasks as if she were a woman of African origin. ["Si mi marido fuera de buenas intenciones no havría pensado en hacer Víctima de mi persona con exigirme al trabajo y demas

As a consequence of mistreatment by her husband, Don Manuel Aguilar, Doña Mercedes Heredia miscarried. Don Manuel saw an opportunity not to be missed and immediately looked for a wet-nursing position for his wife. In notable contrast to the case of Vicenta, Doña Mercedes could not seek a wet-nursing job because she was a "Doña"; her husband found one for her, and, consequently, he had greater control over his wife's earnings because he knew where to collect the pay. Doña Mercedes earned 150 pesos a month, an amount that, according to her, "took her breath away." The availability of her service spread, and she soon added new clients. In the meantime, however, Don Manuel kept all her earnings, leaving her nothing, not even enough for food. For several months, Doña Mercedes was terrified and did nothing to change her dire circumstances. At one point, when she and her parents went before the judge, they recanted the charges because Manuel had threatened "to drink their blood" if they insisted on pressing their suit.

Eventually, they pursued legal recourse for their predicament. However, Doña Mercedes based her argument on her firm belief that because she was a white woman, her husband had no right to ask her to work. From her viewpoint, only *casta* and black women worked, rode on mule-back, and sold produce in the market. She attested that many men in Lima married darker-skinned women to exploit their labor and make money, but as a white woman, such a fate was unacceptable.

In reality, however, wet-nursing, unlike prostitution, was a morally legitimate way in which lower- and middle-class women could help earn money to support their families. Inducing a woman (and even worse, a wife) to become a prostitute was another matter because the fact offended public morality. However, judges responded to both solely in moral terms: there was nothing wrong with women wet-nursing and husbands taking away the earnings; however, when prostitution was added to the mix, judges would recommend a husband behave more decently. In neither case was women's access to their income or control over their bodies addressed. The relationship of abuse and survival went unexamined.

Whereas some husbands urged their wives to earn money by wet-nursing or "rubbing elbows with men," others displayed extreme jealousy over their

---

maltratos y ópreciones a que me redujo, y tiene, qual si fuese sierva suya, ó de Casta africana, como se ve que otros de su clase casados con estas, han echo plata montando encima de una bestia, y vendiendo verduras en la plasa, entonces pues le havría quadrado, y acomodadole yo."] Being pregnant, she asked to be returned to her parents' house. Her petition was granted.

marital rights. But control was an issue for both, and wives who worked or engaged in public activities were particularly problematic. It was easier to control a wet-nursing wife than one who managed a booth in a busy marketplace.

Wives engaged in small commerce often were married to soldiers, and most soldiers stationed in Lima were *castas*, or more specifically, *pardos, morenos,* and *mulattos.* Around 1810 a first sergeant's monthly pay was less than 6 pesos, far too little to live on. Military superiors recognized this and expected their men to marry women who would not need to be supported. Because soldiers had to ask for permission and approval to marry, it was widely held that men from the lower military ranks married laborers. Drinking and beating were common accusations against soldier-husbands, perhaps because their wives were more independent than the average *limeña.* Between 1800 and 1820, 10.5 percent of recorded marital conflicts involved military personnel. Military wives frequently were completely on their own in providing for their children. Yet when they ran a small business or became vendors (that is, when their activities were "public"), it could provoke a husband into a jealous rage.

Martina Cerbantes, an Indian married to a free *pardo*, Cipriano de León, maintained that after six years of marriage, her husband's alcohol consumption was so great that he sometimes "came home on all fours or his friends would carry him home half dead."[30] Martina sold vegetables in a Lima market to feed them both. Because Cipriano would not help her pick and carry loads of vegetables (particularly heavy pumpkins) from the fields, she was forced to hire a day laborer, Felipe, with whom she was in daily contact.[31] Perhaps Martina's financial success or his own inadequacies drove Cipriano to accuse her of adultery. Cognizant that she had made a "military marriage," Martina eloquently put the appropriate question to the *provisor:* "So now I want to hear from Your Excellency, the answer to whether in a marriage the woman must obey and pay the upkeep for her husband, whereas he has no obligation to feed her, dress her, or pay the rent? For more than seven

30. Case 157, AA, LM, L 8, 1810, Cerbantes vs. de León.
31. This made that Cipriano "se olvidase de sus obligaciones sugetándose á la alimentación que yo le proporcionaba con mis industrias mugeriles ... [y] corriendo esta tragedia sin esperanza de reforma ... me puse á trabajar en esta Plaza Mayor poniendo un pequeño Asiento de Legumbres.... Ha sido preciso comprar Vestias para el carguio del recado que se saca de las chacaras. También tener un Ayudante que maneje los Serones de Sapayos como lo es Felipe a quien se le paga su jornal. Como Leon no ha querido hacer lo que este Peon efectua, por eso és preciso mantenerlo."

months, León has done absolutely nothing. He wants me to submit to him, but he forgets to fulfill his marital obligations."

To have any control over money, women needed an established source of revenue, such as a stall in the public market. The one or two clients a wet-nurse could accommodate might easily disappear or, at best, fall prey to a greedy husband, but the volume of customers in the open market provided security. Thus it was a woman like Martina who, in spite of the special assumptions underlying a marriage to a soldier, stepped forward to ask her husband's superior and the *provisor* how to reconcile her husband's obligation to feed her with her own decisive contribution to the couple's survival. In doing so, Martina questioned the patriarchal assumptions underlying her husband's rights, and her questions document yet another scenario in which the "natural order" was subverted by daily experiences.

Only the threat of physical violence can explain why women like Vicenta handed money over to their husbands. Only a few, such as Martina, were able to stand before the judge to defend not only their personal case but the case of women in general. Unlike Vicenta, Martina did not seek refuge in a *beaterio* but asked for direct judicial intervention on her own behalf. In her arguments, she stressed how unfair it was for her to turn her earnings over to her husband without receiving any support in return. Worse yet was his accusation of adultery when, after all, she had been forced to hire a laborer to do the work her husband refused to do. She put the judges on the spot. Did they listen? We do not know the outcome of this case, but Martina's argument made a direct, blunt, and conscious connection between unfulfilled marital obligations and women's obligation to obey their husbands. Women were pouring into judges' ears evidence of the wide gap between the reality of daily life and the legal and male rhetoric about social standards and expectations. Even if judges hesitated to acknowledge these claims, they had something to think about.

Once a couples' allegations reached the legal arena, reality and expectations clashed openly. Reality showed women succeeding in controlling the family's income by circumventing or avoiding a husband's intrusion. In extreme cases, women ventured to describe a reversal of gender roles. Rather than begging for their daily rations, these women took control from their husbands, and husbands were often painfully aware of their weakness.

José Laynes, an Indian of noble ancestry, explained: "For more or less fifteen years, I have been working for my wife[!], bringing fruit to be sold from the nearby *haciendas* of Macas, Santa Olaya, and other orchards around Vellavista [*sic*; Bellavista, a suburb of Lima]. I gave all I earned to her, but she ignored my needs and concerns, always keeping all the profits for herself. Out of our most recent earnings, she tried to keep 400 pesos, which the Commander of Indians [Comandante de Naturales] Don Manuel Alvarado, now has in his possession."[32] José added, "It seems that if my wife wants to split up for her own convenience, she is obliged to do the same with the aforementioned money because it was earned by both of us and especially because when we married she had nothing, and I clothed her."

She had had nothing, and he had provided for her, but over time this arrangement completely reversed itself. Now she was in control, and he depended on her. The similarities to Martina's case—marketing vegetables—is not surprising since agrarian life required all family members to work on the farm and, when necessary, sell in the marketplace. Because women most often sold the produce at market, it was they who directly received the money, enabling them to control the cash flow of the family.

Around 1816 Gregorio Dávalos, from Magdalena Huaca in Lima's outskirts, worked land belonging to his wife, Estefania Quispilloc. These fields, about forty miles apart, were *tierras cacicales* (that is, land of the ethnic chief or cacique) that she had inherited from her parents in the village of Santa Eulalia. The land in Magdalena was in Estefania's care, and she worked hard cultivating, harvesting, selling, and even preparing food for the hired workers. Gregorio managed the tract in Santa Eulalia, which by leasing to others produced a rent that went directly to him (with perhaps some control exerted by Estefania's family).

In Estefania's name, the lawyer of the Real Audiencia, Don Pablo Ramíres de Arellano, wrote: "About fifteen years ago, when she was only thirteen or fourteen years old, my client, the defendant, married Dávalos. Ignoring her weakness and inexperience, he ordered her to carry all by herself the heavy produce from the orchard in the Huacas of Magdalena to the central plaza of this city. . . . She also had to do the laundry, prepare food for the day laborers and the family, and to cut alfalfa for the livestock."[33]

Estefania had worked hard on the land, but she was also in charge of selling crops in Lima's market. After fifteen years, she knew that it was she who had "contributed the lion's share." Now she was tired of the "incredible dejection" in which she lived. In response to her complaining, Gregorio began beating her. She finally fled to Santa Eulalia, probably in search of family support. He asked a priest to convince Estefania to go to a *beaterio*

---

32. Case 253, AA, LM, L 7, 1803, Laynes vs. Gusman.
33. Case 490, AA, CD, L 87, 1816, Quispilloc vs. Dávalos.

in Lima. She obeyed, and she found shelter in the Copacabana *beaterio*, to which Gregorio paid a monthly allowance of 8 pesos. Estefania was not surprised that her husband was willing to pay this allowance, quite in contrast to what other husbands did: it was only a small portion of the rents from her lands in Santa Eulalia, which Gregorio was pocketing. Estefania—following the stipulated morale of the time—was willing to stay in the *beaterio* on the condition that those rents be turned over to her.

Thus, Estefania accepted the norm of remaining in the *beaterio* until the conflict subsided or a divorce was decreed. But she set a condition for fulfilling this social and moral expectation: she must regain the rents from the lands that she believed rightfully belonged to her. Estefania—not the judge—linked moral rules to income by refusing to submit to prevalent norms unless she regained her rents.

The case is representative of the survival strategies used by Indian agrarian producers. Indian women participated in both growing and selling produce. Because they played an important role in the family economy, women were well positioned to fend off misbehavior by their husbands. This was especially true when land or livestock belonged to them. In addition to her direct participation in the family's economy, Estefania's backing from the Indian community undermined her husband's overarching economic power and control.

This suit was also representative of Indians who were well-off and knew how to use the city's legal system and resources. Indian men with city-based ventures resorted to the mainstream judicial system when quarreling with spouses over assets and income, whereas the elders or *caciques* and *alcaldes* in the rural community dealt with most peasant conflicts.[34]

In forcing his Indian wife into the *beaterio*, Gregorio was imposing on her—conveniently for him—the moral rules of white society. Gregorio also defined himself as a *mestizo*, indicating that he was well acquainted with white moral expectations and behavior. He specifically used the racial claim to further himself in Lima and in ecclesiastical court, where being an Indian would have been a drawback. By calling himself a mestizo, he self-identified

34. See, for example, Case 484, AA, CD, L 83, 1803, Pujada vs. Segarra. An Indian couple from the pueblo of Lancon had been married for twenty years and had had several children. Segarra, the husband, had lived with another woman for a long time, but his wife accepted this, complaining only when he hit her in public. The *alcalde* (mayor), as the representative of the community, ostracized him because he was a known to be *amancebado* (a man cohabitating with a woman who was not his wife). When he wanted to reimpose his "marital rights" and ask for money, she threw a stone at his head.

as "whiter" and distanced himself from the Indian community. He escaped communal control in a locale where he—having been born in a different community—was perceived to be a stranger. In spite of Gregorio's clever moves, Estefania regained her rents.

Similar arguments arose in a case involving one of the most prominent guerrilla leaders in the central highlands during the wars of independence. In 1812 Ignacio Ninavilca's wife portrayed her husband in a way far different from the heroic image historians and some contemporaries have promoted. Josefa Rodríguez had inherited no fewer than fifty-five cows and thirty-three beasts of burden (mules and horses) as well as land, yet she complained that Ignacio had never given her even a pair of shoes. But, she noted, he had always been there to "take away from me whatever he could." Josefa described his attitude in the following manner: "Without doubt, Ignacio only thought about taking away the few belongings I had inherited or worked for. When he tried to become a *cacique* after we had been married for a few months, he asked me for 500 pesos. I talked to my father, and he gave the money to Ignacio, who squandered it on pastimes and diversions."[35]

Ninavilca's claim that he hoped to buy the title of *cacique* may have been true. Among Indians, this was a common premarital promise since it would enhance the future wife's position in the community. Ignacio probably was strongly motivated to marry Josefa since her anticipated inheritance brought with it fewer constraints than a more traditional dowry.

When the marriage began to fall apart, he appealed to the white courts since in this venue inherited goods were customarily assigned to a husband's management. But he lost his case. Perhaps the judge opposed Ignacio's political ideas, but it is more likely that his wife had a strong backing from her community, and the mainstream judges wished to prevent more tensions in an already strained political climate.

The prevalence of Indian female participation in the family income also accounted for husbands' much humbler demands when brought to court. We see Indian men accepting almost anything the *procurador* (state assigned lawyer for "Indian problems") decreed.[36] The Indian Segarra claimed he had no money to hire a lawyer "given his lack of resources." He asked to be pardoned, and timidly suggested his wife should be deposited in her mother's house. In the area just outside Lima, where women shared agricultural

35. Case 520, AA, CD, L 86, 1812, Rodrígues vs. Ninavilca. Their marriage had lasted for five and a half years. Both spouses were born in the town (pueblo) of Pachacamac.
36. Case 484, AA, CD, L 83, 1803, Pujada vs. Segarra.

chores within the family and where the influence of "white legality" was strong, material convenience and marital quarrels became a mechanism by which Indians were drawn into a set of legal rules pertaining more closely to the urban white and *mestizo* population. However, the backing from the Indian community remained decisive because communal solidarity was extended to its female members against abusive husbands, especially when these men were "different." The community exerted control on marital apportionment and income distribution between spouses, and it also imposed moral behavior. In Indian communities, women's right to assets and earnings was recognized to a greater degree than within the city's judicial system. Communal authorities, such as the *alcalde*, helped rectify injustices against women, especially when outsiders (ethnically and geographically) threatened communal assets by imposing their mainstream marital rights. As a result, *castas* (soldiers' wives) and Indian women (peasants' wives) were encouraged to ask questions that white judges perceived to be threatening.

In 1814 Ursula Salasar, a woman who both "had" and "made" money, quintessentially expressed such threats: "There can be no doubt (and I can prove it) that I was the man when it came to work, and he was the woman whom I, wishing to satisfy, dressed with the utmost decency, even giving him golden buckles, a fine cape, and everything he has now taken away from me, including a saddled horse. . . . I have given him five reales a day for his amusement in addition to his daily maintenance, and I bought clothes for him."[37]

Oddly, this was exactly how husband's complaints about their wives often sounded. Ursula had dressed her husband, had provided for both, and had even given him an allowance much more generous than husbands normally gave their wives—an allowance for him to have fun. Women, in contrast, were not supposed to have fun, especially if fun cost money.

Ursula was a coal supplier and owned a warehouse. Forty loads was her daily turnover at one of Lima's market booths. Her husband usually went with her, but it was only "to steal what I earned in order to give it to his concubine, who lives in the Calle de los Vorricos." José Antonio Manrique, her husband, had a violent temper. He threatened to kill her if she refused to give him money. To prove the sincerity of his threat, he slit the throats of her two dogs in front of their apartment. Confronted with reversed roles, José Antonio neither sought out nor responded to the courts. He had but one response: violence and brutal intimidation.

---

37. Case 544, AA, LM, L 8, 1814, Salasar vs. Manrique.

More economic independence brought with it more domestic violence. The church's recommendation of better behavior would no longer be enough. To halt violent husbands, the criminal court had to jail husbands, depriving them of their rights as citizens. In such cases, the control of a family's earnings and assets fell into wives' hands almost by default. The private offender became a public offender; the moral issue became a criminal issue. Women who, even early in the nineteenth century, showed economic independence, convey a dramatic representation of how it was possible within the law to exercise power and defend their interests. Success, whether economic or judicial, at times resulted in women's victimization as a result of domestic violence. This was no victory for women, but it can be interpreted as the price to be paid in the negotiation for independence. Female autonomy and freedom ran counter to societal expectations, and by releasing husbands from the obligation to provide for their families, it undermined male authority. Men used domestic violence not only to impede women's self-sufficiency, but also to express their need for empowerment.

Without diminishing the horrors of domestic violence, its presence indicates a struggle. At least in some cases, women subjected to violence had overcome—in the eyes of their husbands, overstepped—gendered economic and social boundaries. In pragmatic terms, increased violence led to court intervention, which ultimately denied economic control to some husbands. As society began to deal with more independent women and increasingly violent husbands, the arena for conflict shifted from ecclesiastical to civil court, from moral recommendations to active police intervention, from deaf ears to awakening fears.

The majority of men fulfilled their marital obligations through both hard work and chastity. Nevertheless, notions of responsibility were invariably associated with some fear. From neighborhood gossip to accounts of court cases, men heard, read, and saw what happened when a man lost control of his wife. Over time, the forms of conflict and meaning of reconciliation changed.

Men's Fears: Divorce and the Limits of Control

There was nothing husbands feared more than divorce—not so much the process as the decree. During the proceedings, the outcome was still uncertain, and the husband remained in control of all marital assets. For the husband, divorce not only meant losing authority over the family, but it also meant losing assets and income. Following the law, after divorce was decreed, a husband was obliged to return the dowry and the *arras* to his wife in addition to half of the accumulated acquest. Although the consequences of divorce varied according to class and individual fortunes, a divorce increased women's leeway to dispose of assets and earnings.

For Doña María del Carmen Santiago and Don Juan de Luque Mármol and their children, a 13,000 peso dowry and a 40,000 peso inheritance represented the family's start-up capital at the time of marriage. As bookkeeper for the Tribunal Mayor (Central Accounting Office) and the Real Audiencia, Don Juan was a member of the colonial high bureaucracy. When he retired, his monthly income was 95 pesos.[38] In 1801, after twenty-six years of marriage, Doña María del Carmen asked for and obtained a divorce. Beyond that, she petitioned to manage her assets. The judges granted her petition, after she had proven mistreatment and adultery. Her comments speak for changing perceptions: "He thought it would be easier for me to sacrifice my belongings than go back to him. I knew very well what I could expect. Now I am aware that there is a straightforward solution: divorce. I had not entertained such a possibility earlier because I tried not to offend my deceased father who had helped me very much during my sufferings. But now it was time to do it, now I could no longer count on his help, without which I could not survive unless I opted to take advantage of the benefits law grants."

Her husband tried to challenge this court decision, but to no avail. Because Doña María had contributed a dowry and an inheritance worth 53,000 pesos to the marriage, her husband would have to return the full amount of this contribution to her, plus half of the accumulated acquest from dowry and inheritance investments. Because all of her contributions had been carefully registered with a notary, Doña María had a strong case and regained direct access to her personal wealth. Acquest went unpaid for both, because there was not enough money left, and Don Juan was left with his meager pension. Divorce depleted all his liquidity.

Because the husband might misuse her assets during the procedure, one

---

38. Case 567, AA, CD, L 82, 1801, Santiago vs. Mármol; AGN, RA, CCI, L 24, C 259, 1802. These 95 pesos were spent in the following way: 5 for *montepío* (social security), 30 for the house's maintenance, 15 for salary paid to a nanny, 30 for rent of a house, and 15 for small daily expenditures (i.e., a distribution of family income that very much resembles the one noted earlier for a military's household).

key to women's success in retaining control over assets was the expediency with which the divorce was granted. But speedy decisions depended on the efficiency of the courts and on the opinions and preconceptions of "propriety" held by the judges. Judges occupied a specific and special place in society: they were both male and members of the elite. Because they were men, and divorce threatened men, they may have been disposed to delay deliberations on divorce cases—even more so when a dispute involved their social peers. When judges finally had to decide to hand over assets to a divorcing wife, this always meant a diminishment of a man's economic power—a step that weakened class interests. Moreover, when business was a family enterprise involving collateral kin, a divorce could jeopardize such joint ventures by diminishing the available capital for investments.

However, this gender/class congruence contained a contradiction: a willingness on the part of the judge to side with a woman in the struggle over assets may have been shaped by the perception that the disputed wealth, originally consolidated and held legitimately by the parents of a well-to-do wife, was now under threat from a dissolute or dishonorable man. In defending a daughter from beating and adultery, upper-class parents were at the same time rescuing the family fortune. And a judge who sided with such a woman was doing the same. Out of this contradiction, and whatever the motive of a judge, a decision in favor of a wife opened the gateway to female vindication and set legal precedents.

From the perception that divorce weakened men's control and access to assets a legal mechanism emerged to benefit economically threatened men. It was based on the traditional interpretation of marriage as a sacrament and a mutual obligation: "A husband has an obligation to feed his wife when she does not have anything and he has money; to the contrary, if he is poor, and a woman has assets, she is called on to support him." This was the solution proposed by a lawyer defending a well-to-do male Indian client[39] in the early nineteenth century, and it was deemed to be a fair solution. Nobody bothered to acknowledge that when women were the claimants, this principle had often been ignored. It is significant that, in the original of this excerpt, men had an "obligation" to feed their wives, whereas the term used for women, *reato,* may be translated as 'mindless obedience' or 'following,' involving some kind of a basic human decency. This subtle use of language still underlined the maintenance/obedience trade-off, and thus, male authority; but in the economic realm, it stressed

39. Case 595, AGN, RA, CCI, L 15, C 161, 1801, Tello de Gusmán vs. de Mesa Tupayupanqui.

a woman's responsibility to worry about her husband's well-being without subjecting him to obedience.

Among middle-class men with steady incomes, husbands feared that divorce would increase their alimony payments. María Loayza and Carlos Orresqui had been separated for eleven years. During that time, Carlos had paid 10 pesos per month to his wife, which represented less than 20 percent of his income (48 pesos and 2 reales), from his position as a customs agent at the Tesorería de la Real Aduana de Lima (customs office).[40] This financial arrangement obliged them to keep in touch and explains why they decided to resuscitate their marriage. The reunion lasted but a year and a half, and more than one priest became tired of listening to their complaints and trying to mediate their conjugal fights. Carlos Orresqui believed he deserved sympathy. In writing to the *provisor*, he tried to invoke compassion by inviting all married men to compare his woeful fate to their own. Nobody would fail to recognize, he argued, that it was judicious to flee before facing financial ruin. Moving beyond the argument of male solidarity, he declared that no clergyman could tell him to suffer and carry his cross any longer. He described with passion and exclamations María's shortcomings as a housekeeper[41] and how she imposed her wishes on him. Invoking Saint Augustine, he claimed that every man who allowed his wife to carry the whip was perpetuating eternal sin, since this countermanded the order of things established by God himself.

In response, María asked her husband's superior, the accounting officer at the customs office, for a part of Carlos's salary. This infuriated him, and he refused to pay further alimony on the grounds that "this would help to perpetuate her crimes [given that she] neither understands nor accepts a husband's dominion and power." Perhaps because she lived near her brothers, she was in a position to challenge her husband. Nevertheless, Carlos viewed her "independent" behavior as socially aberrant, and he was not ready to pay to support it. Because Carlos was a bureaucrat with a steady income, once the divorce was final it was relatively easy for María to obtain

---

40. Case 297, AA, LM, L 8, 1819, Loayza vs. Orresqui.

41. Giving credence to this assertion, Edward Alsworth Ross (1915, 191–92), a traveler at the beginning of the twentieth century, claimed: "In the tropical countries [and here he was referring to Arequipa and Cusco], the abundance of cheap and inefficient servants coupled with the inherited stigma on labor, makes for wretched housekeeping. . . . In the sick room, the women are quite as helpless as in the kitchen. . . . Thanks, however, to the better schooling of girls"—he added—"the numbers of women who can make homes is very noticeably on the increase."

the one-third of his salary to which she was entitled by law. After the second divorce, she was awarded more alimony than before. Although it was still less than necessary for survival, Carlos's effective control over his ex-wife was greatly jeopardized. The judges perceived that Carlos was right when he asserted that he had lost control, been "subdued to her wishes," and, consequently, the natural order of things had been turned upside down. However, he was blamed for allowing it to happen. Carlos harvested disdain rather than compassion, especially because he was a state bureaucrat, that is, a person whose "flaws" were publicly visible. He lost on all counts.

Just as not all men were adulterous wife-beaters, not all women were saints. Between 1800 and 1820, from 120 files brought to the ecclesiastical court by men, 72 (60.0 percent) were accusations against women for adultery. In the same period, women filed 278 suits, 97 (34.8 percent) (see Table 8.3) of which included accusations of adultery. It must be recalled, however, that the cases reviewed above reveal that adultery accusations against women were often a male ploy in court to make men look less guilty; and when the charges were true, the act might have resulted from a husband having forced his spouse into prostitution. Moreover, whereas in some cases adultery was undoubtedly a voluntary decision, in others it may have been the result of licentious seduction.

In 1806 Juan Baptista Laugier and Petronila Rodríguez had two legitimate children. Nevertheless, he claimed, she was more interested in enjoying herself with strangers, whereas he felt utterly neglected.[42] Petronila had abandoned him and the home on two occasions, and both times when she returned, she was pregnant with someone else's child. He had accepted his lot; however, when it happened for the third time, Juan asked for a divorce.

In contrast to the strict moral values imposed on women, this case and others[43] reveal a deep gap between behavior and ideals. Similar to the case of Carlos Orresqui, Juan's patience was perceived as either odd or exaggerated. In society's eyes, he was at fault because he had overextended the boundaries of social consent. People were dubious: adultery was common, but a husband who tolerated it was not. Welcoming a wife back after she had borne children

---

42. Case 521, AA, CD, L 84, 1806, Rodríguez vs. Laugier.
43. For a case later in the century, see Case s.n., AA, CD, L 92 (1854–56), 1854, 3 ff., Hercelles vs. Rossío. In this case, the husband, Francisco Rossío, had been born in Italy and had married a Peruvian wife, Juana Hercelles. Juana left her husband and had a child by another man. Several people interceded on her behalf, and he took her back. However, the conflicts continued. Shortly afterward, Francisco accused her of not obeying him and forgetting about her promises. Many witnesses confirmed Francisco's accusations.

out of wedlock simply did not fit the proper standard of behavior for men and women. Juan had not only been sexually cheated, but he had also been economically abused because he was supporting his wife's illegitimate children. Above all, he was perceived to be stupid, because he hadn't understood how to use his money to control his wife. Thus, he was estranged from social sympathy. This extreme case also shows that there was little husbands could do if their wives decided to find a better match. Morality was a strong inhibitor, but not for everyone to the same degree.

Similarly, some men wanted their wives to participate in business affairs, but their wives reacted with no interest or willingness, or simply were incapable of sharing responsibilities with their partners. Antonio Portilla, a Spaniard, leased a *casa mantequería* (lard-producing workshop) in the Calle de las Mercedarias. Soon he realized that his wife, rather than helping him, was spending all their money, neglecting the house, and, worse yet, having an affair. Following a series of confrontations, she left, only to return after an entire year. Replacing financial punishment with sexual punishment, he retaliated by avoiding their matrimonial bed for another twelve months.[44]

Even in the face of economic (or sexual) reprisal, some women were simply unwilling to submit to moral and matrimonial control or to accept a share of domestic economic responsibility. Husbands were customarily entitled to command, but in practice they could not control their wives at all times or in all situations. Most women exerted some degree of control over their own lives. When a woman gained control over assets, even if these were only clothes and jewelry, or when she physically fled from a domineering husband, reexerting control over her could become more expensive than paying alimony or support to a *beaterio*. This realization probably increased the willingness of some husbands to take a wife back even after the birth of illegitimate children. Love may have been a factor, but this argument rarely appears in divorce cases. "Transgressions" of women like the ones just described, were continually cited by judges and husbands to justify their moral and economic impositions. Men basically argued that women were behaving according to their natural ignorance, their poor education, or a feminine inclination toward vice. Thus, it was a husband's duty to supervise his wife as closely as possible.

In nineteenth-century Lima, men carried with them deeply entrenched suspicions about wives. (Remember the short story by writer Ascensio Segura

44. Case 136, AA, LM, L 7, 1808; and CD, L 85, 1808, Collazos vs. Portilla.

in Chapter 2?). To learn whether another man coveted one's own wife, men would set traps by giving a wife money to go to a bullfight or to buy ice cream in the street. If the wife returned without having spent the money, the husband would assume that a lover had paid for her amusement.[45]

The records contain a few cases that confirm that some wives were not above trading sexual favors for economic support when their husbands failed to provide it. One husband complained that his wife had told him to his face "that she would find somebody who would support her and throw me out of the house so they can live together, that this is the way other women survive, that being married they separate from their husbands because they don't give them any money."[46] Other women in similar circumstances took the initiative and actually left, eventually producing illegitimate children with another man.[47] Thus, while some men wondered why their wives had not—or could not—find someone else to care for them, a few pragmatic women went out and found that "someone." As our cases show, women's responses to the "extramarital" alternative were divided: some took it; others turned to the courts to punish their husbands for suggesting such a thing. In either case, women showed that this was a latent alternative that undermined the holy sacrament and society's expectations of men and women.

Some women were placed several times in *beaterios*, jails, and bakeries (the punishing agency for rebellious slave wives [Hunefeldt 1994]), and still they refused to behave. In the meantime, their husbands had to support them, although—as documented earlier—they often did not comply with this rule. In extreme cases of madness or anger, a wife might destroy furniture and other objects, which the husband then had to fix or replace. She could drain a family's earnings and savings and defame her husband's social image through her conduct. Other wives could—as one husband put it—"just drive me mad."[48]

---

45. Case 87, AA, LM, L 8, 1810, Berau vs. Flores. In this case the husband was a barber from Cusco, and she had been born in Tarma. Their witness was an *alcalde de naturales* (a mayor for Indians).
46. Case 141, AA, CD, L 84, 1807, Cormier vs. Semino.
47. Case 965, AA, CD, L 94 (1860–61), 1860, Rodríguez vs. Castillo. Manuela and Francisco had been married for four years when the suit began. Because Francisco did not provide her with food, Manuela engaged in a different relationship. In 1865 no legal solutions were in sight, and Francisco was petitioning that his wife be deposited in a *beaterio*. In the meantime— according to Francisco—she had had two children and many miscarriages. Manuela was the daughter of an artisan.
48. AA, CD, L 92 (1854–56), 1854, 3 ff., Cárdenas vs. Solari. Juan Solari wrote: "[No puedo seguir casado por] trato cruel, é incapacidad en que me encuentro para poder seguir en

These acts of sabotage within marriage represented rebelliousness or madness, depending on who was interpreting them. Slaves could rebel, why couldn't a wife? A husband could resort to extreme solutions as well. He could kill or attempt to kill his wife. Mercedes Carrasco recalled that while lying in bed after a premature delivery due to a beating her husband had inflicted on her, he asked for a divorce. When she answered that "only death could separate the marriage," he jumped on the bed, and choking her neck, answered that "this could be solved easily."[49] Attempted homicide—mostly interpreted by judges as a gross exaggeration—was a frequent reason given for a divorce by both men and women. Between 1800 and 1820, 1.2 percent of the conflict cases reviewed involved the threat of homicide in addition to the main demand reason; between 1840 and 1860, the percentage rose to 5.6 percent; and between 1890 and 1910, it was 4.9 percent. In some cases, at least, judges' interpretation of attempted-murder accusations as exaggerations may have met the letter of the law. "Minor beatings" were a part of a husband's prerogatives, an acceptable way of teaching a lesson and bringing a wife to heel. Often, however, attempted homicide and "teaching a lesson" were hard to distinguish.

Whereas Rudecinda Falcón asserted that her husband, Jacinto Felices, had beaten her so badly that she had vomited blood, he claimed that he "would—of course—never deny that his wife's bad behavior and frequent infidelity had obliged him to moderately punish her with paternal forbearance, but not seeking revenge."[50] And, even when miscarriage followed beatings, judges would still agree that this was a deserved "lesson." Men even admitted that if their wives refused to go to a *beaterio*,[51] or at least get out of the house, they ran the risk of becoming victims of well-justified male ire.

On the other hand, husbands were particularly afraid of their wives leaving the house with everything they could carry. Such nightmares became reality more than once. Men could never be completely sure about what their wives had in mind. After all, their doubts were a consequence of how womanhood was defined: women were seen as threatening and inscrutable creatures. Demonstrations of love by wives were merely persuasions to win decisions not necessarily in the couple's common interest but aimed at the

---

vida conyugal, como los pleitos repetidos y las cóleras que me ocasiona la dicha mujer, hasta ponerme a pique de perecer de resultas de sus molestias incorregibles."

49. AA, LM, L 9 (1820–49), 1841, Cárdenas vs. León.

50. Case 801, AA, LM, L 10 (1850–69), 1853, Falcón vs. Felices.

51. See Chapter 5 on *beaterios* and Case 206, AGN, RA, CCR, L 91, C 1116, 1800, Figueroa vs. Manis. In this case he was a Spaniard, and marriage had lasted for four years. In the end, she promised to behave well and was "returned to her husband."

wives' more selfish goals. And these falsehoods could not be deciphered until it was too late. Fears of this kind may be summarized in one expression: "She took everything and left nothing."[52] In only a few cases could a watchful *sereno* or *alcalde de barrio*, in combination perhaps with a timely bribe, reveal where a wife, her children, and the family fortune had vanished.[53]

Husbands' fears had very real foundations. In the course of the century, an increasing number of women—as shown earlier—refused to enter a *beaterio*, choosing instead to strike out on their own when they filed a suit. Although many women endured poverty, mistreatment, and the presence of their husband's concubines, it was those who left *and* who managed to take everything with them who created the stereotype: any woman could resort to the "escape option," and thus every woman represented a potential threat to a husband's belongings, well-being, and social image.

Wives' enlarging moral and economic options loomed over all men, even those who had very little to lose. A soldier in the archbishopric, whose wife had claimed her one-third of his 24-peso monthly income, was appalled. Hurling a timeless imprecation against women, he asserted that they "ruin and annihilate everything they can of what belongs to a husband, only because men are willing to get married out of respect to the wishes of God and to live peacefully. Women, though, have different things in mind, and

---

52. "Se alzó con los bienes todos, dejándome absolutamente con lo encapillado." Case 168, AA, CD, L 87, 1805, Chabarría vs. Sierra. In this case, the woman had returned to marriage with "a feigned hypocrisy." Both owned land and slaves. In this context, Segura's short story (see Chapter 2) should be remembered.

53. Case 184, AGN, RA, CCI, L 81, C 825, 1808, Echenique vs. Sánchez. In this case the woman's reaction was a response to a decree issued by the archbishop that she be transferred to a *beaterio*. Also, Case 033, AGN, CS, CCI, L 577, 1854, Tourmier vs. Otayza. Don Luis Otayza wrote: "Doña Mercedes ha forjado un verdadero cuento de grandezas y ensueños, que pueden figurar mui bien entre las *Mil y Una Noches*.- Inventa haber tenido pulseras de brillantes, cruz de idem, anillos, aretes de idem, cadenas de oro, prendedores, etc. etc. *Todo esto es falso; y por tanto, que Doña Mercedes no podrá ni siquiera indicar cuando se compraron, en donde, ni a quien.- Algunas alhajitas que tenía, cuidó mui bien de llevárselas cuando se fugó de mi casa. Eso era mui natural, porque una mujer que tiene el proyecto de abandonar la casa del marido, al realizarlo, es imposible que deje, no diré alhajas de valor, pero ni un fustán. Así ni mas ni menos sucedió con Doña Mercedes; se llevó lo que pudo, y no solo lo de ella; sino aun lo mío, sin embargo de lo cual tiene la serenidad de suponer que dejó alhajas, y de pedir su devolución, forjando ademas la existencia de los que nunca tubo.*" And he added: "It is impossible that a woman who has decided to leave her husband's house forgets to take not only her jewelry but every little item she can find." Don Luis was a merchant, and the spouses had been married for five years when Doña Mercedes decided to leave him. They had two children. With all her claims, Doña Mercedes wanted to make sure her husband would not resort to transfer or sell his merchandise, which she valued at 10,000 pesos. At the end, the judge decreed that 5,000 pesos be retained from Don Luis' earnings for his wife.

every day there occur examples to prove this."[54] It was necessary to be alert and circumspect. Utmost surveillance was advisable.

Through these stereotypes, husbands learned to fear their wives. The subtle cultural definitions of what made a female formed questions in everyone's minds and lay at the heart of an often covert and unconscious division between men and women. This dividing line became explicit in conjugal conflicts, but as part of a gender ideology that cut across racial and class divisions, it was latent all the time.

Beyond divorce and its consequences, the threat of divorce also had devastating effects on social image. Especially for merchants, whose economic success required social connections, divorce proceedings could be a disaster.

Damaged Social Images: The Merchants' Lot

It was, above all, couples involved in trade—from selling potatoes in the market, owning a bakery, or running a small shop, to merchants engaged in regional and international trade—who fought over resources. Women in this social class had alternatives that enabled them to gain control of resources. Occasionally, a woman even took a business enterprise away from her husband. Among large merchants, transactions involved considerable sums of money, but wives usually had to wait for their husbands' death to find out how much of the family assets belonged to them. Rich merchants could prove to be elusive. Commanding "movable" property (that is, goods that were subject to continuous transaction), merchants could more easily resist paying alimony, acquest, or legal costs. It was difficult to determine a merchant's liquidity, and women had to be clever to secure what they considered their fair share. Merchants were not averse to faking bankruptcy, entrusting the storeroom keys to third parties, or even transferring money or assets to others in order to avoid their wives' claims. For women, gathering proof was laborious. In some cases, only a declaration in the last will made in the hope of avoiding a creditor's claims would finally clarify the family finances.

The lawsuit between Don Manuel Pérez and Doña Mercedes Cora had been going on for eighteen years in the Tribunal del Consulado and, simultaneously, at the ecclesiastical curia, when Don Manuel Pérez died

54. Case 648, AA, LM, L 7, 1808, Yamas vs. Ramires.

in 1847.⁵⁵ In his will, he admitted having invented debts to evade Doña Mercedes' claims for alimony. His actions were a retaliation because his wife had abandoned him after their first year of marriage, taking their son with her. In his will, he was forced to admit all this in order to avoid third parties from claiming his assets. Over the years, Doña Mercedes had remained ignorant of her husband's ruse.

In contrast, smaller merchants, such as vendors or bakery owners, needed the good will of their wives to prosper. But a wife's participation in the family business gave her access to cash that could also be used to open a suit for divorce. In some cases, they even had their husband's notarial permission to engage in civil litigation, which they could use against their spouse.

In 1805 Estefa Calderón bitterly complained about her husband, Juan de Dios Reyes, because he had been wooing the woman who lived next door and who also had a booth next to theirs in the central plaza. Estefa protested, "It is impossible to live with a man like this." After five years of marriage, happiness was elusive. As a result of physical closeness, both at home and in the market, frequent confrontations and beatings occurred among husband, wife, and mistress. More than once, neighbors had to call upon the *alcalde de barrio* to settle the dispute.

The marriage went on despite the disagreements and violence. When Juan de Dios wrote his will in 1808, he stated that neither he nor Estefa had any goods when they married. After eight years of selling potatoes in the market, everything they had was the fruit of their shared struggle. By law their earnings would be divided in equal shares,⁵⁶ and being well-known small merchants, public scrutiny put evasion and secrecy beyond their reach. Juan de Dios could not deny that his wife had contributed to the couple's progress, despite the unhappiness of the marriage. Her involvement in their work made it difficult for Juan to resort to "economic reprisal." Estefa did not depend on daily allowances, and she knew how much they earned.

Doña Isabel Baset and Don Marcos Guiyon owned a bakery together. In 1805, when they had been married for three years, tensions began to appear. Doña Isabel, even bolder than Estefa, was determined to gain full

---

55. Case 778, AGN, Tribunal del Consulado, L 479 (1829–47), Pérez vs. Cora. Although faking bankruptcy or transferring goods or money to third persons was frequent above all among merchants, landowners could resort to similar strategies. See Case 825, AGN, CS, CCI, L 568, 1854, Causa seguida por Dominga Gómez contra Manuel Mendoza por alimentos para su menor hijo, Callao.

56. Applied for instance in Case 110, AA, CD, L 7, 1805, Calderón vs. Reyes; AGN, Escribano Juan José Morel de la Prada, Libro 437 (1808–11).

control of the business. One day her husband left on a trip to Cerro de Yauricocha, in the central highlands. Immediately afterward, she went to a judge to declare that her husband had left for Spain (that is, very far away), and that it was necessary for their business that she assume control and be given the power to make contracts without her husband's explicit permission. Before the judge could make a decision on her petition, Don Marcos returned from his trip. He reported that he had told his wife that he was traveling to Cerro de Yauricocha (and had certainly not mentioned any trip to Spain!). He accused Don Francisco Dias, Doña Isabel's lover, of influencing her in order to get hold of the bakery's capital and fixtures. Don Francisco had indeed taken over. When Don Marcos tried to return, the bakery's *mayordomo* and slaves, having switched loyalties, threw him out with his personal belongings.

This divorce initially was not channeled through legal and ecclesiastical courts, where a husband could have remained in control at least for a time. Instead, from the outset, violence was used to disempower Don Marcos. In 1810, when Doña Isabel wrote her will (she was sixty at the time), she mentioned the bakery, but there was no mention of either Don Marcos or Don Francisco.[57] We can only guess what happened between 1805 and 1810, but it seems that Doña Isabel was successful in keeping the bakery. It is possible that she even hired a "lover," that is, somebody strong and determined enough to unseat her husband. This was an option that, in principle, resembled that of a wife who disappears with household items, leaving her husband "naked." In both scenarios, the husband was forced to take the initiative—and the expense and embarrassment—of seeking legal restitution. Only those wives with assets—in most cases, those who participated actively in merchant activity—could threaten a husband with the kind of violence described above. And it was the husbands of these wives who found negotiation and flexibility a less costly solution to marital strife. Moreover, the burden of proof was with the husband.

Don Nicolás Gárate Inca, who was a member of a distinguished military association (the Cuerpo de Lima de la Concordia del Perú), earned his living by buying and selling locally manufactured clothes in Arequipa and Santa Fe (Argentina). While he traveled, his wife, Doña Josefa Vega, was in charge of his household and business. During one of his trips, he sent her

---

57. Case 74, AA, LM, L 7, 1805, Baset vs. Guiyon; PR 133, José de Cárdenas, Testamento 5/11/1810.

money meant to pay his creditors. Once he returned to Lima, he found out that his wife had not transferred the money to the creditors and was instead cohabitating with another man. The amount of money involved was 1,279 pesos, which he claimed Doña Josefa owed to him. He also asked that his wife be placed in a *beaterio*. The money was not returned, Josefa did not go to the *beaterio*, and Don Nicolás could only resort to a long-lasting legal action, in which he had to prove his wife's adultery.[58] In the meantime, Doña Josefa and her lover used the assets of the business and the money entrusted to her.

It comes as no surprise that it is among smaller merchants that we find extreme measures to control wives. These could include renting a room for a friend who would watch a wife's doings and regularly inform the husband of her whereabouts. But such efforts could backfire, not only because those entrusted with watching a wife were also men, but also because it put private problems in the public eye. Merchants had to maintain an unsullied social image so that their credit would remain good, and a merchant's wife could easily damage her husband's good social standing with her suspicious behavior. Although it was highly important for merchants, other social groups, such as military officers, also depended on "good moral standing." In other words, access to marital assets and money in addition to social pressure expanded women's bargaining grounds. Women could use their sexuality and the moral constraints it implied as the ultimate bargaining weapon to retain economic control. In spite of the fact that women had little recourse to male-dominated institutions—court and government—the expansion of mercantile activities that came with economic liberalism provided new opportunities to counter husbands' control.

Turning the Page

The cases discussed above show women who "worked" at specifically "female tasks" (prostitution and wet-nursing) and who had their earnings controlled by their husbands; women who had brought goods or money into their marriages; and women who neither "made" nor "had" money, but who were simply poor. Of all occupational groups, agrarian producers and merchants

---

58. Case 625, AA, LM, L 8, 1815, Vega vs. Gárate Inca.

were the most likely to share work loads with their wives. For both groups, female participation was essential to production and distribution. Consequently, women's contribution was more visible and explicit and thus tended to be taken seriously. In addition to occupation, skin color, age group, and social standing shaped women's options.

The cases reveal women's voices becoming louder. Lower-class women showed judges and priests that they were the family providers and that their husbands, contrary to general expectations, forced them to work, sometimes even by making them resort to prostitution. Quite frequently husbands responded to these accusations by denigrating their wives racially. Those who were darker-skinned were expected to work and "give money to men."

Women who "had" money did not have to listen to race and status accusations, but they were pushed out of public dealings once their husbands took over—as law entitled them to do. In a fashion similar to that of the women who were abused because of their reproductive capacities, middle- and upper-class women began, very early in the nineteenth century, to challenge male prerogatives, the judiciary system, laws, and the morality of society at large. Even for elites, divorce was emerging as a suitable solution to hardship and injustice. Divorce became a vehicle to release daughters from unbearable situations and recapture the family fortune. Judges recommended divorce more frequently to civil authorities, and civil authorities, in turn, had to intervene more often to restrain husbands' violent outbursts. Out of the 15.4 percent of ecclesiastical cases presented by men that received a final decree between 1800 and 1820, 7.7 percent favored the man. In cases presented by women during the same time period, out of the 10.3 percent resulting in a decree, 8.4 had a positive sentence. Between 1840 and 1860, the respective percentage for men had climbed to only 9.2 percent (out of a total of 12.3 percent of cases with a decree), while that for women jumped to 19.2 percent (out of a total of 21.8 percent). These percentages indicate that in the course of time divorce proceedings were pursued more systematically, and that women were more successful than men in ecclesiastical court.

Although judicial decrees favored women in individual cases, this did not bring about changes in the law. For the time being, all women—no matter what their sexual and marital resolutions were—had to bear economic control by their husbands. This was true even if some women went to court with complaints that went beyond their own grievances. Although a more general awareness of the conditions of women was emerging, marital bonds and impositions were still stronger and had the upper hand, even when women actually worked in the public sphere. Women both provoked and sensed these changes, and began to verbalize different outlooks on divorce. The next chapter delineates the multiple layers of the "conflict morphology" that took place in the course of the nineteenth century, and evaluates their social repercussions and outcomes. Tendencies visible in the first decades of the nineteenth century became much more intelligible in the following decades.

9

Redefining Female Domains

By midcentury, Lima's inhabitants looked ahead to calmer days. Political conflicts had diminished, and the export of guano provided the republican state with funds to rebuild infrastructure and undertake long-overdue reforms inspired by liberal ideals. While Peruvian reformers were envisaging possible strategies to spur progress, European women writers were publishing path-breaking works addressing women's civil and political rights. Diaries and biographies of English, French, and German women revealed their active participation in society and posed a direct challenge to the notion of woman's intrinsic, biologically determined inferiority. European women writers were not widely read in Peru, but their radical ideas were explored by Peruvian women writers such as Manuela Gorritti and Clorinda Matto de Turner. These opinion-makers, well-known and respected in the eyes of both men and women, were part of the intellectual climate that allowed for a reassessment of women's role in society.

Until recently many historians portrayed nineteenth-century women as mute historical witnesses or mere victims. The preceding chapters have provided ample evidence to the contrary. Silence is a matter of interpretation and depends on our willingness to listen with care. Court records from the beginning and mid-nineteenth-century Lima reveal that women were systematically voicing their issues, although these issues had not coalesced into a political agenda. These lawsuits show that gender relations were changing in subtle ways: women's arguments in court shifted from personal claims against a husband's abuses to issues of social injustice that took as their focal point the widespread double standard practiced by men and the hypocrisy of a judicial system that supported that double standard. Female voices demanded recognition that women were vital to social progress and that without the recognition of their contribution, no progress was possible. This straightforward message had many facets if not fissures. The counterattack took the form of social and legal pressure on women to keep their personal unhappiness to themselves and within domestic bounds.

Peru's booming midcentury economy created a class of *nouveau riches* who were deeply concerned about social appearances. A decisive asset for social ascent was reputation, which could easily be damaged by a lawsuit. What had been especially true for merchants at the beginning of the century now applied to the broadening middle class.[1] Even at the end of the century, a perceptive observer claimed that in Lima "to know someone personally and the opinion people hold of this person is enough for everyone to know what that person's signature is worth" (Morse and Copelo 1973, 84).

People were gradually reinterpreting laws meant to enhance a husband's control over the family and guarantee society's stability. Behind the emergence of more gender-centered legal arguments and the courtroom manipulation of the contradictions between expectations and reality, three influences came into play around midcentury: the pressure on women to conform to heightened moral standards, a greater social sensitivity toward the role of the husband (especially *his* obligations to his offspring), and a higher success rate for women arguing their cases in court, based on the recognition by judges of the drawbacks existent in women's legally defined financial subordination to men.

Patterns and Tendencies

Two cases illustrate the new arguments brought forward in Lima's courtrooms and the reactions of men and judges to those arguments. In each case, the woman involved, speaking on behalf of herself and her children, focused on the overwhelming male responsibility for the well-being of the

1. See case 791, AN, CS, CCI, L 600, 1855, Díaz vs. Ojeda.

family. The tactics used involved a balancing of a portrayal of the woman's self-sufficiency and economic acumen against the husband's irresponsible behavior, both morally and economically. By invoking the morality of responsibility, these suits are in sharp contrast to suits that focused on isolated complaints such as beatings, public quarreling, or neglect. These cases also illustrate how class separated women. Two women of different class backgrounds facing similar domestic crises must each construct an argument aligned with their social milieu if they are to succeed in winning over the court. Most importantly, an examination of these cases reveals that a dialogue had begun between women and lawmakers. Instead of individual grievances, women asserted their rights as wives and mothers; consequently, judges and lawmakers pondered the social implications of their sentences and laws, and the effects on gender and, more generally, on social relations.

As revealed by many divorce cases without a final sentence, judges remained silent whenever they could. As more personal histories (in contrast to isolated complaints revealing beatings, quarrels on the streets, or lack of food) were filed, some lawyers—touched by a more liberal outlook—sided or had to side with their female clients.

The Marquise and the Sergeant

Around 1840, Lima's gossip-mongers were enjoying themselves at the expense of Doña Clara Buendía, the thirty-two-year-old former marquise of Castellón, who was divorcing Manuel Sota y Poller, a forty-two-year-old retired infantry sergeant.[2] As a lower-rank military man, the sergeant was Doña Clara's social inferior. Although she was just twenty-two when he married her, she was already twice widowed. In the eyes of her contemporaries, Doña Clara was a peculiar and dangerous woman who had little to offer besides her money. When the couple separated, Manuel wanted to retain control of the marital assets contributed by his wife, and to achieve this he used all the arguments that were part of the common perception of women's tendencies toward moral "corruption" and economic ineptitude.

Manuel asserted that Doña Clara had convinced him to abandon his military career. At the time of the wedding, he had refused a dowry. Now he proffered this as proof of his altruism, because the widow was not a virgin.

2. Case 746, AA, CD, L 89; AN, Corte Superior, CCI, L 249, 1840, Buendía vs. Sota y Poller.

Doña Clara, for her part, denied that she had offered the sergeant a dowry. "He did not receive and I did not want to give him a dowry. [Although] widowed from two husbands, I did him the honor of marrying him. He married me because he wanted to try his luck and to have a decent living." Now, the marquise complained, the sergeant had squandered her assets and damaged her reputation with his behavior. In 1837 Doña Clara suggested he "leave the country and avoid a noisy and touchy fight." She offered him money to go as far away as possible so that they could avoid a lawsuit and the social criticism that would come with it. The offer was tempting: 4,000 pesos (once he was safely aboard the ship), all the necessary silverware for his personal use, and the usufruct and possession of entitled estates. This, Doña Clara recognized, was the price for her liberation. In spite of the offer, Manuel remained in Lima, where, inebriated, he spent his days in frivolous pastimes.

Manuel told a different story: Doña Clara's claims were a farce, he said. He had traveled to Huancavelica (a highland city) and later to Spain as a representative for his wife's business interests. During his absence, he empowered her to manage their affairs, but she had abused this trust by spending money, selling properties, and making contracts. When he returned, "everything concerning the family business had altered."

Doña Clara agreed that she had "altered" the family business, which, by the time the sergeant had returned (from wherever he had been), was much improved. Unable to deny her economic shrewdness, Manuel stressed Doña Clara's "moral shortcomings." She was not a virgin, she had misused his power of attorney by engaging in deals beyond those officially stipulated in the document, and upon his return he found her vacationing in Chorrillos instead of sitting at home waiting for him.

Manuel, desperate to paint his own moral portrait, emphasized his concern for and stewardship of Doña Clara's assets. He had not accepted a dowry, and he had tried to shield his wife from "needless" involvement in business worries. Manuel concluded by asserting, "Your Excellency knows well that a conjugal society slowly develops into a civil society and that from the order within simple societies results the stability and tranquility of the complex society. In one word: if women don't respect their husbands' rights, a monstrous turn of social relations will result; I can even assure You that the key to morality and social well-being depends on the order and domestic submission of the wife and the family to its head."

It was his word against hers, and he had one big advantage: his argument was based on commonly accepted gender privileges and women's economic subordination. Her primary advantage lay in her social position, based on her great wealth. In the first court decision, gender considerations prevailed. While the acquest remained to be divided, Manuel had full rights because he was the head of the household. By linking the power of male heads of household to the maintenance of social stability, natural law supported civil law.

In appellate court, where socially high-ranked judges evaluated her case, however, Doña Clara obtained two favorable decrees, one regarding her divorce and the other her assets. Thus in appellate court, consideration of class prevailed over the good-husband argument. Doña Clara used this momentary class allegiance to address sexual discrimination. In one of her many letters to the judge, Doña Clara stressed her rights, as a woman, to use the power of attorney her husband had given to her. A wife's decisions—she argued—should have the same weight and validity as a husband's "unless it is believed that a woman cannot sue her husband, which would mean she has fewer rights than a slave, who is able to proceed against his or her master." In addition, Manuel's scandalous behavior fulfilled neither social expectations nor his marriage vows to the marquise. The judge granted her control because the sergeant was a social inferior, both financially and morally. Class interests were served (that is, wealth was *conserved*) by means of Doña Clara's financial management; it was unnecessary to allow an outsider (that is, a lower-class man) into the picture.

The Housewife and the State Accountant

In 1854, after many years of marriage, Don Pedro José Loyola, an accountant for the government, and his wife, Doña Dolores Valensiano, began quarreling over the administration of their assets.[3] Don Pedro José had always had assignments that had taken him away from Lima, and when absent, a third party had overseen the administration of his household. Then, Doña Dolores wrote, "When he left for Cerro [in 1848], he named Don José Damián Aguilar as his representative in spite of my opposition. I even cried to try to make him reconsider, because I knew his decision would cause suffering and deprivation to our family. What followed confirmed my anxieties, because during the time Aguilar was in charge, he not only denied my children the money necessary to see a doctor and to buy clothes, but he

---

3. Case 042, AGN, CS, CCI, L 570, 1854; L 746, 1859; L 629, 1856; L 560, 1854, Valensiano vs. Loyola.

was elated when creditors from whom we were forced to borrow persecuted us. According to him, my husband had ordered him to treat us rigorously." She implored her husband to put her in charge of family expenditures. Eventually, Don Pedro José himself became suspicious and filed a lawsuit demanding that Don José Damián explain how he had spent the family money. Around the same time, Don Pedro José lost a lot of money during a business trip to Cerro de Pasco, and this apparently made him feel so guilty that he finally signed a general power of attorney to transfer the management of the family funds to Doña Dolores.[4]

Health problems were added to Don Pedro José's financial pains. Doña Dolores rushed to his side "to fulfill my duties." With her care, he was able to recover, but his "mental strength had been weakened" and Doña Dolores continued using the power of attorney without renewing her husband's permission. Once she had succeeded in recovering a part of the family's assets, her "enemies and his insanity" drove Don Pedro José to publish a newspaper article accusing her of pursuing business ventures, investing money, and buying and selling properties, all activities well beyond the power he had given her.[5] Six months later, Doña Dolores petitioned for alimony for herself and their seven children. This petition listed her husband's sources of income: a 150 peso monthly pension as a retired accountant, 32 pesos rent from a shop, 14 pesos and 5 reales from a *capellanía*, as well as some smaller sources of income, for a total of 219 pesos. The judge ruled that Doña Dolores receive a monthly alimony payment of 90 pesos, an amount insufficient to pay for family expenditures:

> Is it possible to maintain seven with ninety pesos? Isn't it utterly unfair to assign 129 pesos . . . for one individual and only 90 for

---

4. "En vista de estos acontecimientos y cuando ya sintió el remordimiento de su conciencia por haber hecho la desgracia de su familia me dió un poder jeneral para que yo entendiese en la administración del resto pequeño de intereses que nos quedaban en papeles, la ajencia de mis hijos ha dado por resultado el hacer efectivo el cobro de algunos medios para la conservación de ellos á si que cuando mi familia poseía algo, mi esposo ya no tenía nada en el Cerro" (ibid.).

5. "En estas circunstancias cayendo gravemente enfermo lo hize traér para llenar con él los deberes que me impuciera la condición de esposa, logrando con mis cuidados restablecer su salud hasta donde fue posible. El decaímiento de sus fuerzas mentales me ha hecho vivir en paz, ejerciendo el poder que él me dió mientras ha durado ese estado de abyección y mientras creyó que mi familia estubiese en un estado de miseria: hoy que se ha desengañado, que sabe que conservamos algo y que ha sido también influído por mis enemigos se ha esforzado en este estado de insanidad tocando en frenesí ó locura é intentando amenazarme que desará cuanto yo he hecho por el poder jeneral dando á la prensa un artículo en el que supone que eccediendome de mis facultades he hecho algunas transacciones indebidas" (ibid.).

seven? Is it perhaps because Your Excellency thinks my husband has more rights? . . . One single child costs a family more money than the father, because in addition to clothes, shelter, and food, a child needs education, which is why the expenses for a child increase. . . . A father cannot eat and let his family perish, he cannot surround himself with comfort while excluding his wife and children. . . . In a marriage, either all enjoy well-being or no one does.

In his response, Don Pedro José told the court that in the last four years he had given Doña Dolores jewelry and 40,000 pesos. Therefore, he argued, it was she who should return acquest to him that had resulted in interest payments accumulated from this capital. He also accused her of appropriating all of their commonly held assets "by using the power of attorney I incautiously gave her, resorting to the most despicable and low-down means, such as depriving me of my last cent, forcing her way into my room and breaking open my trunk where I had put the last bit I had been able to save from her voracious claws and her insatiable thirst for gold."

Doña Dolores turned this argument upside down by highlighting that she was a woman and that it did not matter whether she had ever managed money, because now she was destitute. To invoke social support, Doña Dolores did not claim alimonies for herself but stressed her husband's responsibility to their seven children. Moreover, she requested that her husband prove "with papers" that he had given her anything: "I can count on the testimony of my conscience that whatever money I have spent from our marital assets has only been invested in my children's subsistence, and if there has been any handicap due to the circumstances or because I, being a woman, was not predisposed to making large business deals and the money vanished in my hands, I cannot be held accountable for this, nor should my husband blame me for the amounts that I controlled." Thus she was even willing to state that due to her sex she could not be held responsible for financial losses. The lawsuit, however, showed her in a different light: over and over again, the descriptions of her economic involvement document her shrewdness and success. In the end, Don Pedro José had to recognize that he had acted "foolishly." He recognized that by giving his wife the power of attorney, he had lost control over their marital assets and his family.

With the singular goal of winning the right to administer the conjugal goods, both parties presented alternating accusations of financial squandering, adultery, sickness, and desertion. In this conflict, class differences between the spouses cannot account for the outcome of the suit. The wife's ultimate victory in court resulted from her ability to construct an argument combining a series of issues: the absence (first physically and then mentally) of the husband, the suspicious interference of a third person, and the welfare of their children. Doña Dolores capitalized on social values and the law—women's assumed weakness and the definition of gender roles—to obtain a favorable decree in court. Women were not as defenseless as they appeared to be under the law, as Don Pedro José acknowledged, but there was nothing more he could do.

New Frontiers

These two mid-nineteenth-century cases reveal the upper and the middle classes at the brink of new frontiers in gender relations, especially in regard to the control of conjugal assets. The marquise uncovered the class rationale behind gender relations: the control of assets was subject to bargaining. The housewife revealed the gaps between law and daily life: the way in which the control of assets was defined was unjust. Although some aspects in both cases were reminiscent of earlier arguments brought forward by men and women, some new twists were added.

Dowries were absent in both cases, as expected, given the disappearance of dowries in notarial records. (Although the first case mentioned a dowry, no exchange occurred.) Neither woman worked outside the home, but both participated in economic decision making and had power of attorney to engage in public dealings in the husband's absence. Both women were accused of engaging in activities beyond the stipulations of the power of attorney; both husbands thought they had been "foolish" to trust their wives. The two central differences were that Doña Clara had brought the larger portion (if not all) of the assets to the marriage, whereas Doña Dolores and the state accountant had started married life with no assets. In the first case, the wife regained access to her wealth; in the second, she successfully bargained over acquest.

As in similar cases at the beginning of the century, arguments forwarded in these court cases differed according to whether a woman "had" or "made" money. Doña Clara could fall back on class interests to obtain a favorable decree in appellate court; Doña Dolores was forced to use contradictory logic. First, she disclosed her weaknesses as a married woman: she had to beg to be allowed to manage family resources; and if that were granted, it would apply only when her husband was absent or physically or mentally ill. Nevertheless, the lawsuit revealed her capacities as a financial administrator of the family wealth. But when accused of misspending the money, she portrayed herself as a caring mother (any money she had spent was spent on her children) and a financially ignorant woman (she could not be blamed for any debts because the law protected a woman's naivete). With parallel reasoning, she insisted that she had fulfilled her marital obligations when she rushed to her husband's bedside to help him recover from his disease; now her husband must fulfill his part of the bargain. In other words, she had complied with all the rules and had even assumed her defined dependent status. The judge noted the implicit contradiction, but all her arguments were "right"—that is, legally compelling—and he had no other choice but to rule in her favor. In addition, the lawsuit showed Don Pedro José in a decidedly unfavorable light. Thus, the judge reasoned, Doña Dolores would take better care of the couple's children.

Among upper-class women, courtroom arguments could be straightforward: these women should be in command because the class they represented needed them to be in command. Doña Clara, with the maturity of a woman twice widowed, concluded that when it came to financial matters, she was as competent as all three of her husbands and, by extension, as competent as *any* man. Don Pedro José's "good-husband argument" resonated with class interests, but the support of those interests ultimately led to the assertion of her personal rights as a woman. Thus, class interests could subvert hierarchically defined gender relations.

Within the middle class (that is, the group of people without titles but financially well-off), arguments were more muddled. Class interests within this group were not well defined, so a middle-class person could not count on shared self-identity to generate solidarity in the courtroom. As a result, Doña Dolores's arguments were more gender-centered: women were weak because they were defined as weak. Weakness had become a rhetorical device by which women could help circumvent husbands' accusations of mismanagement in the domestic realm and escape accusations of "improper behavior." Accusing a wife of mismanagement of conjugal assets was a tacit recognition of her control over those same assets. When it came to showing a woman's inability to manage assets, a husband was forced to prove the obvious. By accepting her gender-defined weakness, a wife actually underlined her husband's socially reproached weak standing in the family, and thus she was turning law, and the social assumptions behind it, upside down. Such an explosive escalation of arguments had to be countered, and given the impeccable reasoning brought forward in court, the only alternative left open was to keep women from going to court by increasing moral pressure onthem.

Heightened Moral Pressure on Women

After the wars of independence, women took pains to remind the courts that they too had suffered from the turmoil of the period. Having shared the bad times with their husbands, they argued that now they should share in the prosperity. Women had "spent their whole life in serving and helping [and now were being] left without support, in misery and with no resources whatsoever, . . . whereas their husbands were living in complete comfort and abundance, [dissipating] their fortunes without one thought to she who had saved him more than once from bankruptcy and social criticism," complained a lawyer on behalf of his female client.[6] Women's criticism of the wars was double-edged: reproach against the nation *and* against husbands. Neither the state nor husbands recognized the value of women's war-time participation. Women had been information carriers, provisioners, and sometimes combatants, but they also made less dramatic sacrifices, such as being the sole provider for the family while the husband was in the battlefield or after he had been killed.

Now women were excluded from the "imagined community" of the new nation-state (Pratt 1990). The government was unwilling to recognize their contribution with monetary compensation, nor did laws concerning women's rights change. Empty state coffers made it difficult to provide welfare for "poor and honest" white women or to pay pensions to widowed state employees. Husbands reasserted their patriarchal rights and took back from women whatever control they had gained over their own lives during the chaotic years of bloodshed.

By stressing the dangers of public exposure, husbands countered their wives' growing assertiveness, derived from women's economic involvement and their demonstrations of moral superiority. Although women and men recognized the value of female contributions to the family income—often expressed through giving the power of attorney—working women were subject to reprisals by their husbands and to social criticism. Parallel to

---

6. Case 870, AGN, CS, CCI, L 752, 1859, Machado vs. Revoredo.

the recognition that women worked hard and deserved to be rewarded for their labor, a notion emerged that women who worked like men were "lost" (*malogradas*).[7] Thus women, especially wives, who supplemented the family's income had to stress their virtuous behavior. When a husband was a poor provider, his spouse had to work; yet once she worked, he could claim the moral high ground.

The spread of liberalism, which undergirded women's increasing participation economically and socially, was thus counteracted. People resisted socioeconomic change by means of a heightened discourse on "morality"— in this case, focused on the "proper" position of women in society. Wives were increasingly expected to accept with silence both physical abuse and "lesser" vices, such as a husband's gambling and drunkenness. The ever-forgiving wife became the social standard, and divorce suits based on "lesser" vices no longer swayed the courts. The consequences were twofold: between 1840 and 1860, fewer women resorted to lawsuits; and a woman filing suit had to find the "right" mix of arguments—for example, demonstrating poverty and suffering coupled with her own virtuous behavior—or present dramatic evidence of extreme abuse. Short-term personal suffering no longer constituted a sufficient reason to win a judge's compassion; women now had to prove on-going, moving grievances to win their cases.

In 1857 an Indian woman, Victoria Matres, wrote: "I have had to suffer the most distressing life a human can ever suffer. My husband has not given me and the children anything to survive on, yet he subjects me to continuous work and hardship. In the morning, I worked in the dairy at the Calle de los Huérfanos; in the afternoon, I cooked in Doña Matea Aguero's house. My husband took all my money to get drunk, thus depriving his children of the bare necessities. After such irresponsible behavior, he had the nerve to beat me until I could not move."[8]

Victoria worked two jobs, and her husband kept her pay, but unlike cases registered at the beginning of the century, this alone was not enough to win her suit. She had to give evidence that their children were starving and that she was severely physically abused. Thus, both Victoria and the couple's "innocent" children were in danger. This additional issue invoked the need for social justice, going well beyond the merely personal. It gave Victoria's complaints the necessary social anchor to find support in the legal system that would enable her to live free from her husband's control.

7. Case 012, AA, CD, L 93, 1859, Soto vs. Ugarte.
8. Case 878, AA, CD, L 93, 1857, Matres vs. Melgarejo.

Battered and mistreated wives had more difficulty in finding the courage to turn to the less-than-sympathetic court system. Following the same new "privacy code" that was pushing women out of the courtrooms, a woman's extended family now hesitated longer before interfering in conjugal strife. A woman could endure hardship for years before bursting open the courtroom doors. Carmen Ruis waited twenty-two years before she finally filed a suit in 1853: "In order to have something to eat, I had to work, taking in sewing jobs, first easy ones, later on men's clothes, which are very hard work, and that made me fall ill on several occasions. I am still suffering from a disease of the lungs."[9] Her husband had squandered all of her inheritance by "mortgaging my properties and making me sign the papers without telling me what they were about. . . . I have to kill myself (as people say) to feed and clothe him and give him everything he needs." When her daughter became pregnant, Carmen mortgaged the last piece of property to pay for a doctor. By then, Carmen could tolerate no more, and she sought refuge in the Trinidad monastery. She was forced to leave when her husband failed to pay support, but fearing his abusive behavior, she did not return to him. Her hardships had taught her something about economic independence, and she was ready for divorce.

Before Fermina Godoy finally went to court, many prominent people had intervened to save her marriage. Her husband José regularly insulted and beat her, and he kept concubines. Following each episode, he would promise to treat his wife better, but he always broke his word. Fermina wrote: "I know it would be better for me to get divorced, but I do not want to bring to light evidence that will disparage the behavior of the father of my children. I will only resort to this if he insists on continuing his cruelty toward me."[10] In Fermina's explicit reasoning, we can see she ignored personal vindication in favor of proving her own moral superiority. In contrast to an undeserving husband who ruined marital life and threatened the well-being of wife and children, she conformed to the rules, working as hard as a man. She even hesitated to present negative evidence against her husband in spite of all she had endured.

The notion that women were "weak and sly creatures," naturally inclined to promiscuous behavior, remained strong. This led, in extreme cases, to husbands preventing their wives from working outside the home. In 1855

---

9. Case 980, AA, CD, L 91, 1853, Alva vs. Ruis. For a similar case, see Case 998, AA, CD, L 93, 1857, Sabalata vs. Ruiz Pineda.
10. Case 832, AA, CD, L 91 (1848–53), 1851, Godoy vs. Godoy.

Pedro Romero took his wife's clothes to stop her from leaving the house to work, and he beat her every time he found her in Lima's streets. Ursula, his wife, reacted by claiming that without her earnings, she and her children would starve. Thanks to the declarations of witnesses, she could prove her statements, and not only was her petition accepted, but the police intendant was ordered to help protect her against Pedro.[11] This husband's overreaction to his wife's economic independence surely expresses men's anxiety over the threat of "immoral behavior" on the part of their wives.

In the decades following independence, the *content* of marital conflict cases did not greatly change, in large measure because the legal stipulations for granting a divorce had not changed. However, the legal stipulations were continuously manipulated, especially by women: fights over acquest replaced fights over dowries but were still embedded in laws pertaining to dowries; women asserted their rights to conjugal assets but still claimed to be weak. Parallel to these shifts, the contrast between expectations and reality became stronger. In the second half of the nineteenth century, social hypocrisy became a central argument in women's allegations, while men more insistently demanded "proper behavior." This was true for Doña Dolores, our middle-class case, and was also true for Lima's lower-class women. However, although Doña Dolores stressed the legal and social contradictions and selectively resorted to widely held truths, lower-class women openly talked in court about obsolete conventions.

In 1859 Manuela Campos had been married for eight years to a man her godmother had imposed on her when she was twenty. Throughout her marriage, she had earned the income, while (in a manner similar to other cases) her husband asked her for money to "maintain his vices." She had accepted such irresponsible behavior in order to comply with ideals of honor and discretion. When she refused him money, he mistreated her. "Although I know my rights and that my husband cannot speak against me because he does not give me what I need to survive, I have endured his mistreatment out of a sense of honor and delicacy, and to avoid having people think it was my fault that my husband deserted me, or that I had initiated this lawsuit only to be able to lead a loose life or commit adultery."[12] Manuela anticipated social criticism in her exculpatory letter to the *provisor* in which she both anticipated social reaction and reproduced it, but she was also questioning the premise that women's subordination was necessary to sustain order in

11. Case 737, AA, LM, L 10 (1850–69), 1855, Bernaola vs. Romero.
12. Case 756, AA, LM, L 10, 1859, Campos vs. García.

society. She saw the inconsistency: she fulfilled her wifely duties, was chaste, and worked as hard as a man; her husband, in a very "unhusbandly" way, contributed nothing and squandered her money. Her fulfillment of social expectations indicated that Manuela had interiorized the social ideals of the day, but this worked in her favor because her initiative in preventing accusations of unvirtuous behavior on her part helped to undercut the possibility of a male counterattack.

It was symptomatic of the times that husbands explicitly insisted that male authority was essential to the survival of Western society. The legal precedent for male authority lay in centuries-old canonical law, but around the middle of the nineteenth century, we find husbands categorically reasserting the importance of their authority to civic order. This renewed emphasis came in response to socioeconomic challenges posed by women. As one lower-class husband put it, "Can the husband who does not have resources or credit avoid moral decay in his wife? Whether a husband is rich or poor, he has a sacred duty to reestablish the authority vested in him by the laws relating to marriage or put his wife into secure circumstances so that she does not venture into moral disorder."[13]

The implicit assumption was that women were, by nature, open to moral corruption. No matter how poor, a husband had the "sacred duty" of monitoring his wife's behavior. This male entitlement was sacrosanct, according to Nicolás Nicolini and many other men: "When I got married I thought I had rights that had to be respected, that my wife belonged to me and that she would behave in a rational and decent way, according to our mutual interests." When his wife left to live with her godmother, he averred that "there is no law or logic that can oblige a husband to support his wife when she has decided on a whim to desert him. If this were to become commonplace, the conjugal bond, which is one of the most important social and sacred institutions, would collapse; *morality—the central issue in domestic life*—would be wiped out, because there would be no way to stop a married woman from deserting her husband whenever she felt like it, especially if she was assured that the courts would help her find the means for survival [!] . . . such a system would provoke women's complete licentiousness and . . . order would disappear" (italics added).[14]

His assertion ignored the fact that increasingly many women were no longer financially dependent on husbands, although he acknowledged the

13. Case 909, AA, CD, L 91, 1848, Mosquera vs. Laynes.
14. Case 922, AGN, CS, CCI, 1859, Daniño vs. Nicolini.

"dangers" of allowing this to happen. In his depiction of a society where women followed their "whims," Nicolás imagined an apocalyptic catastrophe. A "tacit divorce," based on a woman's greater economic independence, loomed nightmarishly in the imagination of many men, whose personal fears evolved into a shared social concern. Male power depended on female dependency. And male power supposedly was the glue that held society together. A court ruling that enabled a woman to survive independently endangered the social order.

Echoing the complaints of Doña Clara, Doña Dolores, Carmen, Victoria, Manuela, and many others, Nicolás's wife, Doña Clorinda Daniño, replied: "When I married, I did not intend to become a slave. . . . From what I know in my heart, based on what we both know about our lives, . . . my conscience is at rest." Arguing that she was too modest to reveal details about their private life, she rejected his flamboyant rhetoric. This tactic was part of the period's increased ideology of virtue. A woman was not supposed to divulge secrets from her domestic life, but in return, a husband was to respect his wife's contribution to protecting the family reputation. Doña Clorinda, without providing any details, was explicit in her complaint. She felt victimized by male hypocrisy: "Privately he used all ignoble means to create boredom and even desperation, but to others he tried to hide what he made me suffer."[15]

In spite of the standard of decorum, "silent sufferings" found their way into court records, and when they did, they were long, explicit, and revealed entire personal histories to document a wife's "willingness" to suffer. Women complied with heightened moral standards by being silent longer before going to court and by making explicit the reasons for not resorting to court mediation. At the same time, because they had been silent for so long, the accumulation of grievances helped women portray the long-term consequences of a husband's misconduct for the whole family. Portraits of long-standing injustices expanded the realm of the "moral" to encompass a criticism of how gender roles were defined and performed.

A woman whose occupation involved extensive interaction with men undermined not only her husband's control over her income but also over her sexuality. Jealousy and beatings were often the result.

The case of Espinoza vs. Urbano illustrates both society's tolerance for violence perpetrated by men and the heavy-handed "moral" scrutiny to which even economically active women were subjected. The wife operated a small restaurant in the home she shared with her husband, Valerio Urbano.

15. Case 974, AA, CD, L 93, 1857, Rodríguez vs. Vernaza.

One evening, after spending considerable time chatting with one of her clients, the customer told her that next time he came by he would bring his guitar to entertain everyone. Valerio had been watching, and as soon as the customer left, he forbade his wife to ever talk to that man again. When she started to protest, he cut her with a knife and a broken bottle. Valerio was imprisoned, and the state filed *de oficio* charges against him for provoking a public nuisance. In the 1851 Pajarey vs. Villareal case, a drunk twenty-one-year-old laborer injured his concubine simply because she talked frequently with one of the men who made purchases at the small store she operated. But she dropped all charges and asked that Manuel be freed, because otherwise both would be financially ruined. In each case, the wife had to explain extensively why *she* had provoked her husbands' jealous outburst. This required providing details about how she normally dealt with customers and why the incident leading to the attack was different. In the first case, the difference was the guitar; in the second case, the frequency of the talks.[16]

The economic boom of the 1850s attracted artists from all over the world to Lima. An Italian actress, Lucrecia Miechiarelli, had had an international career before settling in Lima with her Italian husband, José Marconi, and several children. Lucrecia's story exposes the absurd dimensions of control exerted by an insecure husband. She wrote: "My life is a series of painful deprivations, of undeserved outrage, and scandalous offenses, which have caused indignation among everyone who knows about our domestic misfortune."[17]

José Marconi lived off his wife's earnings and had not contributed a single penny to the family, yet he repeatedly indulged in jealous outbursts. This went on even during the trial, when José accused Lucrecia of receiving male visitors (even though they were only the actors with whom she had to rehearse). Summoned to court, Lucrecia declared that she would support José if he would give her liberty, but she would never return to live with him again. This was too much for the judge; he could not allow such an unconventional solution (although a similar proposition by Doña Clara, the marquise, had been accepted by the courts). In a compromise, the judge proposed that Lucrecia continue to rehearse, but only under the supervision

16. Case 799, AGN, CS, CCR, 1853, Espinoza vs. Urbano; and Case 930, AGN, CS, CCI, L 113, 1851, Pajarey vs. Villareal.
17. Case 900, AA, CD, L 91, 1848, Miechiarelli vs. Marconi.

of people selected by her husband as chaperones. Thus, a mechanism was found to extend a husband's control, and Lucrecia failed to gain her independence.

As women's participation in the domestic economy increased and an awareness of the importance of financial independence spread, women began actively to protect their earnings from their husbands. Lucrecia's case was extreme, but the reversal of economic dependency clearly carried a threat for men. Women who supported the family subverted patriarchal rules and assumptions. As seen in Chapter 5, women who were the sole support for their families argued that they could not be placed in a *beaterio*. This not only evidenced growing economic freedom, but it also clearly undercut a man's ability to control his wife's use of money and, hence, her morality. As in Lucrecia's case, judges were eager to rule women back into their place, especially when women in court proffered blunt assertions of their "independence," some going so far as to declare, "I don't need a single penny from my husband."[18]

Whereas records from the first part of the century reveal a questioning of what marriage was all about (a highly unequal "leonine contract" or an agreement for mutual support), by the middle of the century, marriage was clearly perceived as a covenant of mutual responsibilities agreed upon by both spouses. For many, the appropriate arena for resolution of marital conflicts was private, personal, and between the partners. But the marriage contract was inherently unequal. Those in authority, believing that rectification of this inequality would lead to social chaos, did nothing to alter the terms of the contract. The image of sound domesticity was the goal of the rules regarding discretion and honor, and it was widely believed that only transgressions that threatened the social order should be brought to court.

Women, as the subordinate partners in this unequal contract, were powerless to challenge these social norms on a grand scale, especially when they ventured into courtrooms. Women's behavior, arguments, and language had to conform to social expectations. However, although women complied with social decorum, once in the courtroom, they could engage in a struggle to unlink domestic and personal issues from notions of social or public order. Men were linking the two notions; women had to unlink them in order to be heard.

18. Case 800, AA, LM, L 10, 1851, Espinoza vs. Coronel. This case involved a navy lieutenant-colonel who repeatedly sought reconciliation with his wife. She always rebuffed him.

Questioning Husbands

By midcentury, the stringent moral requirements imposed on women had become embedded in broader ethical values, which included men's role as husbands. As the century progressed, selfish or abusive behavior on the part of husbands was viewed as contravening social expectations about marriage as an institution. When a man married for convenience—that is, for economic gain—he did not merit being called a husband. Regardless of the pressures to maintain domestic decorum, the general public as well as judges censured men who lived off their wives.[19]

Although men were becoming more hesitant to expose their problems publicly (including, as in the above case, economic problems), or—depending on how we read the argument—their shortcomings, when a woman dared to pursue her economic rights openly, she was much more likely to be subjected to social criticism. Consequently, women couched their complaints in moral terms. The moral discourse that men were already manipulating to control women's enhanced social and economic freedom was being taken over by women, who expanded its logic to encompass men. Women insisted on the "sacrament" of marriage in order to criticize adulterous husbands, claim support for their children, rescue assets, and eventually escape unhappy marriages. Women appropriated society's moral ideals and sought the church's support. This was the reason, perhaps, why contemporaries perceived that women were so prone to go to the church and participate in processions, and, more generally, the reason that the church had been "feminized" (in contrast to the masculinization of civil society).

The ongoing involvement of nosy neighbors, who restrained abusive husbands and gave testimony on the witness stand, had built up a consciousness of right and wrong that was laid at the feet of the ecclesiastical authorities. The church had been adjudicating marital disputes for centuries, but now it was forced to adjudicate moral issues (the traditional domain of the church) through the lens of gender injustice. How could moral conventions be upheld when men did not fulfill their marital obligations? The nature of marital conflict (not the discourse in the courtroom but the actions that

---

19. An especially clear-cut instance of censorship is documented in Case 974, AA, CD, L 93, 1857, Rodríguez vs. Vernaza. Cornelio Vernaza wrote forty pages—subsequently published in a local newspaper—to slander his wife and her stepfather, because she had publicly claimed that Cornelio owed all his success to them.

underlay suits) altered perceptibly in mid-nineteenth century, and thus the church came to voice women's long-standing grievances. As a result, there were facets of marital life that were now interpreted as being "unacceptable."

In 1851 Doña Carmen Manrique de Lara had been married for twenty-five years to the Venezuelan consul, Don Andrés María Alvarez. In 1832 she had named her husband as her sole heir and executor, believing him to be a decent man with good intentions. As the years passed, she realized that Don Andrés, far from being a good husband, was only after her fortune.[20] She offered three pieces of evidence. First, he had influenced her to make him the sole beneficiary of her will. Second, he had no property or money at the time of marriage. Third, after the will had been written, his attitude toward her had changed to such an extreme "that he started to get sexually involved with my slaves and servants." There was proof. With one of these slaves, he had fathered a son, who was now seventeen years old, living in their house, and studying medicine. Doña Carmen's money paid for all this. Her husband had "publicly shown his weakness" by seducing or raping their domestic servants, while Doña Carmen endured the situation with patience, which made clear that she was beyond moral recrimination. The existence of the son was widely known, and this sort of "morally deviant" behavior was increasingly censured, *especially* when it was public knowledge. The evidence was concrete, and Don Andrés pled diplomatic immunity.

This case again shows that by midcentury women were hesitating longer before seeking judicial intervention. At the same time, women's allegations in court became more detailed as greater proof was required to demonstrate a husband's misconduct. In other words, women were forced to recollect past grievances and, moreover, to interpret how a husband's shortcomings evidenced longstanding "moral corruption" and, more directly, how through his shortcomings he had provoked the family's misery. This was a new rhetorical device imposed on women by heightened moral standards and virtue ideology that impeded women from going to court, but that also helped reinterpret injustices done to them. Divorce involved high social and monetary costs, but the moral wrongs committed prior to the divorce suit had even higher costs because they jeopardized domestic life. Women could now invoke a male argument to claim that a husband's long-term, ongoing moral transgressions diminished marriage and the family, two cornerstones of social order. Social pressure was particularly strong when children were involved.

20. Case 880, AA, CD, L 91, 1851, Manrique de Lara vs. Alvares.

In a divorce suit against her husband, Don José Saldívar, in 1860, Doña Josefa Beramendi constructed another such retrospective argument. At marriage, she had used her jewelry as capital so they could purchase a popular cafe. Husband and wife worked together in that enterprise and lived in rooms adjacent to the establishment. Five or six years later, her husband asked her to move out in order to better organize the business, and he began to work and share the profits with someone else. He rented a room down the street where Doña Josefa would live, and he sent the furniture that she would need there. His "visits" to Doña Josefa became more sporadic, and finally he stayed at the cafe with the remaining household goods. "In this he tricked her because she firmly believed that they were going to continue their marital life in the newly rented room," explained Doña Josefa's lawyer.[21]

One night, twelve years after Don José had rented the room for his wife, he went to visit her once more to ask her to sign the extension of the rental agreement on the room. Doña Josefa, who was suffering from an eye disease, signed, not a rental agreement, but a document in which she agreed to release any claims she had on the rented room. A few days later, Don José visited her again. This time he commanded her to vacate the place. If she did not obey within two or three days, he threatened to throw all her belongings out on the street and return the keys to the landlord. In this way, he hoped to get rid of her without having to go to divorce court where he would risk losing his business's start-up capital and, worse yet, where he might be liable for acquest—to say nothing of problems of a damaged personal reputation that a court case would entail. Even when Don José wrote his will in 1860, he did not mention marital strife or separate living quarters, and he declared that Doña Josefa brought no property to the marriage; seemingly, he did not consider her jewelry to be "goods" or "capital."[22]

His plan failed, however. Doña Josefa filed a civil suit petitioning for alimony. Don José promised to pay support if she dropped her suit, but he broke his word, so Doña Josefa reopened the case. Then, in 1861, Don José died, and his mother was named as executor. Only after reading his will did Doña Josefa discover that Don José had been involved in numerous business enterprises in addition to the cafe. He had bought and sold merchandise in Cerro de Pasco, a trade valued around 12,000 pesos, and he had owned six contracts—worth a total of 1,350 pesos—to import Chinese coolie workers. He also had a house in Chorrillos. Nevertheless, his most important source

21. Case 740, AGN, CS, CCI, L 772, 1860, Beramendi vs. Saldívar.
22. AGN, PR 846/263v.

of income had been the cafe, in which Doña Josefa had an important stake. In addition to the contribution of her jewelry and her labor, she had also co-signed on loans. During a violent strike in the city, the cafe had suffered damages in the amount of 33,000 pesos. Without his wife's signature for the second mortgage, Don José would not have obtained the loan to repair the establishment, nor would he have acquired the credit to engage in the Cerro de Pasco trade. Despite all the property, however, the deceased had debts worth 45,000 pesos.

The mother-in-law continued the court battle, using the argument that Doña Josefa had not participated in the business for twelve years and thus had no right to acquest. She also claimed that Josefa's legal battle had damaged Don José's good credit and social standing. Doña Josefa, for her part, reminded the court that it had been *her* jewelry and *her* work that had provided her husband with the means to succeed in the business. Moreover, Don José had deserted her and taken advantage of her illness.

By recounting the high points of her unhappy history, Doña Josefa selectively focused on certain strategically critical events to build her case. She publicly demonstrated that her husband had systematically ruined her physical health and financial security. Don José's mother ultimately admitted that her son had cheated Doña Josefa. The lawsuit led to financial disaster for both women because court costs put each in debt. So, ironically, in the end both women suffered from the consequences of Don José's contravention of the institution of marriage.

Recalling personal history to showcase a husband's immorality was different from denouncing a husband's nonfulfillment of marital duties. In the eyes of the court, complaints against miscreant husbands could be remedied with moral recommendations. But systematic transgressions of the marital bond could lead to social decay. While women's long-term personal histories kept accumulating in the courts' archives, the only way for women and children to avoid men's transgressions and their consequences was to take power from men.

The evolving definition of morality was paralleled by shifts in the pattern of men's and women's economic contribution to marriage. In the course of the nineteenth century, women gradually contributed fewer and fewer assets to a marriage. Of all married and/or widowed women who wrote wills in 1810, 43.9 percent declared having had financial assets at the time of marriage; in contrast, only 25.5 percent of the men made a similar claim. Ninety years later, we find a figure of 17.5 percent for women, and the same percentage (17.5) for men (Table 7.4). In contrast to the measurable value of dowries and paraphernalia—the main contributions of women at the beginning of the century—female labor—increasingly the sole and most important contribution of women toward the century's end—could not be measured. Labor, unlike assets, was "invisible" and thus much harder to recapture, even when using legal channels. Moreover, to whatever degree it could be measured, a wife's work was automatically discounted. By placing her work and sacrifice in the context of a multiyear marriage, a woman could gain some recognition of her contribution. Personal histories were told in a language of morality because judges would listen to that. This moral discourse, however, had a definite economic component. The women whose voices we have heard all mentioned capital and/or earnings, and most moral arguments were aimed at regaining access to those assets. The heightened moral discourse was the vehicle used to vindicate women's labor, assets, and more generally, their expanding role in the family and in society.

Gaining Judges' Ears

Although husbands insisted on their right to control family property, the existence of conflicts over domestic assets in itself shows that women actually participated in economic decision making. The law stipulated that "a wife was the legitimate guardian of marital goods if her husband was incapacitated and that she assumed legal defense of conjugal property whenever her husband was absent" (García Calderón Sr. 1879, 1396).

By defending their dowries, or what they interpreted to be their dowries, women also defended their right to wealth accumulated communally during marriage, that is, their share in acquest. At the end of the life cycle, acquest turned into inheritance for the couple's offspring. To obtain control of conjugal assets, women increasingly used the argument that they were protecting the inheritance of their offspring, supplementing that argument with proof of a husband's incapacity, mental illness, poor judgment, or maliciousness.[23] Poor financial administration for whatever reason threatened the well-being of wives *and* children. In this way, women enlarged the logic of their morally based arguments to encompass men, and thus they made nonfulfillment of marital obligations a moral issue. If society's moral expectations of role fulfillment applied to women, they must also apply to

23. See also Case 883, AGN, CS, CCI, L 781, 1860, Molina vs. N.

men. A man who failed to fulfill his socially assigned role as husband and father required court sanction.

In the eyes of society and the law, however, the institution of marriage still took precedence over justice for women. As long as a marriage held together, the man was in charge. At least, as a judge cautiously put it in 1860: "It is well-known that while marriage or its appearance exists, all the woman's goods are administered by her husband and nobody bothers to find out whether these belong to him or her. So it is that, in marriage, goods appear to belong to the husband who is in charge of them."[24] But during the century, as deserted women banged at the courtrooms' doors, judges were more willing to grant abandoned women the management of conjugal assets, especially when it was obvious that a wife had helped to create those assets.

The 1854 case of Francisca Valenciano vs. Francisco Padilla provides an apt illustration of the arguments men and women used, and which ones the judges were beginning to find persuasive.[25] Don Francisco was a silversmith, and his wife, Doña Francisca, worked in a shoemaker's shop. He claimed she had deserted him without cause. He had pursued her and placed her in a convent, where he paid for her support. This did not change her attitude, and he recognized that she would never be a docile wife. Rather than paying alimony forever, he gave Doña Francisca a lump sum to buy a modest house. In addition, Don Francisco claimed that he had bought another house for her with money he had earlier lent to a Don Zavala. According to Don Francisco, he had allowed his wife to keep this house for her own use until she died. "When we married she brought nothing but herself and very few clothes for her own use. And in our divorce (which is only tacit), she obtained capital with which to work." In other words, he was the source of everything she possessed. Notably, Don Francisco also stressed that no formal divorce had been granted and that, consequently, he was in charge of whatever Doña Francisca had.

Contrary to Don Francisco's story, Doña Francisca declared that she had been the victim of mistreatment and had sought refuge in the Copacabana monastery. Initially, her husband paid 12 pesos in support. She sold a sofa and borrowed money from her godmother in order to have something to eat. After writing several petitions to the ecclesiastical judge, she obtained permission to eat meals at her mother's house, but at night she had to return

24. Ibid.
25. Case 043, AGN, CS, CCI, L 565, 1854, Valenciano vs. Padilla.

to the monastery. Making use of her limited freedom, she began working and saved 500 pesos. She then lent this money with interest to Señor Zavala. Señor Zavala went bankrupt, but "being troubled by his conscience because he owed me money, he transferred a *finca* to me that had belonged to his wife. . . . This is the *finca* [she asserted] that Padilla was bold enough to claim as having been bought with *his* money." Apparently, the house was not the only asset she possessed. All other things, she continued explaining, "were obtained with the sweat of my brow working in a shoe shop where I still am." It had been eighteen years since she had escaped her husband's control, "naked, without anything."

After all these years, no formal divorce had been declared. In the meantime, Doña Francisca had successfully organized her own strategy for survival. Now, however, her husband was claiming acquest from her earnings and investments. The question became how much he had spent on her support and how much money he had directly given to her. These figures would be a measure of how well he had fulfilled his marital obligations. If she could prove the absence of alimony and that she had obtained the house or the *finca* without Don Francisco's help, then all that she had earned since the separation would be considered *her* property, and he could not claim acquest.

Don Francisco could not prove he had contributed alimony, which is why he stated so insistently that he had made the initial capital contribution. Another central piece in his argument was the existence of marriage by which, of course, he also could claim an acquest. Don Francisco was unable to present a convincing argument, whereas Doña Francisca's witnesses gave her ample support. Perhaps more important, Don Francisco had admitted explicitly that the couple had been "tacitly" separated. So even in the absence of a formal divorce decree, the civil court verdict overruled a husband's claims to acquest, in overt contradiction to its own stipulations. In the end, Doña Francisca asked: "Is it, by any chance, fair that this man who has disgraced me now attempts to impede my free administration of those goods I have obtained through my own work? No. Your Excellency is a talented man and knows very well that a woman is not her husband's slave, but a companion with equal rights." Doña Francisca did not ask for acquest by the right of divorce. Unlike cases discussed earlier, she was asking for and obtained legal recognition of her work by denying her husband control over what she had achieved independently. His Excellency *was* a talented man, and Don Francisco finally accepted the court's decision and relinquished his right to acquest.

In court, no matter how a woman argued her right to marital property (by demonstrating mental illness, dissoluteness, a husband's general incapacity, or desertion), she had to overcome many legal hurdles. Two criteria were necessary when making a case for taking over the administration of family assets: first, the husband had to be shown to be completely incompetent or irresponsible; and second, the wife had to be shown to be entirely capable, responsible, *and* virtuous. All criteria required ample, legally binding evidence, which meant it could take years to resolve a suit or petition.

Church, and increasingly the state, adjudicated cases in which no formal divorce was granted but in which a division of marital assets seemed fair and necessary. When a woman did not want or did not have the resources to file for divorce, and especially if her husband had deserted her (demonstrated by his nonpayment of alimony or by means of neighbors' testimony), it was impossible to apply the existing rules governing the control of conjugal assets. Circumvention of these rules amounted to unspoken recognition of distorted family arrangements and the importance of women's work. Ecclesiastical and patriarchal authority was circumvented by civil judges who could not wait for a divorce decree from the church to solve the needs of a starving family.

Women's legally defined economic dependency had wider implications as well. They could not enter into contracts, a concept dear to liberal ideology. Women with resources who wanted to lend or borrow money or who wanted to engage in the formalities of conducting business were forced to ask a man to act on their behalf. The involvement of a third party posed some risk, but it was nevertheless a strategy that could help women gain rights, resources, and respect.

In the 1830s Doña Narcisa Mendoza, an Indian, worked with her husband in their butcher shop. He was frequently absent, during which time she was in charge of the family assets.[26] While her husband was buying cattle in the highlands, his *compadre* approached Doña Narcisa with a deal to buy sheep and split the profits. Trusting the *compadre* because of his close relationship to her husband, she gave him 220 pesos. Soon afterward she got cold feet and asked for her money back. Initially he agreed, but then news reached Lima

---

26. "Que habiéndose contrahido el citado mi Marido al giro de bajar y matar ganado mayor y menor con el capital de los bienes de mi propiedad que lleve al Matrimonio, yo lo ayudava en el con mi trabajo personal, y asistencia á los Camales en donde se hacia la matansa y á la Plaza del Mercado en que se aprendían las Carnes, principalmente en las frequentes ausencias que hacia de esta Capital á la Costa y á la Sierra á traher dicho ganado, en cuyos casos todos los negocios del giro corrían a mi cargo." AGN, CS, CCI, L 162, 1835, Mendoza vs. Ibañes.

that Narcisa's husband had died. This broke the ritual kinship, and Narcisa, without moral or economic leverage, never recovered her money. Without a man to defend her, the legal stipulations prohibiting women from making contracts made it extremely difficult for someone like Narcisa to recover invested or borrowed money. A man's presence represented security for a woman; its absence could mean her financial ruin.

Maria del Rosario Solórzano was married to an Indian master shoemaker. When he died, his goods, worth 226 pesos, were to be divided between his wife and the church (for the eternal salvation of his soul). The husband apparently had made a bad choice in selecting the executor of his estate, because María del Rosario claimed he was plotting "to keep her goods and her inheritance" by ruining her social image and her good credit.[27] He tried to have her declared insane, accused her of having a lover (even though she was already elderly), and even petitioned to put her in a *beaterio*. Law-defined gender inequalities had reached a point of absurdity. Women, and more importantly, the family and the institution of marriage, were suffering from obvious economic injustice.

Financial Contracts and Women's "Special Rights"

Before a wife could gain control of family assets, legally complicated matters often had to be disentangled. The most difficult scenario arose when a wife's special legal rights were invoked with the goal of saving a husband from his creditors. Laws protecting women (that is, those laws that excluded them from entering into contracts) could be manipulated to avoid debts and safeguard the family fortune. Women had been raised not to accept economic responsibility and to see themselves as dependent on men. However, their status as "legal minors" could serve multifarious purposes: the avoidance of creditors had little to do with women's "incapacity" to engage in financial matters. According to article 189 of the 1852 Civil Code, even when a woman entered a civil contract with her husband (not an infrequent occurrence given the many women who contributed the lion's share to the marriage),

---

27. Case 583, AA, Testamentos, Expediente 10, 1805, Solórzano. In spite of her allegations, she was sentenced to pay court costs, and the executor was congratulated on behalf of his well-thought-out arguments.

the agreement was invalidated if it led to a couple's indebtedness.[28] Consequently, in case of bankruptcy, seizures would proceed only against the husband's portion of the assets.[29] As seen in our discussions of dowries, paraphernalia, and acquest, the emergent distinction between a "woman's" or a "man's" property was multilayered.

Understandably, business partners were suspicious of agreements involving wives. In Peru, as in Mexico, "the protection of women's property made all their transactions suspect" (Arrom 1985a, 80). Before entering into a transaction, partners might require incontestable proof—such as an irrevocable waiver—that a wife had relinquished her rights as a woman protected by the law. Based on the accepted male supremacy in matters of family economics, such documents stated that a wife "had not been coerced by her husband nor any other person and that, ultimately, she believed that the proposed transaction was meant to benefit her."[30] Although the business enterprises represented by these contracts were usually successful, occasionally they were not. In such cases, couples sometimes alleged that the wife had simply not understood what was at risk in signing a contract. This argument could succeed if a woman presented witnesses who would declare that she had been coerced into signing the contract, whether as a result of pressure by her husband, her "natural subordination," or more general anxieties resulting from wider pressures following social convention, a parallel interpretation, this time in civil court, of the expanded definition of consent.

The case of Gregoria Berrospe brought together all these "female arguments" involving a wife's paraphernalia, dowry, *arras propter nuptias*, and labor, in an attempt to save her assets. In 1860 her husband's debts led to the seizure of all the family property. According to her statements, when the couple married, she had provided all the capital to launch them in their new life. This was carefully documented in the *capital de bienes* signed before their marriage.[31] As such, that capital should be considered part of

---

28. Case 708, AGN, Tribunal del Consulado, Juicio Contencioso, L 44, 1830, Aliaga vs. Alfino. In this case, the couple jointly agreed to back up a contract. The husband died in serious debt. Referring to the Civil Code, Josefa Aliaga later stated that her share should not be liable to creditors because she was a woman.
29. Case 848, AGN, CS, CCI, L 668, 1857, Huamán vs. Soria.
30. Case 708, AGN, Tribunal del Consulado, Juicio Contencioso, L 44, 1830, Aliaga vs. Alfino.
31. The *capital de bienes*, defined in articles 937, 938, and 939 of the Civil Code, was a notarial record signed by each spouse, stating what he or she had brought into marriage.

her paraphernalia and not subject to claims by her husband's creditors.[32] Additionally, she owned a business and ran it independently of her husband, something witnesses verified. The creditors, of course, were eager to demonstrate that the couple's assets were owned in common. They asserted that women did not have a legal right to establish a *capital de bienes* because this was a male prerogative. Thus, they tried to undermine Gregoria's allegations on the grounds of legally sanctioned sex discrimination.[33] Nevertheless, Gregoria's defense was successful. The judge declared, "It is not and never can be right that a woman should have to answer for her husband's debts." Because she had documented her capital contribution to the marriage,[34] she proved that her husband's share of acquest was very small.

Special rights were also problematic when women invested their capital to earn interest. It was quite common for a woman to hand over money to a man (not necessarily her husband!), who would then invest it and share with her in the profits. Women could thus assert economic independence while remaining at home. When the risk went bad and the creditors appeared, the woman's male "financial manager" often claimed that the money had not been his (and neither were the debts incurred), and he had stepped in only to help the lady out because investing "required a man's strength."[35]

In a period of social flux, such "female strategies" were crucial to avoid downward mobility.[36] The traditional property rights of wives represented a legal device that opposed the mechanisms of the market economy, which was

---

32. She based her claim on article 901, section 3 of the Civil Code.

33. "Sea por malicia o por inadvertencia, no se ha comprendido bien el tenor de esos artículos. Allí se habla solamente del marido y se le sujeta á la obligación de formar capital de bienes; pero esta no se hace extensiva á la muger, y como quiera que no puede ampliarse la letra de la ley, cuando esta ampliación no se deduce naturalmente de su espíritu, como lejos de allí, parece que el Código ha querido libertar á la muger de la capitalización de sus propiedades; se deduce que el argumento no es aproposito en la cuestión que se ventila." Case 736, AGN, CS, CCI, L 754, 1860, Berrospe vs. Laflor.

34. However, she (or her lawyer) had not read the law very well. The law did, indeed, state that women were not entitled to establish a *capital de bienes* document. By ignoring the letter of the law, the family won their legal battle against the creditors.

35. "La sola administración del establecimiento no dá rasón poderosa para concluirse que soy el propietario, . . . como muger no podía por si hacer su compra, ni menos practicar cuanto requiere el establecimiento, tenía necesidad de fuerzas de hombre y siendo yo una persona allegada y de su confianza, no titubeo en presentarme al frente para la sola administración." Case 986, AGN, CS, CCI, L 652, 1857, Doña Rosa Sáenz contra Don Manuel Pikimans y Don José Higinio Romero.

36. See also Case 885, AGN, CCI, L 571, 1854, Arana vs. Mena; and Case 784, AGN, Superior Gobierno, CCI, L 609, 1856, Cuéllar vs. Ruis.

based on the idea of financial contracts and individual responsibility. As a consequence, judges were faced with determining which "principle" should be safeguarded—individual freedom to make contracts or "special rights." Thus, as the flourishing market economy enabled women to take increasing financial responsibility for themselves and their families, women themselves, their husbands, and their creditors asked that women's special status as legal minors be rescinded. Although "special rights" were still sometimes used to evade creditors, judges increasingly favored creditors over women by denying special treatment for a wife's property.

Both women and men invoked discriminatory laws to manipulate the system. Women used men to engage in business; men used women's second-class legal status to protect themselves. This overt complicity had two consequences. First, it disguised women's real participation in the urban economy because they were often invisible in transactions in which they took part. Second, it could undermine male supremacy in cases when a woman was seeking her own advancement by accepting her unequal legal and economic position. The first assertion calls for a rereading of economic statistics regarding women's involvement in Lima's economy. The second assertion provides an explanation as to why judges became more lenient in accepting women's involvement and responsibility in handling family assets. After all, through strategies of male-female complicity and "special rights," the concept of a contractual obligation was weakened.

Contradictions that arose over the issue of race and civil responsibility also made judges broaden their notions of equality. Race was an additional stumbling block for women who wanted to participate economically. Specific regulations governed Indian (although not black or mulatto) women. Indian women were legally the most sheltered, and at the same time the most marginalized, group within society. To participate in legal or economic activities, an Indian woman had to obtain the permission of both her husband and the *protector fiscal* (or *procurador,* a state-assigned bureaucrat responsible for "Indian problems," a position originally also called the *protector de indios*). These guardians sometimes represented the interests of Indians, and by extension Indian women, but they also posed one more hurdle in the struggle for economic freedom. How well those hurdles were overcome affected the balance between the development of new liberal ideals and the maintenance of paternalistic practices. Simona Torres wrote:

> This petition [made to the *protector fiscal*] is indeed a scandal, because [it suggests . . .] that I cannot freely choose what to do with my

goods. . . . If this were so, there would be nothing more regrettable than having Indian ancestors, and this would be a tyrannical subjugation of the liberty with which every human has been endowed and which is even prevalent in the most barbaric nations. . . . And this is even a worse crime when inflicted on a mature, civilized, and widowed woman, in whom nobody can find the impudence and rudeness one can perceive in others born in the highlands, without education or good manners.[37]

Although racially an Indian, Simona felt she was different from other Indian women born in the highlands. She was civilized, had a business, and had lived in Lima for a long time. According to her own statements, hers was not an isolated case, because if it were true that the *protector* had a right to interfere, "it would be necessary that the countless Indian women working on their own and who have money would not be allowed to use it." There were many Indian women who worked in Lima, and Simona (and/or her lawyer) perceived that it was unreasonable to try to subject all of them to a guardian's control. What is striking, though, is that shortly after making these statements, Simona asked for an annulment of a contract she had signed without the *protector*'s presence. The creditor involved in the case tried to lay bare the contradiction in Simona's arguments, and he also tried to prove that she was not Indian. He even claimed that her "unknown" father was a Spaniard, making her a *mestiza* who could sign a legally binding contract without the presence of a guardian.

Although Indian women were the most sheltered group in society, the double guardianship of husband and *protector* provided them with an expanded defense when they were called on to repay debts. From the creditors' point of view, dealing with an Indian woman involved a double hazard, because they had to make sure that she was acting with her husband's permission and that she would not resort to the *protector* and invoke her status as a legal minor. In spite of this, Indian women were active participants in Lima's labor market. As peasants, house servants, and small merchants, they made up approximately 25 percent of the female urban labor force by 1908 (see Table 9.1). Simona's allegation that other Indian women in the city should not be required to resort to the *protector* was at the same time a gender and a racial vindication.

Simona's contradictory logic—claiming herself as a financially capable person and simultaneously as an Indian woman in need of protection—

---

37. Case 608, AGN, RA, CCI, L 25, C 276, 1802, Torres vs. Palas.

Table 9.1 Working women and race, 1908 (percentage)

Profession	Black	White	Mestiza	Indian	Asian
Cultivators	54.3	16.4	11.1	18.2	0.0
Day-laborers	23.5	5.0	21.8	49.7	0.0
Wash-women	19.9	4.8	55.2	20.0	0.1
Cooks	17.7	4.3	41.9	36.0	0.1
Houseservants	15.8	10.7	34.1	39.2	0.2
Iron-women	15.1	10.6	60.9	13.4	0.0
Commerce employees	14.9	41.9	14.1	29.0	0.0
Housekeepers	13.6	18.4	42.2	25.9	0.0
Industry workers	9.1	16.1	53.7	21.1	0.0
Merchants	6.2	54.0	8.0	31.9	0.0
Prostitutes	9.0	38.1	28.4	20.6	3.9
Wetnurses	15.1	6.8	41.1	37.0	0.0
Weavers	5.7	22.3	60.5	10.8	0.6
Street vendors	5.5	2.2	38.0	54.2	0.0

SOURCE: Censo de Lima, 1908. Prepared by Susan Stokes (Miller et al., 1987).

resembles Doña Dolores' argumentative spin in court (see page 319). However, an Indian challenging the intervention of the *protector* was not equivalent to a wife challenging her husband, although both cases addressed the issue of legal minority. In Dolores's case, gender minority was successfully used to circumvent a husband's claims; in Simona's case, gender and race led to greater protection (and control) of women, but it did not preclude the questioning of the legitimacy of the *protector*, a state bureaucrat, to intercede. Consequently, Indian women arguing against mediation and for the free exercise of their businesses were disputing not only male prerogatives but also state policies. The racial content of such allegations was one more reason—following general liberal tendencies—to cancel what was initially meant to protect and control. The final verdict in Simona's case—she was held responsible for the incurred debts—signal these changes.

The most significant legal change that emerged from the bargaining over the idea of shared responsibility and greater economic equality was the right for both men and women to record with a notary a document registering the existence of separate property. With this record, which could be obtained against a husband's will, wives achieved an important safeguard that allowed them to freely dispose of certain goods or sums of money.[38]

---

38. See, for example, AGN, Notario Valdivia, Protocolo 991 (1880–81), Rojas vs. Arias. What Gregoria Berrospe (or her lawyer) implemented in 1860 became a common procedure. See above, notes 32 and 33.

Some Small Achievements Around Midcentury

The basic moral code vis-à-vis gender issues prevalent in Lima during the mid-nineteenth century lasted at least until the end of the century. Patriarchal assumptions were barely challenged even after 1900, and women who broke the gender code were subject to severe legal and social reprisals. Married and unmarried women had expanded their economic participation, but their greater involvement encountered a heightened moral pressure to conform to ideals of virtue. Even when market economics and conjugal desertion forced them into poverty, they were vulnerable to the accusation of improper moral conduct when they entered the workplace and or other public arenas. The clash between this pressure and increasing female independence led to more violence in the bedroom but also to new arguments in the courtroom.

Women—unable to free themselves from society's emphasis on virtue and morality—brought to bear the question of husbands' obligations, especially in regard to children. Women accomplished this by recounting personal histories that documented the long-term effects of their *husbands*' "immorality." By midcentury, children had become essential in measuring morality and maintenance. The ability to prove that one was a "good parent" could be critical to gaining control of assets when a marriage fell apart. Yet the definition of "good mother" and "good father" remained worlds apart. Only rarely did fathers petition to take custody of their children; rearing children was still solely a female task.[39] Nevertheless, the marriage-contract was gradually reversed: when men did not fulfill their responsibilities as husbands, women were freed from their obligation to obey. The rationale was simple, if a wife was obedient, the children might starve. Thus, the clash between expectations and reality portrayed in women's life histories found resonance in judicial verdicts. Women's individual hardships were coalescing into a broader picture of the social disadvantages of civil inequality. Although by midcentury judges had compelling reasons to reinterpret the law, and husbands to search their souls, many more decades elapsed before liberal notions of equality created the conditions for more equality among people.

---

39. In only two of 1,070 conjugal conflict cases did fathers request custody of their children. The reasons given were the moral incompetence of the mother in one case and the possibility that the stepfather would mistreat the children in the other.

10

Final Thoughts

The End of the Century and Backward

Women's overall role in Lima's economy was on the rise during the last quarter of the nineteenth century. Within the new liberal milieu, men who worked and men who had financial or business dealings were entitled to their wages and their revenues, and by extension, women who participated in the economy could not be denied the same right. But the backlash evident in the heightened moral discourse of the time sometimes forced women to invoke the complex legal and social rights embedded in the dowry practice and in other conventions of matrimony. Despite the reality that most single women lived in dire poverty, women's economic involvement led many people to assume that women could look after themselves, which strengthened the position of those men who no longer wanted to support a wife and children. Thus, although the prejudices against working women were being transformed into a recognition of both the necessity and the importance of women's work, perceptions of women's role in society were not changing at the same pace.

The end of the century actually saw a slight reversal of the "achievements" that had appeared around the middle of the century. Symptomatically, between 1890 and 1910 ecclesiastical suits filed and won by women dropped to 11.5 percent from an average of 19.2 percent between 1840 and 1860, whereas for men the percentages grew from 9.2 percent between 1840 and 1860 to an average of 13.8 percent between 1890 and 1910. Perhaps most important, toward the end of the century, suits filed by women were constructed less through direct descriptive testimony and more through quotations from the civil code, thus impeding women's expression of individuality and voice in the courtroom.

In spite of the accelerating economic changes at the turn of the century and a more progressive awareness of women's role in society, it was not until the 1920s that women's increasing participation in the labor force generated political and legal changes, and even then the changes were limited. In 1919 a law finally acknowledged that mothers and daughters (not women!) had to sell their labor and that new laws to protect them were necessary.[1] Even feminists feared that a redefinition of gender roles might bring about a subversion of social order. At the turn of the century, Clorinda Matto de Turner, a well-known *indigenista* author, wrote that women's mission was to be subservient to men.[2] Women were allowed to attend the university only beginning in 1908,[3] and it was 1922 before women (but only those over thirty years of age) could publicly enter charity institutions.[4] It would be the 1960s before Peruvian women would win the right to vote. Even as late as 1923, during the debates over the new civil code, people argued that society would function only if women "voluntarily" submitted to husbands. In this way, natural law was transformed into an act of "free" will. Customs and "common sense" of the nineteenth century still prevailed, and marriage and family were the unquestioned pillars of society.

1. Ley 2851 Sobre Trabajo de Mujeres y Niños. And in *Anales de la Inspección de Trabajo de Mujeres y Niños del Concejo Provincial de Lima,* Genaro F. Salmón (Lima, 1924), p. ii, quoted in Miller (1987, 23): "Es menester enajenar los esfuerzos de la madre y las hijas."
2. According to the interventions in the debate of Señor Calle in ACR, "la mujer casada depende de su marido, siendo éste el administrador de los bienes de la sociedad conyugal y aun de parte de los bienes parafernales cuando no hay dote constituída . . . en la necesidad de reconocer al marido el rol de jefe de familia, que no se opone al principio ya admitido de la capacidad plena de la mujer fuera del matrimonio [y todo ello] desde luego, no procede del sexo sino de la natural dependencia en que voluntariamente se coloca dentro del matrimonio y de la necesidad de que la dirección de la familia y sus intereses de todo orden fuera única . . . nunca se podría llegar hasta el punto de implantar como sistema legal el de la separación de bienes, ajeno por entero a nuestras costumbres."
3. There were some exceptions. As early as 1874, Trinidad María Enriquez, a young teacher of the Colegio de Educandas in Cusco, wrote a letter to President Manuel Pardo asking to be admitted to study law at the University of San Antonio Abad. She graduated three years later. The same was true for Margarita Práxedes Muñoz (medicine), Felícita Balbuena (dentist, 1886), and Laura Esther Rodríguez Dulanto (surgery, 1899) in San Marcos University in Lima.
4. Mentioned in "Mujeres en Lima: su historia," *Cuadernos del CEDHIP* 8 (Lima) (1985):14.

In the 1920s one of Peru's earliest feminists, María Alvarado, wrote a petition in which she criticized the outmoded Civil Code of 1852, still prevalent in her day:

> We see that a married woman does not have any guarantees, neither for herself nor for her interests. She is under the complete authority of her husband, every right has been taken away from her! . . . today, after seventy-two years, after the philosophical foundations of our society and customs have completely changed, at a time when the new challenges of survival have imposed on her the need to fight for daily bread and have driven her out of domestic seclusion. Today women work in factories, workshops, in offices, in the liberal professions, places in which her work not only equals that of men but, in many cases, surpasses it. In these places she not only earns her own living but also that of her family and contributes to public wealth. In this context, it is impossible to deny her under any pretext her civil equality with men.[5]

Tellingly, the answer to María Alvarado's petition, signed by the female president of the Peruvian National Council of Women, reasoned that to support "more liberal" ideas would undermine the family, *the* pivotal institution in a country that was neither stable nor modern enough to withstand such change. Women's well-being depended on Peru's development, but the reverse—that equality might hasten modernity and stability—was (and still is) unthinkable. To accept the reversed equation would be tantamount to admitting that everything and everyone hampering equality is at root accountable for Peru's underdevelopment and hence its "instability" and "backwardness."

Long-Term Changes and Economic Survival

Given the existing civil and canonical laws, as well as Peruvians' beliefs about the validity of natural law, it is not surprising that the descriptions of marital and familial conflict registered in court records changed very little between 1800 and the 1920s. Nevertheless, by the mid-1800s, a new emphasis was

---

5. Cited in Villavicencio (1990, 13). No references for María Alvarado's memorial are given.

being placed on certain reasons for seeking divorce or annulment, and this shift in accent became stronger toward 1900. Women litigants were experimenting with the manipulation and circumvention of existing laws, and two circumstances within society proved particularly useful. First, the guano boom (1845–65) brought with it familial instability that led to a sharp rise in the number of suits filed for abandonment. Second, women were learning the lessons of "marriage economics" through their increasing participation in the work force. Women were successfully justifying their entrance into the public sphere with a deft double-punch based on those two developments.

Abandonment cases provided a perfect arena in which to present evidence of men who were ignoring their socially defined roles as husbands and fathers while forcing the women around them to remain within the tightly constrained roles of wives and mothers. Women in court skillfully combined these complaints against this social double standard with stories of desperation in the face of material need. Irresponsible husbands who did not fulfill their marital obligations to wives and children endangered the survival of the family both in a direct material sense and institutionally as well. Women thus strengthened the ideal of the family while widening their negotiating room within the family.

In regard to the lessons of marriage economics, at first glance the statistics appear to indicate that women filed fewer and fewer suits during the course of the century. Around 1800, 68.0 percent of marital lawsuits were filed by women; by 1900 this figure had dropped to 45.3 percent (see Tables 8.3 and 8.5). But this decline masks important trends. First, dowries decreased in importance at the same time that women were entering the labor force in significant numbers. Dowries were legally defined and defendable; labor and the earnings derived from it were not. Women's participation in the labor market was being stripped of its traditional meaning: women no longer argued that their labor (whether domestic or formal) was part of the dowry. Among the middle and lower classes, it was becoming common for a bride to marry "empty-handed" but to work to earn an income during marriage. An incipient consciousness of "his" and "hers" in economic matters contrasted sharply with earlier notions that a husband must support his wife because her parents had endowed the couple with money. Women began to see their earnings as their own, and that shift in perspective had important ramifications.

In the absence of laws to deal with assets earned by women, legal mediation was gradually being replaced by a direct assertion, within the private sphere of the family, of the wife's economic rights. Women were making money, and the liberal logic of the time could not deny them access to those earnings. Moreover, it was not just that fewer women went to court. By the end of the century, the declining percentage of women filing marital lawsuits may also reflect an increasing number of men being forced to initiate lawsuits to protect themselves from assertive wives seeking control over family assets they had helped to accumulate.

Thus, within an understanding of marriage as a contract, "social bargaining" (that is, legal, public, and official intermediation) was being replaced by "family bargaining" (between the couple). The heightened morality of midcentury, making familial conflict "shameful," made its private resolution more desirable. But it did not quell conflict. Working women from the middle and lower classes began to demand control over family expenditures, and in a reversal of roles, their husbands were now heard accusing wives of squandering conjugal assets. In their own defense, women would argue that they had spent only what belonged to them.[6] Women also fought for control over the husband's business enterprises, which they had often helped to erect.

As the husband's sole control over assets and income was contested, either because of abandonment or according to the logic of "marriage economics," the claim that women did not need to depend on a husband expanded to include the idea that many women did not *want* to depend on a husband.[7] Women's perceptions of their economic involvement shifted from an assertion of being able to live on their own ("not needing a penny") to a direct challenge to their legally defined economic dependence ("not *wanting* any of *his* pennies").

As women became more active economically, they began to demand more liberty in their day-to-day activities. This liberty, they knew, was necessary to their economic participation. Work thus became an important means for self-assertion socially as well as financially. Whereas earlier in the century a woman might have left her home to find "by chance" her stray husband

---

6. See Case 0582, AA, CD, L 119, 1905, Gonzales vs. Zavala. In this case, the accusing husband was a colonel.

7. Later in the century, a woman would no longer argue that she had better administrative skills than her husband; instead, she would explicitly state that she did not *want* to depend on her husband. In 1892 Doña Dalmira, the wife of a police inspector, Don Reynaldo Alvarado Ortiz, managed a liquor store, and he bought the stock. According to Doña Dalmira, it was she who worked most "in order to increase our income and have a little more for our own and our childrens' subsistence." In court Doña Dalmira petitioned to take over the entire management of the store, arguing that for the well-being of the family she could no longer rely on her husband. Case 0272, AA, CD, L 113, 1892, Zúñiga vs. Alvarado Ortiz.

walking down the street with a concubine, now she left the house "on purpose" to go to work. That meant to be in public, where she could observe her husband's activities. Women began to file suits asking the courts to help them keep a job or to allow them to work in the face of a husband's opposition. "Male privileges" that had reproduced the double standards were becoming "shared prerogatives."[8]

Modernization and industrialization had a strong bearing on women's consciousness, but there were drawbacks. Economic transactions, such as buying shares of stock or taking out loans, could be complex. Women increasingly fell victim to forgeries or fraud, and sometimes they simply did not understand the meaning of documents they had signed.[9] Faced with their own ignorance of financial dealings, women fell back on moral arguments and demanded proper and just behavior from men. Lawyers, judges, and even politicians, in turn, reminded the public that women needed protection, and they called for special legislation. In a sense, the "special legislation" on dowries was replaced by a "special legislation" on labor, which, under the pretense of protecting women, set up new barriers that reinforced gender inequality.

Exclusion abided in the face of modernization.[10] Increased legal scrutiny of women's position as economic actors and the "protective" measures that arose from it also meant a higher degree of state control as opposed to church control. This, in turn, privileged secular over moral arguments. Free-market principles, including financial responsibility and the enforcement of contracts, replaced notions of virtue and support from the extended family.

The Ideology of Virtue

Changing economic conditions did not immediately influence values and beliefs. As the century progressed, liberal ideals of justice and equality were gradually integrated into women's discourse and legal reasoning, but

   8. Case 0605, AA, CD, L 120, 1907, C. vs. Mercado. The best target for gossip was a working woman whose husband had no job; reversed roles were wonderful reasons for social mockery. In the few cases in which women had a public function, such as being a school director, the situation could be embarrassing.
   9. Case 0616, AA, CD, L 120, 1906, Deglave vs. Roggero.
   10. The consequences of "special legislation" can be seen in Case 0494, AA, CD, L 117, 1901, Chinsipoma vs. Macasana. Both spouses were peasants.

this went hand in hand with the heightening of the discourse on morality. Husbands and legislators stubbornly reiterated the assumptions of natural law embedded in the 1852 Civil Code.

Although there was an overall "devaluation" of moral arguments in the wake of secularization, when it came to a woman's individual behavior, the moral argument remained full-blown. As women grew more independent and sought more liberty in their day-to-day activities, husbands' suspicions and fears grew, resulting in a backlash that attempted to circumscribe women's freedom. Even a short separation was interpreted as a social liability that clouded a husband's honor. If a married woman talked to other men or even looked at them, it was a betrayal. Said one husband: "Neither as a husband nor as a man can I accept these temporal separations, like the one that has been going on now for fifteen days. These separations injure my honor, as it is wellknown that she is accompanied by men who do not have any kinship to her."[11]

As part of the heightened moral discourse, men accused women of adultery with greater frequency. Between 1890 and 1910, out of 239 cases filed by men, those involving adultery accounted for 71 percent, an increase of 11 percent over that figure at the beginning of the century.Whereas around 1800, women sued men for adultery more frequently than men sued women; by the end of the century, the reverse was true (see Tables 8.3 and 8.5). While women were probably not more adulterous than they had been in 1800, husbands resorted more frequently to the accusation of adultery because it was charged with moral overtones. By the century's end, it was the most efficient argument to get rid of a wife. Everything was surmountable but adultery, and nobody could ask a husband to accept it. Wrote Señor Lostanau in 1892: "The various and troubled displeasures and griefs one suffers throughout marriage can be endured with some resignation, but not a wife's unfaithfulness. Such a crime is an obstacle, poses an eternal impediment between the honest husband who has been fooled and victimized, and the adulterous woman who did not know how or wish to preserve her decorum, her honor, and the dignity of her status."[12]

Despite access to civil courts, the prejudices against women still worked to prevent anything resembling legal equality with men. The law still read that valid reasons for divorce were a wife's adultery or a husband's *public* concubinage (García Calderón Sr. 1879, 780). The slightest sign of extramarital

11. Case 0160, AA, CD, L 113, 1896, Igorbini vs. Alcazar.
12. Case 0271, AA, LM, L 11, 1892, Zenteno vs. Lostanau.

sexual relations on the part of a wife could be used against her in court. The same would be true for a husband only if his transgressions were overt, that is, offensive to social sensibility. While men would take a woman to court for adultery, a woman might not have legal grounds to dissolve the marriage. Thus, as women gained some economic independence through their work, it became easier simply to dismiss an unfaithful husband than to prosecute in court.

Foreign contemporary observers were alarmed by the gender inequalities they observed in Lima. An American traveler, Edward A. Ross, reported: "In the case of divorce granted for the unfaithfulness of the wife, she loses all right to profits from their joint property; but male legislators have taken care to preserve the rights of the husband to such profits when the divorce has been granted on account of his offending. . . . The illegitimate child may institute legal inquiry to ascertain who is his mother but not to ascertain who is his father because this would 'threaten the peace of the home.' Strange that the law does not think of this 'peace' when it scents the trail of an erring wife" (1915, 202).

Men's moral outrage against women often disguised their own shortcomings. It was reasoned that women who damaged a husband's good social image prevented him from fulfilling his obligations and excelling in his business. A wife's drunkenness or promiscuity offended a husband's self-esteem,[13] even if the husband had married for money, had a lover, or physically abused his wife.[14] Gender injustice reflected men's fear of social scandal, something that could only be held in check by immobilizing a wife. And the easiest way to achieve that was by recreating and reproducing commonly held assumptions about virtue.

Men reproduced the ideology of virtue by portraying the dreadful social consequences of divorce. A letter written by a husband in Chile, whose wife was divorcing him in Lima, succinctly illustrates this. In 1900 Don Juan Manuel de Ezcurra wrote:

> I will allow myself to convey some observations about the consequences a divorce will carry for you. This is something I intend to do for your own good. Once divorce is approved you would have all the liberties and independence of a married woman, but without

---

13. Case 0391, AA, CD, L 114, 1894, Landa vs. Pellegrino.
14. Case 0574, AA, CD, L 119, 1905, Oré vs. Rodriguez. Both spouses originally came from Santa Eulalia, a valley on the road to Peru's central highlands.

the support and the umbrella, without the respect from your husband. You are young, and you are pretty, your social background is noteworthy. You will be accountable to society for what you do with the independence and liberty you have allowed yourself, and even assuming you would not do anything wrong, do you believe that the world would agree? Wouldn't those who tarnish your reputation be the same people you will have to call upon to prove your innocence? And given the general tendency to misjudge events, will you not be condemned and rejected? With a divorce you are pursuing your downfall, it will come sooner or later, and with it you will find desperation, shame, and isolation. And this is not all. Will your parents survive you? Rationally one must answer, no. Have you thought about what will become of you, alone, abandoned, and with no one around to support you for the rest of your life? . . . Your name and your honor will suffer; it is well known that a woman's honor is like a crystal, when carried in everyone's mouth, it either breaks or smudges. . . . If you insist on getting divorced, you can do it. Everything is now in your hands.

This letter was signed "your unfortunate husband." Doña María Eugenia Freundt went ahead with her claims: 80,500 soles of unpaid alimony. It was 1906 when the judge granted her claim, but he reduced her alimony from 500 to 100 soles per month.[15] The commonly held perceptions about the meaning of divorce for a woman—a loss of family, friends, and social status—could make an unhappy marriage based on her endurance and forgiveness appear better than no marriage at all. The fear of social ostracism was a crucial component of women's subordination and silence.

The "dreadful divorce scenario" also allowed men to present themselves as protecting women from social condemnation. These "deceived saints," betrayed by a misguided wife, were generous enough to keep her at their side. In men's discourse, neighbors who perhaps sided with the wife had become "society," ready to condemn her solely on the grounds of her separation from him. Husbands claimed they had fulfilled their marital duties, so a wife seeking a separation must be deviant or have received bad advice from a third party. "My poor wife, see where bad advice has taken her!" Enrique Tovar wrote in 1891. "My honor," he continued, "has been uprooted today by the same woman to whom I extended my hand at the holy

15. Case n.n., AA, CD, 1900, Freundt vs. Ezcurra.

altar. . . . Although I am poor, I have always fulfilled the sacred marital duties, my house has always merited respect. . . . Your Honor can hardly imagine how huge the deception of a husband can be after six years of marriage." Everything surrounding marriage had become even more "sacred": holy altar, holy marital duties, holy honor. Thus, wives petitioning for divorce were held accountable for deceiving their husbands, society, and God himself. This sanctimonious husband had beaten his wife in moments of outrage— he explained—"because of his wife's worries and willful contradictions."[16] Yet husbands could not accept that a wife could seek a divorce simply because she was unhappy. Women's social and moral duties gave them no right to be unhappy.

Institutions Come to Husbands' Rescue

In the guise of providing protection to women, *beaterios* were the institutional means of expanding a husband's control beyond the bedroom and the home. Lima's many *beaterios* are evidence of how much society was inclined toward moral control and how greatly it feared the disruption of family life.[17] At the turn of the century, Lima's heightened moral climate in the wake of secularization was evident in the founding of the Casa del Buen Pastor (House of the Good Shepherd), which served as a "secularized institutional response" to husbands' demands for the moral improvement of their wives. Its secular-liberal traits were limited to its management by the state, a uniform monthly fee (which meant that all transgressions, regardless of their severity, cost the same), and "democratized" access that accepted women of all social backgrounds. But these were the precise limits of how much liberalism was allowed to touch gender relations. The mission of the Casa was the instruction of women in their role as "good" wives and their protection from "misguided steps." Often, as had been the case in the *beaterios,* a woman was safe from seclusion if she could demonstrate that she was her family's main source of support. As this became the case more frequently, the Casa's moral mission was continuously undermined by women's economic assertiveness.

16. Case 0220, AA, CD, L 113, 61ff., 1891, Ramírez vs. Tovar.
17. In England no similar or comparable entities existed (Horstmann 1985).

The arguments put forward by men and women at the beginning of the twentieth century were not only masked in an impersonal legal language, quite in contrast to the spontaneity observed in earlier lawsuits, but also show how women's claims aligned with prevalent social notions concerning a husband's "proper" behavior. Personal pain and grief retreated behind general arguments about the moral and economic well-being of society. And those arguments were different depending on whether they were voiced by a man or a woman. Women had a better chance of winning a lawsuit against a husband when a husband was being sued by a third party. Accusing a husband of mismanaging a dowry or squandering his income while he was being prosecuted (or had been prosecuted) by third parties for embezzlement of funds gave the woman a greater chance of success.[18] Judges would listen more carefully, especially if these other suits were in line with the wife's demands. In such cases, a woman's private plight was sustained by a general bad public opinion on her husband; otherwise, matrimonial conflicts were "her" problem because she was not capable, fit, or intelligent enough to make her husband and her family happy.

Although around midcentury we encounter changing social and economic circumstances, the moral pressure on women increased, and conflict resolution moved into the bedroom. For moral reasons, going to court became more difficult, and when women eventually resorted to court, their allegations had to provoke an extreme moral outrage that could no longer be solved in the bedroom. When independent economic claims were openly put forward, the response from judges and husbands, unfailingly, warned of the damaging consequences of divorce. Only slowly did women in Lima develop a consciousness about society's limitations on women that grew out of the discrepancies between changing economic life and prevailing moral attitudes. From early in the century, women knew, based on daily experience, that their liberty was circumscribed, and that they were subject to unequal and hypocritical rules and assumptions. But this long-term accumulated awareness only gradually began to be heard in the political and legal arenas. The final stage of mounting gender contradictions toward the end of the century became a catalyst toward some minor changes: the notion of character incompatibility and the paternal and maternal obligations toward children. In both areas, there was a progression from

---

18. Case 0470, AA, CD, L 117, 1900, Granadino vs. Tafur. They had been married for four years.

ecclesiastical, moral assumptions and recommendations to the secular realm of civil law code.

Children Revisited

Children played a pivotal role in redefining gender relations in nineteenth-century Lima—indirectly because sexual problems endangered their future health, and directly because they needed parental support and guidance. The low fertility and high mortality rates at the beginning of the nineteenth century made children almost not worth mentioning. Around the middle of the century, they appeared as a measurement of "good" or "bad" parenthood in court records on litigation over alimonies, support, and divorce. By the end of the century, however, children's emotional well-being had been added to their right for economic support. Emotional well-being was construed as depending essentially on a mother's care for her children. The welfare of children became part of legal and political arguments posed in newspapers, theater plays, and congress debates; and in line with these arguments, couples in court often remarked that as a result of improper moral behavior children were inadequately educated, or that the nonfulfillment of support or housekeeping duties had detrimental effects on children.[19] Moving in the same direction, the law, as mentioned earlier, protected working mothers; divorcing women shifted their arguments to gain support for their children's sake;[20] and there emerged a notion of fair distribution of responsibilities for children between the parents.[21]

19. Case 0139, AGN, Expedientes Judiciales, CCI, L 376.2, 1890, Juicio ordinario sobre entrega de una menor, Huapalla vs. del Pino. Don Lucio del Pino, 23, was a soldier born in Cusco who had had a daughter with Doña Rosalía Huapalla. First, he abandoned the mother and the child, but later on he successfully obtained his daughter's *patria potestad* by accusing Doña Rosalía of improper moral behavior. Although Doña Rosalía denied the charges and claimed that a soldier's life was too unstable to allow him to take care of their daughter, the judge ordered that the girl be transferred to her father. Doña Rosalía was allowed to visit her daughter twice a week for one hour.
20. "I implore you, Señor, not to think that I am asking to get money for myself, the only thing I am interested in is my children's food and education. They need to go to school . . . and just the school costs about 200 pesos a month in addition to at least 100 pesos a month for their support" (Case 824, AGN, CS, Expedientes Judiciales, CCI, L 565 and 566, 1854, 21ff, Autos seguidos por Doña Manuela Gil con Don José Manuel Ayulo sobre alimentos).
21. Ibid. This was clearly expressed in the final sentence to this case: The children would go to a boarding school, and their father had to pay for it; the mother had to do the laundry for them.

Women had to be educated to become good mothers. In Lima the Victorian ideal was couched in current perception: "Even if women cannot directly influence the administrative and political order in societies, they have a powerful indirect leverage. They are called upon to be wives and mothers, and to intervene in this double function in their husbands' decisions and in their children's education." Consequently, women were to enjoy an "appropriate religious, intellectual, and moral education, sufficient to fulfill their mission in society." (García Calderón Sr. 1879, 1396).[22] Thus, women's success or failure to forge happy families depended on how "misguided" they intrinsically were and on how properly they performed as mothers. Fathers had to work and could not take care of children; thus they were not accountable for the children's unhappiness.

However, as part of the moral counterattack, children also became an instrument of male control.[23] Children were a part of domestic life and happiness, and as such, they were used as a means to ensnare women. "She left our home and children, taking away from them the necessary care of a mother, that special care that can not be entrusted to any father because he has to work," thought Señor Lostanau.[24] Children were there to remind women of their duties toward their families, especially to their husbands: "Now there was nothing left, because without the pressure of caring for a child, she went ahead and squandered everything while I was sick," mentioned Señor Torrico.[25] Not having to care for children gave women more liberty, and more liberty meant lewd behavior. "This couple doesn't have children, and this has given this wife more liberty than to any of her sex to come and go as she pleases and perhaps be exposed to social criticism," explained Señor Elisalde.[26] Motherhood became a priority for people involved in divorce cases, and it also became a pivotal issue in the struggle for modernization and progress. In other words, the enhancement of motherhood "upgraded" women's role in society while also being an instrument of male control.

22. For a list of available schools for women, see Córdova y Urrutia (1839, 50–51) and Guardia (1985, 51).
23. Case 0261, AA, CD, L 113, 1891, Troncoso vs. Paredes.
24. Case 0271, AA, LM, L 11, 1892, Zenteno vs. Lostanau. In this case, the woman was placed in the *Buen Pastor*, where, according to her husband, she would have food and "she would be able to surround herself with more comfort resulting from her manual work and she would be able to improve her misbehavior."
25. Case 997, AA, CD, L 90 (1843–47), 1847, Salguero vs. Torrico.
26. Case 0339, AA, CD, L 113, 1891, Minaya vs. Elisalde.

Conclusion

Exceptional women have always upset their contemporaries with actions and expectations that exceed established rules and convention. In literature and war, breaches have been tolerated and even praised (at least in the aftermath), but the women portrayed in the preceding pages were neither writers nor war heroes in a traditional sense. They waged a war on a different front and in a different context. Their own writings, the ones written on behalf of them, and the ones written against them fill many more shelves than the recorded writings of nineteenth-century Latin American women writers. Their battlefront was a search for survival and happiness; the context was the courtroom. The personal rights to express a longing for one's happiness and to criticize its impairment were basic liberal assumptions that these women made their own.

None of these "rights" was easily accepted by society or the church. In the wake of ongoing courtroom disputes, a general questioning of social rights emerged. Throughout the nineteenth century, women used their domestic experiences as a seedbed to nurture challenges to traditional gender hierarchies, thus giving personal meaning to the liberal assumptions of their day. These women were "active meaning makers" (Mahoney and Yngvesson 1992, 44–45). The psychology of a whole century is embodied in the court records of their struggles.

In spite of women's "mission" of seclusion and privacy in which the family hearth represented the retreat from public and social aggressions and in which it was a wife's responsibility to secure a safe harbor for her husband and children, domestic life in nineteenth-century Lima presented another reality. As is the case in all societies, not everyone fit the ideal, nor did circumstances always allow for "proper" behavior. In the daily struggle to feed and clothe their families, little time was left for bourgeois contemplations. This was especially true for Peruvian women, living in a country characterized by political unrest, economic problems, socioeconomic inequality, and racial discrimination. Moreover, the pace of change within the political economy varied from the pace of change within families. Together with the economic and racial restrictions imposed on women, law and morality, embedded in the Victorian ideal of womanhood, weighed heavily against them.

For women, liberal ideology created an ideal of domesticity that kept them from pursuing their political rights. Because the courts, the church, and the government were male-dominated institutions, women had little recourse to institutional grievances; and the manipulation of the period's ideology of virtue further constrained women's struggle on their own behalf. Women did not file more lawsuits, but they changed the emphasis of their arguments to bring to the forefront changing economic and family circumstances. Many social pressures and agents were against women in their endeavor, starting with the church itself, through its *defensor de matrimonios* and the *provisor*, both of whom persistently argued against divorce or tried to reconcile quarrelling spouses with their (often contradictory) reading of canon law, the moral whip of Christian responsibility, and their exhortations of godly expectations. In Lima, as in many other societies, there were social avenues of recourse, beyond courts and lawyers, to resolve or at least dampen marital conflicts. Family members, neighbors, policemen, and last but not least, judges, helped to make marriage "work." In spite of this hostile context, women responded because, rather than disputing moral propriety, they were arguing that it be honored (while deftly using the same moral codes to reformulate their arguments for access to material goods). Taking the "moral whip" from the hands of judges and husbands, women invoked God's word to challenge them: "When Our Holy Mother Church instituted the sacrament of marriage He told men: '*I give thee a wife, not a serf.*' But, my husband has not understood the difference," said one woman in court.[27]

Radicalization of women's response was most obvious in women's defense of assets. At the beginning of the century, this occurred in their defense of dowries, *arras*, and inheritance; then—as the importance of these contributions decreased—the issue became the claim to acquest, and the recognition of domestic and public labor. Starting out with a reinterpretation of consent, followed by a claim for women's right to their dowries and acquest, women began very early in the nineteenth-century to question the adequacy and fairness of marriage as a social institution. They compared themselves to slaves, they wondered aloud if marriage was meant to be a contract without reciprocity, and in many cases they proved that their contribution to the family's survival was crucial and that they, not their husbands, were the ones who adequately provided for their families.

Dowries were pivotal in the transition to more radical claims. Established as a way to display social status and to find a suitable husband, dowries were also a moral compromise in two contradictory ways: they implied the husband's reciprocal duty to care for his wife, and they were a device to conceal the lack of virtue (especially the loss of virginity). As the practice of dowry exchange became appropriated by the lower and middle classes, it took on a

---

27. Ibid. She defined herself as an Indian born in Cerro de Pasco, resident in Lima.

socially disruptive nature. While dowries reproduced upper-class alliances, they also fractured horizontal alliances and could even became a weapon to obtain monetary compensation. For lower-class women, dowries were a bargaining chip rather than a device that emphasized social homogeneity. The content of the dowry itself was diluted as many more items came to be accepted as constituting a dowry. Ultimately, there were even instances when the content of a dowry was considered to be nothing more than a woman's work outside the home or even merely her domestic chores and childbearing. What was designed to be a cohesive force among elites came, among the lower classes, to be an argument for the value of women's work that reinforced their rights to acquest.

This had two important consequences: first, it allowed women to show that some husbands were untrustworthy because they did not fulfill their marital duties; and second, implicit to a fight over acquest is the recognition of the importance and necessity of women's labor, even in the domestic sphere. At the beginning of the century, women had argued that their special status as women (symbolized by the practice of dowry exchange) entitled them to a set of specific rights. Moral arguments, codified by the church, were used to win compensation in individual cases; and this limited many court cases to a fight over the rights and obligations of an individual but not over the "rights of women" as a group. By midcentury, women were still using the dowry as the focal point in arguing for economic and personal rights, but the decay of the practice of exchanging dowries had led to confusion in the courtroom. Alimony, earnings, and even childbirth were attached to the traditional meaning of dowries, expanding and changing its implications. Specific acts that were now being performed as part of the exchange no longer fit the traditional model, which thus had to be reinterpreted. This enabled women to present arguments in court that manipulated that reinterpretation. At the same time, the appearance within those arguments of the liberal ideas prevalent in nineteenth-century Peruvian society shifted the focus of court cases from personal vindication for a specific wrong to a larger issue that viewed the individual as a member of society with specific rights. It also added an additional layer to mundane suits over property and divorce. And within that additional space, lower-class women found they now had greater latitude to shape an argument on their own behalf.

Toward the end of the century, men faced increasing economic challenges from women, who were using liberal arguments to protect their assets and their personal liberty, that is, their right to enter into contracts. Men could not fight back on the ground that the contracts were invalid, because that would nullify liberal capitalist premises. So they turned to the church and its morality-based arguments in an attempt to retain power (or disempower women). Then, following that argumentative spin, women used scandal as a weapon against husbands. Women's allegations sprang from applying to men's activities in the domestic realm the same set of morals that were applied to women. This was possible, in part, because the church and legal arguments were grounded on a discourse of morality, whereas women struggled in an economic terrain, where they fought for control of marital assets. Throughout the century, women remained vulnerable to male abuse: men controlled women's property, their bodies (even their physical mobility in many cases), and usually the household income. But women were not helpless.

In their courtroom struggles, women did more than attack gender inequality. Their actions and allegations had a wider social meaning. Lima was governed by a white elite, yet spatial and social mobility increased in the course of the century, especially for Indians, mestizos, and blacks. Elites sought to control mobility, which could be accomplished by accentuating social distances through the mechanisms of racism, higher moral expectations, and notions of "decency," and by selectively "transforming," educating, and assimilating class newcomers (applying upper-class moral rules to others). Elites' attempts in this direction had limited success, in part because the upper classes themselves did not live up to their own ideals of virtue; and those who served and observed them were not blind. In describing what their masters did, women from various racial and economic backgrounds questioned family ideals. They did this not by overtly rebelling against principles and ideals but by reminding elites (and priests!) of the weaknesses of all human beings. Recognition of the shortcomings of the upper classes left elite moral discourse open to continued scrutiny.

Once women moved their allegations and justifications into the legal arena, an enlarged public bargaining ground appeared in which daily life occurrences were turned into vindicative principles. By contesting, ignoring, accepting, or imposing such principles, domestic and legal struggles coalesced, and in the long run, this bargaining ground helped to crystallize social contradictions based on gender differences and to question the validity of moral assumptions.

The church also helped to reproduce social stratification through church-imposed sanctions and, psychologically, through its hold on people's consciences. Among the upper classes, purchasing dispensations was the device by which wealth and class were held together. At the other end of the social structure, blacks, *castas*, and especially Indians were subdued by the mere existence of dispensations to Catholic marriage rituals. In spite of their diverse social functions, dispensations fulfilled one role in women's hands: they became a weapon to dissolve marriage. In this way, although the church was clearly responsive to the state and the upper classes, it also opened unforeseen spaces in which women from all classes could reassess their lives as wives. Sanctions designed to mark social differences had a leveling edge in women's arguments in court. Consequently, the appropriation of dispensation arguments by women from all colors set in motion a questioning of social inequalities.

The arguments concerning consent made this even clearer. Whereas dispensations had a definite social flavor, consent involved a woman's direct will. The lack of consent, or what was understood as the lack of it by women and ecclesiastical judges, could jeopardize marriage on its very foundations. It was probably the only realm of marriage in which a woman's opinion was explicitly asked for. While civil right denied women almost any access to worldly goods, even if they belonged to her, consent gave women the sense that they voluntarily entered a marriage contract with all its consequences. Consequently, free consent was not only a way to escape forced marriages— that is, parents' will—but also a mechanism to resist marriage and eventually escape from it. Moreover, women used the "free consent" argument to spell out the many ways in which their will was curbed by social expectations, and thus they pushed recognition of the hypocrisy of such unequally applied social expectations.

Very strict rules of behavior existed. But beyond what was judiciously tallied among legislators, people with or without lawyers frequently portrayed another kind of society—a more humane society that challenged legal rigidity and called upon justice in the name of common sense and existing reality.

Reformulation of expectations in light of social reality happened on several fronts, starting with the definition of family. "Family" could mean different things: female-headed households; women with children living in unconventional unions, at a variety of points in the life cycle; couples who had formed a household within a household by living together with their parents, especially the wife's parents; slaves or servants who engaged in sexual relationships with their masters, which could result in the birth of children. None of these relationships was exclusive to any specific social group in Lima, not even the master-slave relationships, because slave ownership was widespread. Single mothers with a child or several children living with friends or parents was common among the lower classes, but it was also a practice that sheltered white women who had lost their virginity from social criticism. Two generations living together in one household was common across the class spectrum and was used as a substitute for more traditional dowry contributions among upper classes. Widows from all social strata remarried or lived with a "male protector," a practice that frequently resulted in two or more sets of children.

In most settings, and regardless of the level of bargaining, it became evident that material interests were at stake. In the bargaining ground left open by the abyss between expected domestic and marital responsibilities and men's actual performance of their responsibilities, women expanded their legal battleground. "Distorted family situations" often unavoidably led to unacceptable male behavior, to such a degree that judges had to side with women's allegations, hand over the management of family assets to them, save their dowries in order to guarantee a family's sustenance, and recognize their ability to engage in business. The recognition of this necessity to protect the well-being of women and their children spread throughout the legal system and society at large; and in the long run, it not only changed the meaning of spouses' complaints in court, but also gave these processes a "dangerous" class and race ingredient. By the end of the century, suits over dowries led to arguments about the intrinsic value of women's work, about child rights, and about the inviolability of economic contracts; and these angles had particular importance for the racially segregated lower classes.

The coexistence of a sensitive moral discourse, high illegitimacy rates, unorthodox family settings, and abandoned women had a common setting: racial segregation. Racial hierarchies within society led to the marginalization of darker-skinned men because—out of wedlock—women's social mobility was greater. They could bear whiter children; darker-skinned men could not. Consequently, nonwhite men fought to retain the same social order as white men but for different reasons.[28] Accusations of adultery made by men against their wives increased over the course of the nineteenth century, until merely speaking to a man could be considered adulterous behavior. On the other hand, the widespread licentious behavior of Limeños

---

28. In this sense, I share Johnson's (1983, 108) assertion that "Racism, while affecting the descriptions of members of both sexes, may have surfaced more in relation to nonwhite women because they had been able to progress through the social ranks by marrying Spaniards, an option denied to males of similar racial make-up. These men had remained on the periphery of society and posed no threat to the order established by the Spanish."

left many women on their own. Middle- and lower-class women (the working mestizas, Indians, and black women) gave evidence in court that in the absence of a responsible mate, they were in charge of the "family." This notion subverted patriarchal assumptions.

Given the racial composition of Lima's society, such claims questioned the superiority of white-male domination. Lower-class women were aware of the existence of Christian moral ethics and white honor codes, and they used the legal system to manipulate these values. By participating in the legal system, the lower classes imposed a certain reading on upper-class values, which arose out of their daily marital experience and conflicts. The argument that women in the lower echelons of society drove the reformulation of gender relations within a more rigid moral environment is at the same time an argument of social subversion along class and race lines. In other words, "the 'public' life arises out of the dense determinations of the 'domestic' life" (Thompson 1978, 7), but this connection is established by concrete historical actors (Lima's women) in concrete historical circumstances (rising liberalism), and has political implications (the questioning of social hierarchies).

A weak state and an increasingly weaker church placed the burden of social responsibility on the shoulders of the family, and within the family, on husbands and fathers. Social groups adapted to this challenge in quite different ways, and it was in the process of this adaptation that women expanded their bargaining ground. At all social levels, strategies to control women were also ways to reproduce ethnic and economic subdivisions, no matter how much or how little was involved economically. The erosion of the control over women was at the same time an erosion of ethnic and class boundaries. Women's actions in court are spread out across a whole century. It was a slow process that transcended the very fabric of daily life and was—very literally—the way in which liberalism flowed into bedroom, or the way in which—depending on how we want to phrase a dialectic causality—bedroom issues (from virginity to dowries) patterned liberalism. The importance of such patterning gains a spectacular momentum when we remember the multiple class and race aspects of apparently "simple" gender vindications. Discrimination is most visible in how men treated and perceived women. Thus, gendered allegations unravel deep-seated class and race cleavages, from stereotypes to the meaning and adaptation of honor codes.

Finally, women's protest predated middle-class feminism and had its roots simultaneously in the race-class hierarchies and in the domestic sphere. We wonder if, in this context, patriarchal social perspectives and husbands' control of the family was not challenged from the very outset of the century (or maybe even earlier), as a result of how this society thought of itself. It seems that in the nineteenth century Lima's inhabitants were not moving from a model of patriarchal control of the extended family to one of a male-dominated nuclear family. On every front, women continuously readapted their discourse to changing economic and moral conditions, and contested patriarchal and male prerogatives. Women forwarded their views on the legal system and questioned male supremacy in the domestic sphere, in the market place, and in society.

Striking as it is, these long-term messages, exposed through so many lives in the course of the nineteenth century, were ultimately ignored, most prominently among feminists in the 1920s. Women in Lima's courtrooms had expressed the social dimensions of gender inequalities well before feminism became a middle-class political agenda. Much could have been and can be learned about the many faces of oppression, about defense strategies, and about the possible long-term effects of liberalism on gender and the family, by looking into the bedroom.

Bibliography

Acosta-Belén, Edna. 1994. *Opening New Paths: Research on Women in Latin America and the Caribbean.* Washington D.C.: Woodrow Wilson International Center.
Actas de las sesiones de la Comisión Reformadora del Código Civil Peruano (ACR), 2d ed. 1928. Lima: Imprenta C.A. Castrillón.
Aguirre, Carlos. 1991. "The Penitentiary and the 'Modernization' of Penal Justice in Nineteenth-Century Peru." Paper presented at the American Historical Association, December, Chicago, Illinois.
Anna, Timothy. 1979. *The Fall of the Royal Government in Peru.* Lincoln: University of Nebraska Press.
Anderson, Michael. 1980. *Approaches to the History of the Western Family, 1500–1914.* London: Macmillan.
Arona, Juan de. 1891. *La Inmigración en el Perú: Monografía Histórico-Crítica.* Lima: Imprenta del Universo.
Arrom, Silvia M. 1978. "Marriage Patterns in Mexico City, 1811." *Journal of Family History* 3:376–91.
―――. 1985a. "Changes in Mexican Family Law in the Nineteenth Century: The Civil Codes of 1870 and 1884." *Journal of Family History* 10:305–17.
―――. 1985b. *The Women of Mexico City, 1790–1857.* Stanford: Stanford University Press.
―――. 1991. "Perspectivas Sobre Historia de la Familia en México." In *Familias Novohispanas: Siglos XVI al XIX*, ed. P. Gonzalbo, 389–99. Mexico: El Colegio de Mexico.
Babb, Florence. 1989. *Between Field and Cooking Pot: The Political Economy of Marketwomen in Peru.* Austin: University of Texas Press.
Balmori, Diana. 1985. "Family and Politics: Three Generations (1790–1890)." *Journal of Family History* 3:247–57.
Balmori, Diana, and Robert Oppenheimer. 1979. "Family Clusters: The Generational Nucleation of Families in Nineteenth-Century Argentina and Chile." *Comparative Studies in Society and History* 21:231–61.
Balmori, Diana, Stuart F. Voss, and Miles Wortman. 1984. *Notable Family Networks in Latin America.* Chicago: University of Chicago Press.

Banner, Lois W. 1973 (1971). "On Writing Women's History." In *The Family in History: Interdisciplinary Essays*, ed. T. Rabb and R. Rotberg, 159–70. New York: Harper Torchbooks.

Bayle, Constantino. 1945. "El Concilio de Trento en las Indias Española." In *Razón y Fe* 131 (January–April): 257–84.

Behar, Ruth. 1989. "Sexual Witchcraft, Colonialism, and Women's Powers: Views from the Mexican Inquisition." In *Sexuality and Marriage in Colonial Latin America*, ed. A. Lavrin, 178–206. Lincoln: University of Nebraska Press.

Bendezu, Juan C. 1874. Tesis para Optar el Grado de Doctor en la Facultad de Jurisprudencia en la UNMSM Sobre el "Caracter del Matrimonio." Lima: Imprenta Liberal de "El Correo del Peru."

Bishop, Jane. 1985. "Bishops as Marital Advisors in the Ninth Century." In *Women of the Medieval World*, ed. J. Kirshner and S. F. Wemple, 53–84. Oxford: Basil Blackwell.

Black, Donald, ed. 1984. *Toward a General Theory of Social Control*. New York: Academic Press.

Blanchard, Peter, ed. 1991. *Markham in Peru: The Travels of Clements R. Markham, 1852–1853*. Austin: University of Texas Press.

Blank, Stephanie. 1974. "Patrons, Clients, and Kin in Seventeenth-Century Caracas: A Methodological Essay in Colonial Spanish American Social History." *Hispanic American Historical Review* 54:260–83.

Blasius, Dirk. 1985. "Scheidung und Scheidungsrecht im Neunzehnten Jahrhundert: Zur Sozialgeschichte der Familie." *Historische Zeitschrift* 241:329–60.

Blom, Ida. 1991. "The History of Widowhood: A Bibliographic Overview." *Journal of Family History*. 16(2): 191–210.

Bonilla, Heraclio. 1982. "The War of the Pacific and the National and Colonial Problem in Peru." *Past and Present* 81:92–118.

Bourque, Susan C., and Kay B. Warren. 1981. *Women of the Andes: Patriarchy and Social Change in Two Peruvian Towns*. Ann Arbor: University of Michigan Press.

Bourricaud, François. 1972. *La oligarquía en el Perú*. Buenos Aires: Amorrortu Editores.

Brennan, Eileen. 1978. Demographic and Social Patterns in Urban Mexico: Guadalajara, 1876–1910. Ann Arbor, Mich.: University Microfilms.

Bromley, Juan, and José Barbagelata. 1945. *Evolución Urbana de la Ciudad de Lima*. Lima: n.d.

Bunster, Ximena, and Elsa Charney. 1989 (1985). *Sellers and Servants: Working Women in Lima, Peru*. Granby, Mass.: Bergin and Garvey Publishers.

Burkett, Elinor C. 1975. "Early Colonial Peru: The Urban Female Experience." Ph.D. diss., University of Pittsburgh.

———. 1977. "In Dubious Sisterhood: Class and Sex in Spanish Colonial South America." *Latin American Perspectives* 4(12/13): 18–26.

Calisto, Marcela. 1984. "La Práctica Dotal a Fines de la Colonia." Paper presented at the Congreso Nacional de Investigación Histórica, Consejo Nacional de Ciencia y Tecnología, November 11–16, Lima.

Cancian, Francesca M., L. W. Goodman, and Peter H. Smith. 1978. "Capitalism,

Industrialization, and Kinship in Latin America: Major Issues." *Journal of Family History* 3(4): 319–36.
Cavieres, Eduardo, and Rene Salinas. 1991. *Amor, Sexo, y Matrimonio en Chile Tradicional.* Serie monográfica 5. Valparaíso: Universidad Católica.
Censo Nacional. 1940. Banco de Crédito del Perú. Lima: Empresa Gráfica.
Chance, John K., and William B. Taylor. 1977. "Estate and Class in a Colonial City: Oaxaca in 1792." *Comparative Studies in Society and History* 19:454–87.
Charney, Paul. 1989. "The Destruction and Reorganization of Indian Society in the Lima Valley, Peru, 1532–1824." Ph.D. diss., University of Wisconsin.
———. 1991. "The Implications of Godparental Ties Between Indians and Spaniards in Colonial Lima." *The Americas* 47(3): 295–314.
Cherpak, Evelyn. 1978. "The Participation of Women in the Independence Movement in Gran Colombia, 1780–1830." In *Latin American Women: Historical Perspectives,* ed. A. Lavrin, 219–34. Westport, Conn.: Greenwood Press.
Clavero, José. 1885. *Demografía de Lima.* Lima: Imprenta de J. Francisco Solis.
Collier, Simon. 1967. *Ideas and Politics of Chilean Independence.* Cambridge: Cambridge University Press.
Cordova Y Urrutia, José María. 1839. *Estadística Histórica, Geográfica, Industrial, y Comercial de los Pueblos que Componen las Provincias del Departamento de Lima.* Lima: Imprenta de Instrucción Primaria.
Costeloe, Michael P. 1993. *The Central Republic in Mexico, 1835–1846: Hombres de Bien in the Age of Santa Anna.* Cambridge: Cambridge University Press.
Cotler, Julio. 1978. *Clases, Estado, y Nación en el Perú.* Lima: Instituto de Estudios Peruanos.
Couturier, Edith. 1985. "Women and the Family in Eighteenth-Century Mexico: Law and Practice." *Journal of Family History* 3:294–304.
Couturier, Edith, and Asunción Lavrin. 1979. "Dowries and Wills: A View of Women's Socioeconomic Role in Colonial Guadalajara and Puebla, 1640–1790." *Hispanic American Historical Review* 59(2): 280–304.
Crane, Elaine F. 1987. "Dependence in the Era of Independence: The Role of Women in a Republican Society." In *The American Revolution: Its Character and Limits,* ed. Jack P. Greene, 253–75. New York: New York University Press.
Crawford, Patricia. 1994. "Sexual Knowledge in England, 1500–1750." In *Sexual Knowledge, Sexual Science: The History of Attitudes to Sexuality,* ed. Roy Peter and Mikulás Teich. Cambridge: Cambridge University Press.
Cutter, Martha J. 1992. "Beyond Stereotypes: Mary Wilkins Freeman's Radical Critique of Nineteenth-Century Cults of Femininity." *Women's Studies* 21:383–95.
Deere, Carmen Diana, and Magdalena León de Leal. 1982. *Women in Andean Agriculture.* Geneva: International Labour Office.
De Guevara, A. 1884. *Carta a una Joven Sobre lo que Debe Saber Antes de Casarse: Por el Doctor Salustio.* Lima: Imprenta del Universo de Carlos Prince.
De Mello, George. 1968. "The Writings of Clorinda Matto de Turner." Ph.D. diss., University of Colorado.
Denegri, Francesca. 1996. *El Abanico y la Cigarrera: La Primera Generación de Mujeres Ilustradas en el Perú.* Lima: Centro Flora Tristan/Instituto de Estudios Peruanos.

De Oliveira, Orlandina. 1989. *Trabajo, Poder, y Sexualidad*. México D.F.: El Colegio de Mexico.

Donzelot, Jacques. 1980 (1977). *Die Ordnung der Familie*. Frankfurt: Suhrkamp.

Dowdall, Raymund M. 1944. *The Celebration of Matrimony in Danger of Death*. Rome: Vatican Polyglot Press.

Escobar, Arturo, and Sonia E. Alvarez. 1992. *The Making of Social Movements in Latin America: Identity, Strategy, and Democracy*. Boulder, Colo.: Westview Press.

Extracto Estadístico del Perú. 1935. Ministerio de Hacienda y Comercio, Dirección Nacional de Estadística. Lima: Imprenta Americana.

Fisher, Jo. 1993. *Out of the Shadows: Women, Resistance, and Politics in South America*. London: ZED Books.

Flores Galindo, Alberto. 1984. *Aristocracia y Plebe: Lima, 1760–1830*. Lima: Mosca Azul Editores.

Flores Galindo, Alberto, and Magdalena Chocano. 1984. "Las Cargas del Sacramento." *Revista Andina* 2 (December): 403–23.

Ferry, Robert J. 1989. *The Colonial Elite of Caracas: Formation and Crisis 1567–1767*. Berkeley and Los Angeles: University of California Press.

Francke, Marfil. 1984. "El Trabajo de la Mujer en Lima, 1876–1920." In *Documento de Trabajo de la Investigación: Raíces del Movimiento de Mujeres en el Perú*. Lima: Centro Flora Tristán.

Fuentes, Manuel A. 1866. *Estadística General de Lima*. 4 vols. Paris: Tipografía de A. Laine et J. Havard.

———. 1861. (comp.) "Disertación Primera, en la que se Proponen las Reglas que Deben Observar las Mujeres en el Tiempo de la Preñez." In *Antiguo Mercurio Peruano*, 19–28. Lima: Felipe Bailly.

———. n.d.(comp.) "Examen Histórico-Crítico de la Fundación, Progreso y Actual Estado de la Real Casa ó Recogimiento de las Amparadas de la Concepción." In *Antiguo Mercurio Peruano*, 88–162. Lima: Felipe Bailly.

Galvez, Aníbal. 1905. *Cosas de Antaño: Crónicas Peruanas*. Lima: Imprenta de "El Tiempo."

Galvez, José. 1965 (1931). *Una Lima que se va*, 3d ed. Lima: Editorial Universitaria.

Ganster, Paul. 1990 (1986). "Churchmen." In *Cities and Society in Colonial Latin America*, ed. Louisa S. Hoberman and Susan M. Socolow, 137–63. Albuquerque: University of New Mexico Press.

———. 1991. "Miembros de los Cabildos Eclesiásticos y sus Familias en Lima y la Ciudad de México en el Siglo XVIII." In *Familias Novohispanas: Siglos XVI al XIX*, ed. P. Gonzalbo, 149–62. México D.F.: El Colegio de México.

Garcia, Jacinto Sixto. 1919. *San Martín, Bolivar, Gamarra, Santa Cruz, Castilla y las Constituciones del Perú*. Lima: Oficina Tipográfica "La Opinión Nacional."

García Calderon Sr., Franciso. 1879. *Diccionario de Legislación Peruana*, 2d ed. Lima/Paris: Author/Libreria Laroque.

García Calderon Jr., Francisco. 1954 (1907). *En Torno al Perú y América: Páginas Escogidas*. Lima: Juan Mejía Baca & P. L. Villanueva.

García Jordán, Pilar. 1987. "Progreso, Inmigración, y Libertad de Cultos en Perú a Mediados del Siglo XIX." *Siglo XIX Revista de Historia* 2(3): 37–61.

———. n.d.(1992). *Iglesia y poder en el Perú contemporáneo, 1821–1919.* Cusco: Centro de Estudios Regionales Andinos "Bartolomé de las Casas."
Garrioch, David. 1986. *Neighborhood and Community in Paris, 1740–1790.* Cambridge: Cambridge University Press.
Gibert, Rafael. 1947. *El Consentimiento Familiar en el Matrimonio Según el Derecho Medieval Español.* Madrid: Instituto Nacional de Estudios Jurídicos.
Gilbert, Dennis L. 1982. *La Oligarquía Peruana: Historia de Tres Familias.* Lima: Editorial Horizonte.
Giesecke, Margarita. 1978. *Masas Urbanas y Rebelión en la Historia: Golpe de Estado, Lima 1872.* Lima: Centro de Divulgación de Historia Popular.
Goffin, R. J. R. 1981. *The Testamentary Executor in England and Elsewhere.* Buffalo: Williams, Hein & Company.
Golte, Jürgen, and Norma Adams. 1987. *Los Caballos de Troya de los Invasores: Estrategias Campesinas en la Conquista de la Gran Lima.* Lima: Instituto de Estudios Peruanos.
Góngora, Mario. 1975. "Urban Stratification in Colonial Chile." *Hispanic American Historical Review* 55(3): 421–48.
Gonzalbo, Pilar. 1987. *Las Mujeres en la Nueva España: Educación y Vida Cotidiana.* México D.F.: El Colegio de México.
———, ed. 1991. *Familias Novohispanas: Siglos XVI al XIX.* México D.F.: El Colegio de México.
Gonzalbo, Pilar, and Cecilia Rabell, eds. 1994. *La Familia en el Mundo Iberoamericano.* México D.F.: Instituto de Investigaciones Sociales/Universidad Nacional Autónoma de México.
Goode, William J. 1963. *World Revolutions and Family Patterns.* New York: Free Press.
———. 1969 (1956). *Women in Divorce.* Toronto: Collier-Macmillan.
Goody, Jack. 1983. *The Development of the Family and Marriage in Europe.* Cambridge: Cambridge University Press.
———. 1990. *The Oriental, the Ancient, and the Primitive: Systems of Marriage and the Family in the Pre-Industrial Societies of Eurasia.* Cambridge: Cambridge University Press.
Gootenberg, Paul. 1989. *Between Silver and Guano: Protectionist Elites to a Liberal State in Peru, 1820–1850.* Princeton: Princeton University Press.
———. 1990. "*Carneros y Chuño*: Price Levels in Nineteenth-Century Peru." *Hispanic American Historical Review* 70(1): 1–56.
———. 1991. "Population and Ethnicity in Early Republican Peru: Some Revisions." *Latin American Research Review* 26(3): 109–58.
———. 1994. *Imagining Development: Economic Ideas in Peru's 'Fictitious' Prosperity of Guano, 1840–1990.* Berkeley and Los Angeles: University of California Press.
Gottlieb, Beatrice.1993. *The Family in the Western World: From the Black Death to the Industrial Age.* Oxford: Oxford University Press.
Guardia, Sara B. 1985. *Mujeres Peruanas: El Otro Lado de la Historia.* Lima: Empresa Editora Humboldt.
Gutierrez, Ramón.1985. "Honor Ideology, Marriage Negotiation, and Class-Gender Domination in New Mexico, 1690–1846." *Latin American Perspectives* issue 44, vol. 12, no. 1 (winter): 81–104.

———. 1991. *When Jesus Came the Corn Mothers Went Away*. Stanford: Stanford University Press.
Guy, Donna J. 1985. "Lower-Class Families, Women, and the Law in Nineteenth-Century Argentina." *Journal of Family History* 3:318–31.
———. 1990. "Prostitution and Female Criminality in Buenos Aires, 1875–1937." In *The Problem of Order in Changing Societies*, ed. L. L. Johnson, 89–115. Albuquerque: University of New Mexico Press.
Habakkuk, H. J. 1955. "Family Structure and Economic Change in Nineteenth-Century Europe." *Journal of Economic History* 15:1–12.
Haenke, Thaddaus. 1901 (1808). *Descripción del Perú*. Lima: Imprenta "El Lucero."
Hagerman Johnson, Ann. 1978. "The Impact of Market Agriculture on Family and Household Structure in Nineteenth-Century Chile." *Hispanic American Historical Review* 58:625–48.
Haitin, Marcel. 1983. "Late Colonial Lima: Economy and Society in an Era of Reform and Revolution." Ph.D. diss., University of California, Berkeley.
———. 1986. "Urban Market and Agrarian Hinterland: Lima in the Late Colonial Period." In *The Economies of Mexico and Peru During the Late Colonial Period, 1760–1810*, ed. N. Jacobsen and H. J. Puhle. Berlin: Colloqium Verlag.
Hardwig, Julie. 1992. "Widowhood and Patriarchy in Seventeenth-Century France." *Journal of Social History* 26(1): 133–48.
Hareven, Tamara K. 1973 (1971). "The History of the Family as an Interdisciplinary Field." In *The Family in History: Interdisciplinary Essays*, ed. T. Rabb and R. Rotberg, 211–26. New York: Harper Torchbooks.
———. 1974. "The Family as a Process: The Historical Study of the Family Cycle." *Journal of Social History* 7:322–27.
———. 1978. *Transitions: The Family and the Life Course in Historical Perspective*. New York: Academic Press.
———. 1982. *Family Time and Industrial Time: The Relationship Between Family and Work in a New England Industrial Community*. Cambridge: Cambridge University Press.
———. 1991. "The History of the Family and the Complexity of Social Change." *American Historical Review* 96(1): 95–124.
Hareven, Tamara K., and Andreis Plakans. 1987. *Family History at the Crossroads: A Journal of Family History Reader*. Princeton: Princeton University Press.
Helmholz, R. H. 1978(1974). *Marriage Litigation in Medieval England*, 2d ed. London: Cambridge University Press.
Hoberman, Louisa S., and Susan M. Socolow, eds. 1986. *Cities and Society in Colonial Latin America*. Albuquerque: University of New Mexico Press.
Hobsbawm, Eric. 1997 (1971). "From Social History to the History of Society." Reprinted in E. Hobsbawm, *On History*, 71–73. New York: New Press.
Holloway, Thomas H. 1993. *Policing Rio de Janeiro: Repression and Resistance in a Nineteenth-Century City*. Stanford: Stanford University Press.
Horstmann, Allen. 1985. *Victorian Divorce*. London: Croom Helm.
Humphries, Jane. 1977. "The Working Class Family, Women's Liberation, and Class Struggle: The Case of Nineteenth-Century British History." *Review of Radical Political Economics* 9(3): 25–40.
Hunefeldt, Christine. 1983. "Comunidades y Comuneros Hacia Fines del Período

Colonial: Ovejas y Pastores Indomados en el Perú." *Revista Latinoamericana de Historia Económica y Social* 2:3–31.

———. 1992. *Lasmanuelos: Vida Cotidiana de una Familia Negra en la Lima del Siglo XIX: Una Reflexión Histórica Sobre la Esclavitud Urbana*. Lima: Instituto de Estudios Peruanos, serie mínima.

———. 1994. "Los Beaterios y los Conflictos Matrimoniales en el Siglo XIX Limeño." In *La Familia en el Mundo Iberoamericano*, ed. P. Gonzalbo and C. Rabell, 227–62. México D.F.: Instituto de Investigaciones Sociales/Universidad Nacional Autónoma de México.

Informe Demográfico del Perú. 1972. Del Centro de Estudios de Población y Desarrollo. Lima: Tipografía Sesator.

Jacquette, Jane, ed. 1989. *The Women's Movement in Latin America*. Boston: Unwin Hyman.

Jelin, Elizabeth, ed. 1990. *Women and Social Change in Latin America*. Atlantic Highlands, N.J.: Zed Books.

Johnson, Julie G. 1983. *Women in Colonial Spanish American Literature: Literary Images*. London: Greenwood Press.

Johnson, Lyman C., ed. 1990. *The Problem of Order in Changing Societies*. Albuquerque: University of New Mexico Press.

Johnson, Lyman C., and Susan M. Socolow. 1980. "Población y Espacio en el Buenos Aires del Siglo XVIII." *Desarrollo Económico* 20(79): 329–49.

Jordan Rodriguez, Jesus. 1956. *Pueblos y Parroquias de el Perú*, 3er tomo, n.a.

Kicza, John E. 1985. "The Role of the Family in Economic Development in Nineteenth-Century Latin America." *Journal of Family History* 10(3): 235–46.

Kirshner, Julius. 1978. "Pursuing Honor While Avoiding Sin: The Monte Delle Doti of Florence." *Quaderni di Studi Senesi* 41. Milano: Dott. A. Giuffre Editore.

Klaiber, Jeffrey L., S.J. 1977. *Religion and Revolution in Peru, 1824–1976*. Notre Dame: University of Notre Dame Press.

———. 1980. *Independencia, Iglesia, y Clases Populares*. Lima: Centro de Investigación de la Universidad del Pacífico.

———. 1992 (1988). *The Catholic Church in Peru, 1821–1985: A Social History*. Washington, D.C.: Catholic University of America Press.

Klapish-Zuber, Christiane. 1985. *Women, Family, and Ritual in Renaissance Italy*. Chicago: University of Chicago Press.

Kriedte, Peter, Hans Medick, and Jürgen Schlumbohm. 1977 (1986). *Industrialización antes de la Industrialización*. Barcelona: Editorial Crítica.

Kruggeler, Thomas. 1993. "Unreliable Drunkards or Honorable Citizens? Artisans in Search of their Place in the Cusco Society (1825–1930)." Ph.D. diss., University of Illinois at Urbana-Champaign.

Kuehn, Thomas. 1991. *Law, Family, and Women: Toward a Legal Anthropology of Renaissance Italy*. Chicago: University of Chicago Press.

Kuznesof, Elizabeth A. 1980. "The Role of the Merchants in the Economic Development of Sao Paulo, 1765–1850." *Hispanic American Historical Review* 60:571–92.

———. 1986. *Household Economy and Urban Development: Sao Paulo, 1765–1835*. Boulder, Colo.: Westview Press.

———. 1989. "The History of the Family in Latin America: A Critique of Recent Work." *Latin American Research Review* 24(2): 168–86.

———. 1991. "Raza, Clase, y Matrimonio en la Nueva España: Estado Actual del Debate." In *Familias Novohispanas: Siglos XVI al XIX,* ed. P. Gonzalbo, 373–88. México D.F.: El Colegio de México.

Kuznesof, Elizabeth A., and Robert Oppenheimer. 1985. "The Family and Society in Nineteenth-Century Latin America: An Historiographical Introduction." *Journal of Family History* 10(3): 215–34.

Ladd, Doris M. 1976. *The Mexican Nobility at Independence, 1780–1826.* Austin: University of Texas Press.

Lafond, Gabriel. 1840. "Viaggio nell' America Spagnuola . . . in tempo delle Guerre dell' Independenza etc." Translated into Spanish in *Colección Documental de la Independencia del Perú* (CDIP), ed. Estuardo Nuñez, tomo 27, Relaciones de Viajeros.

Larriva de Llona, Lastenia. 1919. *Cartas a mi hijo. Psicología de la mujer.* Lima: n.p.

Laslett, Peter, ed. 1972. *Household and Family in Past Time: Comparative Studies in the Size and Structure of the Domestic Group over the Last Three Centuries in England, France, Serbia, Japan, and Colonial North America, with Further Materials from Western Europe.* Cambridge: Cambridge University Press.

Lauderdale-Graham, Sandra. 1988. *House and Street: The Domestic World of Servants and Masters in Nineteenth-Century Rio de Janeiro.* Austin: University of Texas Press.

Lavalle, Bernard. 1986. "Divorcio y Nulidad de Matrimonio en Lima (1651–1700): La Desaveniencia Conyugal como Revelador Social." Document de travail, no. 2. Université de Bordeaux III, CNRS.

Lavrin, Asunción, ed. 1978. *Latin American Women: Historical Perspectives.* Westport, Conn.: Greenwood Press.

———. 1986. "Sexuality in Colonial Mexico: A Church Dilemma." In *Cities and Society in Colonial Latin America,* ed. L. Hoberman and S. Socolow, 47–85. Albuquerque: University of New Mexico Press.

———, ed. 1989. *Sexuality and Marriage in Colonial Latin America.* Lincoln: University of Nebraska Press.

———. 1995. *Women, Feminism, and Social Change in Argentina, Chile, and Uruguay, 1890–1940.* Lincoln: University of Nebraska Press.

Lavrin, Asunción, and Edith Couturier. 1979. "Dowries and Wills: A View of Women's Socioeconomic Role in Colonial Guadalajara and Puebla, 1640–1790." *Hispanic American Historical Review* 59(2): 280–304.

Lewin, Linda. 1979. "Some Historical Implications of Kinship Organization for Family: Basic Politics in the Brazilian Northeast." *Comparative Studies in Society and History* 21:262–92.

Lewis, Jane. 1985. "The Debate on Sex and Class." *New Left Review* 149 (January–February): 108–20.

———. 1986. *Labour and Love: Women's Experience of Home and Family, 1850–1940.* Oxford: Basil Blackwell.

———. 1991. *Women and Social Action in Victorian and Edwardian England.* Alderhot: Edward Elgard.

Little, Cynthia. 1978. *The Society of Beneficence in Buenos Aires.* Ann Arbor, Mich.: University Microfilms.

Lizaur, Marisol, and Larissa Adler Lomnitz. 1987. *A Mexican Elite Family, 1820–1980: Kinship, Class, and Culture.* Princeton: Princeton University Press.

Lobo Guerrero, Bartolomé, and Fernando Arias de Ugarte. 1987. *Sínodos de Lima de 1613 y 1636.* Madrid: Centro de Estudios Históricos del Consejo Superior de Investigaciones Científicas, vol. 6.

Lockhardt, James, and Stuart B. Schwartz. 1983. *Early Latin America: A History of Colonial Spanish America and Brazil.* Cambridge: Cambridge University Press.

Lohmann Villena, Guillermo. 1974. *Los Ministros de la Audiencia de Lima en el Reinado de los Borbones (1700–1821): Esquema de un Estudio Sobre un Núcleo Dirigente.* Sevilla: Escuela de Estudios Hispanoamericanos de Sevilla.

Lorence, Bogna W. 1974. "Parents and Children in Eighteenth-Century Europe." *History of Childhood Quarterly* 2:2–30.

Lowry, Lyn.1988. "Religión y Control Social en la Colonia: El Caso de los Indios Urbanos de Lima." *Allpanchis,* año XX, no. 32, 11–42.

Lynch, John. 1989. "The Catholic Church." In *Latin America: Economy and Society, Cambridge History of Latin America,* ed. L. Bethell, 301–29. Cambridge: Cambridge University Press.

Macera, Pablo. 1977. *Historia,* 4 vols. "Iglesia y Economía," 2:139–213; "La Enseñanza Elemental en el Coloniaje," 2:215–301; "Sexo y Coloniaje," 3:297–352. Lima: Instituto Nacional de Cultura.

Mahoney, Maureen A., and Barbara Yngvesson. 1992. "The Construction of Subjectivity and the Paradox of Resistance: Reintegrating Feminist Anthropology and Psychology." *Signs* 18(1): 44–73.

Mallon, Florencia. 1995. *Peasant and Nation: The Making of Postcolonial Mexico and Peru.* Berkeley and Los Angeles: University of California Press.

Manrique, Nelson. 1987. *Mercado Interno y Región: La Sierra Central 1820–1930.* Lima: DESCO.

Mariluz Urquijo, José Maria. 1960. "Victorián de Villava y la Pragmática de 1776 Sobre Matrimonio de Hijos de Familia." *Revista del Instituto de Historia del Derecho* 11:89–105. Buenos Aires: Facultad de Derecho y Ciencias Sociales.

Marks, Dorritt K., ed. 1993. *Women and Grass Roots: Democracy in the Americas.* New Brunswick: Transaction Publishers.

Marshall, C. E. 1939. "The Birth of the Mestizo in New Spain." *Hispanic American Historical Review* 19:161–84.

Martin, Cheryl E. 1990. "Popular Speech and Social Order in Northern Mexico, 1650–1830." *Comparative Studies in Society and History* 32(2): 302–24.

Martin, Luis. 1983. *Daughters of the Conquistadores.* Albuquerque: University of New Mexico Press.

Martinet, J. B. H. 1977. *Carestía de víveres en Lima (1875).* Lima: Centro Peruano de Historia Económica.

Martinez-Alier, Verena. 1974. *Marriage, Class, and Colour in Nineteenth-Century Cuba: A Study of Racial Attitudes and Sexual Values in a Slave Society.* Cambridge: Cambridge University Press.

Mazet, Claude. 1976. "Population et Societe á Lima aux XVIè et XVIIè Siècles: La

paroisse San Sebastian (1562–1689)." *Cahiers des Ameriques Latines,* nos. 13/14, 51–100.
McCaa, Robert. 1983. *The Demographic Transition in Chile: The Population History of the Petorca Valley.* Boulder, Colo.: Westview Press.
———.1991a. "Introduction." *Journal of Family History* 16(3): 211–14.
———.1991b. "La Viuda Viva del México Borbónico: Sus Voces, Variedades, y Vejaciones." In *Familias Novohispanas: Siglos XVI al XIX,* ed. P. Gonzalbo, 299–324. México D.F.: El Colegio de México.
———.1994. "Marriage Ways in Mexico and Spain, 1500–1900." *Continuity and Change* 9(1): 11–43.
McCaa, Robert, Stuart B. Schwartz, and Arturo Grubessich. 1979. "Race and Class in Colonial Latin America: A Critique." *Comparative Studies in Society and History* 21:421–33.
McCreery, John L. 1976. "Women's Property Rights and Dowry in China and South Asia." *Ethnology* 15:163–74.
Medick, Hans. 1983. "Plebeian Culture in the Transition to Capitalism." In *Culture, Ideology, and Politics,* ed. G. S. Jones and R. Samuel. London: Routledge & Kegan Paul.
Medick, Hans, and David Sabean, 1982. "Neue Themen in der historisch-ethnologischen Familienforschung." *Sowi,* Heft 2: 91–100.
———, eds. 1984. *Interest and Function: Essays on the Study of Family and Kinship.* Cambridge: Cambridge University Press.
Méndez, Cecilia. 1987. *Los Trabajadores Guaneros del Perú, 1840–1879.* Lima: Universidad Nacional Mayor de San Marcos.
Menefee, Samuel P. 1981. *Wives for Sale: An Ethnographic Study of British Popular Divorce.* New York: St. Martin's Press.
Merino Arana, Romulo. 1966. *Historia Policial del Perú en la República.* Lima: Imprenta del Departamento de Prensa y Publicaciones de la Guardia Civil.
Mesgravis, Laima.1977. *A Santa Casa de Misericordia de Sao Paulo (1554–1888).* Sao Paulo: Conselho Estadual de Cultura.
Miller, Laura, Susan Stokes, Katherine Roberts, and José A. Lloréns. 1987. *Lima Obrera, 1900–1930,* tomo II. Lima: El Virrey.
Miller, Rory, ed. 1987. *Religion and Class in Modern Peruvian History.* Liverpool: University of Liverpool, Institute of Latin American Studies.
———. 1988. "The Population Problem of Late Nineteenth Century Lima." Paper presented at the International Congress of the Americanists, July 4–8, Amsterdam.
Minchom, Martin. 1994. *The People of Quito, 1690–1810: Change and Unrest in the Underclass.* Boulder, Colo.: Westview Press.
Mitterauer, Michael, and Reinhard Sieder. 1988 (1977). *Vom Patriarchat zur Partnerschaft: Zum Strukturwandel der Familie.* München: Verlag C. H. Beck.
Monografías Históricas de la Ciudad de Lima. 1935. Lima: Concejo Provincial, Librería e Imprenta Gil. Monographs by Domingo Angulo, Jorge Guillermo Leguía, and Pablo Patrón.
Moreno Cebrián, Alfredo. 1977. "La Descripción del Perú de Joaquín Bonet, y la Ordenanza de Intendentes de 1803." *Revista de Indias* 149/150:723–88.

Mörner, Magnus. 1980. *Estratificación Social Hispanoamericana Durante el Período Colonial*. Stockholm: Institute of Latin American Studies, research paper series no. 28.
———. 1983. "Economic Factors and Stratification in Colonial Spanish America with Special Regard to Elites." *Hispanic American Historical Review* 63(2): 335–69.
Morse, Richard M., and Joaquin Capelo. 1973. *Lima en 1900: Estudio Crítico y Antología*. Lima: Instituto de Estudios Peruanos.
Moses, Claire G. 1982. "Saint-Simonian Men, Saint-Simonian Women: The Transformation of Feminist Thought in 1830s France." *Journal of Modern History* 54(2): 240–67.
Muñiz, Pedro E. 1893. *Memoria de Prefecto*. Lima: Imprenta del Universo.
Muriel, Josefina. 1974. *Los Recogimientos de Mujeres*. México D.F.: Universidad Nacional Autónoma de México.
Nazzari, Muriel. 1991. *Disappearance of the Dowry: Women, Families, and Social Change in Sao Paulo, Brazil (1600–1900)*. Stanford: Stanford University Press.
———. 1994. "Composición y Transformación de las Dotes en Sao Paulo, Brasil (1660–1870)." In *La familia en el mundo Iberoamericano*, ed. P. Gonzalbo and C. Rabell. México D.F.: Instituto de Investigaciones Sociales, Universidad Autónoma de México.
Nizza da Silva, Maria Beatriz. 1989. "Divorce in Colonial Brazil: The Case of Sao Paulo." In *Sexuality and Marriage in Colonial Latin America*, ed. A. Lavrin. Lincoln: University of Nebraska Press.
Nye, Robert. 1993. *Masculinity and Male Codes of Honor in Modern France*. Oxford: Oxford University Press.
Oliart, Patricia. 1994. "Images of Gender and Race: The View from Above in Turn of the Century Lima." M.A. thesis, University of Texas at Austin.
Owen-Hughes, Diana.1978. "From Brideprice to Dowry in Mediterranean Europe." *Journal of Family History* 3:262–96.
Palma, Angélica. 1936. *Angélica Palma*. Lima: Sociedad Amigos de Palma.
Pareja Paz-Soldan, José. 1954. *Las Constituciones del Perú*. Madrid: Ediciones Cultura Hispánica.
Paz Soldan, Mariano Felipe. 1863. *Reglamento para el Servicio Interior de la Prisión Penitenciería de Lima*. Lima: Imprenta de José Masías.
———. 1877. *Diccionario Geográfico Estadístico del Perú*. Lima: Imprenta de José Masías.
Pescador, Juan Javier. 1992. *De Bautizados a Fieles Difuntos: Familia y Mentalidades en una Parroquia Urbana: Santa Catarina de Mexico, 1568–1820*. México D.F.: El Colegio de México.
———. 1994. "Entre la Espada y el Olivo: Pleitos Matrimoniales en el Provisorato Eclesiástico de México, Siglo XVIII." In *La Familia en el Mundo Iberoamericano*, ed. P. Gonzalbo and C. Rabell, 193–226. México D.F.: Instituto de Investigaciones Sociales, Universidad Autónoma de México.
Phillips, Roderick.1988. *Putting Asunder: A History of Divorce in Western Society*. Cambridge: Cambridge University Press.
Pinto, Honorio and Alvaro Goicochea. 1977. *Ocupaciones en el Perú, 1876*. Lima: Universidad Nacional Mayor de San Marcos, Seminario de Historia Rural Andina.
Porro, Nelly R. 1980a. "Conflictos Sociales y Tensiones Familiares en la Sociedad

Virreinal Rioplatense a Través de los Juicios de Disenso." *Boletín del Instituto de Historia Argentina y Americana "Dr. Emilio Ravignani,"* no. 26. Buenos Aires: Imprenta de la Universidad.

———. 1980b. "Extrañamientos y Depósitos en los Juicios de Disenso." *Revista de Historia del Derecho.* Buenos Aires: Instituto de Investigaciones de Historia del Derecho.

———. 1980c. "Los Juicios de Disenso en el Rio de la Plata: Nuevos Aportes Sobre la Aplicación de la Pragmática de Hijos de Familia." *Anuario Histórico Jurídico Ecuatoriano,* vol. 5. Quito: Corporación de Estudios y Publicaciones.

Portocarrero, Felipe. 1995. *El Imperio Prado, 1890–1970.* Lima: Universidad del Pacífico.

Portocarrero, Gonzalo. 1987. "Conservadurismo, Liberalismo, y Democracia en el Perú del Siglo XIX." In *Pensamiento Político Peruano,* ed. A. Adrianzén. Lima: DESCO.

Poster, Mark. 1978. *Critical Theory of the Family.* London: Pluto Press.

Powers, Karen V. 1995. "The Battle for Bodies and Souls in the Colonial North Andes: Intraecclesiastical Struggles and the Politics of Migration." *Hispanic American Historical Review* 75(1): 31–56.

———. 1995. *Andean Journeys: Migration, Ethnogenesis, and the State in Colonial Quito.* Albuquerque: University of New Mexico Press.

Pratt, Marie Louise. 1990. "Women, Literature, and National Brotherhood." In *Women, Culture, and Politics in Latin America: Seminar on Feminism and Culture in Latin America.* Berkeley and Los Angeles: University of California Press.

Rabb, Theodore K., and Robert I. Rotberg, eds. 1973 (1971). *The Family in History: Interdisciplinary Essays.* New York: Harper Torchbooks.

———. 1982. *The New History: The 1980s and Beyond: Studies in Interdisciplinary History.* Princeton: Princeton University Press.

Remy, Maria Isabel. 1988. "La Sociedad Local al Inicio de la República: Cusco, 1824–1850." *Revista Andina* 6(2): 451–84.

Rípodas Ardanaz, Daisy. 1977. *El Matrimonio en Indias: Realidad Social y Regulación Jurídica.* Buenos Aires: Fundación para la Educación, la Ciencia y la Cultura.

Rodman, Hyman. 1966. "Illegitimacy in the Caribbean Social Structure: A Reconsideration." *American Sociological Review* 31(51): 673–83.

Rodríguez P., Humberto. 1989. *Hijos del Celeste Imperio en el Perú (1850–1900): Migración, Agricultura, Mentalidad, y Explotación.* Lima: Instituto de Apoyo Agrario.

Rosenbaum, Heidi. 1982. *Formen der Familie: Untersuchungen zum Zusammenhang von Familienverhältnissen, Sozialstruktur, und sozialem Wandel in der deutschen Gesellschaft des neunzehnten Jahrhunderts.* Frankfurt: Suhrkamp.

———, ed. 1980(1978). *Seminar: Familie und Gesellschaftsstruktur.* Frankfurt: Suhrkamp.

Ross, Edward Alsworth. 1915. *South of Panama.* New York: Century.

Ross, Ellen. 1993. *Love and Toil: Motherhood in Outcast London, 1870–1918.* New York: Oxford University Press.

Ruggiero, Kristin. 1992. "Wives on 'Deposit': Internment and the Preservation of Husbands' Honor in Late Nineteenth-Century Buenos Aires." *Journal of Family History* 7(3): 225–67.

Ryan, Mary P. 1982. "The Explosion of Family History." *Reviews in American History* (December): 181–87.
Sacchetti, Alfredo. 1904. *Inmigrantes para el Perú.* Turín.
Safa, Helen. 1994. *The Myth of the Male Breadwinner.* Boulder, Colo.: Westview Press.
Saffioti, Heleieth I. B. 1978. *Women in Class Society.* New York: Monthly Review Press.
Sanday, Peggy R. 1990. *Beyond the Second Sex: New Directions in the Anthropology of Gender.* Philadelphia: University of Pennsylvania Press.
Santibanez Salcedo, Alberto. 1947. *Santuario y Beaterio de Nuestra Señora del Patrocinio.* Lima: Consejo Nacional de Conservación y Restauración de Monumentos Históricos.
Saragoza, Alex M. 1990 (1988). *The Monterrey Elite: The Mexican State.* Austin: University of Texas Press.
Scardaville, Michael C. 1977. "Crime and the Urban Poor: Mexico City in the Late Colonial Period." Ph.D. diss., University of Florida.
———. 1980. "Alcohol Abuse and Tavern Reform in Late Colonial Mexico City." *Hispanic American Historical Review* 60(4): 643–71.
Schneider, Jane. 1985. "Trousseau as Treasure: Some Contradictions of Late Nineteenth-Century Change in Sicily." In *Beyond the Myths of Culture: Essays in Cultural Materialism,* ed. Eric B. Ross, 323–56. New York: Academic Press.
Seco Caro, Carlos. 1958. "Derecho Canónico Particular Referente al Matrimonio en Indias." *Anuario de Estudios Americanos* 15:1–112.
Seed, Patricia. 1985. "The Church and the Patriarchal Family: Marriage Conflicts in Sixteenth- and Seventeenth-Century New Spain." *Journal of Family History* 10(3): 284–93.
———. 1988. *To Love, Honor, and Obey in Colonial Mexico: Conflicts over Marriage Choice, 1574–1821.* Stanford: Stanford University Press.
Segalen, Martine. 1986. *Historical Anthropology of the Family.* New York: Cambridge University Press.
Segura, Manuel A. 1963. *Las Tres Viudas, Comedia de Costumbres.* Lima: Ediciones Markham.
———. 1968. *Artículos de Costumbres.* Lima: Editorial Universo S.A.
Sheehan, M. M. 1978. "Choice of Marriage Partner in the Middle Ages: Development and Mode of Application of a Theory of Marriage." *Studies in Medieval and Renaissance History* 1:1–34.
Shorter, Edward. 1971. "Illegitimacy, Sexual Revolution, and Social Change in Modern Europe." In *The Family in History: Interdisciplinary Essays,* ed. T. Rabb and R. Rotberg, 48–84. New York: Harper Torchbooks.
Smith, Raymond T., ed. 1984. *Interpreting Kinship Ideology and Practice in Latin America.* Chapel Hill: University of North Carolina Press.
Socolow, Susan. 1978. *The Merchants of Buenos Aires, 1778–1810.* Cambridge: Cambridge University Press.
———. 1980. "Women and Crime: Buenos Aires, 1757–97." *Journal of Latin American Studies* 12:39–64.
Stern, Steve J. 1995. *The Secret History of Gender: Women, Men, and Power in Late Colonial Mexico.* Chapel Hill: University of North Carolina Press.
Stevenson, William Bennet. 1829. *Historical and Descriptive Narrative of Twenty Years'*

Residence in South American. 3 vols. London: Longman, Rees, Orme, Brown & Green.

Stone, Lawrence. 1965. *The Crisis of the Aristocracy, 1558–1641.* Princeton: Princeton University Press.

———. 1983. "Interpersonal Violence in English Society, 1300–1980." *Past and Present* 101 (November): 22–33.

———. 1990. *Road to Divorce: England 1530–1987.* Oxford: Oxford University Press.

Stoner, Lynn K. 1989. "Directions in Latin American Women's History." *Latin American Research Review* 22(2): 101–34.

———. 1991. *From the House to the Streets: The Cuban Movement for Legal Reform, 1898–1940.* Durham: Duke University Press.

Szuchman, Mark D. 1988. *Order, Family, and Community in Buenos Aires, 1810–1860.* Stanford: Stanford University Press.

Tamayo Vargas, Augusto. 1940. *Perú en Trance de Novela: Ensayos Crítico-Biográficos Sobre Mercedes Cabello de Carbonera.* Lima: Ediciones Baluarte.

Tantalean, Javier. 1983. *Política Económica-Financiera y la Formación del Estado, Siglo XIX.* Lima: CEDEP.

Teichman, Jenny. 1982. *Illegitimacy: A Philosophical Examination.* Oxford: Basil Blackwell.

Thompson, E. P. 1978. "Folklore, Anthropology, and Social History." *Indian Historical Review* 3(2): 247–66.

———. 1979. *Tradición, Revuelta, y Conciencia de Clase: Estudios Sobre la Crisis de la Sociedad Preindustrial.* Barcelona: Grijalbo.

Thorp, Rosemary, and Geoffrey Bertram. 1978. *Peru 1890–1977: Growth and Policy in an Open Economy.* London: Macmillan.

Tibesar, Antonine. 1970. "The Peruvian Church at the Time of Independence in the Light of Vatican II." *The Americas* 26(4): 349–75.

Tilly, Charles. 1987a. *As Sociology Meets History.* New York: Academic Press.

———. 1987b. "Family History, Social History, and Social Change." *Journal of Family History* 12(1–3): 319–30.

Trazegnies, Fernando de. 1980. *La Idea de Derecho en el Perú Republicano del Siglo XIX.* Lima: PUC.

Tristán, Flora. 1986 (1838). *Peregrinaciones de una Paria.* London: Virago Press.

Tutino, John. 1983. "Power, Class, and Family: Men and Women in the Mexican Elite, 1750–1810." *The Americas* 49(3): 359–81.

Unanue, Hipólito. 1940 (1805). *Observaciones Sobre el Clima de Lima y su Influencia en los Seres Organizados, en Especial el Hombre.* Lima: Imprenta "Lux."

Urteaga, Horacio H. 1935. *Monografías Históricas Sobre la Ciudad de Lima,* tomo II. Lima: Librería e Imprenta Gil S.A.

Valverde, Emilio F. 1942. *El Derecho de Familia en el Código Civil Peruano,* vol. 1. Lima: Imprenta del Ministerio de Guerra.

Van Deusen, Nancy. 1987. *Dentro del Cerco de los Muros: El Recogimiento en la Epoca Colonial.* Lima: CENDOC, Cuadernos Culturales, Serie I "La Mujer en la Historia."

Veliz, Claudio. 1980. *The Centralist Tradition in Latin America.* Princeton: Princeton University Press.

Vichery, Amanda. 1993. "Golden Age to Separate Spheres? A Review of the Cate-

gories and Chronology of English Women's History." *Historical Journal* 36(2): 383–414.
Villavicencio, Maritza. 1990. *Breve Historia de las Vertientes del Movimento de Mujeres en el Perú.* Documento de Trabajo 3. Lima: Centro Flora Tristán.
Viqueira Alban, Juan P. 1987. *Relajados o Reprimidos?Diversiones Públicas y Vida Social en la Ciudad de México Durante el Siglo de las Luces.* México D.F.: Fondo de Cultura Económica.
Vovelle, Michel. 1990. *Ideologies and Mentalities.* Chicago: University of Chicago Press.
Walker, Charles, and Carlos Aguirre, eds. 1990. *Bandoleros, Abigeos y Montoneros: Criminalidad y Violencia en el Perú, Siglos XVIII—XX.* Lima: Instituto de Apoyo Agrario.
Wallerstein, Immanuel, Joan Smith, and Hans-Dieter Evers, eds. 1984. *Households and the World Economy.* Beverly Hills, Calif.: Sage Publications.
Wibel, Frederick. 1975. The Evolution of a Regional Community Within Spanish Empire and Peruvian Nation: Arequipa, 1780–1914. Ph.D. diss., Stanford University.
Witt, Heinrich. 1992. *Diario 1824–1890: Un Testimonio Personal Sobre el Perú del Siglo XIX,* vol. 2 (1843–47). Lima: Banco Mercantil.
Worral, Janet. 1973. "Italian Immigration to Peru: 1860–1914." Ph.D. diss., Indiana University, Bloomington.
Wrigley, E. A. 1982. "Population History in the 1930s." In *The Family in History: Interdisciplinary Essays,* ed. T. Rabb and R. Rotberg. New York: Harper Torchbooks.
Zulawski, Ann. 1990. "Social Differentiation, Gender, and Ethnicity." *Latin America Review* 25(2): 93–113.

Index

abandonment, 350
abduction, 110
abortion, 90
acquest, 150, 152, 226, 339
administrative changes, 31
adultery, 284, 303, 354, 365
adulthood, 117
affinity, 98
alimony, 84, 150, 166, 173, 253
annulment, 83, 84, 104
apprentices, 63
Archicofradía, 266
Arequipa, 129, 167, 310
asceticism, 80
authority
   communal, 128
   institutional, 128

banns, 94, 135
baptism, 87
barraganía, 106
Barrios Altos, 21
bars (*chicherías, chinganas*), 43, 63
Beaterio de Copacabana, 138, 152, 165, 170, 296, 337
Beaterio del Patrocinio o Amparadas, 152, 161, 169
Beaterio de Recogidas, 162
Beaterio de Viterbo, 152
beaterios, 63, 154
   fees, 158–60

Beneficencia Pública, 154, 231, 265
bigamy, 94, 122, 145, 276
birth place, 28
Bolívar, Simón, 42
Bourbon Reforms, 10
Buenas Memorias de Dotes y Obras Pías, 231
Buenos Aires, 231
burial, 87
   fees, 87–88

Cajatambo, 207
canon law, 101, 137, 145, 328
Capelo, Joaquín, 20
Casa de Educandas, 131
Casma, 104
*casta*s, 106–7
Castilla, Ramón, 35, 51
cemeteries, 82, 88
Cerro de Pasco, 276, 320
Chancay, 200
charity, 80
Charles IV, 196
chastity, 204, 229
children, 55–56, 69, 76, 162–63, 204, 209ff., 219, 358ff.
   child abandonment, 90
   childbirth, 138, 201, 238
Chinese, 27, 51
Chorrillos, 45, 62, 281
church, 79, 83, 145, 271, 332, 352, 361
   church holdings, 80–81

church rituals, 132
civil
  contract, 246, 261
  courts, 84, 167, 174, 179, 187, 192, 222, 229, 265, 274–75, 312, 347–48
  equality, 346, 349
  matrimony, 82, 85, 88
  register, 87
Civil Code, 84, 85, 86, 148, 150, 151, 173, 224, 227, 266, 275, 340, 349, 353
clergy, 87
Cocachacra, 144
Colegio de la Caridad, 126
Colegio de Niñas Expósitas, 231
Comisión Reformadora 1923, 84
common property, 152, 236, 243
community, 199
compadrazgo, 48
concubines, 106
condemnation, 80
confession, 94
conjugal
  assets, 322, 337, 351
  quarrels, 63, 147, 155, 238
  residence, 151
consanguinity, 98
consent, 93, 110–11, 136, 364
  consent in the deathbed, 136–39
  consent limits, 133
consummation, 129, 138, 146, 205
Corongo, 154
Cosío, Juan Mariano, 43
Council of Trent, 85, 97, 133, 148, 179
court records, 315
cuarta conjugal, 227–28

defamation, 55
Defensor de Matrimonios, 125, 129, 146
demography (Lima), 17ff.
devil, 73
dispensations, 83, 93, 364
dissent, 93, 199
divorce, 13 n. 16, 83, 172
domestic
  chores, 161, 238
  life, 328, 333
  violence, 163
double standard, 57, 144, 193, 219, 316, 352

dowry, 84, 144, 193, 219, 316, 352

Echenique, Rufino, 35
Escobedo, Jorge, 31
ethnicity, 18, 155, 192, 221, 232, 251, 270, 366
Europeans, 28, 38, 53
Eyzaguirre, Miguel de, 53

family
  history, 4
  intervention, 150, 198
  wealth, 168
feminization (of the church), 86, 332
fertility, 21, 358
filiation, 203
filicide, 38
foreigners, 29, 86
fratricide, 38
freethinkers, 82
free will, 178
Fuentes, Manuel A., 61, 80, 93, 231

Gálvez, José, 35
gender, 175–76, 220, 235, 271, 294, 316, 323, 332
godparents, 48, 213
gossip, 71, 74
Guayaquil, 134

homicide, 306
homosexuality, 20, 89, 108

immigrants, 282
immigration, 21, 82, 98
impediments, 93–94
impotence (sexual), 94, 142
income, 273ff.
incompatibility
  character, 140
  sexual, 109, 111
Indians, 48–50, 54, 103, 106, 149, 169–70, 261, 296ff., 339, 343ff.
individual liberty, 118
infanticide, 38
infant mortality, 22
inheritance, 84, 203, 229
Inquisition, 200
Instituto del Buen Pastor, 152, 154, 167, 356

insults, 65, 74, 285
intimacy, 140, 185–86

jails, 35, 37
Jesus Christ, 73
jewelry, 208, 263, 279, 334
judges
    civil, 145, 270, 301
    ecclesiastical, 145
judiciary, 312
Junta de Calificación, 130
justice, 259, 340

Lafond, Gabriel, 45
Lambayeque, 215
legal demand, 287ff.
legal guardian, 117
legal minor, 345
Liberal Convention, 81
liberal ideology, 339, 360
liberalism, 9–10, 35, 58, 85, 177, 272
    economic, 41, 325
liberty of conscience, 84
life expectancy, 21
litigation costs, 130
López Lissón, Manuel, 84
Lucanas, 201
Luna Pizarro, Javier, 75
Lurin, 45

Malambo, 55, 69
manumission, 30
marital duties, 120, 256, 332, 338
market economy, 343–43
marriage, 331
    age, 119
    alliance, 250
    ceremony, 122
    choice, 110, 120
    intraracial, 114
    reconciliation, 161
    rituals, 94, 130
    secret, 97
masculinity, 143
matrimonial license file, 94, 139
mental illness, 230
Mexico City, 234, 341
migration, 25

military draft, 32
Miraflores, 45
miscegenation, 30
money forgery, 38
moral discourse, 336, 353
morality, morals, 108, 188, 269, 312, 317, 328, 332
motherhood, 220
municipal records, 22

Napoleonic Code, 148
natural law, 113, 319, 348, 353
Nazca, 104
negotiation, 310
neighborhood, 31–32, 33, 55, 71, 77, 149, 202
non-Catholics, 85, 132, 282

occupation, 18, 155–57

paraphernalia, 227, 247
parental
    authority, 112, 122
    intervention, 112, 208
parishes, 95
    rural, 122
Paseo de Aguas, 45
Paseo Militar, 45
paternalism, 80
paternity, 206, 212
patriarchy, 110, 140, 193, 224, 236, 241, 270, 294
patricide, 38
Paz Soldán, Mariano Felipe, 35
Pérez de Tudela, Manuel, 84
Peruvian National Council of Women, 349
physical violence, 74, 84
place of birth, 28
Plaza de Acho, 42
plebe, 34, 56
police, 30, 327
polygamy, 276–77
Popes
    Gregory XIII, 103
    Pius IX, 85
power of attorney, 320
Pragmática, 112–14, 118, 226–27
pregnancy, 104, 138
priests, 73, 103, 124, 200

procreation, 123
promenade, 44
property rights, 342
prostitutes, 89
prostitution, 89, 108, 141, 311
Protestant, 98
provinces, 86, 98, 100, 194
provincial elites, 101
public debate, 140

Quito, 137

race
    dispensations, 97
racial stereotype, 53–55
racism, 40, 48, 52, 56, 108, 193
rape, 146, 180ff., 193
Real Cédula, 118
reason, 261
rebelliousness, 306
reformers, 315
religious calling, 119–20
rights, 167
    violation, 125
Roman Law, 110
Ross, Edward A., 56
rural areas, 3, 126

sacrament, 83, 145, 251, 305, 332
    last, 139
Sagrario, 136
San Domingo, 124
San Francisco, 126
San Lázaro, 73
Santa Ana, 63, 122
Santa Eulalia, 123
Santa Rosa, 120
Sao Paulo, 232
seclusion, 120
secularization, 79, 82, 88, 177
    of marriage, 84
sex
    premarital, 179, 184, 206–7
sexual intercourse, 129
sexuality, 140
sexual pleasure, 142
Siete Partidas, 106, 110, 245
slaves, 27, 34, 149, 169, 248, 261, 305

social convention, 118, 161
    criticism, 324, 332
    image, 311, 318, 325
    inequality, 130, 364
    mobility, 193, 226
    order, 76, 179, 185
spacial mobility, 114
spiritual kin, 48
sponsalia, 193ff.
state, 79
    security, 113
Stevenson, William B., 44
suburbs, 21–22, 50
syphilis, 90, 141

theology, 145
Tribunal del Consulado, 249, 258
Tristan, Flora, 80
Trujillo, 196
tolerance, 85
Tridentine Concilium, 133
Trinidad monastery, 326

Unánue, Hipólito, 19
underwear, 68
Unión para las Mujeres, 82

vagrancy, 39
Valverde, Emilio F., 84
venereal disease, 141
Vidaurre, Manuel, 20
violence, 298, 329
virginity, 180, 183, 201, 205

War of the Pacific, 12, 29, 51, 235, 278
wars of independence, 11, 324
wetnurse, 210, 291ff., 311
widows, 171, 202, 227, 229
will executor, 224, 236, 271
witch, 200
wives, 61, 205, 281, 304
womanhood, 57, 62, 218, 229, 360
women
    providers, 324
    writers, 315, 348

Yauricocha, 102, 124, 310